THE MINORITY REPORT

The Minority Report

AN INTRODUCTION TO RACIAL, ETHNIC, AND GENDER RELATIONS

EDITED BY

ANTHONY GARY DWORKIN

AND

ROSALIND J. DWORKIN

UNIVERSITY OF HOUSTON

PRAEGER PUBLISHERS

NEW YORK

Published in the United States of America in 1976
by Praeger Publishers, Inc.
111 Fourth Avenue, New York, N.Y. 10003

Library of Congress Cataloging in Publication Data
Main entry under title:

The Minority report.

   Includes index.
   1. Minorities—United States—Addresses, essays,
lectures.   2. Minorities—Addresses, essays, lectures.
I. Dworkin, Anthony Gary.   II. Dworkin, Rosalind J.
E184.A1M545   301.45′0973   73-17774
ISBN 0-275-52210-5
ISBN 0-275-89010-4 pbk.

Printed in the United States of America

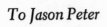

To Jason Peter

Preface

The Minority Report was first proposed in the fall of 1972 as a project to combine a body of theory on minority-group relations with the individual and personal experiences of minority-group members writing about their own people. The book is focused toward the undergraduate who is taking a first race relations or minority-group relations course, and who has had little previous exposure to sociology. The text has two chief themes: (1) that race, ethnicity, and gender relations are social variables subject to social definition and consequences; and that (2) sociology can provide several heuristic orientations toward such social data, definitions, and consequences.

Most minority-group relations texts are written by a single author, expressing the insights of a unitary heritage and perspective. The weakness of such texts is obvious: No single author can present the diversity of understandings which a variety of racial, ethnic, and gender experiences, research, and readings can provide. Although the various contributors to The Minority Report share common sociological insights, they present the diversity of perspective made possible by people of different minority groups with different experiences, all interpreting the minority scene. Together, we have produced a multifaceted textbook which reflects the variations in American minority-group relations and which is timely and exciting, as well as scholarly.

The Minority Report is divided into two distinct sections. Part One, which provides the student with the theoretical groundwork for dealing with Part Two, contains a summary of current knowledge about the minority condition, presented in a fashion oriented toward the undergraduate student.

Chapter 2 deals with the issue of delineating what constitutes a minority group. Out of a presentation of a sociological tradition emerges an emphasis on four necessary conditions: identifiability, differential power, differential and pejorative treatment occasioned by the power differential, and group awareness faciliated by the differential treatment. Groups will be seen as varying relative to one another on each of these conditions. The extent to which these conditions exist will determine the group's chances of overcoming its minority status. Biological, legal, psychological, and sociological components of minority-group status will also be explored relative to the four conditions.

The next three chapters examine minority-group status in terms of the three sociological dimensions: distributive, organizational, and social psychological. Discussion here includes the development of a general theory of minority-group stratification to theories of prejudice and prejudice reduction.

Chapter 6 concentrates on the possible resolutions of minority-majority relations. Two major forms are discussed—assimilation and separatism—and several models presented. The chapter offers a discussion of still other outcomes.

Chapter 7 is a prologue to the individual reports that make up Part Two. Specifically, the chapter attempts to account for the selection of the groups included and to indicate how each of these varies along the several dimensions.

Part Two, which is written by members of the minority groups themselves, provides the substantive material to which the theoretical models can be fitted. Attempts have been made across sections and reports to articulate the diversity of materials presented by the various contributors and the editors. As we shall observe, each contributor tells a slightly different story, tempered by the diversity of each minority group. This diversity exemplifies the parallax of which we spoke earlier. When taken collectively, the different perspectives present with greater clarity the totality of the minority experience in America. The diversity and the synthesis produced by this clarity provides richness to *The Minority Report*.

There are many people who played significant roles in the completion of this book, and to whom we are most indebted. First, to Jim Bergin of Praeger, who persevered through the months of writing, rewriting, and waiting for the final product to emerge, we must extend

Preface

our thanks. We are grateful to Noel P. Gist, of the Department of Sociology of the University of Missouri, for being a constant friend and fine colleague, and for recommending that we undertake this project. To each of the contributors goes our deepest appreciation for holding on while we collectively assembled our act. We wish to thank our colleagues at the University of Houston, including Janet Saltzman Chafetz, chairperson in the Department of Sociology, who worked with us on one of the theoretical models in Chapter 3, and Joshua Weinstein, who chaired the University Publications Committee, which provided funds for the typing and indexing. Special thanks must go to J. Wallace Jackson, who served double duty as a contributor and as a critic and sounding board for many of our ideas.

We wish to thank an excellent team of typists, Suzanne Underwood, Yvonne Anderson, Robin Keene, and Nancy Brooks, who battled the correction fluid and our sloppy handwriting. Finally, we must thank our son, Jason Peter Dworkin, who all too often found us busy at the typewriter and unable to help him master his first two-wheeler. The book is dedicated to Jason and his generation, who we hope can learn that the character of a person, not the characteristics of his group, is all that really counts.

A.G.D.
R.J.D.

The Contributors

ANTHONY GARY DWORKIN, coeditor of *The Minority Report* and co-author of the theory section of the text, is Associate Professor of Sociology, Director of the Program in Child-Youth Services, and Director of the Small Groups Research Laboratory at the University of Houston. He received his Ph.D. degree from Northwestern University.

ROSALIND J. DWORKIN, coeditor of *The Minority Report*, coauthor of the theory section of the text, and author of the report on American women, is Assistant Professor of Sociology at the University of Houston. She holds a Ph.D. degree from Northwestern University.

J. WALLACE JACKSON, author of the report on black Americans, is Assistant Professor of Sociology at the University of Houston. His Ph.D. degree is from Vanderbilt University.

JULIUS RIVERA, author of the report on Mexican Americans, is Professor and Chairperson of the Department of Sociology, University of Texas, El Paso. He received his Ph.D. degree from Michigan State University.

INEKE CUNNINGHAM, senior coauthor of the report on Puerto Ricans, is Assistant Professor of the Department of Epidemiology, Biostatistics, Demography, and Social Sciences of the School of Public Health, Medical Sciences Campus of the University of Puerto Rico. She holds a Ph.D. from Northwestern University. Her coauthor is Sr. Anibal Molina of the Department of Spanish, Temple University.

Contributors

JOSEPH STAUSS, senior coauthor of the report on Native Americans, is Assistant Professor of Sociology at the University of Arizona. During 1975–76 he has been on leave with the Office of Native American Programs in the Department of Health, Education and Welfare. He received his Ph.D. degree from Washington State University. His coauthors are Bruce S. Chadwick, Associate Professor of Sociology, Brigham Young University, who holds a Ph.D. degree from University of Washington, and Howard M. Bahr, Professor of Sociology, Brigham Young University, who holds a Ph.D. degree from the University of Texas.

KENJI IMA, author of the report on Japanese Americans, is Assistant Professor of Sociology at San Diego State University. He received his Ph.D. degree from Northwestern University.

WEN LANG LI, author of the report on Chinese Americans, is Associate Professor of Sociology at Ohio State University. He holds a Ph.D. degree from the University of Pennsylvania.

EUGEN SCHOENFELD, author of the report on Jewish Americans, is Professor and Chairperson of the Department of Sociology at Georgia State University, Atlanta. He received his Ph.D. degree from Southern Illinois University.

ROBERT E. KENNEDY, JR., author of the report on Irish Americans, is Associate Professor of Sociology at the University of Minnesota. He holds a Ph.D. degree from the University of California, Berkeley.

Contents

Contents

PART ONE

Theoretical Perspectives

1.

INTRODUCTION

The American university of our parents is dead. Everyday assumptions about this and other institutions in our society, including the professions, the military, and the family, have so changed that much of our knowledge about the characteristics and role expectations of their occupants must be modified radically. The past twenty years have seen sizable minority entry into careers, roles, and institutions previously denied to them. In the 1940s, 1950s, and even the early 1960s, American universities and the institutions which surrounded them were citadels of white males. Today's greater participation by racial, ethnic, and gender minorities has forced scholars to recognize that no group possesses a monopoly over knowledge. It has also had an impact upon the nature of inquiry in the social sciences.

Although there are canons of scientific inquiry and proof, science, like all systems of knowledge, contains a subjective perception of reality. This perception is defined by the culture in which the scientist lives. Individuals from different cultures or subcultures may see "reality" in a slightly different fashion. The difference may be great or small, depending upon the similarities between the cultures from which the scientists come. Among scientists whose data are remote from cultures and personalities, in such areas as physics, chemistry, geology, or even biology, culture-bound differentials in perception may be very slight, if observ-

3

able at all. However, in the social sciences, where the data are the cultures and societies themselves, the differences in perception may be immense. Even within American society we may extract examples. A black male sociologist and a white female sociologist, each armed with the same body of data, may interpret those data differently. If the data involve interaction sequences among individuals of different races and genders, each sociologist might attribute different motivations to the actors involved. The first sociologist might emphasize the presence of racism in the interaction, the second might stress the presence of sexism. Both may be observing accurately, but each has a less complete view than the composite of the two.

Members of diverse heritages working together can provide a better understanding of the complexities of intergroup relations than can a single individual of a single heritage. The diversity between the observations of Freud[1] and Friedan[2] on women's motives, of Moynihan[3] and Billingsley[4] on black families, and of Heller[5] or Madsen[6] and Romano[7] or Vaca[8] on Mexican American culture illustrates the necessity that social science come from more than a single racial, ethnic, or gender group. We may demonstrate this further with the following metaphor. There is a parallax noticeable when we stare at a point of light with first the left eye and then the right eye closed. We discern two slightly different images. When both eyes are open our view has greater depth and is enlightened by the contribution of the viewpoint of each eye. In the same way each social scientist brings to the study of intergroup relations the uniqueness of his or her own people's perspective on the portrait of American minority group relations, and the composite thus is enhanced with greater precision and clarity.

This book seeks to maximize the contributions of minority group social scientists, while simultaneously attempting to converge these contributions into a general sociological orientation to the data of minority relations. The title of our collective enterprise reflects the diversity we seek to encapsulate. *The Minority Report* has a double meaning. It is first a report by minority group members about their own people, bringing to their presentations the uniqueness of their race, ethnicity, or gender, and is thus a report *by* minorities. But in an historical and legal sense, a minority report is also a dissenting report. It represents a divergence of opinion and view from those of the dominant society and the dominant makeup of the sociological profession. It is thus a critical perspective, filled with different and sometimes uncomplimentary interpretations of the functions and consequences of American institutions and their impact upon people other than the dominant population.

In the past many sociologists writing about minority groups have claimed to assume the vantage point of what was once regarded as value-

4

neutral or value-free social science. Citing an interpretation of Max Weber's "Science as a Vocation,"[9] these authors argued that unbiased objectivity was possible and imperative for the study of any social issue. Other writers allowed sociologists to be human, but required them to be schizophrenic. For them, when the social researcher was performing as a scientist he or she was required to have no values except those deemed by the canons of science and logic—to explore the social issue to its fullest, ruthlessly and without concern for the people involved. However, after working hours, he or she could protest, assume value positions, and behave as a concerned citizen. Robert Lynd[10] and Alvin Gouldner,[11] among several others, have cogently argued that both positions are limiting, untenable, and unreal. The very decision to select a given social issue for study is a value commitment. After all, of the myriad of social issues, of the innumerable areas of human interaction, why have we elected to investigate the conditions of minorities if not because we have more than a dispassionate interest in it? Howard S. Becker[12] suggested that the issue is not whether we espouse values in our research, but "whose side we are on."

Many of the past generation of social scientists who endorsed a value-free position for research, or who argued that values could only be espoused when one was performing the citizen role, negated their contentions in a collective attempt to influence the United States Supreme Court. In 1952 a group of distinguished social researchers, long convinced of the evils of segregation, met to lend scientific credibility to the Brown brothers, Briggs, and Davis' argument that separate education is inherently unequal.[13] These researchers did not attempt to end segregation as individual citizens; rather, in their capacity as social scientists, where their impact would carry more influence, they attacked discrimination. In so doing they chose sides, thereby abandoning a value-neutral orientation.

The contributors to *The Minority Report* likewise cannot remain dispassionately associated with the study of the status of minority peoples. After all, they are themselves members of the very minority populaions about which they write. The future of intergroup relations in America affects the life chances of the contributors. Each contributor thus has expressed a commitment to the study of intergroup relations for personal as well as intellectual reasons—if these two components can actually be separated. Several contributors have published extensively on minority-majority relations or on their own minority group.

The publications and research of each contributor required that each maintain both a degree of objectivity and a degree of involvement. The balance of the two dimensions created *The Minority Report*. Good social science requires that one seek accuracy and truth as goals, but these goals must be pursued with a social conscience—a concern for the human costs to those subjected to investigation. If the data do not support the researcher's political stance, the reaction of the present contributors and other good social scientists is to attempt to understand the data more fully and to alter their political stance. It is never, as in the case with many polemicists, to alter the data to coincide with the political stance.

The contributors to *The Minority Report* also differ from those who shield themselves behind the myth of value-free social science. Many of the contributors, armed with both experiential and research-based knowledge, have engaged in informed social action to correct and attack the fallacies of the myths of racial, ethnic, or gender superiority, to debunk stereotypes, and to improve the quality of the society for all. Each realizes that the oppression and dehumanization of any group ultimately results in the dehumanization of us all.

Despite the fact that each of the contributors to this report brings to the study of minority groups a unique contribution tempered by his or her distinct cultural heritage, there is nonetheless a commonality among them: They are all sociologists. As such, they bring to the study of minority groups an orientation toward the data of social life which includes a commitment to the canons of science and theory construction, and a methodological rigor, including a concern for the logic of proof. Two crucial components of the sociological orientation are synthesis and generalization. Sociologists seek to discern similarities as well as unique components among the experiences of people of different times, places, and backgrounds. Thus, out of the apparent diversity of such groups as the Burghers of Ceylon and the Chicanos of the United States, the sociologist attempts to construct a theory or model of interpersonal and intergroup dynamics and relations which will assist us in understanding past and present contacts among peoples, and to predict the consequences of future contacts. The ability to take from the mundane and the esoteric of social life and to ascertain the trends and patterns of human society depicts the distinctiveness of the social sciences.

The Sociological Orientation

There have been numerous attempts over the past century to portray American minority groups. Sociologists have not been the only ones to observe the complexity of the American minority scene. Journalists, writers, dramatists, historians, and various political actors and strategists have commented on this complex mosaic. Obviously, each of these perspectives has been different, and not all have attempted to avoid polemical stances.

In sociology, too, there have been divergent stances, especially if we examine the sociological perspective historically. E. B. Reuter[14] once noted that the sociology of race relations went through three distinct stages. Early writings assumed an anthropological frame of reference steeped in social Darwinism and emphasizing the biological bases of racial differences (and assumed racial superiorities). A shift then occurred to the cultural orientation, which stressed the diversity not of biology but of heritage, language, and custom. This second stage was followed by the present concern over the interrelations and dynamics of interactions between groups.

Today, despite the distinctions between types of sociological theory, relatively few sociologists would dispute that a study of American minorities would involve three distinct levels of analysis. However, few of them might write or operate on all three levels. The levels widely accepted are the distributive, the organizational, and the attitudinal.

DISTRIBUTIVE, DEMOGRAPHIC, AND STRATIFICATIONAL ANALYSIS

A distributive analysis of minority groups is concerned with the manner in which minority group members are arranged along the various dimensions of the social structure. The emphasis is upon difference. How do groups differ in their life chances? How do groups differ on such important dimensions as income, education, occupation, and political power? What are the bases and functions of minority stratification systems? The distributive level is usually the easiest to measure; it often involves the simple counting of people in different categories, as is done decennially by the U.S. Census. However, the distributive also involves the beginning element in a model of social change. Frequently (Marx would argue always) the root cause of social change is distributive, or material. That is, before people can have a felt dissatisfaction about their objective condition, and effect a new sociopolitical order, there needs to be a distributive condition to which they can point with outrage. In minority group relations, it must be realized, especially in the United States, the distributive differences are most often matters of degree. That is, although there are many objectively very poor people in this nation, the difference in the distribution of resources is one of relative deprivation of one group compared to another group. One group has, relative to another, more or less income, more or less education, a better or worse job, more or less power, and so on. In *The Minority Report* we shall see groups who are more or less advantaged or disadvantaged,

7

relative to other minority groups and relative to the dominant society. The degree of advantage or disadvantage relative to other groups may or may not provoke a collective social action bent on reform, change, or revolution. In our discussion of the manner in which people are distributed in the social structure we shall explore some prevailing theories of minority stratification, and develop a model of our own.

ORGANIZATIONAL ANALYSIS

The organizational dimension refers to the patterned relations and the character of the organizations and associations formed by groups as a consequence of the manner in which they are distributed within the society. Religious life, educational systems, and voluntary associations comprise aspects of the organization analysis. A discussion of minority organizations must encompass their goals (whether assimilationist or separatist) and their strategies (accommodationism, legalism, nonviolence, or violent protest). Essential to the study of minority group relations would be an investigation of the interaction between the minorities and the organization of the dominant society, including corporations, the school system, the police, and the government bureaucracy. But the analysis should not stop there, for the organizational element must also include an analysis of the manner in which ethnic, racial, or gender-based organizations deal with their members and with members of other minorities.

ATTITUDINAL OR SOCIAL PSYCHOLOGICAL ANALYSIS

The social psychological level deals with the imposition of the social structure and its organizations upon the individual and the manner in which he thinks, acts, and interacts. Here we study attitudes, beliefs, and behaviors. Our emphasis will focus on attempts to account for prejudice and to explain, using our knowledge of interpersonal dynamics, how these attitudes develop, change, and become translated into intergroup action. There is considerable controversy at this level of analysis. Some argue that we cannot measure attitudes adequately because we cannot comprehend the individual motivations expressed in the attitudes. Others point to the fact that attitudes and behaviors are not always conjoined, not always consistent. Some even contend that the attitudinal dimension is irrelevant because people are only puppets of the mass society and behave as they are told to behave. Each of these arguments must be examined and an assessment made of the impact of the social psychological dimension.

At each level of analysis the dimension of minority culture, including

8

subcultural norms, plays a role. We do not wish to imply that there is a single minority culture. However, we must realize that a culture unique to the particular group studied provides the general context in which we can comprehend the consequences of the distributive, organizational, and social psychological dimensions. That is, a cultural setting of one type may produce a different set of reactions to the distribution of resources, a different set of organizations and relationships, and a different set of attitudes than another cultural setting.

Social scientists have long argued the respective merits of a functional and a cultural relativist frame of reference in the study of societies. The former concentrates on the forms of society, the systematic consistencies and the functions each performs for the survival of that society across groups, while minimizing a concern for differences in content between groups. The cultural relativist approach emphasizes the unique content of societies, and sometimes ignores the similarities between groups. *The Minority Report* shall remain eclectic. We shall note the similarities between the American Indians and the Chicanos and among the Jews, the Irish, the Japanese, and Chinese. But we shall also explore the impact of their unique belief systems, language, art, and artifacts which interpret their world for them in slightly or very different manners. We shall often assume that dissimilarities in content override similarities of structures among the minority communites. However, because each of these groups is also part of the larger American society, each shares a commonality even in content.

NOTES

1. Sigmund Freud, "Some Psychical Consequences of the Anatomical Distinction between the Sexes," in *The Collected Papers of Sigmund Freud*, Ernest Jones, ed. (New York: Basic Books, 1959), pp. 186–97.
2. Betty Friedan, *The Feminine Mystique* (New York: Norton, 1963).
3. Daniel P. Moynihan, *The Negro Family: The Case for National Action* (Washington, D.C.: Office of Policy Planning and Research, United States Department of Labor, 1965).
4. Andrew Billingsley, *Black Families in White America* (Englewood Cliffs, N.J.: Prentice-Hall, 1968).
5. Celia S. Heller, *Mexican-American Youth: Forgotten Youth at the Crossroads* (New York: Random House, 1966).
6. William Madsen, *The Mexican Americans of South Texas* (New York: Holt, 1964).
7. Octavio I. Romano V., "The Anthropology and Sociology of Mexican Americans," *El Grito* 2 (1968): 13–26.
8. Nick C. Vaca, "The Mexican-American in the Social Sciences," *El Grito* 3 (1970): 3–24, 17–51.
9. Weber was concerned with the politicization of the university by partisan faculty members. He feared that the state would take action and close down the universities. Some have generalized this remark to endorse a rejection of all value orientations in social sciences. See H. H. Gerth and C. W. Mills, eds., *From Max Weber:*

Theoretical Perspectives

Essays in Sociology (New York: Oxford University Press, 1958), pp. 129–56 ("Science as a Vocation").
10. Robert S. Lynd, Knowledge for What? (Princeton: Princeton University Press, 1939).
11. Alvin Gouldner. "Anti-Minotaur: The Myth of a Value-Free Sociology," Social Problems 9 (1962): 199–213.
12. Howard S. Becker. "Whose Side Are We On?," Social Problems 14 (1967): 239–47.
13. "The Effects of Segregation and the Consequences of Desegregation: A Social Science Statement," Appendix to Appellants' Brief, September 22, 1952, in the Supreme Court of the United States, October Term 1952.
14. E. B. Reuter, "Racial Theory," American Journal of Sociology 50 (1945): 452–61.

Suggested Readings

Becker, Howard S. "Whose Side Are We On?" Social Problems 14 (1967). 239–47.

Berry, Bruton. Race and Ethnic Relations. 3rd ed. Boston: Houghton Mifflin, 1965.

Gouldner, Alvin W. "Anti-Minotaur: The Myth of a Value-Free Sociology." Social Problems 9 (1962): 199–213.

———. The Coming Crisis of Western Sociology. New York: Basic Books, 1970.

Lundberg, George. Can Science Save Us? New York: Longmans, Green, 1947.

Lynd, Robert S. Knowledge for What? Princeton, N.J.: Princeton University Press, 1939.

Rose, Peter I. They and We. New York: Random House, 1964.

2.

WHAT IS A MINORITY?

The Varieties of Definitions

If you turned to the want-ads section of most daily newspapers, you would find several advertisements for employment proclaiming, "We are an equal-opportunity employer; women and minorities encouraged to apply." Most of us know what the advertisers mean—women are females of the species and minorities are people who are black or brown. But what about Puerto Ricans, Indians, or Orientals? Are they included as minorities? Not too many years ago Jews would have been included in a popular definition of minorities. In 1880 employers who wished to discriminate in hiring might have advertised, "Jobs available; Negroes, Irish, and Criminals need not apply."

A few years ago a Puerto Rican was refused service at a bar in New Jersey. The man appealed to the courts on the grounds that his rights under the 1968 Civil Rights Act had been violated. The judge ruled that Puerto Ricans were white and therefore not protected under the Civil Rights Act.

It appears that the popular definition of "minority" is highly variable over time and geographic space. Even blacks are not always considered part of the minority. The authors know of a black man who was seeking a teaching position. He visited two areas, one in the Midwest and one in

11

northern New England, along the Canadian border. When he inquired about housing in the midwestern community, the real estate agent showed him a series of all-black neighborhoods. Making the same inquiries in the New England community, the black teacher was shown a wealthy suburban white neighborhood. He asked the real estate agent if he could see some less expensive housing. The agent replied, "I could take you to that part of town over there, but you won't want to live there. Over there are French Canadians, but they don't keep up their property, and they're lazy, dirty, and sloppy." The black teacher later related that this was the first time he had ever been considered part of the majority, in a position to discriminate against others.

Popular definitions of "minority" do not control for variations over time and space. They merely reflect the current thinking in a relatively narrow environment. This produces problems in consistency. Individuals using a word such as "minority" may be referring to different concepts and may make statements which are absurd in the context of another definition.

"Minority" could be defined as a racial group different from the numerically dominant one. Or "minority" could mean a racial group different from the politically dominant group. Or "minority" could mean a cultural group different from the one that is currently dominant. Each of these definitions would compel us to designate different groups as minority in any particular social setting.

Consider the example of South Africa and Rhodesia, or even some areas of our Deep South. Most of the people in each of these areas are black. Using the first definition suggested above, whites would therefore be the minority group and blacks the majority, or dominant group. According to the second definition, whites would become the dominant group and blacks the minority because power, not numerical advantage, is salient. If we were to utilize the third definition, the designation of minority-majority would not be along racial lines but along lines of social class. Middle- and upper-class blacks and whites would both be considered dominant because these groups exercise the power. Lower-class blacks and lower-class whites would be grouped together as minority on the basis of their cultural similarities and relative powerlessness.

Thus we must go beyond the popular definitions of minority groups, because these are too often mere enumerations of classifications which are subject to temporal and regional differences.

The Varieties of Sociological Definitions

Social science seeks to maintain an adequate complement of objectivity, of which we spoke in the introduction, and a degree of methodological and conceptual rigor and precision. To provide for such rigor and precision there must be adequate agreement on the meanings—denotative and connotative—of the variables studied. Definitions of concepts cannot be conceived of in one fashion for one study and then differently for another study. Results would never be comparable and findings could never be combined into a body of knowledge. The social scientific ideal is to create what Herbert Blumer[1] has called *generic variables*. That is, variables are needed about which there is sufficient agreement as to definition and operationalization (the activities, questionnaire items, measures used to represent the variable or concept) so that one social scientist can take the study conducted by another and replicate it, or look at another aspect of the variables and then compare the findings. Without attempts at consistency in definitions we shall forever be comparing apples and oranges, and never building on our knowledge.

A sociological definition of "minority" must have six qualities. A definition must meet the canons of logic to the extent that it is a category which is *mutually exclusive* to its reciprocal, and to the extent that it is *exhaustive*. It is mutually exclusive in that only minority groups will possess the characteristics denoted in the definition, and exhaustive in that all groups considered to be minorities will fit the definition. Majorities will thus not possess the characteristics of our definition of minority, and no group considered to be a minority will be defined out of the category. Our definition must *reflect the social reality* it is intended to describe. It must extract the common denominators from various lay, legal, and other sociological definitions. Further, the definition must be *heuristic* in that it generates explanations for attitudes and behaviors of diverse groups and suggests similarities between groups which possess minority qualities. The heuristic definition should also demonstrate new lines of theoretical development. Thus by showing how groups not usually considered a minority possess the characteristics of a minority, insights into that group's behavior as well as insights into the theory of minorities will be gained. The definition must be *universal* so that it can be applied across societies and regions, rather than being bounded by specific cultures or locales. Finally, the definition must be *dynamic* in that it is not time-bounded and can be applied to emerging and assimilating groups as well as current and commonly recognized minorities.

There are at least two scientific ways in which we can approach the definition of minorities. The first is inductively, the second, deductively. In the first we look at the multitude of groups considered to be minorities and attempt to determine what they have in common. In the second we postulate a set of factors and then determine empirically whether or not minorities possess these qualities. Neither is the perfect solution, and each is used by social scientists. Therefore, in order to construct a sociological definition of "minority" we ought to turn first to definitions previously adopted by social scientists. Should these definitions be inadequate, we may be able to construct our own definition from salvageable aspects of several of them.

The earliest term used by social scientists to denote the groups we shall be studying was "race." Although the term actually refers to groups which have common phenotypical and genotypical (physical and genetic) characteristics, it was also applied to groups which possessed distinctive cultural and other learned characteristics. Thus ethnic groups, language groups, and national groups were aggregated with biological groups under the rubric "race." In the 1920s social scientists like Bogardus studied attitudes toward such ethnic "races" as the French race, the English race, the American race, the Jewish race, and the Turkish race, as well as such biological groups as the Negro race and the Oriental race. Racists, from DeGobineau and Chamberlain in the nineteenth century to Hitler in the twentieth century, spoke of the Nordic race and the Aryian race, and attributed their preferred cultural and linguistic characteristics to biological superiorities. This usage so diluted the concept of race as to make the term almost meaningless.

For that reason Donald Young[2] proposed an alternative. Young chose the term "minority," which would permit one to include racial as well as ethnic groups in a common term, which would not have the biological implication. He observed:

> There is, unfortunately, no word in the English language which can with philological propriety be applied to all . . . groups which are distinguished by biological features, alien national cultures, or a combination of both. For this reason, the phrases, "minorities of racial or national origin," "American minorities," or "minority peoples" are here used as synonyms for the popular usage of the word race.[3]

Since Young's usage sociologists have removed the statistical connotation from the meaning of the term "minority." Thus, although minorities generally are less than 50 percent of the population, the variable of size is of itself not crucial. The past five hundred years has seen countless examples of a relatively small number of Western Europeans dominating and colonizing a vast number of indigenous peoples throughout the world. The numerical disadvantage of the Westerners was more than compensated for by their technological and military advantages. Thus, they held the power and privilege in the region. In these cases the numerically underrepresented whites were the majority, not the minority.

Young does not give us an explicit definition of minority, but in his usage he defines minorities in terms of the groups' "traits." At best Young's definition is subjective, suggesting that minorities are whatever people label as minorities. Thus it is based upon the visibility of the minority group—the extent to which others can identify the group as a minority. Trait definitions such as Young's frequently prove inadequate, because they are based upon current minority groups in a particular society. They are both time and location bounded, which is the same criticism we lodged for lay definitions. The definition we seek must be more dynamic and universal. It must include groups which are emerging as minorities, and must be applicable in diverse locations and time periods.

A more universalistic and objective definition has been provided by Louis Wirth:

> We may define a minority as a group of people who, because of their physical or cultural characteristics, are singled out from others in the society in which they live for differential and unequal treatment and who therefore regard themselves as objects of collective discrimination.[4]

Wirth's definition possesses three components: the group must be visible to others, it must experience differential and pejorative treatment, and its members must be aware of themselves as members of a group which is considered a minority. Many social scientists have adopted Wirth's definition. It meets most of our needs for a definition. However, it does not indicate the power relationships between the minority and the majority groups, which may be more crucial than differential treatment.

Necessary to Wirth's definition is the subjective realization by the minority group. Wirth gives us no clue as to whether all members of the group, only the leaders, some significant number, or some unspecified percentage must possess such a realization of minority statue. This has been a recurrent problem among those employing subjective definitions of group awareness or subjective definitions of social problems or social issues.[5]

Another widely adopted definition of minority has been advanced by Wagley and Harris:

> (1) Minorities are subordinate segments of complex state societies; (2) minorities have special physical or cultural traits which are held in low esteem by the dominant segments of the society; (3) minorities are self-conscious units bound together by the special traits which their members share and by the special disabilities which these bring; (4) membership in a minority is transmitted by a rule of descent which is capable of affiliat-

ing succeeding generations even in the absence of readily apparent special cultural or physical traits; (5) minority peoples, by choice or necessity, tend to marry within the group.[6]

It should be noted that the first three characteristics advanced by Wagley and Harris are in agreement with the definition provided by Wirth. Wagley and Harris elaborate by including two additional elements: ascriptive membership and a norm for endogamous marriage. People do not choose to be minority-group members and do not work to attain minority status (achievement is not the route to the status), but rather membership in a minority group is ascribed at birth through the society's rules of descent. Consequently, one is a minority-group member because one's parent(s) is a minority-group member, and one cannot easily escape the minority label without drastic familial and personal consequences. Rules of endogamy are norms or societal regulations which require members of groups to marry only within their group. Thus minorities are usually prohibited by the majority (and often prohibit themselves) from marrying outside of the minority group. This has beneficial consequences for the majority and may also be beneficial for the minority. It insures for the majority that only they retain the resources needed to continue domination, social control, social power, and wealth. For the minority it insures group solidarity, protects against extinction, and provides for physical and cultural homogeneity.

These last two criteria advanced by Wagley and Harris have been empirically correct and appropriate for groups with long-established histories. Many such groups are commonly included in older trait models advanced for minorities. Today, however, we are experiencing the emergence of groups claiming minority status who do not meet one or both of Wagley and Harris's new criteria. For example, the Gay Liberation Movement's claims of minority-group status for homosexuals calls into question the empirical relevance of the rule of descent as a defining criterion. One is not a homosexual because of his (her) parents' membership in that group; it is a status later achieved. Similarly, the case of women challenges the criterion of endogamy. As R. Dworkin[7] develops later, there is much empirical evidence to support the contention that women constitute a minority group. However, we can plainly see that the rule of endogamy does not hold for them on the individual level. Women may not marry women. It would appear that endogamy is not a necessary component of minority status.

Both the endogamy and rule-of-descent criteria may be relevant for most racial and ethnic minorities.[8] However, they have less applicability for some of the new, emerging minorities in complex societies. Hence

Wagley and Harris have not produced a definition of minority which is entirely universal (something social scientists since Young have sought) or empirically sound.

Several social scientists have argued that the essential quality of minority-majority relations is differential power, and that what makes a minority is the group's lack of the resources and power to determine its own destiny. The power dimension has been central in the models advanced by Blalock,[9] Lieberson,[10] and van den Berghe,[11] among others. In the next chapter we shall assess the role of power in determining minority-group stratification. However, Gelfand and Lee[12] have carried the power dimension to an extreme by positing it as the sole characteristic of groups we label as minorities. These authors argue that if we do not intend the term "minority" to imply numbers, then we ought to substitute the terms "subordination" and "domination," and to ignore the concept "minority."

We must conclude that although power is a necessary condition for minority status, it is not the only defining characteristic. As we have seen, Wirth, Young, Wagley and Harris, and others have pointed to the importance of identifiability, differential treatment, and group awareness as important defining criteria. By combining these with differential power, we may be able to develop a definition which is universal, dynamic, empirically based, and heuristic.

Minority Group Defined

How then shall we define "minority group?" Extracting from previous sociological efforts and satisfying the prerequisites for a good sociological definition, we propose that a minority group is a group characterized by four qualities: identifiability, differential power, differential and pejorative treatment, and group awareness. Minorities are actual groups of people who interact with one another and with the majority group in terms of their group membership. Minority groups are not simply statistical categories, such as all people who wear size nine shoes, or people who wear glasses. Such aggregates are not minorities or even groups; they lack social organization, social relationships between members, and a consciousness of kind.[13] It is conceivable that a statistical category can move in the direction of group, and ultimately minority-group, formation. The statistical category of left-handed people is in the process of becoming a group, and perhaps a minority group, having formed organizations to pressure manufacturers to make equipment which they can use, and interacting with one another to discuss their common problems.

17

Similarly, women represent a statistical category which has progressed to the stage of being a minority group. It must be realized that because some groups are emerging and others are assimilating into the majority, any given minority group may possess more or less of each of the specified qualities. Further, these are group characteristics, and individual group members may possess each of them to a greater or lesser degree. These characteristics will vary over time and geographical region such that there will be variations in the specific operationalization of identifiability, nature and usage of power, form of treatment, and content of self-awareness. Citing relevant examples, let us examine each of these dimensions.

IDENTIFIABILITY

Football players of opposing teams wear uniforms of different colors to assist fans in distinguishing between the teams and to help each player to identify his teammates. In the area of minority-group relations, salient groups must be readily identifiable in order to insure that an individual recognizes members of his own group and members of the others, and treats them accordingly. Without identifiability, group solidarity and differential treatment become difficult, if not impossible.

Selection of the relevant characteristics upon which identifiability is based is neither fixed nor self-evident. Rather, it is variable and socially defined and interpreted. There is nothing intrinsic in the sex, skin color, eye structure, language, or religion of a group that makes it inferior or undesirable. The definitions of such characteristics make them likely foci of identifiability, prejudice, and discrimination. What is often overlooked in minority-group relations is that there are more similarities than dissimilarities between peoples within the same society. Rather than emphasizing that all have human skin, eyes, and the facility for symbolic communication,[14] people emphasize differences in skin color, eye shape and color, specific language, and even accent. People in different societies selectively perceive and define as salient diverse physical and cultural variations.

In America skin color is the central element of identifiability, and black Americans (the most different from the white majority) are the prime outgroup. Until recently a popular maxim has been, "If you're white, you're right; If you're brown, hang around; If you're black, get back." Today, many companies hire a dark-complexioned token black and keep him or her in a visible location as proof of their compliance with civil rights legislation.

Americans have been so sensitized to shades of color that even within minority communities lighter-skinned individuals have greater esteem

18

than darker persons. When a minority group develops a strong group awareness, a pride in the identifiable trait follows, accompanied by slogans such as "Black is beautiful."

Other salient criteria for distinguishing between groups, including religion, dress, speech style, and other cultural factors, tend to be more transitory than biological variables. It is possible to change status merely by adopting the customs and culture of the majority group, thus becoming less identifiable. This is essentially what has occurred with the Irish, Germans, and Italians. Within a few generations, European immigrant minorities became Americanized and blended into the majority population. When biological factors are involved, however, this is not so simple a task, and patterns of minority-group relations are retained as long as these biological factors are considered relevant.

In societies which are physically homogeneous, cultural factors become more critical and both informal social norms and formal legal procedures are instituted to insure that identifiable distinctions remain.

Where identifiability is lacking, artificial visibility is sometimes created. In Nazi Germany, Jews looked like everyone else, so it became Nazi policy to force Jews to wear yellow arm bands to produce this element of identifiability and make possible differential treatment.

DIFFERENTIAL POWER

Power is the actual use of resources to influence and control others.[15] Power is the actual rather than the potential. In his model of racial discrimination, Blalock enters into the equation of power the combination of total resources ("money, property, prestige, authority, and natural and supernatural resources") plus the mobilization of resources (the amount of resources actually used).

Differential power implies relatively greater use of resources by one group compared to another. Hence, we are speaking not of a powerful group versus a powerless group, but of a relatively more powerful group versus a relatively less powerful group.

We must distinguish between a power group (independent of size) and a numerical majority (dependent only upon size). In terms of domination, it is the power rather than the number which matters. In fact, Blalock argues that numbers are not a resource, and may actually drain away a group's strength as they pose coordination and resource distribution problems for the group. Usually the power group is also numerically larger, but one need only look historically and cross-culturally to find examples of the power group being numerically smaller. Parts of the American South during the 1950s and South Africa and Rhodesia today all illustrate the contention that a numerically small group can control a numerically large but relatively powerless group. Similarly, with only a handful of soldiers but with more resources and superior mobilization, Cortez conquered the more numerous Aztec people in two short years. In these cases the "minority group" is actually the numerically larger one.

Numbers can have some effect, however. As the numbers in the (power) minority increase, the resources mobilized by the (power) majority must also increase. Large numbers in the minority group require the power majority to remain on guard. All white Rhodesians serve in a militia, lock themselves in at night, and continually inspect native compounds. However, in this, and most other minority-majority situations, the power group has so many resources at its disposal that it is not easy to overwhelm it with sheer numbers.

When the power majority controls resources, it also controls the life chances of the minority: their access to resources, jobs, education, wealth, even food and health care. So doing guarantees that the minority[16] will remain dependent upon the majority in a colonial-type relationship. The analogy is not accidental. Many (including Blauner,[17] Memmi,[18] J. Moore,[19] and Carmichael and Hamilton[20]) have spoken of "internal colonialism" as typifying the relationships of whites with blacks, browns, and Indians in American society.

DIFFERENTIAL AND PEJORATIVE TREATMENT

The differentials in power permit the dominant majority to exercise control over the minority group through differential and pejorative treatment or discrimination. Discrimination is the behavioral component of prejudicial attitudes of the majority toward the minority. According to Lieberson's[21] model of ethnic stratification, the dominant majority and the minority each seek to maintain their own social order. However, given limitations on resources and given the perception of mutually exclusive goals, the dominant group needs to enforce the subjugation of the minority group through various strategies. Allport[22] itemized these processes and strategies as antilocution (stereotyping), avoidance, discrimination, physical attack, and extermination. Each strategy has been implemented in various societies, including the United States.

Groups which are not economically beneficial to the majority or which are identifiably quite different are often subjected to the more extreme strategies. For example, blacks provided a convenient labor pool enabling whites to maintain a high level of culture and comfort, whereas native Americans were perceived only as an obstacle to white expansion. Thus the treatment of blacks differed significantly from the treatment of native Americans: blacks were enslaved while native Americans were threatened with extermination.

20

Differential treatment, or discrimination, is what group members actually experience as a consequence of their minority status. It is this differential treatment which most directly affects the life chances and life style of the individual minority-group member and which becomes the focus of minority protest and movements.

GROUP AWARENESS

As identifiable groups who are disadvantaged in power receive differential and pejorative treatment, they come to identify themselves as a group. Initially, only a few may be aware of the common bond among them that differentiates their group from the majority. In American society, with its stress upon individual achievement and self-blame for failure,[23] there is a tendency for people not to blame the social system or discrimination. Minority-group status is a process in which increasingly more group members perceive the similarities of their social position and the commonality of their fate. Hence, a minority may exist prior to general group awareness. However, if no individuals in the minority see themselves as a minority and subjected to differential treatment, then minority status cannot be said to exist. Group awareness does not refer to the ability to identify group membership (that is, identifiabilty). Rather, group awareness refers to the perception of common goals that can be achieved only through cooperation, rather than competition,[24] and the realization that differential treatment does not accrue from qualities intrinsic in the minority, but from definitions, evaluations, and actions of the majority.

Development of group awareness is a point of theoretical interest to social scientists, including the contributors to *The Minority Report*. It is heuristic to compare awareness as experienced by different minority groups over time. Such insights, when collected and compared, will enable us to expand upon a theory of minority-group process. A model for such a process will be elaborated in Chapter 3 of this report.

The relationships among the four characteristics of minorities are processual. Further, there are processual changes in the amount of each characteristic possessed by a group at different times in its history. Groups at different times may be more or less identifiable; have more or less power relative to others; be treated more or less differentially; and have more or less group awareness. A frequent pattern is that a group will first be identifiable, then, because of its differential power relative to a majority, receive differential and pejorative treatment, and then over time evolve a group awareness. In some instances differential power and differential treatment may tend to limit opportunities for endogamy, or may impose a given stage of poverty, such that identifiability follows later. Nonetheless, we must consider that, depending upon the vagaries of historical situations, the four components occur as a process.

Specific Minorities and Minority-Group Members

Minority status is shared by numerous groups, not all of which are racial, ethnic, or gender groups. Although we shall focus upon racial, ethnic, and gender groups in *The Minority Report*, political groups, religious groups, deviant groups, social classes, national groups, and so on, can constitute minorities if they possess the four characteristics we have delineated. For example, the Amish of Pennsylvania and the Mormons of nineteenth-century Utah constituted minorities. Catholics in Northern Ireland are clearly minority-group members. Communists, especially during the McCarthy era of the 1950s, Ku Klux Klanners, homosexuals and prison inmates represent other groups which could be covered by a definition of minorities. Each of these groups, while constituting a minority, exemplifies minority status in slightly different ways (although there is sufficient overlap to generalize the definition), and each member of each of the groups possesses more or less of each of the qualities. That is, minority status is variable both across minorities and across individuals labeled as minority-group members.

Once we have determined that a group is a minority, it may still be difficult to place specific individuals into that group. For example, we could agree that black Americans are a minority group, but who is black? Agreement on this issue cannot be assumed.[25]

Georgia in 1927 defined as a person of color anyone who was not white who had Negro, African, or Asiatic Indian ancestry. A white was anyone who had no ascertainable trace of either Negro, African, West Indian, Asiatic Indian, Mongolian Japanese, or Chinese blood in his veins. Louisiana defined color as a person having an appreciable mixture of Negro blood. Texas declares that if a person has had no Negro ancestors for three generations he is white, while Arkansas says that one Negro ancestor anywhere makes one always Negro. Let us imagine the hypothetical case of J. Jones who lives in Texarkana, a community divided by the Texas-Arkansas state line. Suppose that Mr. Jones' great-great-grandfather was black, but that all parents since have been white. On the Texas side he would be white, on the Arkansas side he would be black. Looking for a home prior to the 1968 Civil Rights Act (or since, with the real estate agents willing to violate the law), Mr. Jones would be shown houses in the black neighborhood on the Arkansas side and white neighborhoods on the Texas side. In fact, prior to the 1954 and 1957 Supreme Court rulings on interstate carriers, he would have had to shift from the front to the back of the bus if he were to take the cross-town shuttle.

The legal definition of the native American presents another aspect of the problem. The Bureau of Indian Affairs, the U.S. Census, and Indian organizations themselves use different definitions of what constitutes an Indian. Indians can be people who are defined by others as Indians, who define themselves as Indians, who can claim some specified proportion of Indian blood, or some combination of these criteria. Brewton Berry, in a book about American mestizos,[26] refers to groups of people, mixtures of black, white, and Indian ancestry, who claim recognition as Indians. The Lumbees, the Brass Ankles, and many other such groups along the East Coast have been so recognized by some government agencies but not by others. The confusion of their ancestry, magnified by the confusion of legal definitions, has profound effects upon the future of these groups, as well as on the daily lives of group members.

In all cases of minority-group assignment, the importance of the actual facts of genetic inheritance or cultural background is overshadowed by the significance of the way the individual is socially defined and categorized.

Summary

The term "race" has become a vague, broad word which can no longer be used with precision for social science research. The term "minority" or "minority group" is more appropriate today. However, there are disagreements concerning the best definition of "minority group." Some definitions are lists of traits or lists of actual groups; these are time and location bounded and not particularly heuristic. Other definitions stress identifiability, discriminatory treatment, and awareness. Others have emphasized rules of descent and endogamy. Still others have used differential power as the sole defining characteristic.

In an attempt to develop a definition that is objective, universal, heuristic, and not bounded by time or place, the authors have proposed the following. A minority group is a group characterized by four qualities: identifiability, differential power, differential and pejorative treatment, and group awareness. The definition is processual, in that groups can become minorities and cease to be minorities. It allows for the observation that individual group members may display more or less of these characteristics.

Finally, once a specific group has been defined as a minority it can be problematic as to which specific individuals are members of that group because of conflicting lay definitions.

Theoretical Perspectives

NOTES

1. Herbert Blumer, "Sociological Analysis and the 'Variable,' " *American Sociological Review* 21 (1956): 683–90.
2. Donald Young, *American Minority Peoples* (New York: Harper and Brothers, 1932).
3. Ibid., p. xiii.
4. Louis Wirth, "The Problem of Minority Groups," in *The Science of Man in the World Crisis*, ed. Ralph Linton (New York: Columbia University Press, 1945), p. 347.
5. See the definitions of social problems advanced by Richard Fuller and Richard R. Myers, "Some Aspects of a Theory of Social Problems," *American Sociological Review* 6 (1941): 24–32, and John Kitsuse and Malcolm Spector, "Toward a Sociology of Social Problems," *Social Problems* 20 (1973): 407–18.
6. Charles Wagley and Marvin Harris, *Minorities in the New World* (New York: Columbia University Press, 1958), p. 10.
7. See "A Woman's Report," pp. 373–99.
8. An exception here are the mixed race minorities such as the Anglo-Indian, who exist because individuals marry outside their own group.
9. H. M. Blalock, Jr., "A Power Analysis of Racial Discrimination," *Social Forces* 39 (1960): 53–59.
10. Stanley Lieberson, "A Societal Theory of Race and Ethnic Relations," *American Sociological Review* 26 (1961): 902–10.
11. Pierre L. van den Berge, *Race and Racism* (New York: Wiley, 1967).
12. Donald E. Gelfand and Russell D. Lee, *Ethnic Conflicts and Power: A Cross-National Perspective* (New York: Wiley, 1973).
13. Robert Bierstedt, "The Sociology of Majorities," *American Sociological Review* 13 (1948): 700–710.
14. Racists, even in this century, have attempted to skirt the issue of the commonality between groups by defining particularly hated minorities out of the human species.
15. H. M. Blalock, Jr. ("A Power Analysis"; idem, *Toward a Theory of Minority Group Relations* [New York: Wiley, 1967]), has maintained that power must be used for it to exist. This is distinguished from conceptualizations by Max Weber (*The Theory of Social and Economic Organization*, ed. Talcott Parsons [New York: Free Press, 1964]), who saw power as a potential. The American involvement in Vietnam presents a good case for the preferability of Blalock's position. Although the United States had the potential to destroy all of North and South Vietnam through nuclear annihilation, the costs in exercising such potential were too great, thereby rendering the United States powerless to control the Vietcong and the North Vietnamese.
16. Hereafter "minority" and/or "majority" will be used to refer to a power minority and power majority, respectively. There is no connotation of relative size of population implied.
17. Robert Blauner, "Internal Colonialism and Ghetto Revolt," *Social Problems* 16 (1969): 393–408.
18. Albert Memmi, *The Colonizer and the Colonized* (Boston: Beacon, 1967).
19. Joan Moore, "Colonialism: The Case of the Mexican Americans," *Social Problems* 17 (1970): 463–71.
20. Stokely Carmichael and Charles Hamilton, *Black Power* (New York: Random House, 1967).
21. Lieberson, "A Societal Theory."
22. Gordon W. Allport, *The Nature of Prejudice* (Cambridge, Mass.: Addison-Wesley, 1954).
23. Robert K. Merton, *Social Theory and Social Structure* (New York: Free Press, 1957).
24. We can see that the process of minority-group awareness is similar to that of class consciousness first proposed by Karl Marx.

24

25. John Hope Franklin and Isidore Starr, eds., *The Negro in the Twentieth Century* (New York: Vintage, 1967).
26. Brewton Berry, *Almost White* (New York: Macmillan, 1963).

Suggested Readings

Blalock, H. M., Jr. *Toward a Theory of Minority-Group Relations.* New York: Wiley, 1967.

Blumer, Herbert. "Sociological Analysis and the 'Variable.'" *American Sociological Review* 21 (1956): 683–90.

Gossett, Thomas F. *Race: The History of an Idea in America.* Dallas: Southern Methodist University Press, 1963.

Merton, Robert K. *Social Theory and Social Structure.* New York; Free Press, 1968.

Simpson, George Eaton, and J. Milton Yinger. *Racial and Cultural Minorities: An Analysis of Prejudice and Discrimination.* 4th ed. New York: Harper, 1972.

Wagley, Charles, and Marvin Harris. *Minorities in the New World.* New York: Columbia University Press, 1958.

3.

THE DISTRIBUTIVE DIMENSION

Many are the resources that people need in order to live within a social community. Generally, these resources are ones of property, social prestige, and power, which are unevenly distributed to various groups in the society. Some groups consistently, generation after generation, get more than other groups. In essence this inequality of distribution is a phenomenon of social stratification. When we consider minority and majority relations, we find that the majority group consistently is allocated more resources than the minority groups, and that there is uneven distribution among the minority groups themselves. This chapter will investigate the uneven distribution of resources.

Property

The Bureau of the Census of the United States is the official counter of people in America. This vast social bookkeeping contains information on the distribution of property (economic and economic-related resources). Not only does the census tell us how many members are within the various minority groups, it also gives us a report on the state of their welfare. It indicates their income level, the nature and types of their employment, the quality of their housing, the availability of their health care, and so on.

Working with census data presents some problems. The census is selective in the types of data it collects for its social bookkeeping. For example, it does not provide breakdowns for all minority groups of interest to us. Included in its numerous and complex tables is information about the total population of the United States, whites and blacks, males and females. Other minority groups are sometimes lumped together with blacks forming a category "Negroes and other races."

Recently the census has begun providing breakdowns of persons of "Spanish Heritage." This is not without difficulties. First, grouped under this rubric are such varied classifications as Mexican Americans, Puerto Ricans, Cubans, and Spaniards. There is no way of separating these groups statistically, even though it may be of greatest interest to the sociologists to do so. Second, the category of "Spanish Heritage" is not mutually exclusive vis-à-vis whites and blacks. There is overlap in the categories, so that "Spanish Heritage" persons are counted twice: as "Spanish Heritage" and as either white or black. Hence, percentages do not add to one hundred, and data must be interpreted with great care.

In addition, the census is notorious for its underestimation of blacks and other minorities. Because the census samples residences, it tends to miss individuals who are "hanging" on the street. Estimates are that the census misses as many as one-fifth of all black males between the ages of twenty-five and twenty-nine. Since these individuals may be more likely to be unemployed or underemployed, the income levels for blacks and other minorities may be overestimated, making the differentials between the majority and minorities even greater. For a detailed understanding of the distributive aspect of minority relations, sources other than the census must often be used.

However, the census can give some overall views about the distribution of resources and rewards among groups. For this discussion we will compare those groups represented clearly in the census. For information about other groups, the reader is referred to the reports on individual groups in Part Two of the book.

Of the more than two hundred million persons in the country,[1] slightly more than half (51.34 percent) are female. Some 88 percent of the total population are categorized as white. (This includes the majority white population, plus various "white minorities" such as Jews, Irish, some Puerto Ricans and some Mexican Americans, and, of course, white females.) Of the remaining 12 percent most are black, with relatively small proportions of native Americans, Japanese, and Chinese (.4 percent, .3 percent, and .2 percent, respectively). Persons of Spanish heritage comprise approximately 4.6 percent of the American population.

Property resources are not evenly allocated among these groups. For example, whites have higher incomes. Whereas the median (average) income of persons in the United States (fourteen years and over) is $4,108, the white median is somewhat higher at $4,318, while the black median is considerably lower—$2,917. Spanish heritage persons fall in between with a median yearly income of $3,705. Differences between males and females also are apparent on this level, with males earning significantly more in each of the minority groups as well as in the majority group. The differential is as little as $2,000 between black males and females and as great as $4,000 between white males and females. The differences remain even when incomes of only employed persons are studied.

Differentials in income become more meaningful when percent of families at or below the poverty level is considered. Some 8.6 percent of all white families fall below the poverty level. Among those of Spanish heritage it is over 20 percent, and among black families nearly 30 percent (29.8 percent) have incomes below the poverty level! (It can be noted that because of the overlap involving those of Spanish heritage, the white population will appear less affluent and the black population more affluent than if there were mutually exclusive categories.) Furthermore, unemployment rates are consistently higher for minority groups. In 1970 the unemployment rate of persons in the civilian labor force ranged from a low of 3.6 percent of white males to a high of 8.1 percent for Spanish heritage females. In times of economic crisis, such as experienced in the mid-1970s, the differentials increase even more drastically. In the president's economic report to Congress it was stated that: "In 1974 the unemployment rate of teenagers aged 16 to 19 was 14 percent for white youths and 33 percent for black youngsters."[2]

Translating income into societal costs, blacks, as one might expect, have a higher percentage of families (17.6 percent) receiving public assistance incomes than do whites (4 percent) or Spanish heritage (12.6 percent).

Translated into personal costs, lower income means more minority members living in dilapidated housing, receiving inferior health care, and having lower life expectancies. A black baby born in 1960 is expected to live seven fewer years than a white,[3] and the quality of that life is diminished. Whereas one out of every thirty-two white dwelling units is substandard, one out of every six black dwellings is substandard.[4] So great are the differentials, and so slow the equalization process, that in spite of the civil rights movement it will be well into the twenty-first century before black and white incomes are equalized.[5]

The effects of low income are somewhat cushioned for women as a group. A large proportion of women who have low or no personal income live with a spouse who provides a higher standard of living than their own low income would imply. This applies only to those women who have employed spouses living with them. In households headed by a female, her low income is more likely to be accompanied by dilapidated housing and welfare assistance, as is the case with other minority groups.

Social Prestige

Social prestige is the respect with which an individual or group is held. It is the status honor given to members of any society. Prestige is intertwined with property in an elaborate cycle. Having property resources enables one to command the respect and deference of others. In our society a wealthy person is held in higher esteem than one whose income is below the poverty level. It may be unfortunate, but true, that "money makes the man." With property resources one can purchase prerequisites for high social esteem, including an extensive education at a "good" university. This education will qualify one for a "good" occupation, which is another source of social prestige and also a means of obtaining economic resources.

Usually these three components of social class—income, education, and occupation—are on approximately the same level for any one individual. Thus one with high educational attainment would also have a high income and a prestigeful occupation, and conversely, one with low education would have a low income and a less prestigeful occupation. These are examples of a consistent pattern, but it sometimes happens (and frequently to minority-group[6] members) that the pattern is inconsistent. A typical example is that of a well-educated individual who has been underemployed in a low-income low-prestige job. He has the prerequisites for high status, but it is denied to him. Some sociologists[7] have documented that the vanguard of minority reform movements is composed of status-inconsistent persons. It would appear that inconsistency may be a necessary condition to activism, but it certainly is not a sufficient one, since many inconsistent persons never become active reformers. Unfortunately, research on the effects of status inconsistency has yielded contradictory results and no firm conclusion can be drawn.[8]

Social prestige can be considered on two levels: the individual and the group. American society is characterized by the absence of titles of nobility, so questions of who you are can be answered most easily in terms of what you do. Furthermore, what you do almost invariably refers to what kind of work you do or the nature of your occupation. On the individual level, education is often perceived as the key to unlock the doors to better occupations and middle-class standing for minority persons. However, education has not been equally experienced by all groups in our society. The median number of years of formal education for whites is 12.1; for nonwhites it is only ten.[9] Hence, nonwhites generally have quantitatively less education, and less often receive the diploma critical for job placement. In addition, many writers have verified the qualitatively poorer education given to minorities.

In the 1960s the federal government initiated numerous programs (as part of the "War on Poverty") to improve the educational opportunities of minority group members. The frequent assumption of both the government and the minority groups was that education is the only attainment needed to narrow the gap between minorities and the majority. Jencks[10] has argued that, despite programs to equilibrate educational opportunities, minority gains in occupations and income levels have not met expectations. Some minorities have even experienced a widening of the gap. Thus education has not been the panacea for all.

Individuals with the proper educational credentials still experience discrimination in the job market, resulting in lower prestige and lower-income jobs. Furthermore, success in business often depends upon informal networks formed by "knowing the right people." A well-qualified individual outside these networks experiences great difficulties entering into many occupations. Receiving a bank loan, joining a union, becoming an apprentice, or being a professor's protégé are often denied to minority members who don't "know the right people."

The census reflects the uneven allocation of persons into occupations. Table 3–1 presents the percentages of experienced persons in the labor force (excluding the military) for the year 1970. Each of the groups tabulated is broken down by sex. The table will enable us to make comparisons across groups and between sexes.

The first observation that can be made from the table is that whites (as a group) have a larger percentage of their labor force located in the first five categories than do the black and Spanish heritage groups. These occupational categories—professional, managers, sales, clerical, and crafts—are the white-collar and upper-level blue-collar situses. They carry more prestige, offer greater incomes, and require more education and/or apprenticeships.

Conversely, the black and Spanish heritage groups have greater proportions of their numbers in the unskilled, blue-collar jobs. These are the groups who do the heavy, dirty work for minimal pay and minimal prestige.

Next we can compare males and females and make some additional observations. There are higher percentages of female professionals than male professionals across all three groups. However, as shall be expanded upon later, within the professional category women are concentrated in the so-called semiprofessions such as public school teaching and nursing.

TABLE 3–1

OCCUPATIONS OF EXPERIENCED CIVILIAN LABOR FORCE
BY RACE AND SEX: 1970

	Total		White		Black		Spanish Heritage	
	Male	Female	Male	Female	Male	Female	Male	Female
Total	100%*	100%	100%	100%	100%	100%	100%	100%
Professional/ Technical	13.99	15.30	14.72	15.87	5.67	10.82	8.65	9.11
Managers	10.89	3.55	11.70	3.85	2.90	1.39	6.09	2.34
Sales	6.83	7.41	7.33	8.08	2.03	2.61	4.56	5.91
Clerical	7.58	34.47	7.53	36.43	7.94	20.41	7.48	29.26
Crafts	21.29	1.82	21.94	1.87	15.26	1.46	19.72	2.16
Operatives	13.82	14.53	13.28	14.18	19.78	16.91	18.82	24.74
Transportation Operatives	5.97	.45	5.63	.46	9.80	.39	6.50	.37
Laborers (except farm)	6.96	1.02	6.03	.95	16.20	1.57	10.52	1.37
Farmers and farm managers	2.74	.23	2.94	.24	.88	.16	.69	.08
Farm laborers	1.72	.57	1.51	.48	3.50	1.19	5.63	2.12
Service	8.11	16.60	7.32	15.39	15.52	25.31	11.20	18.35
Private household workers	.08	3.84	.04	2.00	.43	17.53	.09	3.95
Unemployed since 1959	.03	.20	.02	.19	.08	.23	.02	.19

SOURCE: U.S. Bureau of the Census, *Census of Population: 1970* (Washington, D.C.: Government Printing Office, 1973), pt. 1, sec. 2, Table 224, pp. 746–48.

*Raw frequencies have been converted to percentages. Percentages do not total to exactly 100 percent down columns because of rounding error.

These occupations are lower in pay and prestige, and practitioners have less autonomy than do those in other professions.

Women are also well represented in sales, in the broad category of clerical workers, and in the service occupations. Finally, a larger proportion of women (black women especially) than men are private household workers. Housecleaning, maid service, babysitting for a salary can be viewed as an extension of the same traditional tasks performed by women in their own homes.

It is pertinent to note which occupations do not have large percentages of women relative to men. Women are not managers—neither in business nor on the farm. Women, furthermore, are not represented well in the extremes of the blue-collar occupations. They are neither skilled craftsmen nor unskilled laborers. Thus females receive different treatment vis-à-vis occupations. Sometimes this treatment is pejorative; sometimes it is "protective."

Table 3–1 may be misleading in that it paints a more optimistic picture for some minorities than is the reality. First, there are many occupations represented in a given category (e.g., professional/technical includes such diverse occupations as brain surgeons, corporation lawyers, public school teachers, clergymen, and registered nurses), and minority-group members tend to be concentrated in the lower-paying and lower-status end of the scale. Second, when minorities are employed in the same occupation as majority-group members, they tend to be paid less because they do not have seniority, and they tend to be concentrated in positions with "unsteady employment, and in low-wage firms even in the same industry."[11] José Hernandez and Joe Henderson may both be skilled machinists of the same age, but José works for Smalltown Flange Company, earns less than $6,000 per year because his company cannot pay him more, has not had many years on the job, and is subject to frequent layoffs (minorities are the last hired and the first fired). Joe Henderson, on the other hand, works for World-Wide Flange Company, is protected by his union, has experienced few if any layoffs, and is paid over $16,000 per year by a large company with vast control over the economic market.

When we speak of the prestige of groups, the achievement of individuals plays a relatively less significant role. Some individuals within a minority group may have achieved high status, but the group of which they are members will still be ranked very low. Individual mobility is distinct from collective mobility, and sociologically a group is different than the sum of its individual parts. There have been minority-group members who have achieved wealth, fame, and the respect of the majority community. Thurgood Marshall is an associate justice of the United States Supreme Court and a black man; Vicki Carr is a popular Mexican American singer; and part native American Will Rogers was a noted humorist and political satirist. There are numerous other examples, but these few are enough to indicate that individuals can be mobile while the group of which they are members remains of low prestige. In Chapter Six we shall discuss theories of acceptance of minority groups, but suffice it to note that structural assimilation necessitates the widespread acceptance of a group into the clubs and cliques of the majority, not simply the acceptance of a few notables.

Social distance measures have often been used as indicators of the relative ranking of minority groups. These scales are assessments of the extent to which people are willing to enter into close, personal, and intimate relations with members of the minority group qua group. The most widely known of such indicators is the Bogardus Social Distance Scale, first devised in 1926 by Emory Bogardus, and used periodically[12] by him and systematically by dozens of other researchers up to the present day. The scale asks individuals to indicate whether they would interact with members of specified minority groups in the following seven situations: marriage partner, close friend, office coworker, neighbor, casual acquaintance, prefer out of neighborhood, and prefer out of country. The items in the scale are arranged in decreasing degrees of intimacy and increasing amounts of social distance. Groups with which the respondents are willing to have more intimate interactions are thus considered to be of higher status or prestige. Presented in Table 3–2 are the relative rankings of a selection of minority groups studied by Bogardus over a forty-year period. The higher the score assigned to the group, the greater the social distance, and hence the less the minority-group prestige.

Social distance is not identical to minority-group prestige, but it represents one of the less compromised measures of prestige. Assessments of social distance more sophisticated than the Bogardus scale tend to differentiate between classes and subgroups within the minority commu-

TABLE 3–2

RELATIVE BOGARDUS SOCIAL DISTANCE RANKINGS OF MINORITY GROUPS*
(MAJORITY RANKING IN PARENTHESIS)

Group	1926 Sample N = 1725		1946 Sample N = 1950		1956 Sample N = 2053		1966 Sample N = 2605	
	SDS†	Rank	SDS	Rank	SDS	Rank	SDS	Rank
White Americans	1.10	1	1.04	1	1.08	1	1.07	1
Irish	1.30	2	1.24	2	1.56	2	1.40	2
American Indians	2.38	3	2.45	4	2.35	5	2.12	4
Jews	2.39	4	2.32	3	2.15	3	1.97	3
Mexican Americans	(not ranked)		2.52	5	2.51	6	2.37	7
Japanese Americans	(not ranked)		2.90	7	2.34	4	2.14	5
Negroes	3.28	5	3.60	8	2.74	8	2.56	8
Chinese	3.36	6	2.50	6	2.68	7	2.34	6

SOURCE: Adapted from E. Bogardus, "Comparing Racial Distance in Ethiopia, South Africa, and the United States," *Sociology and Social Research* 52 (1968): 152.
* The range of possible scores is from 1.00 (highest prestige and lowest social distance) to 7.00 (lowest prestige and highest social distance).
† Social Distance Score.

nity. In that sense they are better indicators of individual preference for interaction with individual members of minority groups, but they move further from an indication of group prestige. In the construction of his measure of status consistency, Lenski[13] used minority-group prestige as one of four measures of status, along with income, education, and occupation. His measure was even cruder than the use of the Bogardus measure. Lenski simply asked a group of students to rank the groups. Sinha and Sinha[14] measured minority prestige of castes in India in a similar manner by having individuals rank the castes in order of general importance. The task of the latter researchers was aided by the fact that India is a much more rigidly stratified society, with an institutionalized and governmentally ranked hierarchy of groups.

Lieberson argues that in light of the difficulties in measuring minority group rankings, hierarchies ought to be measured in terms of a twofold dimension of stratification: "discrimination against a group in terms of economic opportunity or political power, or both."[15] He contends that because minority groups have the potential of forming their own nation-state (or at least being separatists within the society—a possibility not available to purely social classes), and because minority stratificational systems in a society will affect other stratificational systems (including class solidarity and solidarity across class lines but within minority group lines), one may not be able to use stratificational models in dealing with minority stratification. However, if one defines minority hierarchies in terms of economic opportunities and political power (two of our dimensions of stratification), one eliminates the prestige dimensions altogether, or creates a logical error in defining a concept in terms of two other concepts in the typology. Lieberson would have omitted the prestige dimension, but to do so would ignore the fact that some groups may have prestige without power and property, while others might have power and property without prestige. The Italians and Irish were identified with big-city corruption and with organized crime in the 1930s. Many subgroups of these minorities possessed considerable power and property, but were not held in respect. Similarly, if we explore Table 3–2 we note that in 1966 native Americans had relatively high prestige (fourth among the groups, close to Jews) but possessed little power or property.

As we note from Table 3–2, racial minorities tend generally to be ranked lower than ethnic minorities. Many factors, including historical events, may account for changes in the ranking of groups. Thus during and immediately after World War II Japanese Americans experienced a marked decline in prestige in the eyes of the majority. Three forms of determinants can generally be proposed to account for the rankings of groups: (1) the power of the minority groups relative to one another and to the majority; (2) the extent to which the minority resembles the majority, and hence the probability that the minority may soon assimilate to the majority; and (3) the extent to which the minority is seen as making a substantial contribution to the society in which it lives. These three dimensions are highly interrelated. There are also some instances, although relatively rare, in which achievements by "race men" make it possible for others of their minority group to attain mobility, but the ranking of the group as a whole is usually not altered.[16]

The Irish gained political power through control of ward politics and political machines. They were identifiably very similar to the white Anglo-Saxon Protestant majority (both racially and culturally), and have been identified with much of American history. Thus their status is high. Blacks have, until recently, enjoyed little political control (even of the ghettos). They are dissimilar from the majority in appearance, and their contributions have been ignored in much of the writing of American history. They thus occupy a low status among minorities. However, blacks have attempted through several means (to be discussed in the next section) to gain political power, and they have demanded the correction of history books to include the manifold contributions of blacks to American society. Similar efforts have been made by Mexican Americans, native Americans, and women.

Power

Earlier we noted that power was the actual use of resources to influence and control others. The variables of power are total number of resources and their mobilization. Power is interconnected with property and prestige in that property represents material resources to be mobilized, and prestige represents influence to induce others to mobilize resources or to induce others, out of respect, to comply with one's wishes. Power, when achieved, can be utilized to increment one's prestige and property. In essence, minorities seek to gain power so as to increase their property and prestige. Because they lack property and prestige, poor people are usually unable to run for political office and hence increase their power. The cycle may be vicious: Without property and prestige one cannot gain power, but without power one may not be able to influence others so as to gain property and prestige.

There have been many taxonomies of power, but it may be helpful in discussing minorities to distinguish between two general types; legal and extralegal. Legal power, or authority, is power obeyed because of its legitimacy. As Hopkins, commenting upon Max Weber's use of the term "authority," notes: "People obey when they feel a moral obligation to do so, because specifically, they and everyone else define the statuses they occupy as allowing or requiring them to do so."[17] Thus compliance with and exercise of such power is not a function of coercion or force, but rather of willingness and obligation. Political incumbents do not leave office and surrender power when they lose an election because they fear punishment should they refuse, but because they accept as morally correct and legitimate the rules of political succession. Office holding, legal petitions before the courts, and voting activities represent some forms of legal power available to minorities.

Extralegal power is that power which is not mutually acceptable to the parties involved. In some instances use of such power may involve coercion and force, and is met with the exercise of power by the opposing group. Revolts, riots, protests, sit-ins, marches, boycotts, and similar activities represent some forms of extralegal power available to minorities.

LEGAL POWER

Legal power can be exercised within the formal structure of government. Some European immigrant minorities have assimilated to the extent of acquiring great political power in the highest levels of government. The Irish Kennedy family is such an example. Jews also have achieved national prominence and power. Although not yet gaining the presidency, there have been powerful Jews in Congress, the Cabinet, and on the Supreme Court.

Other minority groups have not fared as well. Blacks have gained elective seats in Congress with some regularity over the past several years, but other groups have been elected only sporadically to Capitol Hill. Table 3–3 shows the distribution of minority-group members in the Congress.

TABLE 3–3

MINORITY MAKEUP OF THE 93RD CONGRESS

Group	Senate	House of Representatives
White	97	418
Negro	1	15
Other	2	2
Males	100	419
Females	0	16

SOURCE: U.S. Department of Commerce, *Statistical Abstracts of the United States,* Tables 695 and 696, p. 433. 93rd ed. (Washington, D.C.: Government Printing Office, 1974).

Minority groups (with the possible exception of blacks in the House) are vastly underrepresented in Congress. Furthermore, minority congressional members usually are relegated to less important committees,[18] and with lack of seniority have relatively little power within congressional walls.

Both females and racial minorities appear to be a long distance from the presidency. Even here there are differentials among groups. As Amundsen notes:

> There is today a greater acceptance of the possibility of having a black man as president than a woman. In 1969, only 54 percent of the electorate said they would be willing to vote for a woman for president, if a generally well-qualified woman were nominated by the party of preference. But 67 percent would be willing to vote for a black man in the same circumstances.[19]

Minorities tend to exert more political power on the local levels of government, and this power is increasing. According to the *Statistical Abstracts of the United States*,[20] black elected officials in county, city, law-enforcement, and education districts in the United States have doubled between 1970 and 1974 (from 1,472 in 1970 to 2,991 in 1974). However, there were over one-half million elected officials in the United States in 1974, and blacks represented only six-tenths of 1 percent of them.

Over recent years some minority groups have achieved a measure of political power—and in some instances even great power. What mechanisms have minority groups used to gain such power?

Ironically, segregation and ghettoization of minorities, while unfortunate for a variety of reasons, is actually functional for the acquisition of political office in this nation. Where members of a minority group have been residentially isolated, they may be able to obtain voting majorities in congressional districts, school districts, and even entire municipalities. Municipal control is enhanced by the majority flight to the suburbs. This isolation has been a recent source of power for blacks and for Mexican Americans; the lack of such isolation has been a handicap for women.

Historically, the Irish and other European immigrant groups were able to achieve much political power and ultimately assimilation through manipulation of the urban political machine.[21] The relationship between the precinct captain and the new immigrant was reciprocal. In return for votes, the petty politicians helped their constituency obtain employment and facilitated adaptation to the new social environment. Thus the new immigrant was able to wield considerable political power in a relatively short time.

Legal power can be exercised not only by gaining elective office, but by using legitimate tactics to influence those who are in office. Lobbying, lawsuits, court appeals, and other such strategies used by reform movements are exercises of power. The most famous of these include the 1954 *Brown Brothers* v. *Board of Education* decision of the Supreme Court, which ruled school segregation unconstitutional.

Often members of minority groups differ in their approval of methods of exercising what power they possess. Within the population of native Americans there is controversy about the utility of lawsuits over such displays of power as the taking of Wounded Knee. Within the black communities of the 1960s there was much debate about the legalism of the NAACP as against the tactics of sit-ins, demonstrations, and protests. The latter tactics can be all categorized as extralegal forms of power.

EXTRA-LEGAL POWER

When legal forms of power are denied, it sometimes becomes necessary to develop extralegal power. The power might be used to call attention to abuses by the majority; to shame the majority into granting concessions to the minority; to gain independence from domination by the majority; or to gain control over one's own destiny. The use of extralegal power to change the social system, alter the societal definition of the minority by the majority, and in turn insure greater resources and prestige for the minority, is thus reform oriented. Techniques of civil disobedience ranging from sit-ins to riots represent uses of reform-oriented extralegal power.

When minorities have few resources to mobilize in order to affect the majority, they may resort to the one resource all have: their bodies. By blocking the activities of the majority (as in a sit-in), attacking the symbols of the majority (the police and fire departments), or destroying some of the majority's property (as well as the minority's) in a riot or violent protest, the minority can achieve an influence over the behavior of the majority. The boycotts, marches, and sit-ins of the black civil rights movement forced the South to abandon many of the Jim Crow practices that had been prevalent for nearly a century. The riots and violent protests that swept the nation in the 1960s forced the white majority to recognize the existence of a serious problem and to induce federal funding to attempt to ameliorate the plight of the urban black.[22] Many researchers have commented on the tokenism of such efforts, and the extent to which these token efforts helped to consolidate black group awareness.[23]

It has been the experience of minority relations in America that as the reform-oriented means to power have become successful, they begin to acquire legitimacy; their effectiveness and impact are diminished; and the majority begins to adopt similar tactics as counterdisplays of power. Initial marches were met by hoses, dogs, and mass arrests; later marches were sanctioned with police protection and legislative support. Protest activities became routinized to the extent that rules for their conduct were established and enforced. For example, parade permits and adherence to a predetermined route of march became necessary. The early years of the 1970s have seen majority marches protesting busing and forced school desegregation.

Some writers have felt that riot behavior was merely aggressive response to total frustration, in which the hopeless minority "explodes" in anger.[24] But others have shown that protesters of all kinds tend to be those who have feelings of personal control over their destinies and convictions of political efficacy.[25] According to these writers, extralegal power strategies are attempted exactly because the individuals in the minority feel that they have a high probability of attaining resources through such exercise of their power.

Majority Responses

The majority, by definition, has relatively greater power than the minority. Thus it has the capacity to retard or defeat minority exercises of power. Generally, minorities are effective only to the extent that the majority is unwilling to mobilize its full resources to halt the minority. The vast changes in intergroup relations in the first half of the present century have occurred in part because the majority was no longer willing to oppose the minority maximally, and in part because the changes were incremental and accompanied by attitude shifts. Further, in hundreds of overt and covert ways the majority has insured its control while granting token benefits to minorities. We may itemize at least six techniques used by majorities to maintain dominance over minorities.

TOKENISM

By minimally meeting some of the demands of minorities, majorities can give the impression of granting resources without actually doing so. By permitting a few minority-group members in an overwhelmingly majority school, majorities have attempted to meet school desegregation orders without changing the balance of power in the schools. Coleman and his associates[26] and Mack and his associates[27] have documented the manner in which southern schools first attempted to bypass desegregation orders by providing better physical facilities for black schools while keeping the schools segregated and unequal. White employers have hired one or two minority-group members, given them executive titles, but provided them with few options to exercise decision making while appearing to be an equal opportunity employer. Often an individual who represents two minority groups (such as a black woman) is hired. Thus the employer gets "two for the price of one."

COERCION

The most common use of majority power has been to force the minorities to comply with their demands. The threat of violence, imprisonment, even death have accompanied these demands. From Ku Klux Klan night rides to mass arrests or loss of job security, the majority has controlled the minorities.

COOPTATION

Here minority groups, minority organizations, or minority-group members are incorporated into the majority to avert threats to the control of the majority. Particularly dynamic and active members of the minority may be appointed to majority-controlled organizations and then given tasks which minimize their effectiveness in leading the minority. In fact, the individual may soon find that his task is to "keep down" or control the activities of other members of his group.

GERRYMANDERING DISTRICTS

Minority political power, although heightened by residential segregation, may be diluted if the majority redistributes voting districts so that minorities do not have a plurality in their district.

DIVIDE AND CONQUER

In this technique majority-group members pit minorities against one another, especially by promoting economic competition between groups.[28] Dr. Martin Luther King, Jr., recognized this strategy and attempted before his assassination to expand his campaign from a black civil rights movement to a poor people's movement, involving all the disinherited of the country.

SOCIALIZATION AND "ANGLO CONFORMITY"

The majority may attempt to educate the young of the minority group to believe in the legitimacy of the majority's control. If these individuals are taught to desire the language, beliefs, values, and customs of the majority, they may be less likely to question the resources owned by the majority. They will identify less with the minority and more with the majority. Thus a minority individual's desire for mobility will be personal and individualistic, and not group oriented. He will achieve not to help "his people" but to help himself.

Another aspect of socialization is the teaching of minorities that only the majority has made significant achievements. Omission of minority contributions from history books has the effect of minimizing minority-group pride and self-awareness and maximizing desires to emulate and identify with the majority. Adults and children alike can be socialized through the mass media, including newspapers, literature, radio, and television. The appearance of minorities and minority-life situations in television programs reflects the initial influence of minority power (especially economic power in terms of buying advertised products) on the identity process. Much of the programing, however, retains the majority group's stereotyped definiton of life in the minority communities.

A System Model for Minority Access to Resources

Figure 3–1 represents a model created by J. Chafetz, A. G. Dworkin, and R. J. Dworkin[29] to attempt to account for the manner in which minority groups may gain property and prestige through entry into the labor force of the majority. The full ramifications of the model cannot be developed in this text. However, the essential components include conditions of the society (A) in which the minority and majority live (population size, level of technology, state of economy, and natural resources), which affect the demand for labor (B). Should the traditional labor force (majority group members) be scarce (C), other sources of labor will be sought (D). These other sources should include minority-group members, provided that subcultural and societal definitions of minority capabilities (E_1) and definitions of the nature of the tasks involved (E_2) are comparable. Minorities, through social movements (F), may exert an influence upon these definitions and compel the majority to utilize the nontraditional labor force(G_1). This in turn influences future role allocations (G_2) and definitions of minority capabilities (H), thereby making it easier for minorities to be incorporated into the labor pool in the future. Obviously minority-group members do perform work and are part of a labor force, even when these mechanisms are not activated. The tasks they perform, however, are usually low paying and low in prestige. The current model attempts to account for changes in allocation of jobs (particularly higher-paying and higher-prestige jobs) to minorities.

Because we have posed a system model, it can be seen that role allocations and definitions are reversible. As the demand for labor

FIGURE 3–1

A SYSTEM MODEL FOR MINORITY ACCESS TO RESOURCES

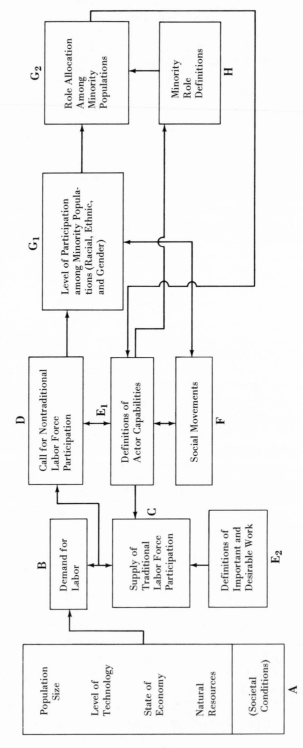

diminishes, minorities may become barred from these higher-paying and higher-prestige occupations. A classic example of the process accounted for by the model is the position of women in the labor force.

Prior to World War II, most women were housewives or in traditionally female occupations (schoolteacher, nurse, salesclerk, typist). The war depleted the masculine labor force and simultaneously created a need for a manufacturing labor force which was literate, skilled, and immediately available. Women could be easily trained to perform the tasks of skilled craftsmen and had a willingness to perform the tasks. They were thus incorporated into this labor pool and "Rosey the Riveter" became a folk heroine. With the end of the war the diminished demand for labor could be satisfied by returning veterans. The female nontraditional labor force was no longer required. Role definitions reversed themselves and women were again relegated to the home. However, the experience of the 1940's was not forgotten, and became a precedent for the new feminist movement of the late 1960's.

Class and Caste:
Open and Closed Models of Minority Stratification

American society has been variously characterized as having either an open *class* system for mobility in terms of power, prestige, and property, or a rigid, closed, color *caste* system of immobility in terms of these indicators.

In societies founded upon a caste system, such as India, a vast amount of a person's status characteristics are ascribed. That is, the person is born into a set of status and role relationships and expectations, as well as other important dimensions of his life. There is no mobility out of one's subcaste, whether it be *Brahmin, Rajput, Chamar,* untouchable, or any other. Marriage across caste lines is forbidden, and since caste determines occupational possibilities, career mobility is rigid. Although caste guarantees that no group will monopolize another's occupational group and steal away jobs, it also prohibits individuals from attaining careers not deemed suitable for their subcaste. The entire social order is maintained, sanctified, by the religious system. To violate the rules of caste is to violate the religion, and to incur considerable sanction.

Class systems are much more open. In the ideal they guarantee that even within a family across generations all members have an opportunity to move up (or down) in the social order. In reality, of course, class system operates somewhat more rigidly than the ideal, but much less rigidly than caste systems. Elites tend to beget elites, and stratificational systems tend to be self-perpetuating. But there remains the potential, through self-improvement and education, for considerable mobility from parent to child. Assignment of roles and statuses ideally is based upon achievement—what you have done and how hard you have attempted to gain it. We know, however, that it is many times easier for a rich man's son to become a rich man than it is for a poor man's son. Aside from marriage to the rich man's son, or through inheritance, the task is somewhat more difficult for a rich man's daughter to become a rich woman.

Some writers have likened American minority-group relations to a caste system of stratification; Warner,[30] Dollard,[31] and Davis, Gardner, and Gardner[32] have characterized black-white relations in America as castelike. In the 1930s and 1940s, when these works were written, there was little black mobility to the status dimensions occupied by whites. Further, most whites could boast that no matter how low they got as individuals, there were always many blacks below them in a lower caste. Changes in the balance of power, prestige, and property occasioned by the civil rights movement have moved the caste barrier from a near-horizontal line, demarcating the white population on the top from the black population on the bottom, to a more vertical line with parallel stratificational systems (social class-based within each caste). There is still little exogamy, but there are many more middle- and upper-class blacks than in the earlier model. Whites no longer assume that most blacks are below them in status regardless of their own low position.

Similar caste models based upon intermarriage have been advanced in the 1940s to account for religious groups. Kennedy[33] argued that there was a triple melting pot, Catholic, Protestant, and Jew, and that intermarriage among these groups was infrequent. Herberg[34] found a similar triple melting pot in the 1950s. But the current generation is not so bounded by pressures against interfaith marriages, and the caste system based on religious groupings is rapidly becoming a phenomenon of the past. Hacker[35] and Andreas[36] have posited a caste system vis-à-vis sex categories.

The caste model has been seriously challenged by many writers. Cox[37] argued nearly thirty years ago that the metaphor of caste adapted from India was being stretched too much to be applicable to the United States. Cox called for some alternative concept to denote the black-white situation. Perhaps what Blauner[38] and Carmichael and Hamilton[39] have termed "internal colonialism" (to be discussed in the next section) may be the preferable metaphor for the black-white relationship. Simpson and Yinger[40] have argued that a caste model is inexorably tied to the religious system of India, and cannot be transported to the United States without suffering irreparable damage. Some, however, have argued that there is a quasi-religious basis for a color caste in the United States—racism.

Class models have been prolific in American sociology. Some writers have viewed classes as discrete categories with clear-cut boundaries separating upper, middle, and lower groups.[41] Others have contended that classes are continuous categories without clear-cut boundaries.[42] When applied to minority-group relations, the models proposed have tended to deal with blacks and whites, and hence twofold parallel class (one for blacks and one for whites) structure models have been advanced, including those by Hunter in Atlanta, Drake and Cayton in Chicago, and Burgess in North Carolina.[43]

Perhaps the most viable model has been that proposed by Milton Gordon.[44] The model, termed "ethclass," is based on the cross-classification of ethnic groups and social class categories. A grid is constructed (Figure 3–2) in which each column represents a group, and each row the social classes (upper, middle, and lower, or some more delineated breakdown). Minority groups are then compared both across columns and rows for given social classes. Gordon had proposed that groups of the same social class, regardless of ethnicity, might have more values, beliefs, and aspirations in common, and hence have a greater common ground on which to develop intergroup harmony, than would different classes within a given ethnic group. Landis, Datwyler, and Dorn[45] have gathered data to suggest that this hypothesis is viable.

Class models, because they assume a greater degree of mobility and permit greater exogamy than do caste models, tend to view the ultimate outcome of minority-group relations as one of assimilation, whereby the minority becomes part of the majority in terms of identifiability, power, prestige, and property. Caste models, on the other hand, maintain minority nationalism or continued minority separatism as a plausible outcome. It appears from the experiences of minority groups, and is the contention of the contributors to *The Minority Report,* that neither model may be applied without caution. Class systems and assimilation models depict the outcomes and goals of ethnic minorities. Caste systems, separatism, and/or a degree of nationalism better depict the conditions of racial minorities. Certainly in terms of power, prestige, and property, there may be viability to the class models for racial groups, but these minorities are often unwilling to surrender their identity and intermarry with the majority. Likewise, the majority is unwilling to admit the minority into intermarriage in any significant numbers.

45

FIGURE 3–2

DISPLAY OF GORDON'S ETHCLASS MODEL. GROUPS ARE RANKED
ACCORDING TO DATA PRESENTED IN TABLE 3–2

GROUPS

		WASP	Irish	Jews	American Indians	Japanese American	Chinese American	Mexican American	Blacks
	Upper–Upper								
	Lower–Upper								
Social Classes (Ranked)	Upper–Middle								
	Lower–Middle								
	Upper–Lower								
	Lower–Lower								

Internal Colonialism

Several authors[46] writing principally about the black and the brown experiences have suggested that, rather than a color caste or class model, a colonial model is more appropriate. To an extent it appears that minority status in general fits the colonial analogy. In such a model the relationship between majority and minority is similar to that between colonizer and native. The colony (or ghetto) supplies the "mother country" with raw materials and buys back the finished product at exorbitant rates. In the internal colonial analogy the raw materials are simply cheap labor, and the finished product is purchased at the inflated prices charged for products in the minority communities. Moore[47] has argued that the analogy is better for Chicanos than for blacks, as the Chicanos did originally own the land occupied and literally colonized by the Anglos.

We have noted that there is a dependency relationship between colony and mother country. The colonizer needs the supply of raw materials (cheap labor) and needs the colonized people as a captive market to buy the finished products. But there will be pressures of several sorts to mitigate the stability of the relationship. First, as technology advances, the tasks requiring cheap labor will diminish, reducing the need of the colonial power for the raw materials. Wilhelm[48] has suggested that, under such conditions, drives may arise to exterminate the minority when it is no longer needed. Second, there will be pressure within the minority community or colony to manufacture its own goods and buy only within its boundaries. There have been some attempts at such actions, but the mother country generally owns the necessary supply of capital to limit this possibility.

Third, as is inherent in all capitalist enterprises, there is a contradiction. Capitalists seek to minimize their costs, especially labor costs, and so they pay low wages. But if they pay too little, their customers, who collectively are the employees of all capitalists, will be unable to afford the merchandise. The solution generally is to turn to imperialism: to seek colonies which will supply a cheap source of labor in order to lower prices, and to find markets abroad to sell their goods. But when the colony is internal to the mother country, the relationship becomes tenuous. If the mother country has no need for cheap labor (because of technology) and the colony lacks the ability to buy the commodities, the internal colony becomes a burden.

Perhaps Wilhelm's prediction may be accurate. It is true that the majority still turns to the minority to buy its commodities. Even when the minority is seeking to attain self-identity, the majority plays a role which enables it to profit. Fortunes have been made off women and other minorities by selling them cigarettes or other products which play on the new feminism, or the new minority self-awareness. Numerous artifacts of group identity are made by the majority and sold to the minority for a profit. Even in the revolt, the majority gains. Further, as the majority finds its commodities obsolete, it often turns to the minority to buy them. The dumping ground for gas-guzzling, oversized, inefficient automobiles of the 1960s and 1970s will be the minority communities of the later 1970s and 1980s. Jackson summarized the major elements of the internal colonialism thesis (as presented by various authors) to include:

(1) The political and socioeconomic status of the black minority in the United States is that of a colonized people.
(2) The white majority has through its values, institutions, and socialization agencies taught blacks to accept their condition as colonized peoples, and this acceptance and socialization has depressed black self-esteem.
(3) The uprisings against colonialism in the Third World, particularly in Africa, have provided a basis of identification for American blacks and have been instrumental in black revolts in America.

(4) The new rebellions have increased self-esteem and diminished the need of blacks for the majority's ideology.[49]

Jackson also tests the thesis. If internal colonialism is a viable conceptualization, he argues, then minority-group members will see themselves as Third World peoples and identify more strongly with other Third World groups than with the dominant society. To this extent their images (stereotypes) of the Third World groups will be more favorable than their images of the dominant society of their own country. Similarly, majority-group members will hold more favorable images of colonial majorities in other countries than of minority groups in their own society. Jackson found this to be precisely true. Black Americans held more favorable images of blacks in South Africa and white Americans held more favorable images of whites in South Africa than either did toward one another in the United States. We should also expect that minority peoples, seeing their common minority status, would identify more closely with one another than with the majority. On this point there is mixed evidence. There have been coalitions between some racial groups, including the Black-Brown Manifesto, the Black Panther party's call for a revolutionary alliance to fight racism, and movements to define all minority groups as Third World peoples. On the other hand, many minority groups have tended to accept majority society stereotypes of other minority groups, although not of themselves.[50]

Summary

The distributive dimension includes resources of property, social prestige, and power. In each of these areas minorities are differentially and pejoratively treated.

According to the U.S. census, minority groups have lower income levels and larger percentages below the poverty level than do the white majority. Unemployment rates are higher, while housing and health standards are lower. These are differentials in property.

Intertwined with property is social prestige. Minority individuals have less education and hold more lower-status occupations than do majority individuals. This inhibits opportunities to secure property. On the group level, entire minorities are differentially ranked, with racial minorities ranked lower than ethnic minorities. There is no comparable data available for gender groups.

There are two general types of power: legal and extralegal. Although minority groups have been gaining power in the past several years, they are still underrepresented in elective government. Ghettoization has become a source of legal power.

Extralegal power, both violent and nonviolent, has been used to change the social system and insure greater resources for minorities. Many of these extralegal strategies have acquired legitimacy.

The majority has reacted to the power of minorities in several ways: tokenism; coercion; cooptation; gerrymandering; divide and conquer; and socialization.

A system model of minority access to resources indicates the ways in which societal conditions affect demands for additional labor forces which can be satisfied by minority groups. This allows minorities (temporarily) to enter nontraditional occupations and to influence definitions of minority capabilities and future role allocations.

The system of stratification of minorities in this society has been sometimes described as a caste system. This conceptualization has been challenged, and perhaps should be replaced by the metaphor of internal colonialism.

Parallel class structures have also been posited. The model of "ethclass" is a heuristic conceptualization of minority class structure.

Class models tend to assume an outcome of assimilation, while caste models generate a minority nationalism as an outcome. The former may be more descriptive of ethnic minorities, and the latter may be more appropriate for racial minorities. Finally, internal colonialism as a model has gained much currency as a heuristic and empirical formulation.

NOTES

1. This and all following statistics, unless otherwise noted, are from: U.S. Bureau of the Census, *Census of Population: 1970*, vol. I, *Characteristics of the Population*, pt. 1, *U.S. Summary* (Washington, D.C.: Government Printing Office, 1973).

2. *Economic Report of the President: Transmitted to Congress, Feb. 1975.* (Washington, D.C.: Government Printing Office, 1975), p. 93, table 25.

3. Howard Ehrlich, "Social Conflict in America: The 1960's," in *Symposium on Violent Confrontation*, ed. Anthony Gary Dworkin, *Sociological Quarterly* 12 (1971): 295–308.

4. Ibid.

5. Leonard Broom and Norval Glenn, *Transformation of the Negro American* (New York: Harper, 1965).

6. Everett C. Hughes, "Dilemmas and Contradictions of Status," *American Journal of Sociology* 50 (1945): 353–59.

7. See Marvin E. Olsen, "Social and Political Participation of Blacks," *American Sociological Review* 35 (1970): 682–97; Jeffrey Paige, "Political Orientation and Riot Participation," *American Sociological Review* 36 (1971): 810–20; and Donald T. Warren, "Status Modality and Riot Behavior," *Sociological Quarterly* 12 (1971): 350–68.

8. Two major problems in status consistency research have been: (1) lack of generic variables (i.e., consistency and inconsistency have been variously defined and operationalized); and (2) status inconsistency not necessarily being perceived by the individual. Without the experiential component and the resultant social psychological awareness, it is doubtful that the initial inconsistency would affect behavior. For a more detailed exposition see Leonard Broom, "Social Differentiation and Stratification," in *Sociology Today*, ed. Robert K. Merton, Leonard Broom, and Leonard S. Cottrell, Jr. (New York: Basic Books, 1959), pp. 429–41, and Kaare Svalastoga "Social Differentiation," in *Handbook of Modern Sociology*, ed. Robert E. L. Faris (Chicago: Rand McNally 1964), pp. 530–75.

9. U.S. Bureau of the Census, *Census of Population*.

10. Christopher Jencks et al. *Inequality* (New York: Basic Books, 1972).

11. Leo Grebler, Joan W. Moore, and Ralph C. Guzman, *The Mexican-American People* (New York: Free Press, 1970), p. 214.

12. For a summary of his results see Emory Bogardus, "Comparing Racial Distance in Ethiopia, South Africa, and the United States," *Sociology and Social Research* 52 (1968): 149–56.

13. Gerhard E. Lenski, "Status Crystallization: A Non-Vertical Dimension of Social Status," *American Sociological Review* 19 (1954): 405–13.

14. Gopal Sharan Sinha and Ramesh Chandra Sinha, "Exploration in Caste Stereotypes," *Social Forces* 46 (1967): 42–47.

15. Stanley Lieberson, "Stratification and Ethnic Groups" *Sociological Inquiry* 40 (1970): 172–81.

16. "Race men" are individuals of their race (or gender) who excel in an area (occupation) previously barred to members of their group. By their excellence they make it possible for others like them to gain entry into these areas. Jackie Robinson was such an individual. He broke the "color bar" against blacks in major league baseball.

17. Terence K. Hopkins, "Bureaucratic Authority: The Convergence of Weber and Barnard," in *Complex Organizations*, ed. Amitai Etzioni (New York: Holt, Rinehart, 1964), p. 87.

18. Kirsten Amundsen, *The Silenced Majority* (Englewood Cliffs, N.J.: Prentice-Hall, 1971).

19. Ibid., p. 67.

20. U.S. Department of Commerce, *Statistical Abstracts of the United States*, 93rd ed. (Washington, D.C.: Government Printing Office, 1974).

21. Robert K. Merton, *Social Theory and Social Structure* (New York: Free Press, 1957).

22. Jerome H. Skolnick, *The Politics of Protest* (New York: Simon and Schuster 1969).

23. J. Kenneth Benson, "Militant Ideologies and Organizational Contexts," in Dworkin, ed., *Symposium on Violent Confrontation*, pp. 328–39.

24. See H. Edward Ransford, "Isolation, Powerlessness, and Violence: A Study of Attitudes and Participation in the Watts Riot," *American Journal of Sociology* 73 (1968): 581–91, and Robert A. Wilson, "Anomia and Militancy Among Urban Negroes," in Dworkin, ed., *Symposium on Violent Confrontation*, pp. 369–86.

25. See Paige, "Political Orientation"; Warren, "Status Modality"; P. Gore and J. Rotter, "A Personality Correlate of Social Action," *Journal of Personality* 31 (1963): 58–64; J. Forward and J. Williams, "Internal-External Control and Black Militancy," *Journal of Social Issues* 26 (1970): 75–92. Robert Blauner, *Racial Oppression in America* (New York: Harper, 1972), and others have shown that ghetto revolt or riot behavior are in fact revolutions against colonialism.

26. James S. Coleman et al. *Equality of Educational Opportunity* (Washington, D.C.: Government Printing Office, 1966).

27. Raymond W. Mack, ed., *Our Children's Burden* (New York: Random House, 1968).

28. Edna Bonacich, "A Theory of Ethnic Antagonism: The Split Labor Market," *American Sociological Review* 37 (1972): 547–59.

29. Janet S. Chafetz, Anthony Gary Dworkin, and Rosalind J. Dworkin, "New Migrants to the Rat Race: A Systems Model for Changes in Work Force Allocation and Role Expectations, by Gender, Race and Ethnicity," mimeographed (University of Houston, 1975).

30. W. Lloyd Warner, "American Caste and Class," *American Journal of Sociology* 42 (1936): 234–37.

31. John Dollard, *Caste and Class in a Southern Town* (New York: Harper and Bros., 1949).

32. W. A. Davis B. B. Gardner and M. R. Gardner, *Deep South: A Social Anthropological Study* (Chicago: University of Chicago Press, 1941).

33. Ruby Jo Reeves Kennedy, "Single or Triple Melting Pot? Intermarriage Trends in New Haven, 1870–1940," *American Journal of Sociology* 49 (1944): 331–39; idem, "Single or Triple Melting Pot? Intermarriage in New Haven, 1870–1950," *American Journal of Sociology* 58 (1953): 56–59.

34. Will Herberg, *Protestant-Catholic-Jew* (Garden City, N.Y.: Doubleday, 1955).

35. Helen Mayer Hacker, "Women as a Minority Group," *Social Forces* 30 (1951): 60–69.

36. Carole Andreas, *Sex and Caste in America* (Englewood Cliffs, N.J.: Prentice-Hall, 1971).

37. Oliver C. Cox, *Caste, Class, and Race: A Study in Social Dynamics* (Garden City, N.Y.: Doubleday, 1948).

38. Robert Blauner, "Internal Colonialism and Ghetto Revolt" *Social Problems* 16 (1969): 393–408; idem, *Racial Oppression in America.*

39. Stokely Carmichael and Charles Hamilton, *Black Power* (New York: Random House, 1967).

40. George Eaton Simpson and J. Milton Yinger, *Racial and Cultural Minorities*, 3rd ed. (New York: Harper, 1958).

41. W. Lloyd Warner, Marchia Meeker, and Kenneth Eells, *Social Class in America* (New York: Harper, 1960 [1949]), and August B. Hollingshead, *Elmtown's Youth* (New York: Wiley, 1949).

42. Gunnar Myrdal, *An American Dilemma* (New York: Harper and Brothers, 1944); Cox, *Caste, Class, and Race*; and John F. Cuber and William F. Kenkel, *Social Stratification in the United States* (New York: Appleton-Century-Crofts 1954).

43. Floyd Hunter, *Community Power Structure* (Chapel Hill, N.C.: University of North Carolina Press, 1953); St. Clair Drake and Horace R. Cayton, *Black Metropolis* (New York: Harcourt, Brace, and Company, 1945); and M. Elaine Burgess, *Negro Leadership in a Southern City* (Chapel Hill, N.C.: University of North Carolina Press, 1962).

44. Milton M. Gordon, *Assimilation in American Life: The Role of Race, Religion, and National Origins* (New York: Oxford University Press, 1964).

45. Judson R. Landis, Darryl Datwyler, and Dean S. Dorn, "Race and Social Class as Determinants of Social Distance," *Sociology and Social Research* 51 (1966): 78–86.

46. See Blauner, "Internal Colonialism"; idem, *Racial Oppression in America*: Carmichael and Hamilton, *Black Power*; Jean W. Moore, "Colonialism: The Case of the Mexican Americans," *Social Problems* 17 (1970): 463–71; Albert Memmi, *The Colonizer and the Colonized* (Boston: Beacon, 1967); and Harold Cruse, *Rebellion or Revolution* (New York: Morrow, 1968).

47. Moore, "Colonialism."

48. Sidney M. Wilhelm, *Who Needs the Negro?* (Cambridge, Mass.: Schenkman, 1970).

49. J. Wallace Jackson, "An Empirical Test of the Internal Colonialism Model," mimeographed (University of Houston, 1975).

50. See Chapter Five of this book for a discussion of this tendency.

Suggested Readings

Blauner, Robert. *Racial Oppression in America*. New York: Harper, 1972.

Carmichael, Stokely, and Charles Hamilton. *Black Power*. New York: Random House, 1967.

Coleman, James S. *Resources for Social Change*. New York: Wiley, 1971.

Gordon, Milton M. *Social Class in American Sociology*. New York: McGraw-Hill, 1963.

Shibutani, Tomotsu, and Kian M. Kwan. *Ethnic Stratification: A Comparative Approach*. New York: Macmillan, 1965.

Svalastoga, Kaare. "Social Differentiation." In *Handbook of Modern Sociology*, edited by Robert E. L. Faris. Chicago: Rand McNally, 1964.

Tumin, Melvin M. *Social Stratification*. Englewood Cliffs, N.J.: Prentice-Hall, 1967.

4.

THE ORGANIZATIONAL
DIMENSION

In a complex society such as this, people are surrounded by organizations. We act in them; we react to them; and we are acted upon by them. Members of minority groups are actors in organizations, not only as individuals, but as members of such minorities. This chapter shall discuss those minority-based organizations which were created as reactions to, or protection from, the majority.

> Organizations are social units (or human groupings) deliberately constructed and reconstructed to seek specific goals. . . . Organizations are characterized by (1) divisions of labor, power, and communications responsibilities . . . (2) the presence of one or more power centers which control the concerted efforts of the organization and direct them towards its goals . . . (3) the substitution of personnel, i.e., unsatisfactory persons can be removed and others assigned their tasks.[1]

Examples of some of the organizations with which minorities are concerned include the police, the school system, welfare agencies, the military, corporations and other bureaucracies, churches, civil rights groups such as the National Association for the Advancement of Colored People, the Congress of Racial Equality, the Anti-Defamation League of B'nai B'rith, National Organization of Women (NOW), the Black

Panther party, the United Farm Workers of America, and a multitude of others.

Minority Experiences with Majority Organizations

When the senior author was interviewing a group of Mexican Americans in Los Angeles in the 1960s, he asked what Anglo organizations cause the most problems for Mexican Americans. One individual responded, "All of them." Most, however, enumerated such organizations as the school system, the police, the Bureau of Public Welfare, banks, realty agencies and retail establishments, and organizations where they were employed. If you were to ask a member of any other minority to specify which organizations cause him problems, a similar list would probably be encountered. The following organizations have been selected because of the typical problems they present.

THE SCHOOLS

The public schools perform two basic functions in society. First, by their instruction they socialize individuals to desire to perform the myriad tasks necessary in a complex society, and transmit to individuals the culture of the majority, including its values and assumptions. Second, the schools create a trained labor pool and, through their system of testing and counseling, allocate individuals to positions within the social structure, thereby maintaining traditional role definitions within the labor force. In the past twenty years schools have also been asked to eradicate and ameliorate quality of performance gaps between the minorities and the majority. The charge that schools should provide equality of educational opportunity raises the ironic fact that schools also tend to perpetuate inequality of opportunity. The educational system is geared toward middle-class white Anglo-Saxon Protestant children. Poverty program projects designed to bridge the gap between the minorities (generally those minority-group members who are poor) and the majority were funded to school systems which had originally created the labels, stigmas, and the gap itself. One of the conclusions of the Coleman and Campbell report[2] was that although most minority children had goals as high as those of majority children, they never were taught how to attain them. For example, school counselors and teachers advise minority students less often than they do members of the majority on how to apply for and get into college.

Colin Greer observed:

The great myth on which our traditional faith in schools is based has been that mobility and social improvement were its goals. Instead, immobility and stratification have been reflected and reinforced by schools and their measures of intelligence.[3]

Thus the school system operates as an arm of the stratification system, insuring that some get the opportunity to do important work and attain property, prestige, and power, while relegating others to menial tasks and relative deprivations. This relegation is not based upon individual merits, but upon group membership. Cicourel and Kitsuse[4] discovered that school personnel counseled students into college preparatory or trade-technical courses on the basis of the student's social class and assumptions of his parents' ability to pay for his education. In a study conducted for the state of Texas, Schulman and his colleagues[5] indicated that teachers interpreted high aspirations of Mexican American students as fantasies and similar aspirations of Anglo students as realistic, and counseled their students accordingly.

Because of the differential treatment of their children in the schools, minorities have focused their discontents on the following issues:

1. Local versus district-wide control of school policy and educational content.
2. Hiring practices.
3. Appropriateness of bilingual education.
4. Minority studies programs.
5. Desegregation guidelines and busing (the latter being an issue of considerable confrontation with majority parents).
6. Career counseling.
7. Intelligence testing.
8. Styles of discipline.
9. Truancy and dropouts.
10. Choice of textbooks and teaching materials.

THE POLICE

In order for society to exist there need to be norms and rules of conduct to regulate the interaction among individuals. In simple societies the regulation may be accomplished informally by every member of the system. But as a society becomes more complex, the process of social control becomes more specialized. Norms become codified into laws, the enforcement of which becomes the task of an agency with the legitimate authority to use coercion and violence. This agency is the police.

Police officers tend to be recruited from lower-class and working-class populations.[6] Such populations are usually identified as being more prejudiced toward minority groups. Further, the role of police officer necessitates that the incumbent expect the worst in people and react immediately to that expectation.

Reported crime tends to be significantly higher in minority business and majority residential areas, so the police are likely to be concentrated in minority areas. Furthermore, the police generally initiate interaction with minorities, while majorities more frequently initiate their interaction with the police. Majorities tend to call the police; the police tend to call on minorities. Therefore, minority group members see more police violence, of which they are most likely to be the targets. When minorities are residentially segregated, as in the case of black Americans, observation and receipt of police-initiated violence tends to be uniform across social classes.[7] Because middle- and lower-class blacks live together in the same ghettos, and are subject to homogeneous experiences with the police, their perceptions of the police are inclined to be more consistent than those of whites of varying social classes.

The police, as Galliher[8] observes, are not the creators of social policy; they only perform the tasks assigned them by dominant classes who make the laws. Minorities are perceptive in their recognition that the police are symbols of the social order that relegates them to less property, prestige, and power. Majorities make laws partly to insure the continuity of their way of life and the stratification system that maintains them as majorities. Stanley Lieberson[9] posited in his theory of majority-minority relations that in the battle to maintain a social order compatible with one's culture, majorities and minorities conflict over institutions. The institution of policing is the focus of numerous battles. These include:

1. Citizen's review boards of police activities.
2. Recruitment practices of the police (more minority recruitment).
3. Police procedures for dealing with minority-group members accused of a crime, including both physical brutality and verbal abuse.
4. Differential enforcement of laws (minorities more often arrested for acts for which the majority is not arrested).
5. As a corollary of differential enforcement of the law, differential adjudication of offenses by the courts (minorities go to prison, while a member of the majority may only get a suspended sentence, a fine, or an acquittal).

GOVERNMENTAL WELFARE AGENCIES

The poverty resulting from differential and pejorative treatment implies dilapidated and deteriorated housing, inadequate health care, and substandard employment and education. These conditions are pervasive across slums of different hues, whether they be "Soulside," "Chinatown," "Spanish Harlem," "Chicano barrio," or a reservation. Accompanying poverty and the poor are a multitude of governmental agencies whose official function is to ameliorate, rehabilitate, direct, correct, consult, refer, or help one to adapt and cope with the exigencies of minority status. The agencies, however, bring to the poor a double-edged sword. In attempting to end poverty, they frequently perpetuate it. The massiveness of the federate state, and the resulting large urban programs, invite great bureaucratic structures which are impersonal and dehumanize the clientele they were created to serve.

By placing a ceiling on supplemental personal income, agencies discourage many welfare recipients from surrendering their welfare checks to accept a low-paying job in industry. Not only would employment in a low-paying job (often too low to support one's family) be economically unwise, but the implications to self-esteem can be as disastrous as welfare itself. In American society one is measured by what one does and how much one gets for doing it. Low pay tells the world two things: that the person's employer thinks so little about him as to offer miniscule wages for his labor, and that he thinks so little about himself as to accept the employer's definition.[10] Furthermore, there are restrictions on the use of welfare payments and food stamps such that the individual, in accepting governmental support, surrenders autonomy as a consumer. Perhaps consumer education is the viable solution, rather than restrictions which foster dependency and treat adults as children.

Welfare agencies also make the assumption that a mother's place is at home with her children. Thus they may discourage women from seeking employment by refusing to facilitate day-care. Since a large portion of a woman's salary might have to be spent on private day-care for her children, she often finds it economically impossible to accept employment.

Aid to families with dependent children (AFDC) requires that the recipient mother not have a spouse living with her. Since her spouse may be unable to find work (especially during recessions), or to find work which pays enough to support his family, he may be permanently or sporadically driven from the home. This produces unusual and sometimes unstable family relations, and a hectic family life at best.[11]

Many social service projects are actually pilot projects based on short-term grants and minimal funds. Agencies, in order to demonstrate high success rates or favorable cost/benefit ratios and thus gain continuation funds, seek out individuals who are likely to be successes, leaving the "hard-core" unemployed or poor to subsist on their own. Other programs, because of their short-term funding, cannot render full service to their clientele. A dramatic illustration of this sort occurred in a large city in the Southwest. According to a city official, a dental program for the elderly was instituted. Dental checkups were given, largely to minority-group members who were indigent; where excessive tooth decay was found, all of their teeth were extracted. Before the individuals could be issued dentures, funds for the program dried up, and dozens of elderly people were left worse off than before the social service program attempted to serve them.

Implementation of federal revenue sharing, rather than facilitating local government in providing social services, actually hampers it. In some instances the monies cannot be used for social services, and in other instances programs provided by the cities which were previously funded directly by other federal sources (libraries, zoos, sewers, streets) are placed in a common pool with local social welfare projects, and thus all compete for these funds. Given the tendency for voters of the majority group to be hostile toward welfare programs and welfare recipients, politicians are pressured into diverting these funds toward services desired by the middle and upper classes and away from the poor.

In response to the conditions of the welfare agencies as perceived by the minority groups, issues of conflict have focused upon:
1. Neighborhood or localized control of welfare strategies and programs.
2. Location of welfare facilities.
3. Debureaucratization of welfare agencies.
4. Collection and immoderate use of confidential, personal information by welfare agencies.
5. Recruitment and training of social workers and social agency employees.

We would be belaboring the issue if we enumerated other examples of minority experiences with majority organizations. Minorities have had similar experiences with credit organizations in trying to secure consumer and business loans, with the realty industry in obtaining housing, with unions, with the military, and elsewhere. In each of these organizations the complaints have been similar. Minorities demand that they be treated as equals; that they not be subjected to dehumanizing bureaucratization; that they gain a share of control over the agencies which regulate and rule their lives; and that they be granted equal opportunities in being hired and recruited into the organizations.

Minority Organizations

Minority group members, especially those with long histories of experience with social service agencies and other majority institutions, have developed techniques for coping with those agencies. In fact, many have learned how to work the system extremely well. This puts some minorities at a relative advantage over majority members who might occasionally find themselves in need of welfare. A medical sociologist[12] tells about a welfare mother in Florida who came upon a technique for gaining immediate service in public health clinics. She borrows neighborhood children—all of them toddlers—to bring with her. The sight of a dozen climbing, crawling, crying children in a waiting room usually compels the nurses to arrange that she be seen by the doctors without delay.

Another coping mechanism is extended familism. The presence of several generations of kinsmen or of many families of kinsmen living either in the same household or in adjoining households provides a functional alternative to social security and unemployment insurance. Not only will the old be cared for, but they can also provide babysitting services, counsel, and social support for the other family members. Further, the mutual interdependence of several nuclear families or several households increases the probability that at any one time there will be at least one wage earner present. When one member loses a job, there are other kinsmen to help. When a group cannot afford insurance premiums, extended familism and close kinship provides a viable and sensible alternative. Burma,[13] Sexton,[14] and Lewis[15] have each reported such mechanisms in the Puerto Rican and Chicano barrios.

Minority groups have also devised less individualistic, more organized techniques for coping with differential and pejorative treatment—for meeting majority power with minority power. We shall enumerate three forms of these organized techniques. The first are culture-maintaining organizations, which function to insure cultural survival and provide emotional support. The second technique creates specifically issue- or problem-oriented organizations, including such areas as economics, self-help, and self-defense. The third involves more generalized civil rights and liberation organizations. The first two may be patterned after majority organizational counterparts and may exist because majorities have excluded minorities from those specific organizations. Groups of the third type are designed to change the majority institutions, beliefs, and behaviors while providing identities for minorities. All are inexorably connected with minority survival and minority success.

CULTURE-MAINTAINING ORGANIZATIONS

This category includes numerous organizations whose main purposes are to sustain the culture—the way of life—of a minority group embedded in a somewhat alien majority environment. These organizations also provide a haven for individuals to be "with their own," to escape temporarily from the ill treatment outside. Many immigrant minorities, even those most nearly assimilated, still maintain this type of organization. The Sons of Italy, B'nai B'rith, and the Japanese-American Citizen's League are only three out of scores of examples.

59

Organized religion also performs culture-maintaining functions. The Roman Catholic church, the Jewish synagogue, the Buddhist temple, and the storefront Baptist church each help their respective groups to sustain at least the religious aspects of their culture. They also provide a large measure of emotional support for their members.

Many have accused religions of not only sustaining minority culture, but also supporting the majority's status quo. By lifting the eyes to the rewards of the "next world," religious organizations have discouraged members from focusing on the injustices of the present. Indeed, religion has resembled the "opiate of the masses" which Karl Marx accused it of being. However, organized religion has produced leaders (e.g., Rev. Dr. Martin Luther King, Jr.) who use the structure of the church to initiate reform movements which challenge that status quo.

ECONOMIC COPING ORGANIZATIONS

When the majority group is unwilling to support minority-group members in their attempt to gain economic independence, minorities may need to seek within their own community for assistance. The white majority is "implicated in the ghetto" not only in terms of its creation, but also in the ownership of businesses located there. Thus minority individuals and the minority communities as a whole may reap few benefits from sales in the ghetto. The Black Muslim's insistence that blacks buy only from Muslim stores and buy only black-made commodities is designed in part to break white domination of blacks. More recently other black groups have made the same demand.[16] Carey McWilliams[17] documented how the Japanese were reproached by whites for attempting to save their earnings and establish Japanese-owned truck farms in California. One cannot help but suspect that the motivation behind the "yellow peril" claims of whites at the turn of the century and the action taken against the Japanese Americans on the West Coast was in part sparked by this anger.[18]

Ivan Light[19] has recently presented a discussion of a mechanism in the Chinese and Japanese communities which provides economic resources in lieu of majority support. The institution is that of revolving credit associations, which are systems organized among kinsmen and friends. When no formal organization, such as a bank, will grant credit, an individual can rely upon relatives and friends. Each member of the association contributes to a central fund; when one needs money he bids an interest rate, and the highest bidder in the association gets the supply of funds to build his business. Credit rotates among members over time. The structure had been brought from Asia by immigrating families of Japanese and Chinese. Thus, when white-owned banks refuse to support their business ventures, the rotating credit associations are ready to step in.

There were similar associations in parts of Africa. Among the Yoruba (from whom many blacks were taken as slaves) the concept was named *esusu*. Light[20] has proposed that slavery so destroyed the traditional family, so broke up tribes, and so decimated the traditional culture of the enslaved that *esusu* was lost. Thus blacks in this society have been slower in developing businesses and economic investments than have the Japanese and Chinese.

Other types of organizations which have helped groups cope with the economic realities of minority status have frequently been parallels to majority organizations, and were created because of exclusionary practices. Minority labor unions (e.g., United Farm Workers of America, Brotherhood of Sleeping Car Porters) have provided protection for minorities when there was no general union for this pupose. These organizations have sometimes broadened their goals, and rather than helping individual members cope with society have sought to reform and change the system itself.

Ghetto life, poverty, crime, and other aspects of minority status often compel minority-group members to band together for their survival. Like the economic organizations, these associations frequently expand their scope. In recent years the Black Panther party grew from a local organization protecting blacks against police harrassment to a multichapter organization encompassing food distribution programs, legal defense programs, and the liberation and control of the black community by blacks as Third World peoples.[21] The party was originally known as the Black Panther Party for Self-Defense, but as Foner observes, it dropped the "Self-Defense" part of its title in 1967 as a realization that it had to take the offensive against racism and for black liberation.[22] It thus ceased to be purely a coping organization.

Marshall Sklare[23] discussed how Jewish organizations, originally local and designed to provide philanthropic aid to Jews, combined together and became national and even international in scope. Some, such as the Anti-Defamation League of B'nai B'rith, are concerned with elimination of prejudice, while others, such as the United Jewish Appeal, have provided refugee relief and aid to Israel.

Throughout the Chinatowns of the United States *tongs*, or benevolent associations, emerged. Wen Li in the present text points out that the ". . . most notable was the Chinese Six Companies, or Chinese Consolidated Benevolent Association. Whenever new immigrants arrived, the various associations serve as caravansaries, credit and loan societies, and employment agencies."[24]

Theoretical Perspectives

CIVIL RIGHTS AND LIBERATION ORGANIZATIONS

Outsiders tend to look at a minority group and perceive a sea of identical faces espousing identical beliefs and desires. This is far from an accurate observation. Just as there is diversity between groups, there is also diversity within groups. And nowhere is the range of heterogeneity within any one minority group more apparent than in intragroup disagreements over the course of social reform.

Although several of the other minority organizations have developed expanded foci, civil rights and liberation organizations *began* with an emphasis on changing the society rather than changing the minority individual or helping him cope with the existing society. Generally these organizations held one of two basic orientations: *separatist* or *integrationist*. The former argued that the majority was too intransigent and minorities would gain their freedom only through physical, cultural, and social separation. Integrationist groups argued that ultimately the day would come when the majority would accept the minority as a full member of society. Although each minority group has some elements of each orientation within its ranks, the black American minority has had the most varied and developed forms.

In addition, there were divergent strategies employed by the civil rights and liberation groups. Some deferred their goals through accommodationism, or the temporary adjustment and cessation of hostilities between groups. Thus the minority endures until it is "ready." Others engaged in legal protest, working through the courts and within the legal structure of the society. Still others engaged in extralegal practices, including civil disobedience, nonviolent protest, and even open, violent confrontation.

A sociologist studying the various civil rights and liberation organizations of minority groups presented in this text is struck by two factors: the diversity of goals and strategies within specific groups, and the similarities to be found across groups. Among Puerto Ricans there are political movements oriented toward independence and nationhood (separatists), and others oriented toward statehood (which implies political equalization and assimilation). There have been black organizations which preached accommodationism, including Booker T. Washington's "Atlanta Compromise"; others have used lawsuits and legislation (NAACP); some have utilized civil disobedience, sit-ins, marches, and boycotts (CORE, Southern Christian Leadership Conference or SCLC); still others have suggested or entertained violent responses to majority provocations (Black Panther party, Black Muslims). Today, some twenty years since the Montgomery bus boycott, there is still debate among blacks about the effectiveness and utility of these diverse strategies.

Among Chicanos, some have used legalism, some have fought with passive resistance, and others have advocated and attempted the violent expulsion of majority persons from land previously belonging to people of Mexican heritage (e.g., Reies Tijerina's *La Alianza Federal de Mercedes*). The feminist movement and the American Indian Movement (AIM) exhibit similar diversity among their members. Historically, the Irish, the Jews, and other minorities also experienced such differences.

There are also striking similarities across groups. The Japanese American Citizen's League and the National Women's Political Caucus support political candidates in ways similar to the Mexican American Political Association and the League of United Latin American Citizens (LULAC). The National Congress of American Indians (NCAI) and NOW bear striking resemblances to NAACP in terms of their legalistic approaches. Within AIM are elements similar to the Black Panthers: each organization was originally created to protect members from police harassment. Finally, the Jewish Defense League (JDL) of today advocates violent responses in defense of Israel against Arab nations in the same manner that, a century before, the Fenian Brotherhood advocated violence in defense of Ireland.

Institutional Racism

Racism and sexism are total ideologies which pervade American society. They represent holistic and encapsulating belief systems and world views which are intertwined throughout the fabric of our society and may be found within each of our institutions and organizations. Although prejudice may be compatible with institutional racism, it is distinct. Prejudice is an individual, personal phenomenon; institutional racism is a societal phenomenon. Institutional racism is the ideology of racism operating within the organizations and institutions of the society. Racism and sexism are world views which define groups of people a priori as inferior or superior and mark as "rational," "sensible," and even "reasonable" organizational and societal behavior which maintains these definitions. There emerges a unity of intent which mitigates efforts at societal change. Because racism is present in all aspects of the society, it is not easy for individuals and groups to divorce themselves from the ideology, unless they divorce themselves from the culture, the language, the everyday assumptions. No group holds a monopoly on the ideological tenets of racism and sexism. Minorities, if they accept their condition, when they deal with other minorities, and even when they rebel against the majority, reaffirm the ideology.

Racism and sexism are not new phenomena. They have persisted throughout our cultural heritage. Gossett[25] noted the presence of sailent racial distinctions in India over five thousand years ago, as well as among the early Egyptians, the classical Greeks and Romans, and the early Hebrews. Racism has served to maintain one group over another. It fitted well with early capitalism, with its need for colonialism and imperialism. If Western Europeans were superior and destined to rule the world, as the ideology preached, then it was only "manifest destiny" that Western Europeans should colonize the New World, Africa, and the Far East; it was likewise only part of the divine nature of things that the native populations were to be subjugated. Van den Berghe noted:

> The egalitarian and libertarian ideas of the Enlightenment spread by the American and French Revolutions conflicted, of course, with racism, but they also paradoxically contributed to its development. Faced with the blatant contradiction between the treatment of slaves and colonial peoples and the official rhetoric of freedom and equality, Europeans and white North Americans began to dichotomize humanity between men and submen (or the "civilized" and the "savages").[26]

In fact, if minorities were less than human, as the enlightened colonizer thought, it would be inhumane to treat them as equals and demand from them the responsibilities of peers and adults. To treat them as children unable to decide for themselves became a humane gesture. How fortunate for the colonizers that they could be humane and get goods and services for almost nothing!

Racism and sexism are manifested in many small, everyday ways. The assumption that a skin-colored Band-Aid is pink is racist. The belief that girls are natural-born mothers with maternal instincts while boys have no paternal instincts is sexist. Racism and sexism are also manifested in much less trivial ways. The assumption that white males are more academically talented and educable produces a self-fulfilling prophecy whereby all others are given inferior education. Inferior education in turn leads to poorer jobs. Poorer jobs mean that the individual is less able to purchase for himself and his family a better standard of living. At each step we are aware of the assumptions of the inferiority of one group and the superiority of the other. Not only in the school, but in the job market and in the consumer market, these assumptions of superiority and inferiority heighten one group's chances of success and the other's chances of failure. We define as inferior; we treat as inferior; and the product appears to be inferior. Further, by the limitations placed upon the parents, we insure that the children will have disadvantages, and the process thus repeats itself.

4: The Organizational Dimension

We have explored minority experiences with organizations and have seen common treatments, definitions, and complaints. We have looked at alternative organizations established by minorities and found many to be patterned after those which they have sought to challenge or which have excluded them. This interconnection of organizations with racist beliefs, goals, and intents confronts the minority-group member. Individual prejudice can be changed because it is an individual problem subject to individual solutions. But the ideologies of institutional racism and sexism, which are mutually comparable and rather similar, are not so easily corrected.

The social science of the 1930s through the 1950s viewed minority-majority relations as solely a problem of prejudice—of misinformed or sick individuals. Techniques were devised to change individuals. The civil rights movement, observes Skolnick, likewise was built upon the assumption that

> racism [prejudice in reality] was a localized [to the South] malignancy within a relative healthy political and social order; it was a move to force American morality and American institutions to root out the last vestiges of the disease."[27]

Because the belief system of racism (and sexism) was so ingrained, the civil rights activists failed to see its pervasiveness. They tended to assume that moral persuasion would correct the evil. But each side saw his cause in moral terms, and so the pervasive ideology blinded both.

The recognition of institutionalized racism, like the organizations it describes, is a double-edged instrument. By contending that the ideology blinds one to the consequences of one's acts, by contending that the causes of the differential treatment of minorities are so ingrained in the very fabric of the society as to be covert and unconscious, is to argue that: (1) only total societal change is effective in dealing with the problem—a point which has validity; but also (2) individuals cannot be held culpable for their discriminatory behavior and prejudicial attitudes—which is not correct. To contend that racism is principally a societal problem is to excuse the actions of prejudiced individuals who are seen merely as victims of the society's system of socialization.

In the next chapter we shall look at the manifold causes of prejudice, and suggest some ways in which such prejudice can be reduced. Even if racism is a societal problem (and in part it is), individuals separately and in groups must be responsible for changing that society. We are not contending that an institutionalized racism perspective is invalid. Rather, we are suggesting that it is one of several viable explanations, and that the error lies in insisting on its predominance and abandoning social psychological models of prejudice and discrimination.

Summary

Organizational analysis provides many insights to minority-group relations. Minorities generally have had similar experiences with majority organizations. The schools are geared to the majority child and tend to reinforce the traditional role definitions of minority groups, while under pressure from both specific minorities and the federal government to relieve minority problems. Similarly, the police have been a source of friction and discontent in most minority communities. The police have, for many, become symbols of that social order that relegates them to an inferior position. Government welfare agencies, ostensibly charged with relieving the problems of the poor and the minority person, often accomplish the opposite. Through top-heavy bureaucracies, impersonal and laden with often contradictory rules, welfare agencies often either discourage needy individuals from using their services or encourage dependency and career welfare recipients.

Minority groups have generated several different types of organizations to react to and serve as a buffer against the treatment of the majority. Most minorities have evolved some types of culture-maintaining organizations; economic organizations as well as self-defense leagues as coping mechanisms; and a range of civil rights and liberation organizations. The last have had two basic orientations, either separatist or integrationist. Strategies also vary from accommodationism to legal, violent, and nonviolent protests.

Noteworthy in the study of minority-group organization is the divergence of opinions within any one minority group, and the similarity in structures and experiences across groups.

Much of the organizational behaviors can be understood in terms of institutional racism and sexism. Racism and sexism are total ideologies that pervade our society. These ideologies have become the rationalizers for minority subjugation, and are so embedded in our culture, so much a part of our organizations, institutions, and expectations, that they operate in very subtle, nearly unnoticeable ways to maintain the power relationships between groups.

NOTES

1. Amitai Etzioni, *Modern Organizations* (Englewood Cliffs, N.J.: Prentice-Hall, 1964), p. 3.

2. James S. Coleman et al., *Equality of Educational Opportunity* (Washington, D.C.: Government Printing Office, 1966).

3. Colin Greer. "A Review of Christopher Jencks's *Inequality*," *Society* 11 (1974): 92.

4. Aaron V. Cicourel and John I. Kitsuse, *The Educational Decision-Makers* (Indianapolis: Bobbs-Merrill, 1963).

5. Sam Schulman et al., *Mexican American Youth and Vocational Education in Texas* (Houston, Tex.: Center for Human Resources, University of Houston, 1973).

6. Jack J. Preiss and Howard J. Ehrlich, *An Examination of Role Theory* (Lincoln: University of Nebraska Press, 1966).

7. Kenneth B. Clark, *Dark Ghetto* (New York: Harper, 1965).

8. John F. Galliher, "Explanations of Police Behavior: A Critical Review and Analysis," in *Symposium on Violent Confrontation*, ed. Anthony Gary Dworkin, *Sociological Quarterly* 12 (1971): 308–18.

9. Stanley Lieberson, "A Societal Theory of Race and Ethnic Relations," *American Sociological Review* 26 (1961): 902–10.

10. Elliot Liebow, *Tally's Corner* (Boston: Little, Brown, 1967), chap. 2.

11. See Andrew Billingsley, *Black Families in White America* (Englewood Cliffs, N.J.: Prentice-Hall, 1968), chap. 7, and Frances Fox Piven and Richard A. Cloward, *Regulating the Poor* (New York: Random House, 1971).

12. Our thanks to Allen Haney, who told us this anecdote.

13. John H. Burma, *Spanish-Speaking Groups in the United States* (Durham, N.C.: Duke University Press, 1954).

14. Patricia Cayo Sexton, *Spanish Harlem* (New York: Harper, 1965).

15. Oscar Lewis, *La Vida* (New York: Random House, 1966).

16. Floyd B. McKissick, "Black Business Development with Social Commitment to Black Communities," in *Black Nationalism in America*, ed. John H. Bracey, Jr., August Meier, and Elliott Rudwick (Indianapolis: Bobbs-Merrill, 1970).

17. Carey McWilliams, *Brothers Under the Skin* (Boston: Little, Brown, 1964).

18. See Ima on Japanese Americans and Li on Chinese Americans in Part Two of this book.

19. Ivan H. Light, *Ethnic Enterprise in America: Business and Welfare Among Chinese, Japanese, and Blacks* (Berkeley and Los Angeles: University of California Press, 1972).

20. Ibid.

21. Philip S. Foner, ed., *The Black Panthers Speak* (Philadelphia: Lippincott 1970).

22. Ibid., p. xix.

23. Marshall Sklare, *America's Jews* (New York: Random House, 1971), chap. 4; see also Schoenfeld on Jewish Americans in Part Two of this book.

24. See Li's report on the Chinese Americans, pp. 297–324.

25. Thomas F. Gossett, *Race: The History of an Idea in America* (Dallas: Southern Methodist University Press, 1963).

26. Pierre L. van den Berghe, *Race and Racism* (New York: Wiley, 1967), pp. 17–18.

27. Jerome H. Skolnick, *The Politics of Protest* (New York: Simon and Schuster, 1969).

Suggested Readings

Coleman, James S., et al. *Equality of Educational Opportunity*. Washington, D.C.: Government Printing Office, 1966.

Etzioni, Amitai. *Modern Organizations*. Englewood Cliffs, N.J.: Prentice-Hall, 1964.

Hall, Richard H. *Organizations: Structures and Processes*. Englewood Cliffs, N.J.: Prentice-Hall, 1972.

Jencks, Christopher, et al. *Inequality: A Reassessment of the Effects of Family and Schooling in America.* New York: Basic Books, 1972.

Knowles, Louis L., and Kenneth Prewitt. *Institutional Racism in America.* Englewood Cliffs, N.J.: Prentice-Hall, 1969.

Piven, Frances Fox, and Richard A. Cloward. *Regulating the Poor.* New York: Random House, 1971.

5.

THE SOCIAL PSYCHOLOGICAL DIMENSION

Up to now we have been concerned with minority-group relations on a societal or institutional level. We have focused upon the minority and the majority as groups. The social psychological level, on the other hand, emphasizes the individual; the unit of analysis is the person. The concern is with the impact of the larger social structure and institutions upon the individual, and upon relationships between individuals.

The essential components of the social psychological dimension in minority-group relations are the elements of *attitudes* and *behaviors*. There have been numerous definitions of attitude, but in general they have emphasized that attitudes are interrelated sets of propositions about classes of ideas, groups, and objects which tend to predispose individuals to behave in ways which are relatively consistent with those attitudes. Attitudes have cognitive (thoughts) and affective (feelings and emotions) components, and through their predisposing tendency imply conditions(behaviors). Behaviors are observable acts committed by individuals. Attitudes are not directly observable, but must be inferred from the behavior. Thus when an individual expresses his opinions or makes statements about an idea, group, or object, he is engaging in written or oral behavior. However, we infer something about his mental images (attitudes) on the basis of these behaviors, and then use these inferences to predict future behaviors. Social scientists usually measure attitudes in terms of responses on questionnaires and direct interviews, often through the use of standard scales (e.g., the Bogardus Social Distance Scale mentioned in Chapter Three). In minority-group relations we are concerned with the attitude of *prejudice* and the behavior of *discrimination*, and their impact on the *self*.

Prejudice

DIMENSIONS

Prejudice represents one of the concepts in the social sciences about which there is little agreement. Clearly prejudice is not a generic variable. The multitude of definitions have some things in common, and perhaps the best single definition has been advanced by Secord and Backman: "Prejudice is an attitude that predisposes a person to think, feel, and act in favorable or unfavorable ways toward a group or its individual members."[1] Prejudice is a prejudgment; the attitude is formed either in the absence of contact with the target group, or with limited contact with that group. In fact, Horowitz[2] and Bass[3] have each observed that individuals learn their prejudiced attitudes about minority groups not through contact with the minorities, but through contact with others who have prejudiced attitudes toward the minority group.

Researchers[4] have enumerated several analytic dimensions of prejudice. Among the more important of these are direction, salience (or generalizability), intensity, commitment, and centrality. Direction is the valence (whether favorable, neutral, or unfavorable) of the attitude. Salience (or generalizability) is the extent to which the attitude can be applied to all, most, some, or a few in the class of such objects, groups, or ideas. Intensity is how strongly a person feels about his attitude. Commitment is the extent to which a person is willing to make sacrifices to hold to his attitude. Centrality is the degree to which the attitude is an integral part of the person's personality and self-conception.

As an illustration of the dimensions of prejudice, imagine a conversation between two friends. The first says, "I really dislike politicians (*direction*) very much (*intensity*). They are all (*salience*) a bunch of crooks. I'd rather vote for my mother-in-law than a career politician (*commitment*). I have become (*centrality*) a thorough politician hater."

The second replies, "I don't let it get to me so much (*centrality*). Some of them (*salience*) seem to be all right (*direction*). Not great, just all right (*intensity*). I won't let Watergate stop me from voting for politicians (*commitment*)."

Not all statements of prejudice are necessarily detailed enough to display all the dimensions as clearly as illustrated above. Sometimes particular dimensions are implicit; sometimes they can be extracted through detailed, probing interviews. Though they are subtle, social scientists must nevertheless be cognizant of these dimensions.

FUNCTIONS

More than a decade ago social psychologist Daniel Katz[5] proposed that prejudice serves four functions. First, prejudice provides a preknowledge of what to expect in a given situation (knowledge function). In a complex world where one meets and interacts with hundreds of different individuals, it becomes impossible to learn personally and make separate judgments about each one. Prejudices relieve one of that burden. It provides a kind of cognitive economy whereby, in applying bits of knowledge to whole categories of persons (such as blacks, Japanese, or males), one does not have to learn about a distinct individual, but can react to him according to a prejudgment of the category to which he belongs. Often this knowledge is accurate, or becomes so through the mechanisms of the self-fulfilling prophecy. But often the knowledge is wholly or partly inaccurate. Nevertheless, one is guided by it and it still serves a knowledge function.

Second, prejudice helps to protect the ego or self-esteem of the individual who holds prejudicial attitudes (ego-defensive function). The prejudiced individual, by holding pejorative attitudes about a group, is able to rationalize his failures and their successes. Thus the anti-Semite who fails in a competition for admission to a university might say, "The professors were all Jews and they helped their own kind first." He never has to admit that his grades, letters of recommendation, or entrance examination scores were not good enough to earn him admission. If the target of prejudice is of low minority status, the prejudiced individual can also take comfort in believing that no matter how many failures he experiences, he is still better off than people in the disliked minority group.

A third function of prejudice is instrumental (instrumental function). Prejudice here serves to maintain patterns of superordination and subordination for economic, political, or social gain. The prejudice is instrumental in helping its user adapt to his environment and thus maximize gains and rewards. Prejudice may aid a merchant to keep low the wages of minority employees, thereby maximizing the merchant's profits. The merchant may assume that members of that group are "lazy" and "stupid." If they are lazy, they won't be doing a full day's work, so they should not be paid a full day's wages. If they are stupid, they won't know that they are being paid less. The merchant's prejudice helps keep his business overhead down, and thus aids him in dealing successfully with his competition.

The fourth and final function of prejudice Katz calls the value-expressive function. Prejudice becomes rewarding for the individual when it permits him to voice his central personal values. As a corollary, prejudice may also permit the individual to express central societal values. We have seen that racism (the societal level ideology) is an integral part of the American ethic. Frank Westie[6] has argued that individual prejudice is normative in our society. There may be two norms with regard to prejudice in our society today: "Thou shall be prejudiced," and (since the civil rights movement) "Thou shall not be caught at it." Prejudice may become such a central part of the individual's personality that he may come to think of himself as a champion of white supremacy or racial purity. To take away his prejudice without giving him a new cause (such as nonprejudice) may be sufficient to destroy him as a personality, as Adorno[7] has observed.

Underlying prejudice is a factor called *ethnocentrism*, or the tendency to use one's own group (racial, ethnic, or even gender) as a standard of reference upon which to evaluate other groups. When people are ethnocentric, they will see other groups as inferior to theirs. To the extent that another group is identifiably different in terms of physical features or cultural practices, they will be evaluated negatively. They may even be stereotyped as a homogeneous class. A related phenomenon of the social psychology of groups is the concept of *xenophobia*, or fear of those who are different. Perhaps because people seek predictability and regularity in their world, they tend to prefer the familiar and shun the different. Individuals who are viewed positively are ascribed values similar to their own, and individuals who are disliked are said to endorse dissimilar values.[8] Milton Rokeach[9] suggested that the basis of prejudice is not race or ethnicity, but assumed dissimilarity of values and beliefs. That is, minorities are not hated by members of the majority because they have a different skin color or speech style, but because they are presumed to hold different and sometimes antithetical values. Downs[10] argues that it is not the fact of a black person's race that leads white property owners to fear residential desegregation, but fear that blacks are not interested in property improvements, real estate values, and providing a middle-class environment for their children.

The view that belief prejudice is the only form of prejudice is not universally accepted by social scientists. Nevertheless, the belief system explanation is yet another facet of the phenomenon we call prejudice.

MANIFESTATIONS

Prejudice is a phenomenon of many faces. It may take the form of beliefs resulting in simple avoidance reactions or in policies which advocate physical extermination of groups. In general, however, there are two principal manifestations of prejudice: *stereotypy* and *social distance*. Stereotypes are the language of prejudice, and social distance is the behavioral intent of prejudice.

More than a half-century ago, journalist Walter Lippman[11] proposed the concept of the stereotype. For him, stereotypes were "accepted types" or "pictures we carry in our heads." Stereotypes—the language of prejudice—provide their users with a vocabulary of motives or a body of rhetoric to rationalize minority-majority relationships. They may be used to justify the status quo, or they may be developed to justify changing the social order. Minorities may attempt to supplant majority stereotypes with counterimages designed to change minority-majority relations. "Black is beautiful" is just such an image.

Stereotypes, like other attitudes, serve the four functions of attitudes: instrumental, ego-defensive, knowledge, and value-expressive. In addition, stereotypes provide a symbolic identification function.[12] By using stereotypes about a given group, an individual tells others whose side he is on. In fact, it is conceivable that if a person wanted to manage his presentation of self to infiltrate an organization like the Klan, he might choose to incorporate negative, antiminority stereotypes in his conversations, thereby telling others he endorses that position.

The best definition advanced for stereotypes comes from Gordon Allport, who proposed that "a stereotype is an exaggerated belief associated with a category. It functions to justify (rationalize) our conduct toward that category."[13] Stereotypes can be favorable and neutral, as well as unfavorable (direction); they are applied to images describing all as well as only some members of a group, thereby allowing for a range of saliency. Allport also notes the rationalizing function of stereotypes, and his definition does not preclude the other functions of attitudes.

Numerous writers have debated whether stereotypes are true or false, whether they are fixed or volatile, and whether they are conservative or liberal. Those who have maintained that stereotypes are false by definition (Bogardus[14] and Klapp[15]) have proposed an alternative term, "sociotypes," to describe images which are true. Some writers[16] insist there is a kernel of truth in every stereotype. The preference among investigators today is that some stereotypes are true while others are false, but what makes them true or false is the extent to which they are applied universally to a category. It is one thing to argue that all Tasmanians are ambitious, and quite another to contend that there is somewhere at least one ambitious Tasmanian. Many stereotypes are somewhat like astrological forecasts or predictions in fortune cookies. They are so general that they can be applied to at least some portion of any population.[17]

Some writers contend that stereotypes never change, or at least are relatively inflexible. If there have not been changes in the nature of the target group, the stereotyper, or the relationship between the two, one would not expect change.[18] But when conditions do change, the stereotypes tend to follow suit. Likewise when the relationship between groups changes, their mutual stereotypes correspondingly change. In some instances the actual words used to describe a group change; in other instances the meanings or connotations of the words change. In their review of stereotypes used by Mexican Americans during the 1960s, Dworkin and Eckberg[19] showed how a word such as "emotional" underwent changes in meaning. "Emotional" first meant "irrational," but in the Chicano movement it came to mean "having soul."

In other instances the social characteristics of the people who use the stereotypes change. The latter point may be illustrated by the changes in observers' images of the Japanese around the period of World War II. The Japanese were seen as "industrious" and "good gardeners" in the prewar period; as "cruel" during the war period; and again as "industrious" after the war. In reality all three images existed throughout the time periods, but before and after the war only a few endorsed "cruel" and most others endorsed the positive images; during wartime most endorsed "cruel" and those using positive stereotypes were considered traitors.[20]

There are some instances when stereotypes persist even in the face of contradictory information or when the groups themselves have undergone change. Richter[21] suggests that stereotypes operate both as stipulative definitions and empirical generalizations. The former specify the necessary and sufficient conditions for labeling objects; the latter are based upon actual observations and hypothesis testing. Thus when a stereotyper encounters an individual from the target group behaving in a fashion consistent with the stereotype, the behavior is used to support the stereotype. However, when a person is encountered who does not conform with the stereotype, rather than reject the image, the stereotyper defines the person out of the category, saying "he's not a typical whatever."

A few writers[22] have debated whether stereotypes are basically conservative or liberal. Stereotypes are both conservative and liberal. They may be used to support a status quo or employed to change the status quo. Further, they may be used by both conservatives and liberals. No political orientation is identified with total refusal to use stereotypes, although the nature of the stereotypes may vary. Liberal individuals may endorse few negative statements about minorities. But as Mackie[23] noted recently, liberals often stereotype "establishment" types. Thus while no liberal would assume that blacks are lazy or stupid, many would agree that corporate capitalists are greedy and endowed with ulterior clandestine motives.

Exploration of the behavior and characteristics which stereotypes describe demonstrates two distinct processes. The first has been called "ingroup virtues and outgroup vices" by Merton.[24] In this process identical behavior by minority-group members and majority-group members is attributed to different and antithetical motivations. Merton makes the comparisons between Abe Lincoln and Abe Cohen. Abe Lincoln labored long hours far into the night, proving he was industrious and hard working. Abe Cohen labors far into the night, proving he is ruthless and will go to any lengths to undercut the competition. Lincoln saved his money and thus was thrifty; Cohen does the same, but he is a miser. The authors once encountered a woman who complained that her gardener, who was black and in his late sixties, was no longer carrying out the heavy trash cans to the curb for garbage collection as he had done twenty years earlier. She contended that the reason he no longer did this chore was because she thought he had become a black militant. When asked if her husband, who was the same age as the gardener, carried out the trash cans, she replied, "Of course not. He's gotten too old to do that kind of heavy work."

A second process in stereotyping has been identified as the "Thomas theorem" after sociologist W. I. Thomas,[25] and is sometimes referred to as "the self-fulfilling prophecy." According to the theorem, if men define situations as real, they will be real in their consequences. Thus by defining a group in terms of a set of stereotypes, one tends to act toward the group in terms of these stereotypes, and in time the group's behavior conforms to the stereotype. Liebow[26] reports that many white employers expect blacks to steal on the job, so they are paid less than those who are not expected to steal. Because the wages are so low, the black individual is faced with either stealing and thereby reinforcing the stereotype held by the white, or taking home too little pay to support his family.

SOCIAL DISTANCE

In Chapter Three we noted that social distance scales could be used to approximate a measure of minority-group prestige. Social distance was first defined by Robert E. Park[27] in 1924 and first measured by Emory Bogardus[28] a year later. These researchers conceptualized social distance as the degree of "empathic understanding" between members of one group and some target population. An alternative definition suggests that social distance is the extent to which one prefers to be aloof and formal rather than to interact in a close relationship with members of another group. Generally, less social distance implies a perception of greater equality between the groups. Groups which are held at a distance are often segregated physically by ghettoization and/or socially through norms of etiquette. Thus, in the urban North, blacks have been residentially segregated to demonstrate that there is a social *distance* between whites and blacks. In the South until recently blacks lived in close geographical proximity to whites. However, racial etiquette, including patterns of deference and demeanor, were more rigidly enforced. Geographical proximity in the North implied equality; not so in the South, which had mechanisms to deny the equality which might be inferred from proximity.

Scales measuring social distance generally contain three elements. They specify a target group, a subject (i.e., one who is answering the questions), and an interaction situation between the two. The target group tends to be presented categorically; the subject is asked to accept or reject an entire category rather than specific individuals within the category. The most widely used social distance scale is the Bogardus measure.[29]

The scale is composed of seven items ranging from most intimate to most distant. The subject is asked if (s)he would be willing to engage in each of the following interactions with the target group:

1. Would marry.
2. Would have as a regular friend.
3. Would work beside in an office.
4. Would have several families in my neighborhood.
5. Would have merely as speaking acquaintances.
6. Would have live outside my neighborhood.
7. Would have live outside my country.

Social distance is measured on many target groups to determine the relative rankings of the groups by the individual. The more groups from which a subject desires to maintain high social distance, the more that individual is perceived to be prejudiced. The scale has also been administered to subjects from various ethnic, racial, and gender groups.

While this scale continues to be the most widely used, it is not without its faults. Some have challenged its appropriateness outside of the United States. Others have suggested that the weighting of items has changed over time, so that having minority-group members in one's neighborhood implies greater intimacy and equality than either the coworker or the friendship items.[30] Rather than the workplace, the neighborhood has become a battleground for majority-minority conflicts. Furthermore, one may have minority-group friends without being necessarily subjected to the sanctions of neighbors.

A more advanced measure of social distance has been developed by

Frank Westie.[31] His measure presents several sets of interaction situations like the Bogardus scale, but it permits variations within a specific target group. Thus if a person feels greater social distance from a black who is of a low social class than from one of a high social class, the scale could be sensitive to that distinction.

Discrimination

Discrimination is a behavior. It is the application of differential and pejorative treatment to individuals on the basis of a person's membership in a particular category rather than upon his individual characteristics and qualifications. In Chapter Three we discussed discrimination on the aggregate level, which is a reflection of institutional racism. However, discrimination also is a personal and individualistic phenomenon. Individuals discriminate and individuals are the objects of discrimination.

Because discrimination is a behavior and is observable, it has often been measured by a technique called *participant observation.* Typical studies have involved placing an observer incognito in a natural situation where discrimination is likely to occur, and then having him record behaviors. Other studies have involved contrived situations in which observations were made. A classic study assessing discrimination was conducted by LaPiere[32] in the 1930s. LaPiere and a Chinese couple traveled widely across the United States, stopping at two hundred and fifty restaurants and hotels. In only one instance were they subjected to discrimination and refused service. The fascinating part of the study was that some time later LaPiere sent a letter to each of the restaurants and hotels they had visited, asking whether they would "take members of the Chinese race as guests at your establishment." Over 90 percent of the restaurants and hotels replied that they would not. LaPiere concluded that attitudes as measured by a questionnaire (the letter) were not identical to behaviors as measured by actual practice. Campbell[33] has suggested that the contrasting situations—the letter and the actual presence of the couple—were dissimilar enough to prohibit comparisons. He contends that it is more difficult to refuse service to someone in front of you than to answer an impersonal letter.

It is generally assumed that a prejudiced person will discriminate and that a nonprejudiced person will not discriminate. Often this assumption is valid. However, the LaPiere study suggests that there are other possibilities. His findings suggest that individuals may verbalize prejudicial attitudes but not actively discriminate. It is indeed true, as Campbell suggests, that it is easier to be a verbal bigot than to behave like one, especially when the weight of the law or public opinion encourages equal treatment and condemns discrimination. In other circumstances, however, the reverse of the LaPiere phenomenon could occur. That is, people may discriminate against others without holding prejudicial attitudes toward them. Such individuals may be constrained to act in discriminatory ways because of economic or peer pressures. An Anglo child may participate in throwing rocks at a lone Chicano, not because he has learned prejudicial attitudes, but because his friends are there, cheering him on.

Adults can feel similar pressures to discriminate despite their personal attitudes. Kohn and Williams[34] report an observational study in which a black couple entered a working-class white tavern and were confronted by the bartender. White observers were located at strategic points in the tavern to record the interactions. At the proprietor's insistence, the bar tender approached the black man and stated:

> Now, mind you, I don't have anything against you people. I went to school with you folks and I've got a lot of friends among you. But some of my customers don't like to see you in here. Five or six of them have already complained to me and left. Now I can't have that. I hope you'll understand if I ask you to leave.[35]

Whether or not we accept the sincerity of the bartender's comments, we must note that he was under a constraint by his boss and that his verbally expressed attitude (that he had nothing "against" blacks) was not supportive of his behavior (to ask the blacks to leave). It is not uncommon that individuals come to find that the exigencies of economic life do not permit them to implement their beliefs in action. The authors of this text once interviewed a black woman who was suing her friend, the president of a local civil rights organization, because he had refused to rent an apartment to her in his complex. He confessed to her that he believed all of his white tenants would leave and he would be bankrupt if she moved in.

Merton[36] used these four possibilities (of the connection between prejudice and discrimination) to construct a paradigm of the following types. The nonprejudiced nondiscriminator, who under no circumstances will discriminate, is called the all-weather liberal. The nonprejudiced discriminator who will discrimnate only when he is pressured by circumstances is the fair-weather liberal. The fair-weather illiberal is the prejudiced nondiscriminator—he would discriminate but circumstances prevent him from doing so. Finally there is the all-weather illiberal; he is the prejudiced discriminator who will discriminate regardless of the circumstances. It is estimated that most Americans are fair-weather types subject to some kind of pressure. Thus one cannot assume the direct connection between prejudiced attitudes and discriminatory behaviors.

There is another faulty assumption: that if an individual discriminates in one situation, he will discriminate in others. Quite the contrary is correct, as illustrated by another classic study. Lohman and Reitzes[37] studied a group of industrial workers and discovered that they supported with equal vigor desegregation of their workplace and segregation of their neighborhood. Killian[38] further supports this observation in his study of southern "hillbillies" in Chicago. Although these individuals had opposed working with blacks on the same job in the South and approved of the southern practice of segregation, very few objected to working with blacks on the same job in the urban North. Most had accommodated to the northern practices despite their previous behavior in the South.

Discrimination, then, is situation specific. Since most Americans are fair-weather types, their willingness to discriminate will depend upon the specific social circumstances in which they find themselves: the kind of pressures they are under, and from whom. Switching the context of the situation from less to more intimate (as in the Lohman and Reitzes study) or switching from one region to another (as in Killian's study) can be sufficient to change the behavior. Merton's fourfold typology was developed into a theory by Yinger[39] and tested by Warner and DeFleur.[40] Four different structural situations were selected: a liberal university neighborhood, a northern city, a southern city, and the rural South. Yinger had predicted that in the liberal situation even the all-weather illiberal might not discriminate. In the rural South (most conservative) the all-weather liberal might discriminate. However, in the two intermediate situations (northern and southern cities) the fair-weather types would behave according to the norms of the area and the all-weather types would behave according to their attitudes. Although there was general support for the Yinger model, Warner and DeFleur found a considerable zone of imprecision in predictability.

Where discrimination and prejudice do not accompany one another, it is generally possible to point to three possible explanations. First, the individual may not have sufficient *commitment* to his prejudicial attitude to back it up with discriminatory behavior. That is, the strength of his beliefs about the inferiority of a group is not so great that he is willing to endure the consequences of acting in accordance with those beliefs. Second, the individual may not have the *volition* or control over the situation to do what he really wants to do. He may be constrained by family, friends, employers, or even the law. Third, the attitude measured may not be equivalent to the behavior predicted. Imagine a subject who would not want to marry a member of a minority group but then signs a petition supporting the candidacy of a minority-group member as mayor of his city (behavior). The two are not equivalent in level of intimacy, and ought not be expected to be equivalent in level of performance.

Several writers[41] have attempted to construct theoretical models to relate attitudes and behaviors (prejudice and discrimination) to situation-bound relationships. Although there are variations in the models, their general form is as shown in Figure 5–1. This chart denotes that the commitment and volitional variables cited above determine the strength of attitudes, and these same commitment and volitional variables enter again to create the behavior. Once the behavior is executed, the individual has increased commitment to remaining consistent and hence reinforces the attitude.

FIGURE 5–1

CONSTRAINTS ON ATTITUDE–BEHAVIOR RELATIONSHIPS

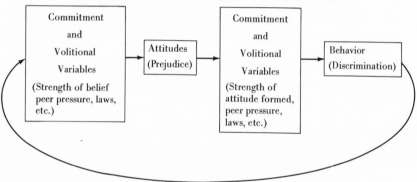

Prejudice, Discrimination, and the Self

Prejudice and discrimination are directed toward groups of individuals, and so they have consequences for both the target-group member and the prejudiced person. The functions that prejudices perform for the individual have already been discussed: preknowledge, ego-defense, instrumentalism, and value-expression. There are also dysfunctions for the prejudiced person. He relies upon stereotypes and other attitudes that may be incorrect, guiding him to behave inappropriately. Furthermore, when a society changes, the prejudiced individual locked into his rigid thought processes does not change along with it, and soon finds himself out of step with his world. Prejudice is a limiting process; it constricts creativity and rationality—costs which are individual as well as societal. The prejudiced person may live in fear of those groups about whom he feels negatively. He sells his house at the first hint of desegregation, moving still further from his workplace. He may send his children to private schools, adding to his financial burdens. His beliefs may alienate his children from him. He may quit his job or lose interest in his workplace because of the presence of minority-group members. Although he is an extreme example of the prejudiced person, Archie Bunker of the popular television program "All in the Family" displays many of the personal costs of prejudice. Archie is not only bigoted, he is also unhappy. His prejudice, which simplifies some of his decisions and interactions in life, also complicates his life, and robs it of much of its pleasure.

There are costs to being prejudiced, but the costs to the target of prejudice are many times greater. Being a target of prejudice essentially means being a victim of rejection. Rejection in turn, if it is seen as legitimate, leads to lowered self-esteem, hatred of oneself and one's own group. It is an insidious fact of prejudice and discrimination that target-group members can become so well socialized through majority organizations and institutions such as the schools and the mass media that they may come to believe the derogatory statements made about them.

The socialization process teaches women that they ought not to pursue careers in the sciences and in technological fields. It tells women that they should seek challenging careers, but then confronts them with guilt feelings because of these ambitions. They fear that their desire to be economically independent means that they are axiomatically "bad spouses" or "bad mothers." This guilt drives many to seek counseling and even psychiatric help. Frequently, the psychiatrists they consult accept the societal definitions and only reinforce their guilt feelings, directing them not to question the societal values, but to look for and deal with internal inadequacies.[42]

The society places a premium upon whiteness and blondness. Dark-complexioned minorities, especially some black Americans, have in the past been driven to buying skin-lightening creams, hair straighteners, and other devices to make them look more white. Grier and Cobbs, two black psychiatrists, observed:

Caution must be exercised in distinguishing feelings of inferiority from emulation of the majority by a minority concerned with survival. But even taking this into account, there remains an increment of feeling which says emphatically: "White is right."

For a black man to straighten his hair chemically, to have what is known as a "process," is a painful, dangerous procedure. The result is a slick pompadour which in no way save one resembles a white man's hair. Only in that it is straight and not kinky does it appear less black and more white.

Negroes have always referred to straight hair as good—and kinky hair as bad.[43]

Other groups have tried equally drastic alterations of their bodies. Some

Japanese have had plastic surgery to give their eyes a more Caucasian appearance. In most instances minority individuals have accepted majority aesthetic judgements, and merely want to look "pretty." But in some instances the motive was to permit economic passing (in which the individual plays the role of a majority member in order to secure better employment opportunities, but emotionally continues to identify with the minority); others sought varying degrees of social passing (in which the individual breaks off all contact with his own group and tries to blend into the majority). The individual who passes socially must be on constant guard against being detected, and lives in fear and suspicion.

Attempts at social passing also incur the wrath of the individual's own minority community. Anger, jealousy, and withdrawal of respect by one's own family and friends may be more damaging to the individual than rejection by the majority. Each minority has a derogatory term to describe individuals of its own group who have become too Anglicized, too much like the majority group in thought and behavior. Blacks refer to such individuals as *Oreos* or *Uncle Toms*; Chicanos use the term *Tío Tacos* or *Tío Tomas*; native Americans call such individuals of their group *Apples* (red on the outside, white on the inside); the Chinese and Japanese refer to them as *Bananas* (yellow on the outside, white on the inside); the Irish referred to their "traitors" as *Lace-Curtain Irish*. One Mexican American recounted to the authors that his own family refused to let him return to their home after he had changed his surname in order to become successful in his law practice. He commented "My own mother told me that she had no son; that he had died; and that she didn't want to have 'ghosts' in her house."

There have been a plethora of studies conducted by social scientists on minority children (usually black) to discover at how early an age minorities learn to emulate whites and prefer to be like them. One classic study was conducted by Kenneth and Mamie Clark.[44] These social psychologists asked black children, some in segregated southern schools and some in desegregated northern schools, to choose between a black doll and a white doll. The children were asked which doll looked like them, which doll looked nice, which doll looked bad, and which doll had a nice color. Black children, especially in the segregated schools, preferred and more favorably evaluated the white doll over the black doll. Similar findings have been reported by other writers, including Miller,[45] who determined color preferences by white, Chicano, and black children and reported the general acceptance of "the rightness of whiteness hypothesis"—the preference for white over brown or black.

The Clark study is not without some critical flaws. The research was done long before black dolls were commercially available, so the black doll was really a white doll with black enamel paint all over its face. Thus it cannot be determined that the children were really evaluating skin color preference, or merely choosing a doll which looked less damaged or soiled and more like their own at home. This procedure required the children to make two cognitive leaps. They first had to see the racial nature of the dolls, and then had to translate their feelings toward that symbolic object into their feelings toward real groups. With two stages of cognitions required, there is twice the probability of miscuing. There is double the chance that the individuals will be unable to make the cognitive leaps. Not only is it problematic that children may accomplish the task, but the experience of those who run consciousness-raising groups suggests that adults also need help in making such leaps. In fact, those studies which have asked minority children to indicate with whom they wanted to play have generally shown that minorities tend to choose members of their own group. This observation was recently noted by Linda Teplin.[46] She compared what she called the "projectively based technique," in which children are to project onto inanimate objects (such as dolls or animals of different skin color) cognitions about self-acceptance or rejection, with the "reality-based technique," in which children choose sociometrically an individual with whom they would want to play and be photographed. Teplin noted that children's choices of friends were nearly unrelated to their preferences for inanimate objects. That is, a minority child may choose a toy that shares the color of a majority-group member, but tends to choose other minority-group members as friends. Teplin argues that we should place greater credence on the reality-based measures than the projective measures.

Exploration of early studies of minority-held stereotypes about the majority and about their own group suggests another area of the psychological cost of prejudice. Minority-group members have tended to evaluate the majority more favorably than they evaluate themselves. Bayton[47] in the 1940s found that black college students stereotyped blacks nearly as negatively as white college students stereotyped blacks, and stereotyped whites as positively as whites stereotyped themselves. Simmons[48] noted comparable findings for Mexican Americans in South Texas in the 1950s. A. G. Dworkin[49] compared foreign-born Mexican Americans, who had just arrived in the United States from Mexico and were consequently not socialized to the majority ideology, with native-born Mexican Americans, who had lived in the barrio in East Los Angeles, California, all of their lives and had been socialized by the Anglo schools and media. The foreign born had favorable images of themselves and of the Anglos, while the native born had unfavorable images of themselves and also somewhat unfavorable images of the Anglos. A second study indicated that in a relatively short time (about six months) even the foreign-born Mexican Americans acquired the negative self-imagery pervasive in the barrio.[50]

Attributions of superiority to men and inferiority to women is another element of the socialization of minority groups which tends to have social and psychological consequences for minority-group members. Goldberg[51] found that, because of this socialization, women were more prejudiced against themselves than they were against men. In fact, women downgraded the accomplishments of female professionals in all fields, even in the traditionally female fields, while upgrading the evaluation of males in all fields.

Social scientists have debated whether minority-held stereotypes generally reflect mirror imagery (they are identical to the majority stereotypes, evolving from them and indicating acceptance of majority-based definitions) or whether they reflect reciprocal prejudice (counters to majority-held stereotypes, reflecting rejection of the majority and attacks upon the majority). Maykovich[52] advanced the thesis of general support for the latter form. Recently published research by A. G. Dworkin and Eckberg[53] has illustrated that both processes are at work within the same individual. Minority-group members may accept the majority stereotypes of other minorities, but they reject majority stereotypes of themselves and hold reciprocal prejudiced images of the majority. These authors found that each minority group in their study (Jews, Chicanos, blacks, and Japanese Americans) accepted between 50 and 60 percent of the images white Protestants held of other minority groups, but less than 30 percent of the images white Protestants held about themselves or about the minority's own group.

Social movements generally tend to have a positive psychological impact upon minority-group members. Movements for civil rights, black liberation, the Chicanos, and women's liberation, each of which stresses system blame for social ills rather than personal blame, tend to aid minority-group members in dealing with majority stereotypes. The movements not only affect the images the majority hold of the minority but also provide minority-group members with a vocabulary of motives to shape new self-identities and to account for majority-held images. The senior author has monitored the stereotypes held by Mexican Americans in the periods of 1963 (pre-Chicano movement), 1967–1968 (during the inception of the movement), and 1971–1972 (a period of movement gains).[54] During the ten-year period of the studies, Chicano images of themselves and of Anglos traded positions. In 1963 Chicanos saw Anglos as their superiors; in 1967–1968 they saw Anglos as their equals; and in 1971–1972 they saw Anglos as their inferiors.

Presented in Table 5–1 are the most frequently mentioned stereotypes and self-images held by the Chicano subjects over the three sampling periods. From the table it is possible to discern several points. First, the rank order of the images has changed, reflecting changes in the overall evaluations of the groups as well as in the content of their perceived characteristics. Second, some images have acquired new "meanings," e.g., "emotional" has changed from unfavorable to favorable in Chicano self-stereotypes, while "high social position" has changed from favorable to neutral in Chicano images of Anglos. Third, the same word applied to one's own group may have a different meaning than when applied to another group, e.g., "ambitious" has become a favorable quality when Chicanos apply it to themselves, but an unfavorable quality when ascribed to Anglos. Fourth, over time several new words have emerged while others have disappeared, or at least were mentioned too infrequently to be prevalent stereotypes. The pattern of images which emerged or disappeared was consistent with the general trend toward more favorable Chicano self-imagery and more unfavorable imagery of Anglos.

The civil rights movement and the black liberation movement similarly have increasingly insulated black Americans from possible ego threats induced by white prejudice. These movements have taught blacks to view as illegitimate and motivated by racism the preponderance of white stereotypy. Researchers have found that blacks and whites now report equally high estimates of self-esteem.[55] The basis for such self-esteem among blacks is within the black community through black and not white evaluations,[56] and most usually through evaluations by one's friends and neighbors.[57]

The movements provide for a transition from psychological marginality to the development of a marginal culture. Park[58] and Stonequist[59] advanced the concept of marginality, and numerous authors have improved upon it.[60] According to the theory, when an individual is part of two societies or subcultures and is accepted in neither, or finds that the subordinate subculture in which he is accepted is unsatisfactory but the superordinate one is blocked to him, he will manifest a series of social and psychological conditions. Stonequist itemized some of the symptoms as a double consciousness, ambivalent feelings, moodiness, tempermentalness, hypersensitivity, and hyperactivity.

If, however, there are sufficient other individuals in his condition so that a social group with a strong sense of identity can evolve, they may be able to develop an alternative society based upon their common marginality. Social movements are useful in focusing the individual consciousness and in-group self-awareness into a viable entity. The new marginal culture is then capable of providing psychic and social rewards for its members, and the condition of psychological marginality terminates.[61]

TABLE 5-1

STEREOTYPES OF CHICANOS AND ANGLOS HELD BY CHICANOS

IMAGES OF CHICANOS

	1963 Sample (N = 174)			1967–1968 Sample (N = 131)			1971–1972 Sample (N = 227)		
	Image	Evaluation	Percent	Image	Evaluation	Percent	Image	Evaluation	Percent
	Religious	Fav.	37.4	Religious	Fav.	37.4	Proud	Fav.	37.9
	Friendly	Fav.	35.1	Friendly	Fav.	30.5	Brown	Fav.	35.2
	Uneducated	Unfav.	30.5	Proud	Fav.	26.0	Friendly	Fav.	32.6
	Catholics	Neutral	29.3	Lazy	Unfav.	22.1	Religious	Fav.	30.8
	Lazy	Unfav.	28.2	Poor	Unfav.	20.7	Intelligent	Fav.	29.5
	Poor	Unfav.	27.6	Hard working	Fav.	19.9	Hard working	Fav.	26.0
	Large families	Neutral	27.0	Uneducated	Neutral	18.3	Poor	Neutral	23.4
	Hard working	Fav.	20.7	Intelligent	Fav.	16.8	Ambitious	Fav.	18.5
	Pessimistic	Unfav.	19.0	Emotional	Fav.	15.3	Uneducated	Neutral	18.1
	Proud	Fav.	17.8	Large families	Fav.	13.7	Emotional	Fav.	17.2
	Shy	Unfav.	15.5	Catholics	Fav.	11.5	Good family life	Fav.	15.4
	Intelligent	Fav.	14.4	—*			—		
	Emotional	Unfav.	13.2	—			—		

Images of Anglos

1963 Sample (N = 174)			1967–1968 Sample (N = 131)			1971–1972 Sample (N = 227)		
Image	Evaluation	Percent	Image	Evaluation	Percent	Image	Evaluation	Percent
Friendly	Fav.	61.0	High economic level	Neutral	29.0	Superiority	Unfav.	28.2
Light complexioned	Fav.	52.3	Well educated	Fav.	25.2	Well educated	Fav.	22.5
Intelligent	Fav.	51.2	Superiority	Unfav.	21.4	Bigoted	Unfav.	22.0
Well educated	Fav.	48.3	Intelligent	Fav.	19.1	Prejudiced	Unfav.	21.1
Ambitious	Fav.	37.4	Bigoted	Unfav.	16.8	High social position	Neutral	18.5
Well dressed	Fav.	29.3	Boastful	Unfav.	13.7	Greedy	Unfav.	18.1
High economic level	Fav.	27.0	Greedy	Unfav.	12.2	Intelligent	Fav.	16.3
High social position	Fav.	25.3	High social position	Neutral	12.2	Boastful	Unfav.	13.2
Well mannered	Fav.	24.7	Prejudiced	Unfav.	11.5	Light complexioned	Neutral	12.3
Religious	Fav.	23.6	Athletic	Neutral	10.7	Ambitious	Unfav.	11.5
Athletic	Fav.	19.5	Ambitious	Neutral	10.0	Average social position	Neutral	11.5
Superiority	Unfav.	19.5	Well dressed	Fav.	10.0	Athletic	Neutral	10.1
Snob	Unfav.	17.4	Well mannered	Fav.	10.0	Social	Neutral	10.1
Humanitarian	Fav.	16.7	Friendly	Fav.	10.0	—		
Social	Fav.	15.5	—			—		

* Less than 10 percent mentioned an image in these ranks.

The Causes of Prejudice

Prejudice and discrimination manifest themselves in numerous ways, and so there are numerous explanations for them. No one theory of prejudice is adequate to explain all of its manifestations, and prejudice itself is probably not a unitary phenomenon. That is, we might do well to consider that there are many kinds of prejudice and that each kind may be caused by combinations of a multitude of factors. Earliest theories of prejudice focused upon instinctive and biological factors, including instinctive fear of difference and instinctive hatreds. Some of these theories have been around since shortly after the French Revolution.[62] It is generally true that we can detect more plausible social, psychological, or cultural factors behind these manifestations of prejudice and discrimination than if we had to rely upon purely organismic explanations. Basically, we can discern three classes of theories of prejudice and discrimination: psychological theories, social structural theories, and normative and cultural theories.

PSYCHOLOGICAL THEORIES

Frustration-Aggression and Scapegoating Theory. Dollard[63] and his colleagues at the Yale Institute of Human Relations developed the hypothesis which maintains that aggressive impulses arise whenever one is frustrated. Prejudice is considered a type of aggression and is said to be a universal response to frustration. When people's needs are unsatisfied or their activities are interrupted, they respond with aggression. But often aggression cannot be directed toward the frustrating object, because that object is too powerful. Thus the aggression is directed toward members of the minority groups, who serve as a "scapegoat." For example, a "poor white," who cannot vent his aggression upon his landlord (because of custom and power structure pressures), displaces his aggression onto a convenient, easily identified object—the black.

Hughes[64] gives the example of French Canadian farmers unable to strike back at the dominant English-speaking Canadian urbanites, who were attempting to do away with the rural way of life. The French Canadians, being too weak to affect the decisions of the English-speaking group, vented their aggressions upon the Jewish minority.

There are weaknesses in the frustration-aggression-scapegoating theory. While the abovementioned cases seem to support the theory, the theory does not explain satisfactorily why aggression may be directed against one minority and not against another. Furthermore, while the theory explains a *possible* force behind prejudice in general, it fails to account for the fact that prejudice against minorities is not the only response to frustration. Berkowitz and Geen[65] and more recently Geen[66] have demonstrated that frustration does not necessarily lead to aggression but tends to require symbols of violence or aggression as intervening variables. That is, unless frustration occurs in the presence of or immediately before exposure to aggressive cues, aggression will not occur. The widespread displays of violence and symbols of violence in the mass media, especially on television, may provide the necessary connective link between frustration and aggression.

The Authoritarian Personality. In the 1930s German philosopher and social scientist Max Horkheimer[67] first proposed that prejudice could be accounted for by a general personality type. In 1950 Adorno and his associates[68] published their massive study on the psychology of prejudice, *The Authoritarian Personality.* Studying over two thousand Americans, the research concluded that about 10 percent of the population was authoritarian and an additional 30 percent had "the seeds of authoritarianism in them." The authoritarian personality is one which has been shaped by fear of authority, as in the relationship between the child and his strict patriarchal father who makes binding and arbitrary decisions and punishes for lack of respect. The child who has such a relationship responds to all authority as he did to his father, submissively, and as an adult becomes authoritarian in turn. Deeper studies demonstrate that obeying arbitrary authority in childhood results in bottled-up fear and resentment. The child who successfully weathers the discipline develops into an adult frightened by and morally indignant about people whose behavior is different from his own conduct. His fears and repressed wish to retaliate can easily be mobilized whenever the proper rationalization is supplied. Generally, the authoritarian is a person who has the following characteristics:[69]

1. He is a supreme conformist who irrationally and unquestioningly succumbs to the commands of a leader.
2. He views the world as menacing and unfriendly, agreeing that the "world is a jungle."
3. He is mechanical and rigid, showing little imagination.
4. He is quite ethnocentric and xenophobic. Because the world is menacing, he can find security only with those who are like him and hence predictable.
5. He is a phony conservative, waving the flag but hating the values of freedom and democracy.
6. He is a moral purist, who has come to reject all emotionality and sensuality.

The Authoritarian Personality has been immensely heuristic, generating volumes of research. Much of the research has brought into question the accuracy of the portrayal of a single personality factor to account for prejudice. The famous F-Scale, which emerged from the study and which was designed to measure authoritarianism, has also been the subject of much methodological criticism. Without the study, work in the analysis of prejudice and its causes would have been slower to develop. Nonetheless, we now know that psychological causes of prejudice cannot explain all or even most of the phenomenon.

SOCIAL STRUCTURE THEORIES

Unlike the psychological theories which posit the cause of prejudice as located within the individual and his or her personality development, social structural theories locate the cause of prejudice within the context of relationships between people in the society. There are numerous structural theories, but those with which we shall deal concern economic competition, economic exploitation, and situational and mass society theories.

Economic Competition and Economic Exploitation. These two economic theories of prejudice are basically rather similar. The economic competition theory sees prejudice arising from groups which are in direct competition for scarce resources. The economic exploitation theory adds that if one group possesses far greater power than the other, the competition is turned into the exploitation of the weaker group by the more powerful. A leading exponent of the economic models in minority-group relations was Oliver C. Cox,[70] who viewed prejudice as a tool employed by the ruling class to suppress the minority class.

In support of the competition theory, McWilliams[71] noted that there was little prejudice against the Japanese in California until Japanese immigrants began to enter types of work which competed with Anglo occupations. Similarly, medieval anti-Semitism in Europe increased greatly when banking and finance, previously left to the Jews, grew to be profitable for the Gentiles. The economic exploitation of Mexican Americans, which kept them in stoop labor jobs at less than minimum wages, rewarded Anglo prejudice with low fruit and vegetable prices. However, when Mexican American field workers tried to unionize in 1931, growers got the police to arrest the workers and to place them into "concentration camps." Those who resisted were deported (repatriated —even though many were American-born). Similar recent attacks on Cesar Chavez and members of the United Farm Workers can be explained by the same theory.

Slavery in the United States also conforms to the economic exploitation hypothesis. Until the invention of the cotton gin in the 1790s slavery was moving toward extinction. With this innovation, slavery was rapidly extended and cemented into the social structure with the rise of racist attitudes of prejudice. Whereas slavery had formerly existed as a weak institution, an economic incentive made it strong and apparently provided the stimulus for the introduction of race prejudice.

Wilhelm[72] has suggested in his theory of economic exclusion that blacks were tolerated only so long as they could provide a pool of cheap labor that could not be technologically displaced. Now machines can do many tasks with minimal expense, especially those normally relegated to unskilled labor. Wilhelm fears that black Americans will no longer be needed by whites and may face wholesale extermination, such as the native American faced a century ago.

Split Labor Market Theory. Within the past few years a new theory has emerged which attempts to combine both economic competition and economic exploitation into a single framework. Bonacich[73] has proposed a "split labor market theory of ethnic antagonisms." The theory does not posit prejudice as an outcome per se, only discrimination. According to her theory two groups, with different levels of skill resources and expertise, are pitted against one another in the labor market. Employers seek to minimize labor costs and hence displace higher-paid labor with lower-paid labor. However, this increases the antagonisms between the labor groups, which often are minority and majority groups. The majority group of laborers, having greater power, engages in two discriminatory practices: exclusion movements, whereby the minority may be deported, and labor caste systems, whereby the minority is relegated to lower-status, less well-paying jobs, and the majority to higher-status, better-paying jobs. Thus prejudices become the rationalization for economic behaviors—both competitive and exploitive. Discrimination becomes the tool for securing and/or maintaining economic advantage. Simultaneously, contact between hostile groups in economic competition tends to validate and reinforce previously held prejudices.

Situational and Mass Society Theories. These theories[74] combine two observations about prejudice and discrimination in complex societies. The first is that prejudice and discrimination are situation specific. Individuals may express prejudicial beliefs and engage in discriminatory practices in one situation, and do and say antithetical things in another situation (recall several studies[75] reported earlier in this chapter). Second, people participate in many organizations which may have contradictory goals. These organizations, sometimes massive in scale, are impersonal and unresponsive to individual imputs, so the actor exerts much less control over the organization than the organization exerts over the individual. Communications, typified by the mass media, tend to be one-way, in which the individual receives but does not send messages. Participation in these organizations (e.g., labor unions, churches, neighborhood associations) does not involve the total self, but only segments of specific roles performed. During participation in a specific organization, one's attitudes, goals, and behaviors must conform to the prescriptions of that organization. Because of the lowered commitment and the segmented participation in these mass organizations, individuals can tolerate a high degree of apparently contradictory behavior and attitudes within themselves.[76] Thus, under pressures to conform to the demands of multiple organizations and a large variation of peers, behavior toward minority groups may vary with the specific situation. Seen in this way, prejudice and discrimination are less individualistic and more organizational in origin. The individual bigot is merely an extension of institutional racism.

The general trend of the mass media and of large organizations has been to diminish prejudice and discrimination. The content of television programs, implementation of governmental policy, and other large organizational policies have been aimed toward more equality among citizens. Thus we might not expect the model depicted by the situational and mass society theory to lead to greater prejudice and discrimination. Nonetheless, there are significant differences in the amount and kind of exposure to organizations that different individuals encounter. Further, the messages from these organizations are not always consistent. A variety of studies of voting behavior has suggested that only individuals caught between conflicting pressure groups are likely to follow the mass media's suggestions. Social structural theories of prejudice and discrimination have proven to be viable explanations. They do not, however, explain the totality of attitudes and behaviors. For one thing, social structural models are embedded within a given culture. They assume the existence of cultural theories in order to operate. We now turn to the normative and cultural explanations of prejudice.

NORMATIVE AND CULTURAL THEORIES

In Chapter Four we spoke of institutional racism as an ideology of American society. Supported by this ideology is the norm for prejudice. That is, people are prejudiced because society teaches them to be prejudiced, rewards them for prejudice, and demands prejudicial beliefs and discriminatory behavior as forms of compliance to the norm.[77] Part of most people's socialization has included being discouraged by their parents from playing with "inappropriate playmates." No individual is born with prejudices, but through his early socialization he quickly learns whom to hate. Many writers have noted that people rarely learn their prejudice from direct contact with minority-group members, but from members of their own group who are already prejudiced.

One must be cautious of a static view of the normative theory of prejudice. To accept the explanation of prejudice as static is to assume that ideas are passed from generation to generation without modification.

We know, however, that there have been changes in the amount and level of prejudice observable in our society over the past three decades. A dynamic normative theory can account for this, because it would suggest that as norms concerning prejudice change, the level of prejudice should change. One should also be cautious not to assume that a normative theory can explain all prejudice. The previously discussed structural and personality theories do account for some of the presence of prejudice.

Prejudice as a Symbol. In some instances prejudice may persist even after it ceases to perform psychological, economic, structural, and other societal functions. In such instances the strength of the prejudice might be less intense. Some researchers have argued that these lingering prejudices stem from historical events in which the minority group was involved and for which it now serves as a symbol. Some aspects of anti-Semitism may be due to the historical view of Jews as "Christ-killers" or as symbols of the city with its strange cosmopolitan atmosphere which frightened many rural peoples.[78] Some prejudice against blacks may be a residual symbol of the South's defeat in the Civil War and Reconstruction.[79] It is quite possible that some of the prejudice encountered by Vietnamese refugees may have resulted from their role as a symbol of America's frustrations in Vietnam, and of the economic and political consequences of the defeat to American foreign policy.

The Linguistic Theory. A final theory of prejudice which operates on the cultural or macrosystem (as opposed to the social structural or interpersonal) level is the linguistic theory of prejudice.

Most linguistic theories of prejudice are based upon an interpretation of the Sapir-Whorf hypothesis,[80] which holds that the characteristics of a language determine how its speakers view their world. That is, "language is not 'merely' a vehicle of communication by which man talks about some objective reality 'out there' that exists previous to and independent of his language, but, rather that language itself represents an objective reality by means of which man structures and organizes the 'out there' in certain characteristic ways."[81]

Much of human interaction involves manipulation of symbols. Without symbols, especially language, individuals would be able neither to think, nor to possess a social self and social identity.[82] The culture which specifies the appropriate modes of behavior, thinking, and dealing with others is transmitted through the language. Thus some theorists have looked to the content of language for the roots and causes of prejudice and discrimination.

In Western societies and, as Allport notes, in many non-Western societies,[83] the term "black" has sinister connotations—witches are black, funerals and death are depicted as black, harmful or evil magic is "black magic," and "blacklisting" and "blackballing" refer to rejection. On the other hand, the term "white" has connotations of cleanliness and purity—angels are white, bridal gowns are white, Ivory Soap is white (and 99 and 44/100 percent pure). Similarly, Orientals have yellowish skin, and since the color "yellow" connotes cowardly, stale, and untrustworthy, according to the theory, these negative characteristics are ascribed to Orientals. Thus the theory holds that because of the cultural connotations attached to them, people with skin resembling one of these three colors are attributed with the characteristics the colors connote.

Similarly, the English language has structured within it several assumptions about sex roles and the nature of males and females. Although gender designations of nouns and pronouns are more conspicuous in other languages (such as Spanish, Italian, and French), it is difficult to compose English paragraphs which do not demand gender designations of pronouns (e.g., his, her) even when gender is irrelevant to the meaning being communicated. In such instances the correct pronoun is considered to be the masculine, because of the assumed importance of the masculine in the entire culture. When various feminist groups rebel against the suffix "man" in words like "policeman," "chairman," and "postman," and insist on the substitution of "person," they are expressing an awareness of the sensitizing and symbolic function of language as a determinant of behavior.

Prejudice and Discrimination Reduction

The previous section began with the observation that there are many causes of prejudice and discrimination, and in fact, there probably are many kinds of prejudice. Hence it is unlikely that a cure-all procedure can be devised to eradicate prejudice and discrimination. The most effective technique would be to prevent a person from becoming prejudiced in the first place. Hence, child-raising practices which permit children to experience, meet, and learn about people of diverse identities and heritages are superior to any technique which seeks to rid an adult of his prejudices. Public television programs and other forms of the mass media are available to provide children with the lesson that all people, regardless of skin color, cultural background, or gender are human beings with equal rights to a productive life on our planet. But it is a reality of social life that people differentiate between groups, that people do evaluate others in terms of their race, ethnicity, and gender. Given that there is prejudice in the world and that children tend to learn that prejudice, the task then becomes one of reducing it.

Early in this chapter four functions of prejudice were enumerated: knowledge, ego-defense, instrumental, and value-expressive. It was further noted that unless changes occurred in the nature of the target of prejudice, the nature of the prejudiced individual, or the relationship between the two, prejudice itself would not change. There have been programs to change minority-group members, including techniques which "Americanized" them. There have been programs oriented toward the prejudiced individual, providing aids such as psychiatric help, counseling, or correcting misinformation about the minority groups. And there have been programs which have attempted to instill better relations between the minorities and the majority. It has been the general experience of many programs geared toward the prejudiced individual or toward tightening bonds between majorities and minorities that the only individuals who attended the sessions were those already committed to nonprejudice, who came only to reinforce their beliefs. The really "hard-core" bigot never came to the various "human relations sessions."

INFORMATION CAMPAIGNS

One of the more dismal failures in prejudice reduction has been public information campaigns geared at debunking stereotypes. Most of the people who come to such sessions do not subscribe to the stereotype in the first place, and those that do believe the stereotype either supplant the debunked image with a new, equally negative one, or define the experience as proving nothing. A student in a class taught by the junior author complained after several myths about sex roles had been attacked, "You're just trying to confuse me with facts."

EDUCATION

There is some evidence that educational programs within the schools, particularly in the universities, can be effective. However, it is the *nature* of the programs that are essential, not simply their presence. In some instances, simply offering black history courses in the public schools may have little or no effect, or may even heighten barriers. This is especially true if the material is presented by a teacher who is hostile to the concepts, or if the issues are freighted with political ramifications in the community which filter into the classroom. Although an integrated education potentially can benefit majority and minority participants, two things tend also to be true. First, much of what is called integrated education is simply desegregated in a token fashion, either with a few minority students in a majority classroom or desegregation at the school level, but not at the classroom level.[84] A school in the latter situation may have many minority children, but all of them may be assigned to a "special educational program," separated from the majority children. Second, the potential benefits which could accrue to both minority- and majority-group members tend to be mitigated when community-wide hostilities arise over issues of busing and school-community politics. Students see the agitation created by their parents and are prepared to expect the worst from the educational situation. Considering that events defined negatively tend to be self-fulfilling, it is little wonder that results have been disappointing.

In college and university studies there is evidence that education, especially desegregated education, can reduce prejudice. The early Bennington studies demonstrated the liberalism fostered by a college environment.[85] The work of Perlmutter[86] and A. G. Dworkin[87] has illustrated that the liberal arts education tends to reduce reliance upon stereotypes. Dworkin found that although college students held a variety of stereotypes about minority groups, the stereotypes were not used to rationalize social distance feelings or discriminatory behavior. The stereotypes lingered as conventions of speech, not as the language of prejudice.

Ehrlich[88] makes two observations about the role of education in attitude change. The first is that education may produce decreased prejudice in instances in which the individual becomes educationally very mobile in relation to his family. He may find himself marginal to the values and social support of his family, and is likely to hold to disparate and more egalitarian values. Ehrlich's second observation is that it is vastly easier to change attitudes than to maintain the stability of those changed attitudes. The college experience may reduce prejudice, provided that the college which the student attends supports liberal values, because of social support (peer support) for the liberalism. However, once the student graduates and enters a world which is not so libertarian, his attitudes may change back to conservativism. The situation-specific nature of prejudice is again apparent.

CONTACT AND PREJUDICE REDUCTION

If prejudice is formed in the absence of intergroup contact, reasoned many thinkers, it could be eliminated in the presence of intergroup contact. This was hoped because intergroup contact was more easily implemented than other techniques, such as those requiring massive resocialization of the populace.[89] But early in the attempts to reduce prejudice it was discovered that not all contact is the same. Contact which maintains social distance, which is based upon the subordination of one group by another, does not breed reductions in prejudice, discrimination, and hostility. It is now known that contact has to be equal status in nature. That is, individuals interacting with one another have to view each other as coequals. Early research by Deutsch and Collins[90] and Wilner, Walkley, and Cook[91] has shown that in desegregated public housing projects equal status contacts will reduce prejudice on the part of whites. Other studies have shown less conclusive results.[92]

Ford[93] recently discovered that the equal status contact between blacks and whites actually tended to decrease white prejudice toward blacks while not reducing black prejudice toward whites. The explanation for the disparity in findings can be found in the nature of the equal status contacts. Whites frequently projected unconscious cues which told the blacks that the situation was not really equal status; they behaved in ways which implied that the blacks were really subordinate. What is clearly needed is a program which will alert majorities to the myriad ways in which they unconsciously announce their majority status. Otherwise majorities will not understand why their attempts at prejudice reduction are met with minority resistance. Faced with such rebuff, majority-group members may become even more hardened in their prejudice, and minority-group members will similarly have their prejudice reinforced.

VALUE CONSENSUS AND SUPERORDINATE GOALS

Vastly more success has been afforded programs which involve the active participation of individuals in reducing prejudice.[94] Two distinct techniques should be noted here. The first is based upon value consensus and has been proposed by Allport[95] and Pettigrew.[96] In the value consensus design, individuals of different groups that are currently conflicting (e.g., blacks and whites) are brought together to explore their common goals, ambitions, beliefs, and so on. Provided that these groups have much in common, they tend to discover additional avenues of dialogue and common understandings, which in turn further reduce hostility. The procedure works well if the individuals share many things in common and are not competing for scarce or mutually exclusive resources. For example, upper-class blacks and whites could serve as tests of the value consensus approach. Economic competition is minimal, and they hold many values in common according to the class principle.

The present authors once worked on a study involving black and white parents in a predominantly white neighborhood. The black parents were concerned about the schools, as were the white parents. The blacks feared that their children might be attacked by white children on the way to school; that the teachers would dilute the curriculum because of the presence of blacks, thereby reducing their children's chances of getting into a prestigious college; and that whites would flee the neighborhood and lower property values. The white parents voiced the identical fears. Once the two groups realized they had so many values in common, most racial tensions in the neighborhood ceased.

If, however, the groups do not have common goals and values, value consensus is unlikely, and so is prejudice reduction. Muzafer Sherif[97] has offered an alternative procedure. Sherif demonstrated the principle of superordinate goals in a study of a boys' summer camp. Through a series of contrivances, Sherif created two hostile and conflicting groups within the camp. Then, by establishing a major goal which neither could attain without the cooperation of the other (hence a superordinate goal), Sherif was able to get the groups to coexist peacefully and to abandon their prejudices against one another.

It is essential that the superordinate goal be one which: (1) is of major importance to both groups; (2) can be attained only through the mutual cooperation of the groups; and (3) is actually attained after the cooperation. Should the third condition not be satisfied, each group may blame the other for the failure and prejudice and hostilities may be heightened. McClendon and Eitzen[98] have shown that prejudice levels among college basketball teams diminish in those teams which are interracial and have successful win-lose records. The teams want to win, they can win only interracially, and they have been winners. All three of Sherif's conditions have been met. In another study, several researchers[99] have been working with the Houston Council on Human Relations in the testing and evaluation of an interracial simulation game which creates interdependence between racial groups. The simulation has been effective in reducing prejudice levels among the participants, who are students in the Houston public schools. However, the most dramatic reductions in prejudice have occurred in those schools which were "balanced"—that is, having nearly equal numbers of black, brown, and white students. In such schools the entire school situation provides an extension of the simulation and is in itself a superordinate goal. No school activity, whether it be a sports activity, a class play, or student government, can be executed without the cooperation of members of each group.

Superordinate goal situations tend to merge into value consensus situations. By working for a common goal, groups explore other areas of common cooperation, and in turn prejudice is reduced. The current era of détente between the United States and the Soviet Union represents a set of superordinate goals: preventing a thermonuclear war, cooperating in space and technology, and coping with the world's food and energy crises. It is apparent that models applicable to individuals can be applied under some conditions to groups, and even to nation-states.

Summary

The social psychological level of analysis emphasizes the impact of the social structure upon the individual. The unit of analysis is the individual and the relationships between individuals. The essential aspects of such a level of analysis in minority-group relations are attitudes, behaviors, and the self. The attitude is prejudice and the behavior is discrimination.

Prejudice is multidimensional, including the elements of direction, salience, intensity, commitment, and centrality. Prejudice serves its users with four functions. It provides knowledge to give meanings to interactions and to reduce the need to interact; it provides the prejudiced individual with ego-defense; it is instrumental in providing rewards to the prejudiced person, including maintenance of the pattern of superordination and subordination; and it is value-expressive, permitting the individual to express his key values, or the key values of his culture. Ethnocentrism supports prejudice and stereotypes provide prejudice with a language and a rhetoric. Changing stereotypes, like reducing prejudice, requires alterations in the nature of the target group, the nature of the stereotyper, and/or the relationship between the two. Nonetheless, there are conceptual mechanisms which may permit stereotypes to persist beyond their immediate functionality. Another manifestation of prejudice is social distance, or the degree to which a person is unwilling to have intimate contact with the minority. Several measures have been divised to assess social distance, including the Bogardus Social Distance Scale.

The relationship between discrimination and prejudice is not mutually contingent. Prejudiced people do not always discriminate, and discriminators are not always prejudiced. The social situation in which the individual finds himself plays an integral role. Commitment to his beliefs and his volition (the amount of control he can exercise over the situation) determine whether or not prejudice and discrimination will be conjoined. A theoretical model was advanced to show the manner in which peer and other influences could determine the relationship between prejudicial attitudes and discriminatory behaviors.

The costs of prejudice and discrimination to the prejudiced individual and to the target of prejudice were explored. An analysis of the concept of minority-group self-hatred was advanced. It is indeterminate whether the concept per se exists, or whether it is a symptom of emulation of the majority. Minority-based social movements tend to reduce the emulation and to heighten a group's self-pride. Evidence for this was demonstrated in material on stereotype change.

Prejudice is caused by many factors, and it is likely that there are many forms of prejudice, each caused by different sets of variables. Basic theories of prejudice can be subsumed under psychological, social structural, and cultural and normative theories. The psychological theories include, but are not limited to, frustration-aggression and scapegoating models and the theory of the authoritarian personality. Social structural theories include economic exploitation and economic competition, economic exclusion, and situational and mass society theories. Normative and cultural theories include ideology theories, symbolic theories, and linguistic theories.

Numerous attempts have been made to reduce prejudice and discrimination. Education and diversity of experience may be effective in preventing prejudice from emerging, but once it is present, information campaigns and other "passive" techniques tend to be ineffective. The techniques of value consensus and superordinate goals tend to be more effective in reducing prejudice, with the latter preferable if the groups initially have little in common. Even these attempts are sometimes problematic, since contact, which is a necessary condition for the two techniques to operate, may not be perceived as equal status contact by all. In such cases prejudice levels might be unaffected or even increased.

NOTES

1. Paul F. Secord and Carl W. Backman, *Social Psychology* (New York: McGraw-Hill, 1964).

2. Eugene L. Horowitz, "Development of Attitudes Toward Negroes," *Archives for Psychology* 28, no. 194 (1936): entire issue.

3. Joseph O. Bass, "Attitudes Toward Negroes of Selected Occupational Categories in Bangkok, Thailand' (Master's thesis, University of Missouri, 1969).

4. See Gordon W. Allport, *The Nature of Prejudice* (Cambridge, Mass: Addison-Wesley, 1954), and Howard J. Ehrlich, *The Social Psychology of Prejudice* (New York: Wiley-Interscience, 1973).

5. See Daniel Katz, "The Functional Approach to the Study of Attitudes," *Public Opinion Quarterly* 24 (1960): 163–204, and Daniel Katz and E. Stotland "A Preliminary Statement to Theory of Attitude Structure and Change," in *Psychology: A Study of a Science*, ed. Sigmund Koch (New York: McGraw-Hill, 1959) pp. 423–75.

6. Frank R. Westie, "The American Dilemma: An Empirical Test," *American Sociological Review* 30 (1965): 527–38.

7. T. W. Adorno, et al., *The Authoritarian Personality* (New York: Harper Bros., 1950).

8. See Donn Byrne, "Interpersonal Attraction and Attitude Similarity," *Journal of Abnormal and Social Psychology* 62 (1961): 713–15, and Donn Byrne and Terry J. Wong, "Racial Prejudice, Interpersonal Attraction, and Assumed Dissimilarity of Attitudes," *Journal of Abnormal and Social Psychology* 63 (1962): 246–53.

9. Milton Rokeach, Patricia Smith, and Richard I. Evans, "Two Kinds of Prejudice or One?" in Milton Rokeach, *The Open and Closed Mind* (New York: Basic Books, 1960), pp. 132–68.

10. Anthony Downs, "Alternative Futures for the American Ghetto" *Daedalus* 97 (1968): 1331–78.

11. Walter Lippmann, *Public Opinion* (New York: Macmillan, 1922), p. 95.

12. F. LaViolette and K. H. Silvert "A Theory of Stereotypes," *Social Forces* 29 (1951): 257–62.

13. Allport, *Nature of Prejudice*, p. 191.

14. Emory S. Bogardus, "Stereotypes and Sociotypes," *Sociology and Social Research* 34 (1950): 286–91.

15. Orrin E. Klapp, *Heroes, Villains, and Fools* (Englewood Cliffs, N.J.: Prentice-Hall, 1962).

16. E. T. Prothro and L. Mellikian, "Studies in Stereotypes," *Journal of Social Psychology* 41 (1955): 21–30; W. Buchanan, "Stereotypes and Tensions as Revealed by the UNESCO International Poll" *International Social Science Bulletin* 3 (1951): 515–28; and W. Vinacki, "Stereotyping Among National-Racial Groups in Hawaii," *Journal of Social Psychology* 30 (1949): 265–91.

17. Muzafer Sherif and Carolyn W. Sherif, *Social Psychology* (New York: Harper, 1969).

18. See Joshua Fishman, "An Examination of the Process and Functioning of Social Stereotyping" *Journal of Social Psychology* 43 (1956): 27–64, and Hubertus C. J. Duijker and N. H. Frijda, *National Character and National Stereotypes* (Amsterdam: North-Holland, 1960).

19. Anthony Gary Dworkin and Douglas L. Eckberg, "Stereotyping: The Language of Prejudice" (Roundtable discussion, American Sociological Association meetings, New York, August 1973), and idem, "Consciousness and Reality: The Impact of the Chicano Movement on Mutual Stereotypy," in *Mexican Americans in the United States*, ed. John H. Burma and Miquel Tirado (New York: Canfield, in press).

20. See Daniel Katz and Kenneth W. Braly, "Racial Stereotypes of 100 College Students," *Journal of Abnormal and Social Psychology* 28 (1933): 280–90; Marvin Karlins, Thomas L. Coffman, and Gary Walters, "On the Fading of Social Stereotypes: Studies in Three Generations of College Students," *Journal of Personality and Social Psychology* 13 (1969): 4–5; and Ehrlich, *Social Psychology*.

21. Maurice N. Richter, Jr., "The Conceptual Mechanism of Stereotyping," *American Sociological Review* 21 (1956): 568–71.

22. Fishman, "Examination of the Process."

23. M. Mackie, "Arriving at 'Truth' by Definition: The Case of Stereotype Inaccuracy," *Social Problems* 21 (1973): 431–47.

24. Robert K. Merton, *Social Theory and Social Structure* (New York: Free Press 1957), chap. 11.

25. W. I. Thomas and F. Znaniecki, *The Polish Peasant in Europe and America*, 2 vols. (reprint ed., New York: Knopf, 1927) (1918).

26. Elliot Liebow, *Talley's Corner* (Boston: Little, Brown, 1967).

27. Robert E. Park, "The Concept of Social Distance," *Journal of Applied Sociology* 8 (1924): 339–44.

28. Emory S. Bogardus, "Measuring Social Distance," *Journal of Applied Sociology* 9 (1925): 299–308.

29. Emory S. Bogardus, "A Social Distance Scale," *Sociology and Social Research* 17 (1933): 265–71.

30. Anthony Gary Dworkin, "Prejudice, Social Distance and Intergroup Perceptions: Exploratory Research in the Correlates of Stereotypy" (Ph.D. diss., Northwestern University, 1970), and Michael Banton, *Race Relations* (New York: Basic Books, 1967).

31. Frank Westie, "A Technique for the Measurement of Race Attitudes," *American Sociological Review* 18 (1953): 73–78.

32. R. T. LaPiere "Attitudes Versus Actions," *Social Forces* 13 (1934): 230–37.

33. Donald T. Campbell, "Social Attitudes and Other Acquired Behavioral Dispositions," in *Psychology: A Study of a Science*, ed. Sigmund Koch, vol. 6 (New York: McGraw-Hill, 1963), pp. 94–172.

34. Melvin L. Kohn and Robin M. Williams, Jr., "Situational Patterning in Inter-

group Relations," in *Race, Class, and Power*, ed. Raymond W. Mack (New York: American Book, 1963).

35. Ibid., p. 130.

36. Robert K. Merton, "Discrimination and the American Creed," in *Discrimination and National Welfare*, ed. Robert M. MacIver (New York: Institute for Religious and Social Studies, 1949), pp. 99–126.

37. Joseph D. Lohman and Dietrich C. Reitzes, "Deliberately Organized Groups and Racial Behavior," *American Sociological Review* 19 (1954): 342–44.

38. L. M. Killian, "The Effects of Southern White Workers on Race Relations in Northern Plants," *American Sociological Review* 17 (1952): 327–31.

39. J. Milton Yinger, *Toward a Field Theory of Behavior* (New York: McGraw-Hill, 1965).

40. Lyle G. Warner and Melvin L. DeFleur, "Attitude as an Interactional Concept: Social Constraint and Social Distance as Intervening Variables Between Attitudes and Action," *American Sociological Review* 34 (1969): 153–69.

41. See Lawrence S. Linn, "Verbal Attitudes and Overt Behavior: A Study of Racial Discrimination," *Social Forces* 43 (1965): 353–64, and Gordon H. DeFriese and W. Scott Ford, Jr., "Open Occupancy—What Whites Say, What They Do," *Trans-action* 5 (1968): 53–56.

42. Phyllis Chesler, "Patient and Patriarch: Women in the Psychotherapeutic Relationship," in *Woman in Sexist Society*, ed. Vivian Gornick and Barbara K. Moran (New York: Basic Books, 1971), pp. 251–75.

43. William H. Grier and Price M. Cobbs, *Black Rage* (New York: Basic Books, 1968), p. 191.

44. See Kenneth B. and Mamie P. Clark, "Skin Color as a Factor in Racial Identifications of Negro Pre-School Children," *Journal of Social Psychology* 11 (1940): 159–69, and idem, "Racial Identification and Preference in Negro Children," in *Readings in Social Psychology*, ed. T. M. Newcomb and E. L. Hartley (New York: Holt, 1947), pp. 169–78.

45. James Miller, Jr., "Rightness of Whiteness Value-Syndrome Among Pre-School Age Children, I, II, and III," mimeographed (University of California, Los Angeles, 1972).

46. Linda Teplin "Misconceptualization as Artifact?: A Multitrait-Multimethod Analysis of Interracial Choice and Interaction Methodologies Utilized in Studying Children" (Manuscript presented at the Society for the Study of Social Problems meetings, Montreal, August 1974).

47. J. A. Bayton. "The Racial Stereotypes of Negro College Students" *Journal of Abnormal and Social Psychology* 36 (1941): 97–102.

48. Ozzie G. Simmons, "The Mutual Images and Expectations of Anglo Americans and Mexican Americans," *Daedalus* 90 (1961): 286–99.

49. Anthony Gary Dworkin, "Stereotypes and Self-Images Held by Native-Born and Foreign-Born Mexican Americans" *Sociology and Social Research* 49 (1965): 214–24.

50. Anthony Gary Dworkin, "National Origin and Ghetto Experience as Variables in Mexican American Stereotypy," in *Chicanos: Social and Psychological Perspectives*, ed. Nathaniel N. Wagner and Marsha J. Haug (St. Louis: Mosby, 1971), pp. 80–84.

51. Philip Goldberg, "Are Women Prejudiced Against Women?" *Trans-action* 5 (1968): 28–30.

52. Minako Kurokawa Maykovich, "Reciprocity in Racial Stereotypes: White, Black and Yellow," *American Journal of Sociology* 77 (1972): 876–97.

53. Dworkin and Eckberg "Consciousness and Reality," and idem, "To See Ourselves as Others See Us Isn't So Simple: Complexities in Stereotype Reciprocity" (Manuscript presented at the Society for the Study of Social Problems meetings, Montreal, August 1974).

54. Data presented here and in Table 5–1 are from Dworkin "Stereotypes and Self-Images"; idem, "Prejudice"; idem, "National Origin"; Dworkin and Eckberg, "Stereotyping"; idem, "To See Ourselves"; and idem, "Consciousness and Reality."

5: The Social Psychological Dimension

55. John D. McCarthy and William L. Yancey, "Uncle Tom and Mr. Charlie: Metaphysical Pathos in the Study of Racism and Personal Disorganization," *American Journal of Sociology* 76 (1971): 648–72, and William L. Yancey, Leo Rigsby, and John D. McCarthy, "Social Position and Self-Evaluation: The Relative Importance of Race," *American Journal of Sociology* 78 (1972): 338–59.

56. Jerold Heiss and Susan Owens, "Self-Evaluations of Blacks and Whites," *American Journal of Sociology* 78 (1972): 360–70.

57. Donald I. Warren, "Neighborhood Status Modality and Riot Behavior: An Analysis of the Detroit Disorders of 1967," in *Symposium on Violent Confrontation*, ed. Anthony Gary Dworkin, *Sociological Quarterly* 12 (1971): 350–68.

58. Robert E. Park. "Human Migration and the Marginal Man," *American Journal of Sociology* 33 (1928): 881–93.

59. Everett V. Stonequist, *The Marginal Man: A Study in Personality and Culture Conflict* (New York: Scribner's, 1937).

60. For a discussion of these writers and for a paradigm on marginality, see Noel P. Gist and Anthony Gary Dworkin, eds., *The Blending of Races: Marginality and Identity in World Perspective* (New York: Wiley, 1972), chap. 1.

61. Ibid.

62. M. P. Huber, *The Natural History of Ants* (London, Longmans, 1810). At one point Huber makes the analogy between the crowding of ants into a too-small nest and the crowding of people into Paris slums; both, he thought, triggered instinctive hatred.

63. See John Dollard et al., *Frustration and Aggression* (New Haven: Yale University Press, 1939).

64. Everett Cherington Hughes, *French Canada in Transition* (Chicago: University of Chicago Press, 1943).

65. Leonard Berkowitz and Russell G. Geen. "Film Violence and the Cue Properties of Available Targets," *Journal of Personality and Social Psychology* 3 (1966): 525–30, and idem, "Stimulus Qualities of the Target of Aggression: A Further Study," *Journal of Personality and Social Psychology* 5 (1967): 364–68. See also Leonard Berkowitz, *Aggression* (New York: McGraw-Hill, 1962).

66. Russell G. Geen, "Some Implications of Experimental Social Psychology for the Study of Urban Disorders," in *Symposium on Violent Confrontation*, ed. Dworkin, pp. 340–49.

67. See Max Horkheimer, "Sociological Background of the Psychoanalytic Approach," in *Anti-Semitism: A Social Disease*, ed. Ernst Simmel (New York: International Universities Press, 1946), pp. 1–10.

68. Adorno et al., *Authoritarian Personality*.

69. Samuel H. Flowerman, "Portrait of the Authoritarian Man," *New York Times Magazine*, April 23, 1950.

70. Oliver C. Cox, *Caste, Class, and Race: A Study in Social Dynamics* (Garden City, N.Y.: Doubleday, 1948).

71. Carey McWilliams, *Brothers Under the Skin* (Boston: Little, Brown, 1964).

72. Sidney M. Wilhelm, *Who Needs the Negro?* (Cambridge, Mass.: Schenkman, 1970).

73. Edna Bonacich, "A Theory of Ethnic Antagonism: The Split Labor Market," *American Sociological Review* 37 (1972): 547–59.

74. Among those identified with various aspects of the mass society hypothesis and the situational theories of prejudice are Karl Mannheim, *Man and Society in an Age of Reconstruction* (New York: Harcourt, Brace, 1940); C. Wright Mills, *The Power Elite* (New York: Oxford University Press, 1959); Edward A. Shils, "Mass Society and Its Culture," in *Culture for the Millions?* ed. N. Jacobs (Princeton, N.J.: Van Nostrand, 1961), pp. 1–27; Philip Olson, *America as a Mass Society* (New York: Free Press, 1963); and Frank Westie, "Race and Ethnic Relations," in *Handbook of Modern Sociology*, ed. Robert E. L. Faris (Chicago: Rand McNally, 1964), pp. 576–618.

75. Lohman and Reitzes, "Deliberately Organized Groups"; Kohn and Williams, "Situational Patterning"; and Killian, "Effects of Southern White Workers."

103

76. Frank Westie, "The American Dilemma: An Empirical Test," *American Sociological Review* 30 (1965): 527–38.

77. Ibid.

78. Allport, *Nature of Prejudice.*

79. Ibid.

80. See, for example, Edward Sapir, "Language and Environment" *American Anthropologist* 14 (1912): 226–42; idem, *Language* (New York: Harcourt, Brace & World, 1921); Benjamin Lee Whorf, "Science and Linguistics," *Technology Review* 44 (1940): 229–31, 247, 248; idem, "The Relation of Habitual Thought and Behavior to Language," in *Language, Culture, and Personality*, ed. L. Spier (Menasa, Wis.: Sapir Memorial Publication Fund, 1941), pp. 75–93.

81. Joshua A. Fishman, "A Systematization of the Whorfian Hypothesis," *Behavioral Science* 5 (1960): 82. More recently the Sapir-Whorf hypothesis has been subjected to a serious challenge. Max Black has argued that those who rely upon the language of a society to explain cultural behavior have often focused only upon supportive aspects of the language and ignored unsupportive ones. Further, some languages have been the vehicle for diverse philosophical orientations, suggesting a much "softer" determinism between language and thought. For more on this issue, see Max Black, *The Labyrinth of Language* (New York: Praeger, 1968), ch. 4.

82. There is a branch of social psychology, known as symbolic interactionism, which looks at the role of language and other symbols in the development of the self. In contrast to psychological behaviorism, symbolic interactionism stresses the shared meanings attached to objects, events, and people. These meanings are communicated through gestures and language. The orientation developed in the works of William James, John Dewey, Charles Horton Cooley, George Herbert Mead, and others. The reader is referred to Herbert Blumer, *Symbolic Interactionism: Perspective and Method* (Englewood Cliffs, N.J.: Prentice-Hall, 1969).

83. Allport, *Nature of Prejudice.*

84. James S. Coleman et al., *Equality of Educational Opportunity* (Washington, D.C.: Government Printing Office, 1966).

85. Theodore Newcomb, *Personality and Social Change* (New York: Dryden, 1943).

86. Howard V. Perlmutter, "Relations Between the Self-Image, the Image of the Foreigner, and the Desire to Live Abroad," *Journal of Psychology* 38 (1954): 131–37.

87. Dworkin, "Prejudice."

88. Ehrlich, *Social Psychology.*

89. Wessley I. Robinson, "Interracial Contact and Desegregation: An Analysis Of Tri-Ethnic Race Relations in the Houston Independent School District" (Master's thesis, University of Houston, 1975).

90. Morton Deutsch and Mary E. Collins, *Interracial Housing* (Minneapolis: University of Minnesota Press, 1951).

91. Daniel Wilner, Rosabelle P. Walkley, and Stuart W. Cook, *Human Relations in Interracial Housing—A Study of the Contact Hypothesis* (Minneapolis: University of Minnesota Press, 1955).

92. Ernest Q. Campbell "Some Social Psychological Correlates of Direction in Attitude Change," *Social Forces* 36 (1958): 335–40; Paul H. Mussen, "Some Personality and Social Factors Related to Change in Children's Attitudes Towards Negroes," *Journal of Abnormal and Social Psychology* 45 (1950): 423–41; and Irwin Silverman and Marvin E. Shaw, "Effects of Sudden Mass School Desegregation on Interracial Interaction and Attitudes in One Southern City," *Journal of Social Issues* 29 (1973): 133–42.

93. W. Scott Ford, "Interracial Public Housing in a Border City: Another Look at the Contact Hypothesis," *American Journal of Sociology* 78 (1973): 1426–47.

94. Kurt Lewin, "Group Decision and Social Change," in *Readings in Social Change*, 3rd ed. ed. E. Maccoby, T. M. Newcomb, and E. L. Hartley (New York: Holt, Rinehart and Winston, 1958), pp. 197–211.

95. Allport, Nature of Prejudice.
96. Thomas F. Pettigrew, Racially Separate or Together? (New York: McGraw-Hill, 1971).
97. Muzafer Sherif, "Superordinate Goals and the Reduction of Intergroup Conflict," American Journal of Sociology 63 (1958): 349–56, and Muzafer Sherif et al., Intergroup Conflict and Cooperation: The Robbers Cave Experiment (Norman: University of Oklahoma Book Exchange, 1961).
98. McKee J. McClendon and D. Stanley Eitzen, "Interracial Contact on Collegiate Basketball Teams: A Test of Sherif's Theory of Superordinate Goals," Social Science Quarterly 55 (1975): 926–38.
99. Anthony Gary Dworkin, Ronald G. Frankiewicz, Helen Copitka, and Wesley I. Robinson, Intergroup Action Project Report ("Balance on the Bayou: The Impact of Racial Isolation and Interaction on Stereotypy in the Houston Independent School District" and "Assessment of Attitudes Towards GROB as a Unit of Study") (Houston, Tex.: Houston Council on Human Relations, 1974).

Suggested Readings

Adorno, T. W., et al. The Authoritarian Personality. New York: Harper, 1950.

Allport, Gordon W. The Nature of Prejudice. Cambridge, Mass.: Addison-Wesley, 1954.

Blumer, Herbert. Symbolic Interactionism: Perspective and Method. Englewood Cliffs, N.J.: Prentice-Hall, 1969.

Ehrlich, Howard J. The Social Psychology of Prejudice. New York: Wiley-Interscience, 1973.

Fishman, Joshua. "An Examination of the Process and Functioning of Social Stereotyping." Journal of Social Psychology 43 (1956): 27–64.

Gist, Noel P., and Anthony Gary Dworkin. The Blending of Races: Marginality and Identity in World Perspective. New York: Wiley-Interscience, 1972.

Pettigrew, Thomas F. Racially Separate or Together? New York: McGraw-Hill, 1971.

Secord, Paul F., and Carl W. Backman. Social Psychology. New York: McGraw-Hill, 1974.

Sherif, Muzafer, and Carolyn W. Sherif. Social Psychology. New York: Harper, 1969.

Warner, Lyle G., and Melvin L. DeFleur. "Attitude as an Interactional Concept: Social Constraint and Social Distance as Intervening Variables between Attitudes and Action." American Sociological Review 34 (1969): 153–69.

Westie, Frank. "Race and Ethnic Relations." In Handbook of Modern Sociology, edited by Robert E. L. Faris, pp. 576–618. Chicago: Rand McNally, 1964.

6.

THE RESOLUTION OF
MINORITY-GROUP STATUS

We have examined the ways in which the minority groups have been treated as people apart. The documentation of an inequitable distribution of power, property, and prestige, the description and categorization of organizations to which minorities belong and/or in which they must react, and the variety of social psychological inputs and effects of prejudice and discrimination are all of interest to the student of minority-group relations. However, the sociologist must do more than document, describe, and categorize. The sociologist is also interested in explanation and prediction, to which ends models must be constructed. These models, or theories, consider the entire phenomenon of minority-majority relationships, and attempt to make some generalizing statements about the process of these relationships: from contact and cause through to resolution. There are many such models in the field of minority-group relations. Some are more complete than others; some are more heuristic than others; and some have more explanatory power than others. Basically they can be categorized into two types, depending upon the kind of resolution they predict. The two models assume distinct outcomes for minority-group relations. The first and more traditional model assumes assimilation of the minority group into the majority. The second and more radical assumes continued separation of the minority group. The separation may be forced upon the minority or initiated by the minority.

Examples range from exclusion and ultimate extermination, through reservation status, to establishment of a new nation-state.

Regardless of the model proposed, a necessary condition for minority-group status and its resolution is intergroup contact. It is difficult to conceive of minorities and majorities who are members of the same society and have never been in contact with one another. Identifiability implies a subject observing and interacting with an object. Likewise, differential power is meaningless unless it is power over some one or some group with whom one interacts. Further, differential treatment cannot occur in isolation, but requires contact. Lastly, group awareness implies an acknowledgment of "us" separate from "them."

The nature of the initial contact has been a dimension explored by many writers. That contact may shape the future course of the minority-majority relationship; determine who will play the minority role, and who will play the majority; establish how great the differentials between them will be; and foreshadow the likely resolution. In some instances the initial contact between groups has been historically documented. Exploration, conquest, colonization, enslavement, or immigration represent the diversity of initial contacts. For some groups the initial contact may have occurred so far in the past that there is no record, so records may be fabricated in the form of a folk history. In the case of male-female relationships, where documentation of initial contact is an absurdity, a mythology or a religio-folk history has been created. Most of the world's religions, however simple or complex, have a story comparable to the Adam and Eve explanation of the initial contact between males and females.

A second necessary condition upon which all the theories agree is that the contact must be prolonged such that the differentials in power and treatment become apparent and entrenched at the distributive, organizational, and social psychological levels.

The divergences which develop as a function of the prolonged contact, the nature of the assumptions about the goals of the actors involved in the contact, and the course of actions which ensue after the initial contact provide the essential distinctions among the diverse theories of the resolution of minority-group status.

Assimilation as an Outcome

ESSENTIAL CONCEPTS

Assimilation is a process by which minority and majority groups are merged into some total societal unit. There have been many divergent interpretations of the concept of assimilation, and perhaps its utility as a scientific concept can be challenged. It certainly cannot be thought of as unitary. In some instances it means that the minority group merges into the majority and loses its own distinct identity. In other instances it means that the minority and the majority form a new hybrid. In still other applications it means that the minority retains much of its identity and distinctiveness, but shares an equal status in the society with the majority, without prejudice and discrimination. Each of these definitions of assimilation have acqured different names. The first is called *Anglo conformity*; the second is the *melting pot*; and the third is called *cultural pluralism*. We shall comment on each of these shortly, for they are distinct goals within the theme of assimilation.

Assimilation also involves other processes which have attained distinct labels. These include *acculturation* and *amalgamation*. Acculturation refers to cultural assimilation of the minority group, in which the minority adopts the culture, including the language, customs, and beliefs, of the majority. Amalgamation refers to the biological blending of the minority with the majority through intermarriage (as well as less formalized sexual relationships). We shall delineate additional aspects of assimilation shortly when we discuss the conceptualization by Milton Gordon.

Gordon[1] has developed an excellent assessment of the goals of the assimilative process (the three models cited previously). He suggests that the most common form imposed upon minorities is Anglo conformity. Here the majority attempts to "Americanize" the minority, socializing it to reject all aspects of its native (usually immigrant) culture and to seek to be a carbon copy of the majority society prototype. The Coles[2] first coined the concept of Anglo conformity in 1954. Gordon indicates that "the 'Anglo Conformity' theory demanded the complete renunciation of the immigrant's ancestral culture in favor of the behavior and values of the Anglo-Saxon core group."[3] The model has had a diversity of manifestations, and has not been enforced uniformly for all groups. In fact, groups which are identifiably closer to the majority than other minorities tend to be subjected to less rigorous and brutal "Americanization." The experiences of English-speaking groups, for example, have been less restrictive than the experiences of eastern European, southern European, or Spanish-speaking groups. Because the members of the majority are unable to understand the non-English speakers, they are less able to monitor their attitudes, beliefs, and conversations, and hence must expend greater effort in order to control them.

The melting pot theory, according to Gordon, "envisaged a biological merger of the Anglo-Saxon peoples with other immigrant groups and a blending of their respective cultures into a new indigenous American type."[4] The melting pot thus consisted of a hybrid culture and an amalgamation of peoples. It is problematic whether the melting pot phenomenon actually characterized the American scene. It may have had limited currency when there was not much diversity among the groups blending together (there is greater evidence for the melting pot among the northern European groups in the United States). However, Glazer and Moynihan[5] contend the phenomenon really did not exist in the United States. Ethnic minorities have retained much of their distinct cultural heritages, albeit with an American flavor, such that Little Italy was not exactly like its European counterpart. The melting pot idea was a romantic view and probably could not have developed in a society in which the majority had so many resources to maintain its dominance over the various minorities. That is, a melting pot requires that the minority be able to exert enough influence over the majority to effect a merger of groups. Lacking that, the melting pot would require a friendlier and more benevolent majority willing to acknowledge that minorities may have some superior cultural elements. The melting pot concept accurately describes the nation of Mexico. Here, the Spaniards crushed the Indian society, but did not replace it with their own. Rather, they intermarried and blended the Indian and Spanish heritage into a mestizo culture.

The experience in the United States was different. What has happened, as Gordon observes, is that American society has evolved a *transmuting pot.*[6] In the transmuting pot the majority selectively samples aspects of the minority group's culture and remakes them in an Americanized mold. Thus pizza is topped with hamburger and cheddar cheese; a manufacturer of Chinese food advertises that its product "swings American"; drive-in Mexican restaurants offer tacos and tamales American-style (without hot sauce); caftans and dashikis are made from colorfast and permanent press fabrics; and strawberry incense is burned before a plastic Buddha to rid the house of stale odors.

The third form of assimilation implies the least homogeneity for the populace. Gordon suggests that cultural pluralism "postulated the preservation of the communal life and significant positions of the culture of the later immigrant groups within the context of American citizenship and political and economic integration into American society."[7] Thus cultural pluralism implies equality of status of diverse groups which retain their identity. If American society cannot be characterized as a melting pot, it is problematic that it could be described as pluralistic. Minorities retain their ethnic character, but inequality of status is still present. Several writers, including Gordon, have argued for the preferability of the cultural pluralist form as an American ideal. It certainly is the most democratic, except in its implementation. In order for cultural pluralism to succeed, the minority must impose restrictions within itself to discourage its members from blending into the majority. Although cultural pluralism has not been attained in American society, Gordon suggests that *structural pluralism* has. In the latter, there is a "structural merging . . . among the nationality groups within each of the three major religions, and in the occupational areas of the intellectual and art worlds."[8] Thus within religious organizations and in certain elite occupational groups, people of diverse backgrounds function together. American artists and scholars are artists or scholars regardless of their ethnicity; they are stratified only against nonartists and nonscholars. Likewise, Catholic organizations may be composed of Irish, Italian, German, and even Spanish American groups, all of whom identify themselves as Catholics.

THEORIES OF ASSIMILATION

Early in the present century sociologists proposed some models which they felt would account for the manner in which the patterns of minority-majority relations evolved and developed. Much of the debate on the issue of such patterns has concerned the universality and complexity of the models. Early models were assumed to be generalizable to all intergroup relations situations and often involved only one or a few variables. Frequently these early models were like some of the early attempts to define minority groups, based upon a limited set of traits observed in a particular society, subculture, or even region of the country. Nonetheless, attempts were made to generalize to the whole of mankind these models based upon limited observation.

Among the earliest theories advanced was Park's in 1926.[9] According to Park, new immigrant groups to a society move through four phases in a cycle from contact, to competition and conflict, to accommodation, to assimilation. Initially two groups, usually an indigenous group and an immigrant group, come into contact with one another and compete for some scarce resource such as wealth, property, or status. Because the resources are scarce and successful gain for one means loss to the other, competition results in open conflict between the two groups. However, because one group (usually the indigenous group) has more resources to mobilize, it maintains control over the market situation. The immigrant group accommodates or withdraws hostilities until some future time when they can have an advantage. As the two groups interact, the subordinate immigrant group copies or emulates the dominant indigenous group. Over time the two groups become more alike, with the immigrant or minority group accepting more of the culture of the dominant group. Eventually the differences are erased and, as holders of common values, the two groups merge into a single dominant group. Park considered the cycle to be unidirectional; that is, groups progressed through the four phases in order and only in the direction hypothesized. Once begun, the process is irreversible, and is repeated in turn with new minority groups. In this sense the process is cyclical.

Basing his race relations cycle upon the West Coast, Bogardus[10] proposed that there were seven distinct stages in the process of assimilation. Initial contact between the majority and the minority sparks the "curiosity" of the majority. Because the numbers of the minority are extremely small, they are not seen as a threat, but are often viewed with sympathy. Curiosity yields to "economic welcome" when the minority becomes recognized as a source of cheap labor. As more members of the minority enter the labor market, members of the dominant society organize to protest the takeover by the minority, a stage Bogardus described as "industrial and social antagonism." (This antagonism is an essential component in Bonacich's split labor market theory described in Chapter Five.) Pressure is put upon political and governmental officials to pass laws limiting immigration and the rights and opportunities of the minority. This is the stage of "legislative antagonism." In time, some citizens react against the laws. Friendship and a sense of injustice may spark this stage of "fair-play tendencies." But as Berry[11] notes, it is rather short-lived because of lack of organization, lack of finances, and extremism within the movement. An accommodation is reached after the full force of the restrictive legislation is felt. In the stage of "quiescence" attitudes become ameliorated and efforts to extend social and political rights emerge. At this point, attempts develop to resocialize (Americanize) the minority, to assimilate the group into the dominant group by making them culturally identical to the majority. In the final stage crises of identity arise between the first and second generations of the minority group. The stage of "second-generation difficulties" emerges because the children become more assimilated than their parents. In some respects the children are true cultural marginals[12] in that they are of both the minority and the majority culture, but fully integrated into neither.

A model by Brown[13] also assumes assimilation as the ultimate end product. It is unlike the others in recognizing that the assimilation process may be extremely slow and that other, albeit less likely, outcomes may occur in between. These alternative outcomes include total isolation of the minority or subordination of the minority into a caste. The former is impractical in a geographically mobile society like the United States, and the latter is unlikely because of espoused societal norms of equality, Constitutional guarantees, and observable social mobility.

Still other cyclical theories of assimilation have been advanced.[14] However, they are basically similar to the three discussed here. The characteristic weakness of the early theories was that they were not universally applicable because they were based upon limited samplings of minority experiences. Lieberson synthesized and expanded the models of

Park and his followers, noting that "many earlier race and ethnic cycles were, in fact, narrowly confined to a rather specific set of groups or contact situations. . . ."[15] Lieberson begins by postulating that intergroup contact initially involves "each population's maintenance and development of a social order compatible with its ways of life prior to contact."[16] Thus developing conflicts center around institutions. Lieberson cited two basic forms of contact: subordination of an indigenous[17] group by a migrant group (e.g., western European contact with American Indian groups) and subordination of a migrant group by an indigenous group (e.g., Anglo American contact with new migrant western Europeans in the late nineteenth century or with the Chinese building the railroad in the mid–nineteenth century).

Lieberson makes problematic whether the indigenous or the immigrant group will be dominant. Thus unlike Park and those he influenced, Lieberson's model is applicable not only to a situation of minority-group entry into existing, well-developed societies (e.g., European and Oriental immigration to the United States). The model is also applicable to the conquest of native populations by colonial powers throughout history. It can account for the outcomes of power majorities who were numerically large as well as power majorities who were numerically small.

Although Lieberson's model accounts for greater diversity than the earlier models, it nonetheless rests upon a single variable—differential power. Power is a necessary condition, but it is not a sufficient condition, and certainly power alone cannot distinguish among the diversity of minority experiences. Berry[18] suggests that other variables must include: (1) the nature of the initial contact; (2) the extent of "tribal" solidarity of the minority group; (3) the effect of the dominant group upon the natural resources in the society; (4) values of the minority group; (5) attitudes of the majority group; and (6) existing norms with regard to intermarriage and sexual contact.

Lieberson's model could be further strengthened by application of Blalock's[19] conceptualization of power. By defining power in terms of its application rather than its potential, Blalock provides for a wider range of minority-majority relationships hinging not only upon differentials in the amount of resources available to each group, but also whether those resources are mobilized by the majority against the minority.

Lieberson's model depends upon a specific, historic point of initial contact between two groups of differing cultures. Hence the model cannot be applied to gender groups which have always coexisted and which share a common (or complementary) culture.

Gordon[20] has delineated a complex seven-stage model of assimilation.

His model was created to be applicable to the conditions of Anglo conformity, melting pot, or cultural pluralism, but is predisposed toward the Anglo conformity format. The first stage is identified as "cultural or behavioral assimilation" and involves the acculturation of the minority group, during which the dominant society's cultural patterns are adopted by the minority. Sequentially, the group then passes through a stage of "structural assimilation," when there is large-scale entry by the minority into the majority's voluntary associations, cliques, and clubs. Gordon maintains that it is not sufficient for a select few members of the minority to be so accepted on an interpersonal level; there must be wholesale acceptance. It is on the structural level that the final outcome depends. Once a group is accepted structurally, all other forms of assimilation will proceed with relatively little difficulty.

Gordon's third stage is identified as "marital assimilation," or amalgamation. Here there is large-scale intermarriage between members of the minority and the majority. It is now clearly evident that structural assimilation is a necessary precondition, as large-scale intermarriage cannot occur without large-scale interpersonal acceptance.

After wide-spread intermarriage, the minority and the offspring from the intermarriages come to see themselves as members of the same group as the majority. Gordon describes this stage as "identificational assimilation." It is not the final stage, because there may still be little reciprocity in the identification. That is, the minority might see themselves as part of the majority, but the majority may not accept them as such. They may be defined only as the spouses of majority-group members.

Sometime after identificational assimilation, however, there is an abandonment of prejudice and discrimination against the group. Gordon calls the stage of cessation of prejudice, "attitude receptional assimilation," and the stage of cessation of discrimination, "behavioral receptional assimilation." Full and total assimilation occurs when the minority has passed into the stage of "civic assimilation." At this last stage there are no value or power conflicts between the groups. In fact, even on specific issues the group boundaries have vanished for both sides, and we can no longer speak of majorities and minorities.

Gordon's model is perhaps more heuristic than it is empirical. It suggests many intriguing hypotheses, including the role of structural assimilation and the multidimensionality of the assimilation process. However, the particular order has not been universal for all groups, and some groups have attained later stages of assimilation without earlier ones.[21] Further, minority groups are not homogeneous enough, as Gordon acknowledges, to permit the model's applicability to a group carte blanche. Thus Gordon observes that class differentiates the degree of assimilation of some religious groups, such as Catholics. Kitano,[22] in his application of the model to the Japanese American case, suggests that age and number of generations in the host society affect the stage of assimilation and the amount of assimilation within each stage. Finally, the fact that Gordon speaks of host and immigrant societies suggests the inappropriateness of the model to nonimmigrant groups. And if intermarriage is a precondition for later assimilation, then gender groups are clearly discounted from the model.

Banton[23] provides six orders of intersocietal relations, and these models, when combined, provide three possible routes for minority-majority relations resolutions. The six orders include peripheral contact, institutionalized contact, acculturation, domination, paternalism (or colonialism), and integration. Peripheral contact involves exchanges between groups that do not influence the internal makeup or structure of the groups involved, and do not affect their attitudes, beliefs, behaviors, or values. The so-called "silent trade" between the hunting and gathering Pygmies of the Ituri forest in the Congo and the Negro settlements of the neighboring agriculturalists is the example provided by Banton. Items to be traded are left separately at a designated location by each group. Each returns to examine the items left by the other and, if they are acceptable, completes the exchange. The parties never see one another. So long as the same kinds of items are exchanged (agricultural products for game and forest products) the relationship remains unchanged, and the impact of one upon the other is minimal.

Should the interaction be continuous and face-to-face, then Banton suggests that two other forms of relations will develop. The first is institutionalized contact, in which the two societies remain essentially intact, except that individuals at the geographical boundary between the two adopt relationships and special roles in both societies—sometimes as liaisons between the two. Banton argues that such a model is possible only if: "(1) one of the two groups has a strong centralized political structure such that a few leaders control the actions of other members, and these leaders use their power to try to dominate the other group; and (2) when two such societies enter into contact through some of the outlying members, there is no strong competition for resources. . . ."[24] Should the societies be small in size, the power structure more diffused, competition between groups minimal, and contact between them gradual, then Banton argues acculturation, or cultural assimilation, will evolve. Here the two groups will tend to merge culturally, including linguistically, with the minority culture making more concessions than the majority. Historically, when racial groups or relationships between nationalities are involved, the pattern is more likely one of domination, in which one group imposes its will upon the other. In such situations slavery or near-slave conditions may prevail for the dominated. There soon evolves a caste-like system to rationalize the social order normatively and to insure that members of the minority group do not intermarry, or become mobile into the majority group.

When the two groups are nations geographically apart, then the nature of domination will involve a home government (the colonial power) determining the internal policies of the dominated society (colony). Such a situation is what Banton has termed paternalism, and involves the same form of intergroup relations described by van den Berghe[25] under the same name.

Having delineated these orders of relationships, Banton arranges them into three sequences representing processes of resolution (see Figure 6–1). The first sequence begins with contact, but because of independent political power resources, the majority enforces a domination over the other group. The domination tends to be self-reinforcing and shifts follow. In the second sequence contact results in paternalism. Over time become more difficult. If the economic base changes, pluralism may the paternalistic power becomes weakened and a shift occurs toward integration. The third sequence also begins with contact, which leads to acculturation and then easily and quickly to integration.

FIGURE 6–1

SEQUENCES OF MINORITY RESOLUTIONS*

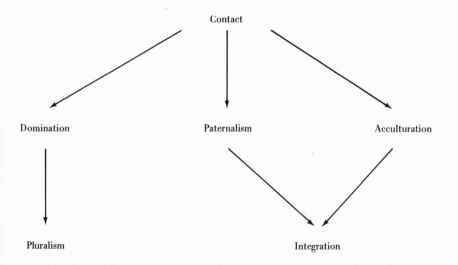

*Modified from Michael Banton, *Race Relations* (New York: Basic Books, 1967), p. 75.

Banton's model assumes an outside force impinging upon some indigenous population. His examples are most often drawn from British and American colonial histories. However, the model is less appropriate to minority-majority relationships which develop from within a given social structure. Thus the process of awakening minorities—women, homosexuals, new religious sects, and so on—cannot be fitted into this model.

Utilizing the orientations of the distributive, organizational, and social psychological levels of analysis, van den Berghe[26] has advanced a multidimensional typology of majority-minority group relations. He has developed two polar or extreme types. No society is thought of as being purely one or another form of the dichotomy, but rather societies can be compared with one another in terms of the type. For van den Berghe the types are the *paternalistic* and the *competitive* systems. The paternalistic relationship is one resembling the "master-servant model."[27] In such a model "the dominant group, often a small minority of less than 10 percent of the total population, rationalizes its rule in an ideology of benevolent despotism and regards members of the subordinate group as . . . inferior, but loveable as long as they stay 'in their place.' "[28] There is little need for physical segregation because contact between the two groups follows set patterns prescribed by the dominant group and never implies equality of interaction (e.g., black-white relationships until recently in the American South, and male-female relationships society-wide).

In the paternalistic system the division of labor is low, such that there are few status-role distinctions among members within each caste. Members of the dominant society tend to do relatively similar tasks, usually overseeing the activities of members of the minority group. Members of the minority group likewise tend to have little task differentiation, all generally engaging in menial, unskilled, and service activities. Race relations in such situations, because of the security of the dominant group's position, rarely are accompanied by deep, psychologically based prejudices. Van den Berghe contends that the paternalistic model is characteristic of the preindustrial, agricultural societies typical of colonialism. An ideology of racial superiority rationalizes the social system, and the caste lines are impenetrable. Although miscegenation is common, almost totally involving sexual relations between majority men and minority women, this is not assumed to imply equality.[29] Stereotypes in the paternalistic system stress the perception of the minority as "childlike, fun-loving, lazy, and good-natured."[30]

In a complex, industrialized, and urbanized society the pattern is of a competitive type of system. Van den Berghe indicates that the "dominant group is frequently a majority or a large minority (more than 20 or

25 percent)."[31] Although there still remains an ascription in terms of race, "class differences . . . become more salient relative to caste."[32]

Without clear race-bounded distinctions in terms of status, rank, and opportunities, threat to the dominant group is more intense. The dominant group must mobilize more of its resources to maintain its higher status. Under such instability, prejudice is a prevalent psychological need of the dominant group. Segregation emerges in order to insure that equal status interaction does not occur. Miscegenation, which was common and did not imply equal status in the paternalistic system, ceases to be open, since it threatens the social order.

Parallel social institutions emerge in the competitive society, and these tend to be counterproductive for the whole society, putting strains on the relationship to eliminate all segregation and distinctions. As the minority gains in the educational, economic, and political prerequisites for equal status, it will demand a greater role in the society and in turn often drive the dominant group to attempt oppressive tactics. Stereotypes in the competitive system stress the perception of the minority as "aggressive, cunning, untidy, and dangerous."[33] The economic competition between the majority and Japanese Americans or Jewish Americans typifies this form of relationship.

Van den Berghe suggests that pluralism is not necessarily a democratic ideal. Rather, he sees pluralism (cultural pluralism involving the amount of cultural variation within a society, and social or structural pluralism involving the institutional segmentation of the social structure) as a concept which can describe conditions in both the paternalistic and the competitive format. Pluralism for van den Berghe indicates the degree of commonality of cultures and institutions in the society, and the extent to which there exist parallel structures for the majority and the minorities. Van den Berghe develops a typology of pluralism conditions operating at four levels of analysis: (1) the group level, indicating the number of groups and the rigidity of their boundaries; (2) the institutional level, indicating the number of parallel institutions and their compatibility with one another; (3) the value level, including the degree of consensus and compatibility of the value systems of the pluralistic groups; and (4) the individual level, including the extent to which "passing" by group members is possible. For van den Berghe:

> The safest conclusion is that there is no necessary or universal association of pluralism with either democracy or tyranny. There are a few cases of moderately pluralistic politics that have also been fairly democratic, such as Switzerland or Belgium. . . . But many highly homogeneous societies, for example, a number of stateless and classless African societies like the Nuer, have also been quite democratic. . . . It is equally true, however,

that most of the world's highly pluralistic societies have been quite undemocratic, albeit in a very different way from modern totalitarianism.[34]

Van den Berghe's usage of pluralism as a concept is unique. Depending upon the mix of the four levels of analysis, pluralism is not a resolution per se, but has potential outcomes of assimilation or separatism.

There have been numerous criticisms lodged against the assimilation models, and the early models in particular. The majority of such criticisms have focused upon the explanatory power of the models when applied to racial groups. Warner and Srole[35] suggest that groups which differ significantly from the majority in skin color and culture are likely to take more time to assimilate than groups which do not so differ. Lyman[36] argues that imposing such a condition makes the models tautological. That is, assimilation involves acculturation and amalgamation, but to contend that because of culture and biology some groups will take longer to assimilate is to engage in a certain degree of circularity.

Similarly, some assimilationist theories tend to be teleological. They posit an end product of a unilineal evolution which is planned either by social forces or social policy. Unfortunately, they never predict deadlines. Finally, the models tend to commit what Barber[37] has called the "the and also fallacy," "which in effect makes an abstract analysis immune to criticism or disproof, by simply attributing all discrepancies between hypothetical scheme and actual observation to 'other factors' in the situation."[38] Brown and others after Park suggested that assimilation might not be the immediate outcome, and other outcomes might intervene. But regardless of the amount of time it takes, assimilation will ultimately triumph. Thus if after several hundred years a group has not assimilated, but has progressed through a series of stages not specified in the model, the model is not challenged. The theorists tell us that we have not given the group and the majority enough time. Since "enough time" is not defined, millennia, even eons, may pass, and the model is still unchallenged. In short, the models are vague enough and possess an "escape clause" to prevent their being tested. They may be supported by a conceptual mechanism similar to the one we mentioned in Chapter Five which permits stereotypes to endure testing. If a negative case arises, it is defined as unsuitable because enough time has not elapsed and the group is in some indeterminate intermediate phase; if the group has assimilated, the model is validated.

Some writers, especially Park and several of his students, committed what has been called the fallacy of misplaced concreteness. They have defined reality as their theory, and in cases in which groups were not progressing through the stages in accordance with the theory, the groups rather than the theory were found to be at fault.[39]

Van den Berghe's conceptualization is not subject to these criticisms.

His model was not designed to predict an ultimate outcome. Rather, it is a typology of relations between groups, the utility of which is to predict clusters of associations between variables within given societies. That is, its explanatory power is in linking a set of social, cultural, and historical conditions to the present development of given societies.

Assimilation models are not without their merits. They have been heuristic and they have been accurate in predicting the dynamics of some groups, particularly ethnic groups. But what may as yet be untested even with ethnic groups is the irreversibility of the models. One can imagine a time when a fully assimilated group may choose to reestablish its ethnic distinctiveness. This is happening in the United States today, partly as a response to the attempts by blacks to regain their African heritage. In reaction to the popularity of being a member of a minority group (provided one does not have to live in deprivation), many individuals whose parents and grandparents fought to become Americanized are today searching for their ethnic pasts.

Separatism as an Outcome

Assimilation is only one possible resolution of the condition of minority status. There is an alternative resolution—separatism. Separatism is based upon the assumption that there can be no satisfactory coexistence between majority and minority groups within the context of a single society. Separatism thus means the formation of a geographically distinct nation-state for a minority group. This separatism might be thrust upon the minority group by the majority, or it might be initiated by the minority itself. The latter usually takes the form of a nationalist movement.

IMPOSED SEPARATISM

Separation imposed by the majority is an extreme tactic. At least two basic forms of imposed separatism have been observable in the past century. The first type has occurred after the collapse of colonial empires. The indigenous people, newly powerful, expel the last remnants of colonialism, including the Europeans and the mixed-race peoples who were born of European and native parents. Under such circumstances Banton's model of domination does not lead to assimilation of the minority into the majority, but imposed separatism of the former by the new majority. There may also occur the explusion of weaker minority groups who had lived in the colony. The emergence of new nations in the African continent has been followed by the departure of many Europeans and expulsion of numerous Asians. Independence for Guyana in South

America was followed by a large-scale departure of mixed-race peoples known as the Guyanese Coloured, who had served the British as petty bureaucrats and as a buffer between the small white majority and the African and Asian minorities.[40]

A second form of imposed separatism involves either deportation of the minority to its former homeland, or restriction of the minority to isolated, semiautonomous reservations encapsulated within the territory of the majority. The first form may arise in order to prevent warfare between minority and majority, while the latter may be a final outcome after warfare. When the latter type occurs it is often initiated by a desire to exterminate the minority, because the minority is either in the way of the majority or serves no function for it. This is done usually with a very small and/or weak minority. Of course, the two examples in American history are the white-imposed "Back to Africa" movements and the establishment of reservations for native Americans. In the period during slavery, many whites feared that unless blacks were deported back to Africa, every American city and town would experience slave revolts and black uprisings. Thus some "Back to Africa" movements were initiated and supported by whites.

NATIONALISM

When the minority group initiates separatism, it frequently takes the form of a nationalist movement. Essien-Udom offered a definition of such nationalism:

> The concept nationalism . . . may be thought of as a belief of a group that it possesses, or ought to possess, a country; that it shares, or ought to share, a common heritage, of language, culture, and religion; and that its heritage, way of life, and ethnic identity are distinct from those of other groups. Nationalists believe that they ought to rule themselves, and shape their own destinies, and that they therefore should be in control of their social, economic, and political institutions.[41]

Minorities have the potential of forming their own geographically distinct nation-states. These groups are usually large enough, with sufficient diversity of abilities and skills, to perform the variety of tasks needed to sustain a society. Further, once a strong sense of group awareness and solidarity is developed, the minority group has the potential to provide its members with all the social and psychological support necessary to establish and maintain a rewarding environment and culture. Three issues that are always problematic are: (1) developing a group awareness and then a consensus that nationalism is preferable to fighting for assimilation; (2) gaining freedom from the constraints imposed by the majority; and (3) securing a geographical territory in which to establish the new nation-state. All three are difficult, but the last poses innumerable problems. Land not presently claimed by one sovereignty or another is very scarce on this earth. Existing nation-states composed of people who were the racial or ethnic kinsmen of the minority group are often unwilling to accept a large influx of their "relatives," and are more likely to see them as an invasion of foreigners rather than returning kin. Finally, the majority is almost always unwilling to cede any of its own land to the minority group, even if the land was once owned by the minority or the minority presently represents the plurality of the population in that particular geographic area.

The migration of European Jews to Palestine after World War II to found the nation-state of Israel suggests that even in this century minorities can form new societies. However, such action also involves the displacement of numbers of people who had previously occupied the territory. Four wars in little more than a quarter of a century and the Palestine refugee question point to the fact that the formation of new nation-states with the displacement of existing groups creates new minorities and new hostility.

There have been several attempts at separatism in America. Black history is filled with "Back to Africa" movements and endeavors to establish black nations in the New World as well. Because white America was unwilling to accept black America, there was a growing pressure for Negro nationalism, which traced its roots back to the American Colonization Society of 1816 and the Negro Convention movements. The most effective leader of those who were convinced that equality was impossible in America was Marcus Garvey. After an initial failure in Jamaica, Garvey formed the Universal Negro Improvement Association (UNIA) in 1916. Estimates of his following range from two to six million by the early 1920s. Garvey solicited money to finance a steamship company, the Black Star Steam Ship Line, but pressure from the NAACP and middle-class blacks, who did not want to see blacks leave the United States, eventually wrecked the movement. The UNIA and the Black Star Line collapsed in 1925. However, Garvey was successful in unifying a large proportion of black people, teaching self- and group pride. His work provided a legacy which fed other forms of nationalism, including the present Black Muslim organization.

The Black Muslims, under the leadership of Elija Muhammed, established an economic nationalism. Muslim-owned stores, farms, and schools have been established in various parts of the nation. Total separation from the "blue-eyed devils" (whites) has been the belief and practice of the organization. The Muslims have been effective in providing an identity for many blacks, and have been successful in running

121

drug rehabilitation programs based upon uplifting and dignifying the individual. Their separatism had taken the form of a continued demand that the "slave masters" (white America) give twenty-five states to the Black Muslims to establish a Nation of Islam for black people. In 1964, after his return from Mecca, Malcolm X broke with the main organization over his conviction that cooperation with whites was possible and rigid separatism was contrary to Allah's plan. A year later Malcolm X was assassinated while addressing a group of his followers. Since the recent death of Elija Muhammed, the Black Muslim organization has entertained the possibility of cooperation with some whites.

There have been numerous other attempts at separatism by minority groups in the United States. The Zionist movement was created to support the establishment of a Jewish state. Since the creation of Israel, however, American Jewish support has been in terms of financial contributions rather than massive immigration.

Reies Tijerina and his followers in *La Alianza* were convinced that Chicanos and Anglos could not live together in a common society. The Chicanos wanted to take back their land seized by Anglos in the nineteenth century and guaranteed to Mexican Americans at the time of Mexico's surrender to the United States in 1848. In 1967 the Chicanos of Tierra Amarilla (in northern New Mexico) elected their own local government and induced *La Alianza* to seize the land in the name of that government. *La Alianza* effectively controlled Tierra Amarilla for ninety minutes, after which the Anglo-dominated local government returned to power.

Although total separatism remains a philosophical goal of some segments of the minority population, it has received little minority support and met with little success. Only Liberia, established by a treaty between the United States and native princes in the region early in the nineteenth century, has been a successful attempt at minority nationalism. However, although Liberia was established to provide a homeland for black Americans, only a small portion of the black population ever sought refuge back in Africa.

Conclusion

It is not possible to make a generalization about the future of all minority groups. There is too much diversity in terms of their sizes, resources, histories, identifiability, differential power, differential treatment by the majority, and degree of self-awareness. Both models—assimilation and separatism—may operate in part for all minority groups. Within any society there are centrifugal and centripetal forces that pull apart a single group or combine parts of diverse groups. At any point in time one of these forces may predominate over the others. A society may first attempt to assimilate one or some of its minorities, and then follow with a period of dissolution of the unity and establishment of separatism. In addition, members of groups within complex societies possess varied and sometimes antithetical loyalties. In some instances members from diverse racial, ethnic, or gender groups may be united along the lines of other loyalties, including social class, careers, and even leisure-time activities. These could form additional dimensions of "structural pluralism" as Gordon described it.

Assimilation and separatism represent two polar types which can be theoretically heuristic and even empirically plausible. However, they can never be seen as a final outcome. If by that phrase we mean a stable relationship that will never again change, we can assuredly say that this will never happen. Human society is dynamic. Final resolutions for one generation are only the starting point for new resolutions for the next generation. If, on the other hand, we wish to speak of the short run, we can assume that there will continue to be individual and personal mobility of racial, ethnic, and gender individuals. This has been the trend, accompanied by less significant gains, and in some instances losses, for the groups as a whole.

There are still other temporary resolutions. There can be continuation of colonial status for many minority groups; there can be coalitions among the poor and the minorities to seize power, prestige, and property, and to change the society and its ideology of racism; there can be limited pluralisms in which the minorities retain some of their cultural or biological identities, but also share a common identity with the majority; there may be the splintering of the total nation-state into various minority enclaves; there can even be the wholesale extermination of some minority groups, which may then focus attention upon other minority groups; or there may be the unification of all groups against some new asd as yet unrecognized out-group.

Summary

There are many models which attempt to predict the outcomes of minority-majority relationships. Most of these models have assumed assimilation as a goal, usually in one of the following forms: Anglo conformity, melting pot, or cultural pluralism. The constructs of Park, Bogardus, and Brown are examples of early attempts to develop a cyclical stage theory of intergroup relations. Lieberson expanded these earlier models into a more complex one which hinges on a single variable—differential power. Gordon delineated a complex model which includes seven stages of assimilation, beginning with cultural assimilation and culminating in civic assimilation. Banton provides yet another model of three sequences of racial orders, all of which are resolved in some type of assimilation—either pluralism or integration. Van den Berghe rejects the single-dimensional conceptualization in favor of a complex, multilevel typology of pluralism, while emphasizing that pluralism is not intrinsically democratic. For van den Berghe, pluralism is not an outcome but a condition of societies. Differing types of pluralism may develop into assimilation or separatism.

Assimilation models generally have had many criticisms lodged against them. They are sometimes tautological, teleological, and untestable. However, several of these models have been heuristic, and have accurately predicted the dynamics of some groups.

Other models have posited an alternative resolution—separatism. Separatism may be imposed on a weak minority by a powerful majority, or it may be initiated by the minority in the form of nationalism. There have been several attempts at separatism in America. Garvey and the UNIA represent one of the strongest such movements for blacks in the past. Today the Black Muslims are among the larger separatist movements among the black minority. Zionism and *La Alianza* are separatist attempts within other minorities. However, we must conclude that although there may be short-run or temporary goals, one must approach the idea of a final resolution with caution. Social life is dynamic and ever changing. The process of assimilation may be reversible. For any one minority group the forces of separation and the forces of integration may operate either simultaneously or consecutively.

NOTES

1. Milton M. Gordon, *Assimilation in American Life* (New York: Oxford University Press, 1964).
2. Stewart G. Cole and Mildred Wiese Cole, *Minorities and the American Promise* (New York: Harper and Brothers, 1954).
3. Gordon, *Assimilation*, p. 85.
4. Ibid.
5. Nathan Glazer and Daniel Patrick Moynihan, *Beyond the Melting Pot* (Cambridge, Mass.: M.I.T. Press, 1963).
6. See Gordon, *Assimilation*, and George R. Stewart, *American Ways of Life* (Garden City, N.Y.: Doubleday, 1954).
7. Gordon, *Assimilation*.
8. Ibid., p. 159.
9. Robert E. Park, *Race and Culture* (Glencoe, Ill.: Free Press, 1950).
10. Emory S. Bogardus, *Immigration and Race Attitudes* (Boston: D. C. Heath, 1928).
11. Brewton Berry, *Race and Ethnic Relations* (Boston: Houghton Mifflin, 1965).

12. See Robert E. Park, "Human Migration and the Marginal Man," *American Journal of Sociology* 33 (1928): 881–93; Everett V. Stonequist, *The Marginal Man: A Study in Personality and Culture Conflict* (New York: Scribner's, 1937); and Noel P. Gist and Anthony Gary Dworkin, eds., *The Blending of Races* (New York: Wiley-Interscience, 1972).

13. W. O. Brown, "Culture Contact and Race Conflict," in *Race and Culture Contacts*, ed. E. B. Reuter (New York: McGraw-Hill, 1934).

14. Others include E. Franklin Frazier, "The Impact of Urban Civilization Upon Negro Family Life," *American Sociological Review* 2 (1937): 609–18; Louis Wirth, "The Problem of Minority Groups," in *The Science of Man in the World Crisis*, ed. Ralph Linton (New York: Columbia University Press, 1945); Clarence E. Glick, "Social Roles and Types of Race Relations," in *Race Relations in World Perspective*, ed. A. W. Lind (Honolulu: University of Hawaii Press, 1955); Rose Hum Lee, *The Chinese in the United States of America* (Hong Kong: Hong Kong University Press, 1960); and Peter I. Rose, *They and We* (New York: Random House, 1964). See Stanford M. Lyman, *The Black American in Sociological Thought* (New York: Capricorn, 1973), chap. 2, for a discussion of these theories.

15. Stanley Lieberson, "A Societal Theory of Race and Ethnic Relations," *American Sociological Review* 26 (1961): 902.

16. Ibid.

17. For Lieberson, "indigenous" is any established group, not necessarily the original or aboriginal group.

18. Berry, *Race and Ethnic Relations*.

19. See H. M. Blalock, Jr., "A Power Analysis of Racial Discrimination," *Social Forces* 39 (1960): 53–59, and *Toward a Theory of Minority-Group Relations* (New York: Wiley, 1967), chap. 4.

20. Gordon, *Assimilation*.

21. See ibid. and Harry H. L. Kitano, *Japanese Americans* (Englewood Cliffs, N.J.: Prentice-Hall 1969).

22. Kitano, *Japanese Americans*.

23. Michael Banton, *Race Relations* (New York: Basic Books, 1967), chap. 4.

24. Ibid., p. 69.

25. Pierre van den Berghe, *Race and Racism: A Comparative Perspective* (New York: Wiley, 1967).

26. Ibid.

27. Ibid., p. 27.

28. Ibid.

29. The mixed-race individuals who issue from such sexual unions often occupy positions intermediate to that of the two parents, or they assimilate with the lower caste. Gist and Dworkin (*Blending of Races*) have observed that if the mixed-race individuals occupy intermediate positions between the majority and the minority station, they may come to serve as those who do the dirty work for the majority in its control over the minority. If the society is one which later gains independence, then the suppressed native population (or minority) may seek retribution against the intermediate group. In many respects the products of the mixed-race unions come to be very marginal persons.

30. Van den Berghe, *Race and Racism*.

31. Ibid., p. 29.

32. Ibid.

33. Ibid.

34. Van den Berghe, *Race and Racism*, p. 147.

35. W. Lloyd Warner and Leo Srole, *The Social Systems of American Ethnic Groups*, Yankee City Series, vol. 3 (New Haven, Conn.: Yale University Press, 1945). See also Lyman, *Black American*.

36. Lyman, *Black American*, pp. 49–51.

37. Bernard Barber, "Structural-Functional Analysis: Some Problems and Misunderstandings," *American Sociological Review* 21 (1956): 129–35.

38. Ibid.
39. Lyman, *Black American*. For a presentation of the "fallacy of misplaced concreteness," see Alfred North Whitehead, *Science and the Modern World* (New York: Macmillan, 1925).
40. Dennis H. Gouveia, "The Coloreds of Guyana," in *Blending of Races*, ed. Gist and Dworkin, pp. 103–19.
41. E. U. Essien-Udom, *Black Nationalism: A Search for an Identity in America* (Chicago: University of Chicago Press, 1962).

Suggested Readings

Banton, Michael. *Race Relations*. New York: Basic Books, 1967.

Essien-Udom, E. U. *Black Nationalism: A Search for an Identity in America*. Chicago: University of Chicago Press, 1962.

Glazer, Nathan, and Daniel Patrick Moynihan. *Beyond the Melting Pot*. Cambridge, Mass.: M.I.T. Press, 1963.

Gordon, Milton M. *Assimilation in American Life*. New York: Oxford University Press, 1964.

Lieberson, Stanley. "A Societal Theory of Race and Ethnic Relations." *American Sociological Review* 26 (1961): 902–10.

Lyman, Stanford. *The Black American in Sociological Thought: A Failure of Perspective*. New York: Capricorn, 1973.

Park, Robert E. *Race and Culture*. Glencoe, Ill.: The Free Press, 1950.

van den Berghe, Pierre. *Race and Racism: A Comparative Perspective*. New York: Wiley, 1967.

Wilhelm, Sidney M. *Who Needs the Negro?* Cambridge, Mass.: Schenkman, 1970.

7.

A PARADIGM OF THE MINORITY GROUPS

Part Two of this book presents reports by members of nine minority groups. Some of the groups are readily recognized as minorities; some are increasingly seen as minorities; some used to be considered minorities but are rarely considered so anymore; and one is emerging as a minority, although its claim to minority status has been challenged by some. When people think of minority groups in American society, they most frequently cite blacks, Chicanos, perhaps Puerto Ricans, and native Americans. With additional prodding the Japanese and the Chinese will be mentioned. If we searched through an early American minorities text such as *Old World Traits Transplanted*,[1] written by Robert E. Park and Herbert A. Miller in 1921, we would also find the Jews and the Irish as minorities. Increasingly, women are coming to be seen as a recognizable minority.

The nine we have chosen are not an exhaustive list of minority groups, past, present, or emerging, but they are representative of the multitude of groups which could be classified as minorities. The groups differ in the extent to which they may presently claim full minority status. Further, there are differences among the groups in terms of the dimensions of minority status, as well as in power, prestige, and property. Some groups are more identifiable than others; some have greater power than others and have had diverse experiences of differential and

pejorative treatment by the majority. Some have attained a group awareness, while others have as yet to gain fully such an awareness. Some
groups are clearly colonial peoples; some seek separatism, while others
seek or have attained assimilation, especially of the cultural pluralist
variety.

Blacks, Mexican Americans, Puerto Ricans, native Americans, Japanese Americans, and Chinese Americans are each racial minorities,
although in another sense they are also ethnic groups. That is, some of
the distinctions between the groups are clearly cultural. Black Americans
differ from Puerto Rican blacks in terms of culture, although Puerto
Rican blacks differ from Puerto Rican whites in terms of race. Puerto
Rican whites (or really mestizos) differ from Mexican Americans principally in terms of culture, although there are some racial factors as well.
Mexican Americans are a mixture of Caucasians and Mongoloids, and
culturally a mixture of Indian, Spanish, and Anglo (North American
white) heritages. They can thus trace some of their heritage in common
with the native Americans. The Anglo part of their heritage is similar
culturally to the Irish Catholics. Native Americans have had considerable intermarriage with whites, and in some instances with blacks. In
fact, some groups legally defined as Indians are triracial.[2] The Japanese
and Chinese differ from one another in terms of culture and some
genetic factors due to centuries of isolation and endogamy. Most Jewish
Americans are white and thus racially similar to the Irish and the Cauca-
sion ancestry of the various mixed-race groups. Because Judaism is a religious characteristic, not a biological trait, we can find some Jews who
belong to each of the groups. To turn full circle, we should note that all
black Americans, due to widespread miscegenation during the two and
one-half centuries of slavery, have some white ancestors. Black culture,
furthermore, is not unconnected to white culture. Women, needless to
say, represent a numerical plurality of each of the groups.

Thus although each has, as a group, experienced a different history
and a different relationship with the majority and with other minorities,
all have some things in common. After all, as we suggested in Chapter
One, minority status is a social definition, involving distinctions which
people impose upon and select from the totality of reality. In a sense, we
are all of mixed races and all of mixed cultures.[3]

Table 7–1 presents a paradigm of the nine groups, their varied minority experiences, and their relative minority status. In all instances the
table presents the current status of the group relative to the majority.
Identifiability may be either cultural or phenotypic and varies from
"none" to "very much". Power is the extent to which that minority
group can influence the majority, and it varies by social class for each
group. The range of variation in power is from "very little" to "very

TABLE 7-1

Typology of the Minority Groups in Relation to the Majority

Group	Identifiability	Power	Treatment (Discrimination)	Group Awareness
Black Americans	Phenotypic: very much Cultural: some	Some (increasing)	Very much	Very much (still growing)
Mexican Americans	Phenotypic: variable Cultural: much	Little (increasing)	Much to very much	Some (growing)
Puerto Rican Americans	Phenotypic: variable Cultural: much	Little (increasing)	Much, but varies by race	Some (growing)
Native Americans (American Indians)	Phenotypic: variable Cultural: variable	Very little (increasing)	Very much	Some (growing)
Japanese Americans	Phenotypic: much Cultural: some to much	Some	Some	Much (slightly diminishing)
Chinese Americans	Phenotypic: much Cultural: some to much	Little	Moderate	Much (growing)
Jewish Americans	Phenotypic: none Cultural: some	Much	Little	Some (diminishing)
Irish Americans	Phenotypic: none Cultural: very little	Very much	Very little to none	Very little (diminishing)
American Women	Phenotypic: very much Cultural: some	Some	Some to much	Some (growing)

much." Treatment is an expression of the amount of discrimination currently experienced, and varies from "very little" to "very much." Group awareness is the final component of minority-group status, involving a consciousness of kind. There are static and dynamic aspects to group awareness. The static reflects the current level, the dynamic the direction of that level. The ranges are thus from "very little" to "very much" (static) and from "emerging" to "diminishing" (dynamic).

This table is intended to serve as a very loose skeletal guide to enable the reader to place each of the nine groups in relationship to one another. It in no way can communicate the intricacy and the individual flavor of each group. One must also recognize that there is considerable variation by social class, generation, and geographic region within each group. For the complexity of each group, for the manner in which each group has experienced the minority situation in America, we must ask each to make its *Minority Report.*

NOTES

1. Robert E. Park and Herbert A. Miller, *Old World Traits Transplanted,* New York: Harper and Bros., 1921.
2. See Brewton Berry, *Almost White* (New York: Macmillan, 1963), and idem, "America's Mestizos," in *The Blending of Races,* ed. Noel P. Gist and Anthony Gary Dworkin (New York: Wiley-Interscience, 1972), pp. 191–212.
3. Gist and Dworkin, *Blending of Races.*

PART TWO

The Reports

J. WALLACE JACKSON

THE AFRO-AMERICAN EXPERIENCE

Five Sociological Perspectives

The Afro-American experience represents the most unique social phenomenon in the history of race relations. The history of Afro-Americans chronicles a people torn from their motherland and brought to America in chains; forced into a position of perpetual servitude and subjected to the brutal perpetuation of that status for several generations; liberated from slavery only to be relegated to the status of serfs in an economic system of tenancy and sharecropping; persistently isolated by law and custom from the mainstream of the society; and deprived of any intellectual heritage and denied any identity other than that of a second-class citizen; and constantly subjected to the negative images of a hostile racial majority who, at best, behaves as though they do not exist. The net result has been an adaptive state of mind and a way of life that is without comparison in modern history—the Afro-American.

The Historical Perspective

The Afro-American experience began with the arrival of twenty Africans to the mainland of Colonial America aboard a Dutch frigate in 1619. Contrary to popular belief, the first Africans came to the New World not as slaves but as indentured servants. It was only after unsuccessful attempts to enslave the native Indian population that the African's status was reduced to that of chattel slave. Slavery quickly developed into a profitable industry. Under the slavery system, the Afro-American was treated more like an economic commodity than a human being, as the Portuguese, Spanish, and British slave traders made huge profits dealing in the precious "black ivory."

During the process of enslavement, Africans were uprooted from societies that were older and, in some cases, more advanced than many Anglo-European societies.[1] The systematic suppression of the transference of African cultural elements to the Americas became standard colonial policy. This process of cultural annihilation began in the West Indies, where the African was subjected to an intense period of "thought reform" before being transported to the mainland. Once on the plantation, the African was stripped of all remaining vestiges of his cultural heritage. The final act was the systematic destruction of the African family structure as the slaves were separated from their kinsmen and friends.[2]

During the seventeenth and eighteenth centuries, the importation of Africans increased to meet the labor demands of the plantation system of agriculture. As the ratio of blacks to whites increased, the whites became obsessed with the threat of widespread insurrections. Numerous historical accounts attest to the fact that African resistance dominated the southern mind during this period. This preoccupation of whites with slave revolts was not unfounded as evidenced by the rebellions led by Gaberiel Prosser in 1800, Denmark Vesey in 1822, and Nat Turner in 1831. The ever-present threat of slave revolt forced whites to maintain a harsh system of order to keep the black slave "in his place." The slave existed under the constant surveillance of the whites, who were ever ready to engage in repressive activities to reinforce the systematic and brutal perpetuation of the slave system.

The slave trade continued to be a profitable industry during most of the eighteenth century, but by the end of the century the growing opposition to slavery in the North coupled with the decreasing productivity of slave labor caused a decline in the trade. However, with the invention of the cotton gin in 1793, which made the production of cotton profitable, the importation of slaves was once again accelerated. As a result, the African slave became the foundation of the American agricultural economy in the nineteenth century. Congress prohibited the further importation of slaves after January 1808. Although this act legally ended the overseas trade in slaves, slavery itself continued until the start of the Civil War in 1860.

In the main, the events of the Civil War and its aftermath only served to aggravate the hostility between blacks and whites. The devastation caused by the war intensified the antagonism of southern whites toward blacks. The demagogues who assumed leadership of the "poor whites" maintained themselves in power by engaging in a racist program which made the Afro-American the scapegoat for the ills of southern society. Moreover, many northern whites resented blacks and blamed them for being forced to fight a war they did not support, a situation aggravated by the influx into the North of blacks who challenged the whites for their jobs.

For a brief period following the Civil War, the South's social structure was sufficiently flexible for Afro-Americans to make some important gains. It appeared that the federal government would be committed to a reordering of southern society to ensure the freedmen some degree of equality. The various constitutional amendments and congressional acts passed during Reconstruction which prohibited southern states from limiting the political and social privileges of blacks tend to support this belief. The brief interlude of Reconstruction temporarily gave to Afro-Americans civil rights, suffrage, and even limited access to public office. But the political events of the period were to negate the beneficial efforts of the federal government.

Disclosures of corruption had greatly weakened the Republican administration prior to the presidential election of 1876. As part of a deal to elect Rutherford B. Hayes president, his Republican supporters agreed to the withdrawal of federal troops and the lifting of other restrictions imposed on the South. With the pullout of federal troops in 1877, the stage was set for the restoration of "white supremacy" in the South. Through all kinds of legal subterfuge and overt hostile action, Afro-Americans were soon returned to a position just above their previous condition of servitude. The plight of Afro-Americans following Reconstruction has been aptly described by Walter Wilson:

By the end of the nineteenth century, black America had been beaten back toward slavery and despair. The black people in the South were virtually no longer citizens. They were often denied mobility, suffrage, the right to own desirable land, and be self-employed. The opportunity for meaningful education, the right to bear arms, the right to serve on juries and the right to testify against whites were also denied to them. In short, the black person no longer had any rights a white person was bound to respect. Violence against blacks, including thousands of lynchings often under official protection, was commonplace. . . . The United States Supreme Court had struck down the early state and federal civil rights laws which attempted to make real the promises of the Black "Magna Carta"—The 13th, 14th, and 15th amendments. Special laws, modeled on the infamous Black Codes, had been carefully reformulated and enacted in the southern states to hold the blacks under the system of forced labor substituted for chattel slavery.[3]

The mass exodus of Afro-Americans from the South following emancipation did not occur as anticipated; instead, they became involved in a legally enforced system of sharecropping and tenancy that allowed white planters to continue their exploitation of black labor. Through a mutual economic arrangement, Afro-Americans consented to live on and farm the land owned by white planters, with the agreement that the income produced would be shared equally after expenses. Such was not the case, and as whites resorted to various forms of cheating and deception, blacks found themselves once again the victims of white domination and exploitation. Moreover, laws were passed that denied blacks the right to move off the land until all indebtedness had been settled. Thus, Afro-Americans were reduced to a status of peonage in the South that persisted for several decades.

The two world wars had a profound effect on the status of Afro-Americans. The decades following both wars witnessed very significant migrations of blacks from the rural areas of the South to the industrial centers of the North. The initial migration of Afro-Americans from the South, which began during World War I, was prompted by the changing economy of the South. The large-scale out-migration from the rural South was the result of a combination of push-pull factors. On the one hand, the war created an enormous demand for labor and blacks were pulled to the North by job opportunities. On the other hand, they were pushed off the land as the mechanization of agriculture in the South made sharecropping and tenant farming obsolete. Mass migration to the North abated somewhat during the depression of the 1930s, but during World War II there was a second major migration as blacks moved to fill the void created by the ten million men and women in uniform. After the war the country continued a period of accelerated growth which gave rise to continued black migration.

The immense impact of World War II had major implications for American race relations.[4] The war precipitated profound changes, many of which did not crystallize until the fifties and sixties. These changes occurred not because of any shifts in white America's racial attitudes but rather because the international situation during the postwar period dictated a new climate of political necessity. Two events were of paramount importance in precipitating these changes: first was the advent of the Cold War and the threat of global communism; second was the emerging independence of Asian and African nations. The American government realized that in a world populated mainly by nonwhites who were primarily uncommitted in the conflict between the United

States and Russia, assigning second-class citizenship to Afro-Americans was an unwise policy.

To understand fully the impact of the international circumstances that prompted the changes in black-white relations following World War II, it is useful to survey what happened in the Afro-American's quest for social equality in the aftermath of the conflict. I suggest that one way to do this is by briefly analyzing the individual histories of the various black protest activities. Specifically, this involves a general statement of the goals, tactics, and organizational structures of the different protest organizations as they led to organizational survival and goal attainment. It also involves the degree of potential support each organization received in the black community, as well as the degree of opposition each encountered from the white community. We will treat each of these factors in turn.

Organizations and Movements: Goals and Strategies

NATIONAL ASSOCIATION FOR THE ADVANCEMENT OF COLORED PEOPLE (NAACP)

The NAACP was organized in 1911 and has been traditionally recognized as the first of the black protest organizations. From its inception the organization took on a somewhat militant stance, despite the fact that white philanthropists and black professionals made up the nucleus of the organization. The NAACP's long-range objective has always been equality for blacks in American society, and its specific strategy has consisted of direct efforts toward legal reform through litigation in the courts. Its most notable success was the 1954 *Brown* decision, which outlawed segregation in public education. As evidenced by its integrationist goals and tactics, the NAACP has operated on the basic premise that major changes in the status of blacks can be obtained within the existing framework of American society. The social changes they have sought were limited to the inclusion of blacks in the existing social order.

THE NATIONAL URBAN LEAGUE

The Urban League was founded in 1911 by white philanthropists to ease the transition of southern rural black families to northern cities. It is essentially a social services agency with black social workers and professionals making up the nucleus of the organization. The League also attempts to find solutions for the problems of the black ghetto. In addition to welfare work, it is involved in vocational guidance and training, job placement, problems of youth, recreation, housing, and health. The basic strategy of the League has been an appeal to the rational economic motives of American businessmen in terms of their enlightened self-interest. In its moderate, middle-class, biracial composition, independent financial base, and nonmilitant orientation the League is similar to the NAACP. In fact, the two organizations have become identified as the more traditional or conservative wing of the black protest movement.

THE CIVIL RIGHTS MOVEMENT

The legal reform forced by the NAACP, particularly the *Brown* decision, served to usher in a new phase in the black protest movement. It soon became apparent to black leaders that the positive rulings of the courts did not ensure that their white adversaries would willingly permit blacks to enjoy their newly won status. It was obvious that test cases would be necessary to determine the extent of white resistance to change and the degree of government commitment to the protection of black civil rights.

THE SOUTHERN CHRISTIAN LEADERSHIP CONFERENCE (SCLC)

The first black protest organization to test white resistance to desegregation evolved in the South in response to segregated busing. The commitment was made concrete through an organization that came to be known as the Southern Christian Leadership Conference. During its evolution Dr. Martin Luther King, Jr., emerged as a charismatic leader who controlled and directed the organization. By virtue of his magnetic personality, King provided the symbol of unified protest and defiance. Adopting the Gandhian philosophy of nonviolence and the strategy of nonresistant, direct, and peaceful action, he consciously set out to expose the flagrant cruelty of southern racism. His objective was to appeal to the public conscience and rely upon the inherent good will of the majority of the American people to correct the nation's social ills.

The SCLC mobilized its membership not in protest against the entire system but against specific injustices. The organization's activities were largely directed against the "Jim Crow" restrictions embodied in the local and state laws and customs in the South. The issues forced in the South made such basic demands as equal access to facilities of public conveyance, public accommodation, cessation of police brutality, and greater access to the political process.

THE STUDENT NONVIOLENT COORDINATING COMMITTEE (SNCC)

The sit-in in Greensboro, North Carolina, in 1960 by four black college students marked the arrival of organized student protest into the ranks of the civil rights movement. SNCC was organized in 1960 at a meeting at Shaw University in Raleigh, North Carolina, to coordinate the protest activities on college campuses throughout the country. This organization represented the impatience of the younger generation with what they perceived as the "gradualistic" and "accommodative" policies of the more moderate leaders and organizations. Although SNCC did not openly repudiate the philosophy of nonviolence, its assertive defiance and resistance assumed a spirit of militancy that seemed almost nationalistic. Because of its more militant stance, SNCC came to be viewed as the most radical of the nonviolent protest groups.

THE CONGRESS OF RACIAL EQUALITY (CORE)

Although organized in 1943 as the first of the nonviolent, direct-action groups, the Congress of Racial Equality remained relatively obscure until 1961, when it organized a series of nationwide "freedom rides" to protest discrimination in buses engaged in interstate transportation. James Farmer, like Martin Luther King, was generally accepted by the public and the membership as the symbol of the organization's integrity and commitment. CORE attracted to its activist ranks the more passionate middle-class blacks and whites who were disillusioned with the nonactivist methods of the NAACP.

THE BLACK NATIONALIST MOVEMENT

By the mid-1960s many militant black leaders had become convinced that the aims and methods of the civil rights organizations were no longer viable. Despite a decade of intense protest activity, they could discern no significant change in the status of the black masses. Thus, to them, the nonviolent methods of persuasion such as litigation, negotiation, and direct-action confrontation were no longer workable strategies for dealing with American racial realities. The growing frustration among blacks, particularly younger blacks in the northern ghettos, caused many to become disillusioned and to bring the nonviolent direct-action approach of the civil rights organizations under scrutiny.

In 1966, Stokley Carmichael, SNCC's chairman, introduced the term "black power" which signaled a major shift in the black protest movement.[5] The black power concept originally derived from the ideas of Malcolm X, who in 1964 had established the Organization of Afro-American Unity through which he planned to implement his ideology.[6] But Malcolm was assassinated before he could bring his ideas to fruition. Carmichael, aided by the mass media, was to successfully articulate the black nationalist theme originally sounded by Malcolm X. The SNCC leader considered black nationalism as synonymous with self-determination. Many black leaders seemed to grasp the essence of this new ideology and immediately began to translate it into concrete programs of action. The main thrust of this new militancy was expressed through a determination of black Americans to settle for nothing less than complete equality, and the strategy was to destroy the forces of racial oppression through any means necessary, including violence.

THE BLACK PANTHER PARTY

The urban riots that occurred in the summer of 1967 gave concrete expression to the issue of self-determination. By their actions the black rioters were demonstrating their determination to rid the black community of outside control and also reflecting a repudiation of the nonviolent tactics of the civil rights leaders. They were calling for new leadership willing to confront head on the problems of racial oppression. It was in this atmosphere of black frustration and hostility that the Black Panther Party evolved. The radical leadership of the Panthers imbued the black community, particularly young blacks, with a new spirit of militancy that showed a strong determination to settle for nothing less than complete freedom and human dignity. The major difference between the leaders of the Black Panthers and the leaders of the traditional civil rights organizations was along fundamental ideological lines. Where the earlier civil rights groups had worked under the basic assumption that fundamental change could be accomplished within the present institutional framework of American society, the Panthers argued that freedom and equality for blacks was impossible under the existing institutional structure. What was needed was nothing short of a revolution to bring about the total destruction of the present institutional arrangements that functioned to perpetuate the American racist system.

Critique: The Effectiveness of the Organizations

Any analysis of the black protest movement must include the reaction of white adversaries. For any black protest effort to be successful, it must first correctly perceive and then respond to the needs of the black community. But its success also depends on its ability to anticipate and overcome the white opposition it is certain to encounter. Any strategy that fails to meet these two basic conditions will almost certainly experience failure. Therefore, we will attempt a critique of the goals and strategies of the major black protest activities to determine their effectiveness in meeting these two basic conditions.

THE NAACP

The NAACP's strategy of a massive legal assault on segregation was initially responsive to the needs for equality of opportunity of blacks as the organization carried case after case to successful litigation in federal courts. But as a consequence of the organization's concrete victories, which culminated in the 1954 Supreme Court decision, the legal approach of the organization appeared to many blacks as no longer relevant to the specific problems blacks were experiencing. Now black leaders felt that black protest activities should shift to the translation of these gains into actual change. Despite the pressures of the more militant protest groups, the NAACP has been reluctant to modify its program to include more active protest. Thus, the NAACP came to be viewed by the more activist black protest organizations as a rather moderate, even conservative, organization. In spite of its obvious limitations, due mainly to its high degree of institutionalization, the NAACP remains a strong organization. Its success is due certainly in part to the respectability it has gained in the white community.

THE NATIONAL URBAN LEAGUE

Like the NAACP, the Urban League has attained a degree of institutionalization that will ensure its survival. Also, like the NAACP, it has continued to emphasize its traditional concerns—economic, industrial, and social service activities—in seeking solutions to the problems of urban blacks. But unlike the NAACP, the League has not been as noticeably effective in attaining its specific objectives. The racist forces that perpetuate the ghettos are clearly beyond the scope of the League's integrationist rationale and programs. A social service approach is grossly inadequate to deal with the myriad problems precipitated by the institutionalized racism found in large cities. In fact, social-service agencies have been accused of helping to perpetuate such conditions. But the programs of the Urban League continue to receive the support of both black and white communities.

THE SCLC

The SCLC was also similar to the NAACP in that the organization's activities were largely directed toward the attainment of specific goals within the existing institutional framework of American society. Redress involved such visible changes as access to public facilities, cessation of police abuse, and greater participation in the political process. The potential for effective action on such concrete issues is great. Thus, the SCLC appeared to have reached many of its objectives by the midsixties. To justify its continued existence it became necessary for the organization to modify its goal and extend its base, and the logical area of expansion was the central cities of the North.

King was cognizant of the limitations of his method for attracting potential supporters from the North, for the major issues confronting the mass of ghetto blacks were economic and cultural rather than political and legal. Thus, he set about reformulating his goals and restructuring his organization. This fact was clearly seen in two major developments in his perspective and organization. First, he began to speak out against the Vietnam War in an effort to relate the problem of civil rights to the broader problem of human rights. Second, he chose a major northern city—Chicago—as a base of operations for attacking the basic problems of blacks residing in urban ghettos. King was under no illusion about the size and complexity of his task but he had no other recourse —his organization was on the wane and its survival depended on the development of a new and effective program that was responsive to the ghetto masses. Martin Luther King was assassinated in April, 1968, before he had a chance to implement his changes.

After King's death, Ralph Abernathy assumed the leadership of the SCLC, taking on the awesome task of directing an organization that had been built around the symbol of a strong charismatic personality. According to Zald and Ashe, following the death of a charismatic leader, two basic changes in movement organizations can be expected.[7] First, there is likely to be a decline of membership and audience as those whose commitment is more to the man than the organization drop away. Second, his death is likely to lead to factionalism. This latter change was evident in SCLC with the breaking away of the Chicago-based Operation Bread Basket under the Reverend Jesse Jackson.

Abernathy faces monumental problems. First, he must establish himself as a strong and capable leader; second, he must formulate and articulate a definite program that attracts a sufficient number of potential supporters. Moreover, since the Poor People's Campaign in 1969, SCLC has reportedly been in serious financial difficulty. Today, SCLC appears to be in a major decline.

CORE

Under James Farmer, CORE had been an integrationist organization relying on the tactics of nonviolent direct action to achieve its goals. But in 1966, Floyd McKissick was named to replace Farmer as national director, and under his leadership the organization seemingly shifted from an integrationist orientation to one of "racial coexistence" through black power. But to McKissick black power meant "economic power." Hence, he began to argue that if CORE's programs were adequately financed, America's present course of self-destruction might be averted. Many of CORE's members were opposed to this strategy because they felt that such a position would render the organization vulnerable to corporate penetration. In 1968, the internal disputes of the organization came to a head at the national conference. Following this convention,

Roy Innis was named national director; shortly after, McKissick left the organization, taking much of its financial support with him. CORE's impact in the black community has declined significantly as has the organization.

THE BLACK PANTHER PARTY

Whenever black militancy assumes a genuinely radical dimension it becomes the object of systematic police repression. To illustrate the suppressive reaction of the system, one can note its response to the Black Panther Party's attempt to effect fundamental change by methods the authorities considered subversive. The revolutionary orientation of the organization represented a direct threat to the established order and, therefore, it was suppressed and destroyed by any means the authorities deemed necessary. It became standard operating procedure to suppress any potentially dangerous black organization by destroying its leadership. Almost every leader of the Black Panther Party has been either jailed, exiled, or killed.[8] Many other members of the organization have been subjected to harrassments, arrests, and raids by police in states throughout the nation. To avert total annihilation the Black Panther Party has had to drastically modify its original objectives and strategies.

Commentary

The compelling reality of American race relations today is that black protest organizations have so far been unable to articulate an appropriate ideology and formulate viable strategies to deal effectively with white racism. Litigation, legislation, nonviolent confrontation, and violence no longer seem to be effective methods for resolving the complex structural problems now facing the ghetto masses. The legal avenues have, for the most part, been exhausted as passive resistance meets with white indifference and a stubborn refusal to change, and violence is met with brutal police repression.

The strategy of separatism which has gained increased acceptance as the only solution to the American race problem also seems unlikely of attainment: first, the idea lacks any substantial support in the black community, and second, such a strategy is dependent on the willingness of the dominant white majority to cede territory—which appears highly improbable. The coming revolution is, at best, far off in the future and, at worst, a myth. Realistically, for such a revolution to be successful would require the support of a significant percentage of the white community.

Today black Americans are faced with a situation of benign intransigence and neglect in which whites are generally opposed to any new legislative programs for change and where the existing programs are systematically undermined and circumvented. For instance, rather than integrate, whites have chosen to move to the suburbs, leaving blacks to confront deteriorating ghetto housing, segregated and inferior public schools, deteriorating social services, high unemployment, and crime. Such stubborn refusals to alter the status of blacks present black leaders with the monumental task of formulating new organizational goals, tactics, and structures to continue the drive of blacks for social equality in American society.

The Demographic Perspective

The demographic perspective entails a review of the population history of Afro-Americans in the United States. Specifically, the concern is with population size, migration patterns, and population distribution. When the first census was taken in 1790, there were nearly four million persons in the nation. Blacks constituted about one-fifth of the total population and remained about one-fifth of the national total until the termination of slave importation in 1810. Within a century the black population had declined to less than 10 percent of the population. Black population growth during this one-hundred-year period resulted almost entirely from natural increase, that is, excess births over deaths. Blacks have remained about one-tenth of the total population until the present time. Today, blacks number about 23 million or 11 percent of the 205 million Americans.[9] Some agree that 15 percent of the population is a more realistic figure.

Of the 4.5 million blacks in the United States in 1860, 90 percent were slaves. The major portion of the slave population resided in the South, and nearly all in rural areas. Despite predictions the mass exodus of blacks from the South did not occur following emancipation, the vast majority staying in the rural areas of the region to become tenant farmers and sharecroppers. In 1910, some 90 percent of the nation's black population still resided in the rural South, a spatial distribution that remained basically unchanged for a half-century. It was not until 1915 that there was any significant black migration to the North and the West. But as early as 1890 the pull forces which held blacks in the South back had begun to weaken.

A basic notion of ecological processes is that large-scale migrations usually result from a combination of "push" and "pull" factors, that is, the "push" of limited social and economic opportunities at the place of origin, and the "pull" of new social and economic opportunities at the place of destination.[10] As we have seen, the large-scale in-migration of blacks to the urban areas of the North resulted partly from employment opportunities in northern industries during World War I, and partly from deteriorating economic conditions in the rural agrarian South.

The international conflict which restricted the immigration of European labor also increased demands on American industry to support the war effort. To fill the needs for unskilled labor, northern industries undertook a mass recruitment effort of southern black workers. This situation, along with the depressed economic conditions in agricultural areas in the South, forced the migration of blacks to northern urban centers in unprecedented numbers. It should be noted that blacks could not find a niche in the southern industrial system because whites who were also being pushed off the land barred their access to the jobs in the factories springing up in the South.

The northern migration of blacks which began with World War I continued unabated until 1930. The economic depression of the 1930s, which further deteriorated the economic condition of southern blacks, also severely restricted job opportunities in the North. The result was a general slow-down in the interstate migration of blacks. This decline, however, was only temporary as the wartime resurgence of northern industry in the 1940s saw a resumption of the large-scale migration of the black population to northern urban areas. This period also saw a significant increase in the westward migration of the black population. This second migration of blacks from the South to the North and West continued unabated until the 1960s, until, by the midsixties, the transmigration of blacks from rural to urban areas had been completed.[11]

Approximately 2.75 million blacks left the South between 1940 and 1960. The black population living outside the eleven states of the South increased from less than four million in 1940 to over nine million in 1960—nearly one-half the total population in the United States. Between 1950 and 1960, all but three of the southern states experienced a net out-migration of black population, while nearly every northern state had a net in-migration of black population. Most of this increase was concentrated in the central cities of the twelve largest metropolitan areas of the United States.

In 1910, every city in the United States had less than 100,000 black residents; a half-century later, more than one-third of the nation's black population were living in twenty-five large cities, with five large cities containing more than one of every six blacks. In 1960, the black population of New York City alone stood at over one million, which constituted 14 percent of the city's total population. In the same year, blacks in Chicago comprised 22 percent of the population, Philadelphia 26.4

percent, Detroit 28.9 percent, Los Angeles 13.5 percent, Baltimore 34.8 percent, Cleveland 28.6 percent, and Washington, D.C., 53.9 percent.

The migration trend of blacks from rural to urban areas has occurred also in the South. The 1960 census report reveals that there were almost 19 million blacks in the United States, of which nearly 60 percent lived in the South. Of the South's 1960 black population, 58 percent was urban and 42 percent was rural. In recent years, there has been a noticeable trend of reverse migration, with many young black professionals returning to the South's urban areas.

During 1940 and 1950, the birth rates of both blacks and whites rose as a result of the postwar baby boom. By 1960, however, the black natural increase of population was about two-thirds greater than that of the white population. This phenomenal increase in black fertility occurred while blacks were becoming rapidly urbanized.

The influx of blacks into the nation's major urban centers has been accompanied by a migration of middle-class whites to the suburbs. The shift in the ecological distribution of the nation's urban population, with the continuing influx of lower-income blacks and the movement of higher-income blacks to the suburbs, is having a number of consequences. The major effect is that the trend has threatened to transform the cities into slums, with large black populations ringed by predominantly white suburbs. Without question, the present energy crisis will have a major impact on future ecological processes, but it is too early to decipher directional trends to predict new demographic patterns.

The Socioeconomic Perspective

The socioeconomic perspective is concerned with the status of Afro-Americans in the educational, occupational, and political structures in American society. Specifically, it focuses on the degree of access to societal values and the equality of opportunity in the structure of racial and ethnic privilege. In this section, I shall describe the status of blacks under the existing institutional structures, the latent functions of these organizations for perpetuating this condition, and the responses of the black minority as a consequence of the pressures of institutionalized racism. Moreover, I have limited my discussion to three socioeconomic areas: education, employment, and crime. (For a discussion of other areas see Chapter 4.)

EDUCATION AND UPWARD MOBILITY

The educational system in the United States is designed ostensibly to equip all of the nation's youth to realize their full potential and to improve their personal and group status. But the ghetto schools have failed miserably to provide the educational experience to help blacks overcome the effects of deprivation and discrimination. Social scientists recognize two basic areas in which inner-city ghetto schools have failed to fulfill their assigned task. First, students in such schools do not continue their public education as long as students in other schools do. James Bryant Conant's *Slums and Suburbs*[12] used "dropout" rates as an index to measure this first level of failure. Comparing the varying percentage of high school graduates from different schools, Conant confirmed the obvious fact that fewer students graduate from predominantly black inner-city school systems than from white suburban systems.

Second, black students in ghetto schools learn less than do students in other schools. James S. Coleman, in his influential study *Equality of Educational Opportunity*,[13] cites the low-achievement scores of black students at all grade levels as evidence of this second measure of ghetto school failure. Using the dubious index of achievement scores of 600,000 American students, the federally sponsored Coleman Report found that in the critical skills—verbal and reading—black students at every level were behind whites, and the gap appears to be widening. The report concludes that these differences in performance between black students and white students result from the fact that white students receive a much higher quality education than black students.

Traditionally, education has been viewed as the route through which disadvantaged groups have achieved social mobility. American society has defined its ghetto schools as the vehicle of black upward mobility, but the current status of ghetto education seems to reflect the failure of these schools to perform their public task. Viewed from another perspective, however, the schools are not failing but fulfilling their assigned function. This view argues that ghetto school practices and policies are instruments of social control in the structure of racial and ethnic privilege.[14] Historically, the American educational system has disproportionately benefitted the more advantaged white class. In many instances, the administration of ghetto schools by the predominantly white state legislatures and local school boards has served to reinforce class inequality. Ghetto schools, in effect, have not functioned to improve equality of educational opportunity; rather, they have functioned to create and preserve social-class divisions.

If, indeed, American educational systems function to maintain race and class divisions, then one would expect to find inherent in educational systems policies and practices that serve as instruments of social control in the structure of racial and class privilege. Such devices would be employed to advance those of privileged status through the system, while depressing the aspirations and performance of those of subordinate status. Three facts common to ghetto education tend to support this view. The first deals with how priorities are set and the allocation of resources are made by state legislatures and local school boards. The quality of education for black children has constantly lagged behind that of white children because of the general practice of allocating fewer resources to schools attended predominantly by blacks. Second, ghetto schools are normally staffed by teachers with less experience and lower qualifications than white suburban schools. It is a common practice to reward good teachers by transferring them to easier teaching duties. And, finally, schools in the central cities not only suffer from overcrowding but also tend to be older structures that are poorly equipped and maintained.[15]

EMPLOYMENT AND INCOME

Black unemployment rates have traditionally been significantly higher than those for whites in every category. Even during the recent period of unprecedented sustained economic growth, the black unemployment rate remained high relative to the white rate. Black unemployment has been continuously above 6 percent, a level regarded by most economic analysts as a sign of economic crisis. Due to technological progress and automation, the number of unskilled jobs are on the decline in the United States. Since blacks are disproportionately represented in the unskilled-jobs category they are particularly vulnerable to unemployment resulting from the termination of such jobs. The great mass of blacks, particularly young black males, are today experiencing unemployment of such crisis proportions that it has been rightly described by many as a "depression."

Since slavery, Afro-Americans have been relegated to the status of a residual element in the American occupational structure. The black labor force has been functional in the American economy because it suited the flexibility of labor that is necessary in the shifting economic conditions of a capitalist economy. During periods of recession, blacks can be ejected from the labor force, and during periods of economic expansion the reserve of black labor can be drawn upon. But to be effective, the system must keep from blacks the realization of the actual role they are playing in the perpetuation of their own exploitation.

The status of blacks in the American occupational structure is described by Richard Edwards and Arthur MacEwan who, using a radical approach, offer an explanation of the plight of a disadvantaged minority in a capitalist economic system:

Unemployment is always present in a capitalist system, and its incidence falls heaviest on the groups already at the bottom of the income ladder. This situation poses a threat to capitalism. Those affected have no stake in the system and become unruly. The preservation of capitalism requires that the misery of poverty be alleviated, or at least that something be done about its appearance. Yet an attack on the basic causes of the problem, the functioning of the basic economic institutions is ruled out.[16]

As a consequence of the civil rights movement, a number of federally sponsored programs were initiated during the sixties designed to ameliorate ghetto unemployment problems. But despite their broad governmental, business, and public support, none of the programs fared too well. Given the less than enthusiastic federal support of these programs, such failures could have been anticipated. For instance, the Manpower Training programs did not seriously attempt major changes in the occupational structure and therefore had marginal effects. Predictably, by 1970, Congress, the business community, and the general public were beginning to express misgivings about many of the "Great Society" programs and began seriously considering their discontinuance.

Of those blacks who are fortunate enough to find jobs, the work is likely to be unskilled and menial and will pay less than is needed to support a family. In addition to substandard wages, these jobs often involve uncertainty of tenure, extremely low prestige, minimal opportunities for advancement, no fringe benefits, and unpleasant or exhausting duties. Such conditions are likely to be reflected in a set of overt acts deemed typical of black male workers—laziness, irresponsibility, apathy, and unreliability. Such limited employment opportunities have led many blacks to go on relief or engage in illegitimate activities—options viewed as less physically and psychologically stressful than the costs associated with legitimate employment.

CRIME

We have noted that illegitimate economic pursuits often offer more status, income, and prestige to black Americans than does legitimate employment. David Gordon correctly perceived this fact when he wrote:

> The prevalence of illegal activity in the ghetto, especially among younger black men, represents a perfectly rational response to their limited employment opportunities with the "legitimate" labor market—to the threat of unemployment, low wages in dead-end jobs, and previously alienating conditions in many jobs.[17]

The decision of many blacks to enter a life of crime is related to Robert Merton's explanation of deviant behavior in terms of social structure.[18] The ghetto youth growing up in the slums accepts many of the values of a society oriented to material success, but he will probably never have the opportunity to gain the symbols of success through legitimate channels. The means closest at hand to attain his desired goals is through criminal activity. Moreover, in accordance with Edwin Sutherland's theory of differential association,[19] young black males may have come to accept the values of a subculture whose definitions are favorable to the violation of established legal codes. In such a setting such criminal types as gamblers, pimps, numbers operators, and dope peddlers may serve as role models to be emulated.

It appears that the urban riots of the late 1960s set in motion a fear reaction among whites which has manifested itself in a preoccupation with urban street crime. Doubtless this white concern gave rise to the persistent "law and order" theme espoused by many public officials. Without discounting the seriousness of such crimes, the fact of the matter is that muggings and armed robbery account for only a small percentage of death, injury, and property loss due to criminal activity. Automobile accidents, suicide, and domestic murders account for more loss of life than street crimes. Employee thefts and shoplifting account for much more property loss than ghetto crime. And ghetto crime is much less expensive than organized crime and corporate crime. It would seem more appropriate that white society's moral outrage be directed as much to these forms of criminal activity as to urban street crime.

Moreover, personal and property loss has consistently been highest in black neighborhoods, a fact highlighted in the 1968 report of the National Advisory Commission on Civil Disorders:

> Two facts are crucial to understand the effects of high crime rates in racial ghettos: most of these crimes are committed by a small minority of the residents, and the principal victims are the residents themselves. . . . As a result, the majority of law-abiding citizens who live in disadvantaged Negro areas face much higher probabilities of being victimized than residents of most higher-income areas, including almost all suburbs.[20]

Empirical studies have shown that certain demographic conditions have a high correlation with crime.[21] For instance, in larger cities crime has traditionally been highest in the "areas of transition" surrounding the downtown business district. Many of these enclaves of crime, which first served as "ports of entry" for poor European immigrants, have since become urban black ghettos. The increased presence of police in these high crime areas does not necessarily mean a decrease in crime. Moreover, the high incidence of crime in these areas will not decline until the social, economic, and political conditions that created them have been treated.

Finally, it should be noted that the biased pattern of law enforcement serves a latent function in the occupational structure. For instance, it facilitates discriminatory hiring practices by allowing the employer to refuse a black person employment ostensibly on the grounds of having a criminal record rather than for his undesirability because of race. Thus, law enforcement functions to "legitimately" deny thousands of blacks access to certain jobs, thereby limiting their upward mobility while at the same time ensuring a cheap source of labor for society's necessary but undesirable tasks.

The Structural Perspective

The structural perspective focuses on the status of blacks as a racial minority in the social structure of race and ethnic relations in the United States. The concern is with the impact of the social structure and institutions on Afro-Americans in their quest for social equality. The most salient feature about the structural relations between blacks and whites in the United States is its racist character. Racism pervades the entire fabric of American society. Considering the racist context within which racial interaction takes place, any discussion of the structural relations between black Americans and white Americans would be meaningless without stressing the effects of racism on the interactive process.

Before entering a discussion of the structural consequences of racism, we should first distinguish between two types of racism. Racism must be conceptualized as operating on two levels—the individual and the institutional. Antiblack sentiments held by individual whites which manifest themselves in discriminatory behavior are examples of individual racism. Therefore, an individual may be considered a racist if he views members of another racial or ethnic group as being biologically inferior to his own, and if his behavior toward members of that racial group is based primarily on his convictions of their inherent inferiority.

However, by far the most critical manifestation of racism in the United States is institutional. Such racism functions to legitimize racial inequality which derives directly from the fundamental institutions in society whose normal mode of operation serve to restrict the opportunities of racial minorities. Inherent in racist institutions are social mechanisms that function to deny equal status and equal access to resources to racial minorities for no other reason than they are minorities. A society can be said to be racist if its major institutions operate with race and ethnicity as deciding factors.

A basic theme of this essay is that the structural patterns of black-white relations have assumed different forms at different periods in American history. Social theorists have attempted to characterize the specific pattern that existed during given periods. It is not my intent in this short paper to critique the various structural models but rather to present them and their basic assumptions about the racial realities in American society.

THE TOTAL INSTITUTION OF SLAVERY AS A CLOSED-SYSTEM MODEL

The status of Afro-Americans during slavery can be best described by two structural models—the closed system and the total institution. Black-white relations during this period were structured almost solely along functional lines designed to serve rational economic ends. The plantation economy, which was intended as a completely rational, self-contained system, was based upon a purely unequal symbiotic relationship between white master and black slave. The plantation policy of absolute containment and control initially adopted to protect the capital investment in slave labor crystallized over time into a closed institutional structure that prevailed throughout the South. Eventually a slave code defining the unequal status between white owners and their black property was made a part of the legal structure of every southern state.

The closed-system model views slavery as a total institution similar to that defined by Erving Goffman. According to Goffman's conception, a total institution is "a place of residence and work where a large number of like-situated individuals cut off from the wider society for an appreciable period of time, together lead an enclosed, formally administered round of life."[22] Although the slave plantation as a total institution was never completely isolated from the larger society, the absolute authority of white master over black slave which extended to the limits of life and death qualifies it as an appropriate theoretical model.

Roy Simon Bryce-La Porte[23] contends that the slave plantation as a total system had two specialized functions. First, it was an instrumental-formal organizational unit whose primary goal was economic profit. Thus it functioned to maximize the exploitation of slaves as producers of profit. Its second responsibility was the maximum confinement and control of a segment of the population that the larger society considered undesirable. Thus, the slave plantation allowed, on the one hand, the maximum exploitation of slave labor and, at the same time, maximum containment of a socially undesirable racial group.

THE JIM CROW SYSTEM AS A
COLOR-CASTE MODEL

Following emancipation and the brief interlude of Reconstruction, black-white relations in the United States became defined by the South's policy of Jim Crowism.[24]

W. Lloyd Warner and Allison Davis[25] conceived a conceptual framework for analyzing black-white structural relations in the Jim Crow South. They viewed black interaction as conforming to a color-caste system that defined unequal social, economic, and political relations between the two races. An entire sociocultural system functioned to distribute power and prestige unevenly between the dominant white caste and the subordinate black caste. Warner and Davis conceptualized a horizontal color bar that separated the two castes which insured no intercaste mobility. Caste relations were reinforced by the legal system and negative sanctions were applied to anyone challenging the caste order.

THE CASTE SYSTEM AND THE ECONOMIC
EXPLOITATION MODEL

Oliver C. Cox's *Caste, Class and Race*[26] argues that the color-caste system in America is based on "exploitation" in the strict Marxist sense. He emphasizes that *economic* exploitation is the root cause of American racial discrimination. Racism in America, according to Cox, evolved as a means of rationalizing the institution of slavery, in which a small white elitist group had a vested interest. Today, the same capitalist class initiates and supports racist policies to maintain an institutional structure that functions in their favor. Thus, blacks are restricted to the lowest strata of the occupational structure to ensure an exploiting class of a depressed source of cheap labor. Other institutions in a capitalist society are subordinate to the economic system, which is dominated by the capitalist class. Thus government, education, and mass media, all instruments of the economic exploiters, are manipulated to maintain the lowly status of the exploited black masses. Institutional racism denies blacks equal access to activities through which the quality of labor is improved. Thus, stratification of the labor force is a primary mechanism by which blacks are prevented from obtaining upward mobility through increased income.

TECHNOLOGICAL PROGRESS AND THE
ECONOMIC EXCLUSION MODEL

A corollary to the economic exploitation argument is the economic exclusion model advanced by Sidney Willhelm.[27] Like Cox, Willhelm subscribes to the notion that slavery came into existence for economic reasons, and racism evolved to rationalize the exploitation of black labor. Willhelm argues, however, that while the exploitation thesis might be valid for explaining the origin of racism, it has become increasingly untenable as a model for today's racial realities. Willhelm proceeds on the assumption that because racism is economic in origin, it does not necessarily follow that racism can be overcome by economic change. That is, if white America no longer needed black labor, this does not mean that racism would no longer exist. In his preface to *Who Needs the Negro?* Willhelm writes:

> While harboring constant antipathy toward nonwhite people, White America could not dismiss the black man until the invention of machines severed its dependency upon labor. Now the economics of technology combines with white racism to make possible the Negro's total exclusion and possibly even extermination.[28]

URBAN MIGRATION AND THE ASSIMILATION MODEL

There has been a prevalent view among sociologists that, over time, the marginal groups in society will gain access to the mainstream of American society.[29] The supporters of this assimilation theory have assumed that blacks, like the European immigrants, would, with time, education, and acculturation, become immersed into Anglo-American culture and social structure. This perspective has led some social scientists to analyze the structural position of blacks in ethnic terms. These theorists contend that the low status of blacks in urban areas is comparable to the inferior status experienced by the European immigrants who flocked to American cities at the turn of the century. They argue that the problems of ghetto blacks are no different from those of European immigrant groups, all of whom experienced an initial period of social, economic, and political domination. But with time, black Americans will ascend to positions of greater prestige and privilege, as did their European predecessors.

BLACK NATIONALISM AND THE INTERNAL COLONIALISM MODEL

In the mid-1950s the historical struggle of Afro-Americans for change in the structure of racial and ethnic privilege took on new impetus. This new mood of active protest in the black community can be traced to two sources. The first was the changing international situation and the rise to power of the Third World nations. The second motivating force was the 1954 Supreme Court decision declaring "separate-but-equal" schools unconstitutional. Together, these events provided the incentive for Afro-Americans to begin a new push for fundamental change in the educational, political, and economic structures of American life. The initial phase of this new protest activity came to be known as the "civil rights movement," but it later evolved into a more militant force for change called "black nationalism."

Black nationalist leaders view the structural relations between the ghetto masses and the predominantly white business and governmental communities as one not unlike the colonial relations between the European imperialists and their Asian, African, and Latin American colonies.[30] This colonial analogy has gained increasing acceptance among social scientists as a basis for analyzing black-white structural relations in the United States. The basic thesis of the colonial model is that the political, economic, and social status of blacks in American society is that of a colonized people, and that the white majority has consistently employed its value system to socialize the black minority into an acceptance of its colonized status. Today, however, as a result of positive identification with the colonial uprising of black African and other formerly colonized Third World nations, the Afro-American community can be characterized as being in rebellion against colonial control. The colonial perspective explains the urban riots of the sixties as an overt expression of the ghetto dwellers' drive for community autonomy by the expulsion of foreign domination in the form of exploitative white businessmen, absentee landlords, and oppressive policemen.

The Behavioral Perspective

The behavioral perspective focuses on the social psychological dimension in black-white relations. The primary emphasis is on the consequences of white prejudice and discrimination for black personality development and the impact of adaptive responses on black self-esteem. We have noted that the structural patterns of black-white relations have assumed different forms at different periods in American history. One would expect to also find characteristic modes of behavior accompanying each of the structural patterns which reflect the adaptive response of blacks to racial oppression. Here we will attempt to characterize the dominant patterns of the adjustive responses of blacks for three major periods in the history of American race relations. It must be stressed, however, that there was no universal acceptance among blacks of the dominant role prescriptions for any given period.

THE TOTAL INSTITUTION OF SLAVERY AND THE "SAMBO" ROLE

During slavery, standard plantation policy was the socialization or coercion of slaves into patterns of behavior considered essential for the survival of the slave economy. Slaves were expected to be obedient, loyal, docile, and hard-working. Stanley Elkins has drawn the analogy between the American slave system and the Nazi concentration camps as having the same devastating effects on personality. Elkins conceptualized both situations as closed and total systems where the absolute power of the dominant group meant absolute dependency for the subordinate group. Within the narrow confines of the dependent-role prescriptions, the slave developed the type of personality the existing social order required, and the plantation owners encouraged the development of a subservient mentality which Elkins called the "Sambo" personality. He describes the Sambo role as follows:

> The typical plantation slave was docile but irresponsible, loyal, but lazy, chronically driven to lying and stealing; his behavior was full of infantile silliness. . . . His relationship with his master was one of utter dependence and childlike attachment.[31]

It is important to note that Elkins points to the necessity of this particular type of behavior response for blacks' sheer survival under the slavery system. He writes:

> It was indeed this childlike quality that was the very key to his [the slave's] being. Although the merest hint of Sambo's manhood might fill the Southern breast with scorn, the child in his place could be both exasperating and lovable.[32]

It must be stressed that there was far from complete acquiescence of the slave population in this socialization process. The success of the underground railroad and the repeated attempts of slaves to escape, the numerous reports of suicide, and the constant surveillance of plantation authorities to avert slave revolts all attest to the rebellious attitudes of blacks against the enforcement of the Sambo role prescriptions.

THE JIM CROW SYSTEM AND THE "ACCOMMODATING NEGRO"

The customs and institutional arrangements that evolved in the South following emancipation were organized about a set of racist beliefs and values that defined the social relations between blacks and whites. The

Jim Crow system of segregation was based on the racist ideology of white supremacy and its concept of the natural differences between blacks and whites. Blacks fully realized that southern whites were determined to perpetuate this racial distinction even to the point of resorting to extreme violence. In light of the racial realities of the period, expediency demanded that blacks accept the prevailing caste system and accommodate themselves to it. As in the earlier socialization process, blacks did not totally acquiesce to the harsh realities of caste status. To be sure, many, like W. E. B. DuBois,[33] vehemently attacked the existing caste order.

The color-caste system that defined black-white structural relations in the Jim Crow South was characterized by the adaptive response of the "accommodating Negro." The social relation during this period conformed closely to the paternalistic model described by van den Berghe.[34] In the paternalist interracial situation, according to van den Berghe, the majority's attitudes and stereotypes toward the minority are an integral part of the society's value system. There is a clear delineation of racial roles and statuses with an "elaborate and rigid etiquette of race relations" maintaining status inequality. In this structure, the black lower caste has "accommodated" itself to its inferior status. By contrast, the white upper caste has adopted an "attitude of benevolent despotism" toward members of the lower caste.

Kardiner and Ovesey's *The Mark of Oppression*[35] and Dollard's *Caste and Class in a Southern Town* offer illustrations of the accommodative adaptive behavior response of blacks to the segregated caste conditions in southern society. Of the accommodative role, Dollard writes:

> Accommodation involves the renunciation of protest or aggression against undesirable conditions of life and the organization of the character so that protest does not appear, but acceptance does. It may come to pass in the end that the unwelcomed force is idealized, that one identifies with it and takes it into the personality; it sometimes even happens that what is first resented and feared is finally loved.[36]

Again, it must be stressed that the accommodative response was not all-pervasive in the black community.

THE INTERNAL COLONIALISM MODEL AND "BLACK MILITANCY"

The internal colonialism that defined black-white structural relations in the urban ghettos evoked a new mood of militancy in the black community. This militant stance evolved in the late 1960s as a result of the emergence of "black power" in the black protest movement. Underlying the concept of black power is the economic, political, and cultural philosophy of black nationalism. Webster defines nationalism as "a sense of national consciousness exalting one nation above all others and placing primary emphasis on promotion of its culture and interests as opposed to those of other nations or supranational groups." The essence of this version of black nationalism is a repudiation of both the traditional institutional arrangements and the value system established by the dominant white society. Characterizing this position, Carmichael and Hamilton write

> Traditionally, each new ethnic group in this society has found the route to social and political viability through organization of its own institutions with which to represent its needs within the larger society.[37]

Coupled with this emphasis on the development of black institutions is a value-oriented aspect of black nationalism. Of this new consciousness, Bennett says, "The mood is, in essence, an affirmation of Negro experience and Negro values. It is not necessarily a rejection of whiteness, but it is quite definitely an acceptance of blackness."[38] and Gary Marx writes, "It [black nationalism] implies pride in being black—a positive regard for Afro-American origins, history, and culture."[39]

The theoretical assumption of the positive identification of Afro-Americans with Third World forces was empirically supported in a 1973 study by J. Wallace Jackson. Jackson's study evaluates two basic postulates of the internal colonialism model: (1) the dissociation of Afro-Americans from an Anglo-oriented value system and (2) an improved self-image among blacks resulting from a cultural affiliation with Third World peoples. Defining stereotypes as a special class of social norm, Jackson employs a modified version of the Katz and Braly adjective list to test the degree of value consensus in the society. He requested a sample of black and white undergraduate students attending two separate universities in the same southern city to assign positive and negative traits to four racio-national groups: Afro-Americans, white Americans, black South Africans, and white South Africans. He offers the prevalence of a significant identification of the black student sample with black South Africans rather than with white Americans as evidence of an increased Third World orientation of Afro-Americans.[40]

Black Personality and Self-Esteem

Two popular, yet contradictory, models have been posited that attempt to explain the consequences of racial prejudice and discrimination for the black psyche. The first views the black protest movement as motivated by a suicidal impulse and as a struggle against self. The second views the movement as an external struggle against inferior status. Both perspectives have their roots in two opposing theories of American race relations—the self-hatred thesis and the power model. We shall consider each theory in turn.

THE SELF-HATRED THESIS

There is a popular notion among social scientists that the historical consequences of prejudice and discrimination for black personality and self-esteem have been devastating.[41] This argument holds that racial oppression has so adversely affected the black personality that it has developed not only a deep-seated hatred of the self but also contempt for one's racial group. The self-hatred model assumes that the contemporary problems blacks are experiencing have their roots in slavery and are manifestations of what three-and-a-half centuries of constant racial oppression have done to the black personality. Supposedly, the self-hatred process began with the trauma of capture and voyage to America and was reinforced by the destruction of the African cultural heritage; the role of Sambo in the authoritarian system of slavery; the role of the accommodating Negro established under the color system in the Jim Crow South; and, finally, the institutional racism and forced ghettoization in the urban North.

The self-hatred thesis is not limited to the problems of individual self-esteem resulting from the negative images of a dominant white majority; it also covers the collective deviance of the black community. According to the argument, collective self-hatred has produced the crime, drug, and alcohol problems that afflict the black community. Moreover, the basic structure in the black community—the black family—is viewed as in a state of deterioration. Perhaps the best example of the self-hatred thesis as it relates to the black family is Daniel Patrick Moynihan's controversial study *The Negro Family: The Case for National Action*.[42]

Typically, the Moynihan Report traces the present condition of the black family back into slavery. Making use of a survey of census data, Moynihan draws the dubious conclusion that "at the center of the tangle of pathology is the weakness of the family structure." It will be found to be principal source of the antisocial behavior which serves to perpetuate the cycle of poverty and deprivation. Rainwater's "Crucible of Identity"[43] and Liebow's *Tally's Corner*[44] further illustrate the application of the self-hatred thesis to the black family. Where Rainwater and Liebow limit their studies to the adjustive responses of lower-class blacks, Frazier's *Black Bourgeoise*[45] and Hare's *The Black Anglo Saxon*[46] similarly treat the pathology of the black middle-class family.

159

The problem with the self-hatred thesis is that, though partially true, it chooses not to stress the effects of individual and institutionalized racism and, therefore, implicitly exempts white Americans from the major responsibility of correcting the present condition of Afro-Americans. This fault derives directly from the basic supposition of the model to give primacy to slavery as the root cause of what is popularly defined as *personality disorganization*. Thus, the resolution of Afro-Americans' problems does not lie in the changing of white attitudes or the cessation of institutional discrimination but in the Afro-American's ability to overcome his slave psychology.

Frequent data to support the self-hatred thesis are taken from clinical evidence gathered by psychiatrists. Grier and Cobb's *Black Rage*[47] represents a case in point. Evidence of the "psychopathology" of the black personality is presented from black patients who have sought the help of these writers. The sample is necessarily biased, since only a small percentage of any population seek psychiatric help for their problems. Further, if all cases are drawn from individuals who are labeled, either by themselves or by others, as psychopathological, it is of little surprise that psychopathological roots will be found behind black problems. In a similar fashion, the 1840 census suggested that freedom caused insanity and slavery caused psychological normality for blacks.[48] In 1840, however, only free blacks were admitted to mental institutions and institutionalization was the operationalization of insanity. Thus, regardless of the actual mental health of slaves, they were defined out of the enumerated category. Finally, self-hatred themes are evoked whenever members of minority groups criticize their own people. However, as Frazier once observed,[49] if a black criticizes blacks, he is accused of displaying minority-group self-hatred, but if a white criticizes whites, he is said to be making critical or constructive observations. The same behavior is defined differentially. Like other labeling processes, the essential element is the relative status of the person creating the label.

THE POWER MODEL

The counterargument to the self-hatred thesis is the power model, which states that the black person's self-esteem suffers not so much from a marginal existence or a crisis of identity, as from a sense of impotence stemming from a lack of power. Silberman, arguing that the apathy and lack of motivation of many blacks results from their sense of dependence and powerlessness, writes:

> What is crucial is that Negroes never have had the sense of controlling their own destinies; they have never had the feeling that they were making, or even participating in, the decisions that affected their lives and

fortunes. . . . Negroes cannot solve their problem of identity . . . until they are in a position to make or to influence the decisions that affect them. . . . Thus, the principle solution to the problem of Negro personality and identity is the acquisition of power: political, social, and economic.[50]

Two interpretations of the urban riots of the 1960s serve to test the validity of the contradictory self-hatred thesis and the power model for explaining American racial realities. The former perspective has viewed black aggressiveness as a struggle against self and interprets the ghetto riots as a form of community suicide. In this view, black hostility is collectively turned inward in an attempt to destroy the symbols of a hated community existence. On the other hand, the latter perspective has viewed black aggressiveness as a struggle against inferior status and explained the ghetto riots in terms of the black people's determination to gain control of their own community. According to the power model, black hostility has resulted not from any collective suicidal instinct but from a collective self-consciousness to take control of those institutions that exist within or are supported by the black community.

A New Strategy: Black Political Awareness

This author sees a new resurgence in the black protest movement, one that can be best understood by noting the Afro-American's demands to be included in political decision-making or power positions. If one is looking for clues to the reality of this new political strategy, he has but to notice the increasing political activity in the black community: voter registration drives, neighborhood-based political awareness sessions, and the decision of more and more black leaders to seek elective office. It appears that black political leaders have heeded Kenneth Clark's wise political counsel:

The Negro must now be aware that no fundamental change in his status can come about through deference to or patronage from whites. He cannot have rights that are given as a gesture of good will. . . . with the implication of the right to withdraw those rights.[51]

The Black Caucus, the black political convention, black mayors, black congressmen and senators, and the decision of blacks to run for a host of minor offices such as school boards, city councils, and the like—all can be viewed as demands for inclusion in the political system. The extreme example of the pervasiveness of this new political strategy is seen in Bobby Seale's decision to enter the 1970 mayoral race in Oakland, Cali-

The Reports

fornia. While it is yet too soon to measure the degree of influence this new political movement is having in effecting fundamental change, it can hardly be denied that the new political awareness of the black community is having an increasing impact in defining black-white structural relations in American society.

NOTES

1. John Hope Franklin, *From Slavery to Freedom* (New York: Knopf, 1948).
2. E. Franklin Frazier, *The Negro Family in the United States* (Chicago: University of Chicago Press, 1966).
3. Walter Wilson, *The Selected Writings of W.E.B. DuBois* (New York: Mentor Books, 1970), p. 27.
4. Rupert Emerson and Martin Kilson, 'The American Dilemma in a Changing World: The Negro American," *Daedalus* 94 (Fall 1965): 1055–84.
5. Stokley Carmichael and Charles Hamilton, *Black Power: The Politics of Liberation in America* (New York: Random House, 1967).
6. George Breitman, *Malcolm X Speaks* (New York: Grove Press, 1965).
7. Mayer N. Zald and Roberta Ashe, "Social Movement Organizations: Growth, Decay, and Change," *Social Forces* 44 (1966): 327–41.
8. Jerome H. Skolnick, *The Politics of Protest* (New York: Simon and Schuster, 1969), p. 152.
9. Bureau of the Census, Department of Commerce, *Statistical Abstracts*, 1973.
10. See the essay on the Puerto Rican Americans for a discussion of similar "push-pull" forces among that minority.
11. Prior to 1915, nearly three-fourths of the black population lived in rural America, mostly in the South. Within a half-century this situation had been reversed, with some 73 percent of the black population residing in the urban centers of the nation.
12. James B. Conant, *Slums and Suburbs* (New York: McGraw-Hill, 1961).
13. James S. Coleman et al. *Equality of Educational Opportunity* (Washington, D.C.: U.S. Government Printing Office, 1966).
14. For a discussion of this viewpoint see Chapter 4.
15. Howard S. Becker, "Schools and Systems of Social Status," *Phylon* 16 (1955): 159–70, and Raymond W. Mack, ed., *Our Children's Burden* (New York: Random House, 1968).
16. Richard Edwards and Authur MacEwan, "A Radical Approach to Economics" in David M. Gordon, ed. *Problems in Political Economy* (Lexington, Mass.: Heath, 1971), p. 20.
17. Gordon, *op. cit.*, p. 276.
18. Robert K. Merton, "Social Structure and Anomie," in his *Social Theory and Social Structure* (New York: Free Press, 1968).
19. Edwin H. Sutherland and Donald Cressey, *Criminology*, 9th ed. (Philadelphia: Lippincott, 1974).
20. *Report of the National Advisory Commission on Civil Disorders* (Washington, D.C.: Government Printing Office, 1968), p. 268.
21. Ernest W. Burgess, "The Growth of the City," in Robert E. Park, Ernest W. Burgess, and R. D. McKenzie, eds. *The City* (Chicago: University of Chicago Press, 1925), pp. 47–62, and Walter C. Reckless, "The Distribution of Commercialized Vice in the City: Sociological Analysis," *Publications of the American Sociological Society* 20 (1926): 164–76.
22. Erving Goffman, *Asylums* (Garden City, N.Y.: Doubleday Anchor, 1961), p. 1.
23. Roy Simon Bryce-Laporte, "Slaves as Inmates: Slaves as Men: A Sociological

Discussion of Elkin's Sambo Thesis" in A. Lane, ed. *The Debate of Slavery* (Urbana: University of Illinois Press, 1971).

24. C. Vann Woodward, *The Strange Career of Jim Crow*. rev. ed. (New York: Oxford University Press, 1957).

25. The first systematic formulation of a caste-class model to explain black-white relations in America appeared in an article by W. Lloyd Warner and Allison Davis, "A Comparative Study of American Caste," in Edgar Thompson, ed., *Race Relations and the Race Problem* (New York: Greenwood Press, 1968), pp. 219–45.

26. Oliver C. Cox, *Caste, Class, and Race* (New York: Doubleday, 1948).

27. Sidney Wilhelm, *Who Needs the Negro?* (New York: Doubleday, 1971).

28. Ibid., p. xv.

29. Philip Hauser, "Demographic Factors in the Integration of the Negro," *Daedalus* 94 (1965): 862–63, and Oscar Handlin, *The Newcomers: Negroes and Puerto Ricans in a Changing Metropolis* (Cambridge, Mass.: Harvard University Press, 1959).

30. Robert Blauner, *Internal Colonialism and Social Problems* 16 (1969): 393–408.

31. Stanley Elkins, *Slavery* (Chicago: University of Chicago Press, 1959), p. 82.

32. *Ibid*.

33. Pierre L. van den Berghe, *Race and Racism: A Comparative Perspective* (New York: Wiley, 1967), pp. 25–34.

34. W. E. B. DuBois. *The Souls of Black Folk* (Chicago: A. C. McClurg, 1903).

35. Abram Kardiner and Lionel Ovesey, *The Mark of Oppression* (New York: Norton, 1951.

36. John Dollard, *Caste and Class in a Southern Town* (New York: Doubleday, 1957), p. 255.

37. Carmichael and Hamilton, *op. cit.*

38. Lerone Bennett, "Confrontation: Black and White" (Chicago: Johnson Publishing Co., 1965), p. 239.

39. Gary Marx, *Protest and Prejudice: A Study of Belief in the Black Community* (New York: Harper and Row, 1967), p. 107.

40. J. Wallace Jackson, "An Empirical Test of the Internal Colonialism Model," mimeographed, University of Houston, 1975.

41. Thomas Pettigrew, *A Profile of the Negro American* (Princeton, N.J.: Van Nostrand, 1964), and Arnold Rose, *The Negro in America* (New York: Harper and Bros., 1948).

42. Daniel P. Moynihan, *The Negro Family: The Case for National Action* (Washington, D.C.: U.S. Department of Labor, 1965).

43. Lee Rainwater, "The Crucible of Identity: The Lower-Class Negro Family" *Daedalus* 95 (1965): 258–64.

44. Elliot Liebow, *Tally's Corner: A Study of Negro Streetcorner Men* (Boston: Little, Brown, 1967).

45. E. Franklin Frazier, *Black Bourgeoisie* (New York: The Free Press of Glencoe, 1957).

46. Nathan Hare, *Black Anglo-Saxons* (London: Macmillan, 1970).

47. William H. Grier and Price M. Cobbs, *Black Rage* (New York: Basic Books, 1968).

48. Pettigrew, *op. cit.*, pp. 72–74.

49. Frank R. Westie, "Race and Ethnic Relations," in Robert E. L. Faris, ed., *Handbook of Modern Sociology* (Chicago: Rand McNally 1964), p. 609.

50. Charles Silberman, *Crisis in Black and White* (New York: Random House, 1964), pp. 193–94.

51. Kenneth B. Clark, "Introduction: The Dilemma of Power," in Talcott Parsons and Kenneth B. Clark, eds., *The Negro American* (Boston: Beacon Press, 1965), p. xvii.

Suggested Readings

Allen, Robert L. *Black Awakening in Capitalist America*. Garden City, N.Y.: Doubleday Anchor, 1970.

Carmichael, Stokley, and Charles V. Hamilton. *Black Power: The Politics of Liberation in America*. New York: Random House, 1967.

Clark, Kenneth B. *Dark Ghetto: Dilemmas of Social Power*. New York: Harper and Row, 1967.

Foner, Philip S., ed. *The Black Panthers Speak*. Philadelphia: Lippincott, 1970.

Franklin, John Hope. *From Slavery to Freedom*. New York: Knopf, 1948.

Grier, William H., and Price M. Cobbs. *Black Rage*. New York: Basic Books, 1968.

Killian, Lewis M. *The Impossible Revolution, Phase II*. New York: Random House, 1975.

Ladner, Joyce A. *The Death of White Sociology*. New York: Random House, 1973.

Malcolm X. *The Autobiography of Malcolm X*. New York: Grove Press, 1964.

Marx, Gary T. *Racial Conflict*. Boston: Little, Brown, 1971.

Parsons, Talcott, and Kenneth B. Clark, eds. *The Negro American*. Boston: Beacon Press, 1965.

Pinkney, Alphonso. *Black Americans*, 2d ed. Englewood Cliffs, N.J.: Prentice-Hall, 1975.

Silberman, Charles E. *Crisis in Black and White*. New York: Random House, 1964.

Wilhelm, Sidney M. *Who Needs the Negro?* Cambridge, Mass.: Schenkman, 1970.

Woodward, C. Vann. *The Strange Career of Jim Crow*. New York: Oxford University Press, 1966.

JULIUS RIVERA

MEXICAN AMERICANS

The Conflict of Two Cultures

The Ways of History

When the Spaniards touched land in the New World in 1492, thousands of tribes inhabited the continent from Alaska to Patagonia, with a total population of over thirty-five million. Ancestors of these tribes had started to colonize the hemisphere from thirty to sixty thousand years earlier. The Europeans, that is, Spaniards and Portuguese, produced a new ethnic group (mestizo) when they mixed with the American Indians, and they did so almost upon arrival. But from the beginning the mestizo was socially a half-breed. He was neither a European nor an Indian unless his occasionally extremely light or dark features betrayed his birth and made him pass as one or the other. The mestizo child was most frequently left with his Indian mother, who only occasionally became a legitimate wife. Thus, added to the stigma of being a half-breed, the colonial society, mainly under the inspiration of the church, bestowed on the mestizo the stigma of illegitimacy. Therefore he could not become a priest nor she a nun, two highly prestigious statuses in a highly Catholic social world.

COLONIAL PERIOD, 1519–1810

The tragedy of the Mexican mestizo and of his lower-class Indian blood kin began with the downfall and burning of Tenochtitlan by Her-

165

nando Cortez and his forces, including Tlascalan natives, in 1521. Cortez had married an Indian princess two years earlier. Other Spanish soldiers and adventurers had sexual encounters with Indian women and eventually mixed blood in the same manner. The miscegenation proceeded at rapid pace; sexual rights over women were considered part of the spoils of war, and during peace they were the tribute of the conquered to the conqueror. Later, in the colonial *encomienda*[1] and in the *hacienda*, the landlord, his sons, and their employees would continue to force Indian women to submit to sexual advances. With the passing of the years, lower-class Indians and mestizos enlarged the labor force to plow the land, guard cattle and sheep, and dig gold and silver mines. There was, however, a significant difference between Indian and mestizo labor. Indian labor was forced labor, nearing the slavery of the Negroes brought from Africa. Indians were organized into *repartimientos*, and each colonist was assigned so many Indians for his work. Cortez himself had around twenty-three thousand assigned to his *encomienda!* The mestizos, in turn, made up a pool of "free labor that developed in the mines, in the town about the mines, and to some extent, in the cities, where [they] congregated and became craftsmen and laborers."[2]

The mestizos were not at the bottom of the social ladder; they were three rungs above it. By birth they were closer to the *patrón* than were Indians and Negroes, although mixed-race status placed them in a lower caste than the Europeans. They tended to identify with the European part of their ancestry, spoke Spanish, and were entitled to baptism rites of the church. Thus their language and religion gave them access to civil and religious administration that few lower-class Indians and fewer Negroes and mulattoes could reach. Eventually some of them became masters and *patrones*. It took the War of Independence (1810) to break this ladder of class-caste subordination, although a new one soon emerged.

THE FIRST HUNDRED YEARS OF MEXICAN INDEPENDENCE, 1810–1910

The new class system developed after independence (1821) was no longer dominated by Spaniards as landed nobles and high administrators and by *criollos* as holders of middle-class positions. It was now dominated by mestizos and some Indians. But to have white children was still considered an improvement of the race. Although an occasional mulatto rose high and an Indian (Benito Juarez) became president of the country, the more the Spanish blood in one's veins, the higher one was socially, all factors being otherwise equal.

It did not take long for the masses of Indians and mestizos to realize inadequacies in the new social order. So the struggle started again.

During independent Mexico's first fifty hectic and catastrophic years, over thirty different individuals served as presidents, heading more than fifty governments. One person occupied the presidential chair on nine different occasions, and three others sat on that rickety pinnacle of power three times each. In a short span (1837–51 inclusive), sixteen different men served twenty-two governments as president. Cabinet ministers changed more often than presidents, and these fifteen years saw forty-eight foreign ministers, sixty-one ministers of government, fifty-seven secretaries of finance, and forty-one secretaries of war. Frequently, two groups claimed control of the government at the same time, and sometimes three. The pendulum swang from empire to federal republic to centralist government to dictatorship and back again.[3]

The upheavals finally came to rest for over thirty years in the dictatorship of Porfirio Diaz, which established the grounds for the bloodiest revolution any country has experienced in modern times: the Mexican Revolution of 1910–1917.

The warfare that raged throughout central Mexico before independence affected the present status of Coahuila, Chihuahua, and Texas. The civil wars that intermittently disturbed central Mexico after independence had repercussions in various forms in Texas, where Mexicans and non-Mexicans tried again for independence as a new republic (1835). The attempts of Santa Ana (1836 and 1842) to retain Texas proved not only useless, but actually damaging to Mexico. War between the United States and Mexico broke out the following year, ending with the Treaty of Guadalupe Hidalgo and the loss of half of the Mexican territory.

During the nineteenth century, even after the United States conquest of the Southwest, Mexicans (now mestizos and Indians) continued to move north, although in very small numbers. In New Mexico they settled in the old ancestral places to lead a rural life. Villages multiplied along the Rio Grande and in the canyons of its smaller tributaries. These villages remained isolated from much of the political struggle occurring during the early nineteenth century. It took the gold rush and the land grab of the second half of the century to shake the tranquil life of the villages. In 1850 the regional population was just over sixty thousand, of which at least fifty-five thousand were mestizos and Indians. That was much less than one-third of what it had been three hundred years earlier.

As in any agrarian society, New Mexico developed a class structure somewhat more complex than the neighboring territories. Small farmers and herders, traders, and merchants bridged the gap between the landed gentry and the peasants. The former soon claimed "Hispano" (pure Spanish) ancestry, creating a cleavage that still exists among the Spanish-speaking people of the Southwest. The clustering around the old colonial capital helped in developing this class consciousness.

The Spanish-Mexican traditions of New Mexico are clearly different from the ones retained in Texas and California. The latter area was inhabited successively by nomads and transients. Cattle brought by the Spaniards populated a vast land extending from San Antonio to Monclova and to the Gulf of Mexico. At the beginning of the nineteenth century a few Americans "invaded" the territory,[4] but by 1835 their numbers had increased to over thirty thousand. During the same time period, the Mexican population in the region only increased from twenty-six hundred to over six thousand,[5] so the Americans achieved numerical dominance in the region. The Mexicans lived mainly by ranching, although deprived of their lands. All Mexican land grants but one in Nueces County would pass to Anglo hands from 1840 to 1859.[6] With the increase in trade between Texas and Mexico, a few towns emerged along the Rio Grande that were populated primarily by Mexicans. Brownsville had a population of seven hundred and Corpus Christi had forty-five hundred in 1903.

In contrast to an agrarian society, a society of ranchers does not develop a complicated class system. Large property owners and their lands plus the few peasants constituted the two main layers of society. Traders were transient and the merchant groups were just beginning to take form. The government bureaucracies were still very small. Within this relatively flat class structure, the Mexicans were ranked low. Few could retain their land. Most became ranchhands and cowboys, and their language and folklore impregnated the new Texas cattle-centered culture. Lasso (*lazo*), lariat (*la riata*), chaps (*chaparreras*), mustang (*mesteno*), dally, dally welter (*dar la vuelta*), and ranch (*rancho*) are just a few examples of their influence.

In contrast to Texas and New Mexico, the society of California was not as deeply tortured with either physical or spiritual bloodshed. The colonization itself was fairly peaceful, although the United States-Mexican War of 1846–1848 and the gold rush of the 1850s did disturb the tranquillity. The mid-nineteenth-century *Californios*, fairly undisturbed by Indian uprisings and protected by isolation, had built a relatively self-sufficient ranching and farming way of life. They had paid tributes faithfully to the Spanish crown and to the new Mexican government after 1821. The bitter disturbances of central Mexico passed them by; they were too far away from the scene. Although they did not fight with Santa Ana against the American armies, neither did they all welcome them, and eventually they tried to repel the invaders by force in Septem ber of 1846.[7] They did not organize guerrilla warfare as the New Mexi cans did during those fateful years. The superiority of the conquering armies overran their resistance. Soon, as in Texas and New Mexico, lands were taken away from the *Californios* through force and devious legal maneuvers. Under these conditions, the class structure that had been built on land holdings crumbled gradually by the end of the cen tury. The elite, of course, lost the land, but retained some power since the invaders showed regard for aristocratic backgrounds. Lower-class Mexicans lost not only their lands but also their civil rights, although less drastically in California and New Mexico than in Texas. The loss of vast territories was a tragedy for Mexico. These territories entered the United States as the "Mexican cession." The Treaty of Guadalupe-Hidalgo, ratified in 1848, legalized the loss. *Tejanos, Hispanos,* and *Californios* (all called Mexican Americans) were hopeful at the stipulations of the treaty that made them full citizens of the United States, with all rights guaranteed. They soon found out that the treaty was not to be enforced. Violence against Mexicans, most of them poor, gave birth to the racial prejudice that was to infect the new society. Even the *Californios* shared the feelings of separation from *cholos* and "greasers." The gold rush reduced to minority-group status all Mexican Americans in northern California. In the southern part of the state (especially in Los Angeles and Santa Barbara) they retained some power for twenty more years. By the end of the century, however, they also became a minority, both numerically and socially.

Toward the end of the nineteenth century the golden era of American agriculture (1895–1914) was unfolding north of the border.[8] "Between 1870 and 1900, the total farm acreage in the West had tripled, and lands under irrigation had increased dramatically from 60,000 to 1,446,000 acres."[9] More lands were irrigated later as a consequence of the Reclamation Act of 1902. Cotton moved farther West from east Texas to southern New Mexico, to Arizona and then to southern California. Sugar beet production was stimulated by the continuing exten sion of the railroads. It should be observed that many of the immigrants of the period were upper- and middle-class refugees from the revolution in Mexico, and many had the means and ability to establish business enterprises, especially in Los Angeles.

TWO WORLD WARS AND THEIR AFTERMATHS

The Mexican labor mobilization during World War I appears small. During the war many Mexicans and Mexican Americans moved to the Midwest and became industrial workers, especially in the automobile and related factories that were then prospering. From this period date the Mexican *colonies* in Chicago, Detroit, and in various cities in Indiana, Michigan, Ohio, and Pennsylvania.[10]

Agriculture suffered a hard depression in the early 1920s except in cotton and other crops that were feeding the industrial complex. Mexican Americans had replaced Negroes in the cotton harvests of the Southwest early in the century. The agricultural depression of the early 1920s hit these early *braceros* hard. Four hundred thousand of them wanted to return to Mexico in 1921. The movement affected people working everywhere, including railroad and sugar beet workers in Idaho and Oklahoma and factory workers in Michigan. Henry Ford paid for the repatriation of three thousand from Michigan. President Obregon of Mexico, concerned with their condition, set up a Department of Repatriation. President Cardenas of Mexico was to use its services heavily during his later administration.

During the Great Depression the need for labor (including Mexican labor) diminished. The repatriation scenes of the early 1920s were to be replaced by involuntary deportations in the 1930s. An eyewitness writes as follows:

> I watched the first shipment of "repatriated" Mexicans leave Los Angeles in February, 1931. The loading process began at six o'clock in the morning. *Repatriados* arrived by the truckload—men, women, and children—with dogs, cats, and goats, half open suitcases, rolls of bedding and lunch baskets. It cost the County of Los Angeles $77,249.20 to repatriate one trainload but the savings in relief amounted to $347,468.41 for this one shipment. In 1932 alone, over eleven thousand Mexicans were repatriated from Los Angeles.[11]

From 1930 to 1932 as many as two hundred seventy-five thousand were deported, of which one hundred thirty-two thousand were from Texas alone.[12] Of course, deportations not only relieved the welfare load, they also weakened Mexican attempts to unionize. Since the gold rush days, and even since colonial times, Mexican workers had learned to ask collectively for better wages and better working conditions in mines, ranches, and farms, so it was only natural that they would utilize this experience in factories. The strikes of the first third of the twentieth century had become more sophisticated. Mexicans did not strike only for wages; they organized strikes against poor housing and discrimination. However, their strikes were met "with violence and gross brutality, with mass arrests, deportations, and 'repatriations.' "[13]

After the Depression, the *bracero* program was initiated in 1942 to provide a pool of stoop labor from Mexico to replace Americans who were needed in the military operations of World War II. This program provided for large-scale legal migration of contract labor from Mexico, and the program persisted until 1965.

> The Bracero Program . . . was an "ideal" solution to labor demands in agriculture from the employer's viewpoint. Since they were single individuals, no housing for families was necessary; wages and other considerations favorable to agribusiness were established; and much of the program was subsidized by the federal government and administered by state employment agencies. In this program, the only persons who were in a disadvantaged position were domestic agricultural workers (United States citizens) willing to work (but for decent wages) and the Mexican nationals.[14]

During the initial months of the war, American losses at Japanese hands were the topic of much fear and anger. Racial sentiments ran high, and with the relocation of the Japanese population away from the West Coast (see report on Japanese Americans, pp. 254–96), Anglos had few available scapegoats other than Mexican Americans. "The Mexican- American teen-age gang member, with his tight-cuffed trousers, long coats, high boots and duck-tail haircut provided an easily distinguishable target group. The police harrassed these 'zoot suiters' who were not in the army 'fighting for their country.'"[15] Encouraged by the local Anglo press in Los Angeles, a ten-day riot[16] broke out on June 3, 1943. The next year the Juvenile Court of the County of Los Angeles took legal action against zoot suiters, forcing them to work for the Santa Fe Railroad as convict laborers.

Despite the Anglo conception of the "zoot suiters," many Mexican Americans served valiantly in the United States Army and Marines, earning proportionately more medals of honor than any other group. After the war many of the veterans took advantage of the GI Bill, went to college, and later organized an assortment of civil rights and political rights organizations to upgrade conditions in the barrios. These individuals were successful in overturning many legal restrictions against Mexican Americans, and paving the way for more advances to be attained in the Chicano movement two decades later.

The Distribution Dimension

POPULATION GROWTH AND MOBILITY

Because the United States census has not distinguished between Mexican Americans and others with a Spanish surname, it has been difficult to estimate precisely the total Chicano population. To compound the matter, the census has changed definitions from decade to decade and

171

has used such categories as mother tongue, Spanish origin, Spanish surname, nationality, and self-identification. Moreover, it has used different samples for different purposes. The situation was so bad in the 1970 census that the United States Commission on Civil Rights published a one hundred twelve-page report criticizing the Bureau of the Census.[17]

Table 1 gives the census estimates for 1970, 1973, and 1974. Legal immigration from Mexico has averaged over fifty thousand a year during the 1950s and 1960s. The population has increased in recent years, as suggested in the table, due to both immigration and, of course, natural growth, or the difference between births and deaths. The total Mexican American population rose from over one million in 1930 to four and one-half million in 1970. It also rose considerably in Texas, from nearly seven hundred thousand in 1930 to more than 1.6 million in 1970, and California, from close to four hundred thousand in 1930 to over 2.1 million in 1970. For the other three southwestern states the increase was proportionately just as high, although in much smaller numbers during the same period.

The census figures do not reflect the growth and distribution of the illegal Mexican alien. Estimates made by researchers suggest two million, and the Immigration and Naturalization Service is currently intensifying efforts to close the border to illegal immigration. Aliens move from the border to the larger cities: to Los Angeles, San Francisco, Denver, Kansas City, Chicago, Detroit, Toledo, Buffalo, Dallas and Houston. Deportations have increased fantastically, from forty-two thousand in 1964 to five hundred seventy-seven thousand in 1973.[18] Many people may be deported more than one time. The remaining ones, however, enlarge the Mexican American population and exert pressures over

TABLE 1

NUMBER OF PERSONS OF SPANISH ORIGIN

	1970	1973	1974
Persons of Spanish origin	9,072,602	10,577,000	10,795,000
Mexican	4,532,435	6,293,000	6,455,000
Puerto Rico	1,429,396	1,548,000	1,548,000
Cuban	544,600	733,000	689,000
Central and South America	1,508,866	597,000	705,000
Other Spanish origin	1,057,305	1,406,000	1,398,000

SOURCE: U.S. Bureau of the Census, U.S. Census of Population *Current Population Reports, Population Characteristics, Persons of Spanish Origin in the United States, March, 1973* (Washington, D.C.: Government Printing Office, 1974), ser. P–20, no. 264, issued May 1974, Table L, p. 9, and ser. P–20, no. 267, issued July 1974, Table 1, p. 1.

community services and employment opportunities, whether or not they are counted by the census.

EDUCATIONAL AND OCCUPATIONAL ATTAINMENT

In order to understand the educational and occupational attainment of the Mexican Americans, two factors must be taken into consideration. One is the residential patterns affecting all of them one way or another; the second is that from one-fourth to one-third of the population are immigrants from Mexico whose economic and educational background is relatively low.

According to the March 1973 report of the Census Bureau,[19] although 83 percent of the Spanish-origin population lived at that time in metropolitan areas, only 76 percent of families of Mexican origin did so, compared with 97 percent of Puerto Ricans. Moreover, whereas 81 percent of the Puerto Rican families lived in central cities, only 43 percent of the families of Mexican American origin lived in central cities; the others preferred nonmetropolitan residence. Since the degree of urbanization of the population affects educational attainment, we would expect that Mexican Americans, as a collectivity, have somewhat less education than do Puerto Ricans.

Retrospectively, the Mexican Americans have gained in the number of years of school attended. Table 2 has been derived from more elaborate tables in decennial censuses. It is interesting to observe in the table that California has been ahead of the other states, and Texas behind. Never-

TABLE 2

MEDIAN SCHOOL YEARS COMPLETED, SPANISH SURNAME POPULATION
25 YEARS OLD AND OVER, FIVE SOUTHWESTERN STATES
1950, 1960, AND 1970

Census Year	Arizona	California	Colorado	New Mexico	Texas
1950	6.0	7.8	6.4	6.1	3.5
1960	8.0	9.5	8.6	8.4	6.1
1970	8.6	9.7	9.4	9.1	6.7
Percent high school graduates in 1970	28.6	34.3	31.0	32.1	20.0

SOURCES: U.S. Bureau of the Census, *U.S. Census of Population, 1960, Subject Reports: Persons of Spanish Surname*, Final Report PC (2)—1B (Washington, D.C.: Government Printing Office, 1963), Table 3, pp. 12–23; U.S. Bureau of the Census, *U.S. Census of Population, 1970. Subject Reports: Persons of Spanish Surname*, Final Report PC (2)–1D (Washington, D.C.: Government Printing Office, 1973), Table 7, pp. 21–23; U.S. Bureau of the Census, *U.S. Census of Population, 1950. Special Reports: Persons of Spanish Surname* (Washington, D.C.: Government Printing Office, 1953), vol. 4, p. 3, chap. C, Table 3, pp. 16–17.

The Reports

theless, the conditions in Texas have improved more rapidly than in the other states (from 3.5 to 6.7). The 1960 census demonstrated that Spanish-speaking people are behind in schooling compared with blacks and Anglos. Although everybody gained, the difference persists in the same direction, with Texas still behind the other states. Table 3 shows how females lag behind males in education, particularly among Spanish-language or Spanish-surname people in Texas (7.6 to 7.0)

Other census data[20] point to another reality: Mexican Americans, regardless of sex, lag in education (9.1) behind Puerto Ricans (9.5) and other persons of Spanish origin (Cubans and other Latin Americans,

TABLE 3

MEDIAN SCHOOL YEARS COMPLETED, FIVE SOUTHWESTERN STATES
POPULATION 25 YEARS OLD AND OVER
BY RACE AND ETHNICITY 1970

	Male			
	Total Population	Anglo	Negro	Spanish Language or Spanish Surname
Arizona	12.3	12.3	9.4	9.3
California	12.4	12.5	11.9	10.8
Colorado	12.4	12.4	12.2	10.0
New Mexico	12.2	12.3	11.2	9.8
Texas	11.7	12.0	9.3	7.6
	Female			
Arizona	12.2	12.3	9.9	8.8
California	12.3	12.4	12.0	10.4
Colorado	12.4	12.4	12.2	9.8
New Mexico	12.1	12.2	10.6	9.6
Texas	11.6	11.9	10.0	7.0

SOURCES: U.S. Beureau of the Census, U.S. Census of Population, 1970. *General Social and Economic Characteristics*, Final Report PC (1)–C4, *Arizona*. (Washington, D.C.: Government Printing Office), Table 51, pp. 98–99; U.S. Bureau of the Census, U.S. Census of Population, 1970. *General Social and Economic Characteristics*, Final Report PC (1)–C6, *California* (Washington, D.C.: Government Printing Office, 1971), Table 51, pp. 392–93; U.S. Bureau of the Census, U.S. Census of Population, 1970. *General Social and Economic Characteristics*, Final Report PC (1)–C7, *Colorado* (Washington, D.C.: Government Printing Office, 1971), Table 51, pp. 146–47; U.S. Bureau of the Census, U.S. Census of Population, 1970. *General Social and Economic Characteristics*, Final Report PC (1)–C33, *New Mexico* (Washington, D.C.: U.S. Government Printing Office, 1971), Table 51, pp. 109–10; U.S. Bureau of the Census, U.S. Census of Population, 1970. *General Social and Economic Characteristics*, Final Report PC (1)–C45, *Texas*. (Washington, D.C.: U.S. Government Printing Office, 1972), Table 51, pp. 439–40.

12.0). On the other hand, the picture derived from intergenerational analysis is very encouraging. Although over one-third (36.5) of Mexican Americans forty-five to sixty-four years old had completed less than five years of school in March 1973, 8.8 percent of Mexican Americans twenty-five to twenty-nine years old had done so, and about half (46.1) in this age category had completed four years of high school or more.

As noted previously, the educational attainment of Mexican Americans is lower than that of black Americans. Because of the close association between educational attainment and occupational status, we might assume that Mexican Americans would also have lower-ranked occupations than blacks. This is not the case, however. Larger proportions of Mexican Americans are found in high-status occupations than are blacks, and thus their overall occupational status is higher. This is probably because of the more pervasive and uniform job discrimination exerted against blacks, and the fact that more Mexican Americans can, because of lighter complexions, pass as white. In comparison to whites, however, neither Mexican Americans nor blacks have achieved high occupational status.[21] Mexican Americans are crowded into the same occupational categories as in the past,[22] such as farm or factory laborers, or as operatives. Two-thirds of Mexican American workers were employed in 1970[23] in blue-collar occupations, and less than one-third were in white-collar occupations. By contrast, half of the Anglos held jobs in white-collar occupations. "The proportion of Spanish workers in the professional and managerial occupations was less than half the proportion for white workers in such occupations."[24] The unemployment rate for Mexican Americans was 7.5, compared with 4.3 for Anglos and 9.3 for blacks. The rate for adult men was 5.3, compared with 7.2 for adult women and 19.8 for teenagers. These, of course, vary by region, city, industry and occupation.

INCOME

The effects of discrimination are pervasive. Limited educational opportunities are accompanied by limitations to career (occupational) opportunities. These in turn lead to commensurate poverty. The 1970 census reported that among persons fourteen years and older, the total median American family income was $9,586. For whites the median income was $9,957, for blacks it was $6,063, and for persons with Spanish surnames it was $7,533. Although as a group Spanish-surname Americans were nearly midway between blacks and whites in income, it must be realized that the figure overestimates Mexican American income, which is substantially lower then the Cuban and other Latin American incomes also merged into the statistic.[25]

Lowered income has its effects on a broad range of life opportunities, including access to basic shelter. The poor and the targets of discrimination have little choice about where they may live. That is, acquisition of attractive, adequate housing depends not only upon individual aesthetic tastes, but also upon the income resources which may be relegated to shelter. Income, in turn, is dependent upon occupation and education. In addition, individuals who are objects of discrimination are limited in their choices of neighborhood, regardless of income. Although overt residential segregation is illegal, informal mechanisms still enforce ghettoization.

The barrios of the Southwest (which are populated mostly by Mexican Americans) look very different from the Spanish Harlems of the East. Instead of seeing the multiple-storied, grim tenement buildings owned by absentee landlords which are so common in the urban East, one may visit poor neighborhoods in cities such as Los Angeles and observe broad tree-lined boulevards and single-family dwelling units—many privately owned.[26] One could quickly but inaccurately conclude that Mexican American housing—even for the poor—is not deprived. However, as is the case with so much of social life, the obvious is not always the accurate. A visit to a sample of these homes would confirm census findings (see Table 4) which assert that in the five southwestern states, more than half of the Spanish-surname families own their own homes. However, the proportion is lower than that of the total American population. Mexican American homes tend to be smaller and more crowded, and more frequently lack complete plumbing facilities. Not

TABLE 4

MEXICAN AMERICAN HOUSING CHARACTERISTICS
COMPARED WITH THE TOTAL UNITED STATES

	Total U.S.	Mexican Americans*
Percent in owner-occupied units	62.9%	53.8%
Median number of rooms	5.0	4.5
Median number of persons	2.7	3.8
1.01 or more persons per room	8.2%	30.0%
Lack of some or all plumbing	6.9%	10.3%
Median value	$17,000.00	$12,800.00

SOURCES: U.S. Bureau of the Census, U.S. Census of Population, *Census of Housing, 1970,* vol. 1, *Housing Characteristics for States, Cities, and Counties,* pt. 1, *United States Summary* (Washington, D.C.: Government Printing Office, 1972); idem, *Census of Population, 1970: Subject Reports—Persons of Spanish Surname* (Washington, D.C.: Government Printing Office, 1973).

* Technically, this column should read "Spanish Surname in the Five Southwestern States."

unexpectedly, these homes are worth $4,000 less than the median value of homes for the total American population. This difference occurs not only because of the characteristics mentioned above, but also because Mexican American homes tend to be old (30.7 built before 1940) and because of general neighborhood characteristics.

DISCRIMINATION AND PREJUDICE

Prejudice against the Mexicans began to emerge early in the history of the Southwest. It was not only a question of ethnicity and culture; it was also an economic matter. Mexicans were dispossessed of their lands. Social class added complications. Poor Mexicans became objects of derision as more of them filled the ranks of the low-paid working force in jobs that few others would take. Stoop labor came to mean Mexican labor. Poverty made Mexicans discriminate against Mexicans and, in recent times, Mexican Americans against Mexican Americans. In the latter instances it has been the same type of discrimination that *blancos* (white) employed against Indians, and mestizos and patrones employed against peones (landlords against their hirelings).

Prejudice and discrimination,[27] intermittent in the past, became critical during and after World War II. Mexican American heroes were returning home from the European battlefields, proud of having fought for their country, to find hotels, restaurants, and public baths closed to them; to be segregated in schools and churches; and to be refused burial in "Christian" cemeteries because of their ethnic identity. An instance of the latter kind originated protest in Texas and the organization of the GI Forum in 1949 under the leadership of Hector Garcia, a World War II surgeon. The previous year the remains of Felix Longoria, a World War II hero, had been denied burial in Three Rivers, Texas. "The story quickly made newspaper headlines" and brought about the intervention of the Texas Good Neighbor Commission and Lyndon B. Johnson, the senator from Texas who "succeeded in obtaining burial for Longoria in Arlington National Cemetery."[28]

The infamous 1943 "zoot suit riots" in Los Angeles were explosions of hidden racial tensions. George Sanchez, writing about these and other incidents, stated that the roots of the prejudicial evil were in "biased attitudes and misguided thinking" that postulated biological and racial characteristics of Mexican youth as motivations to crime. The social conditions of segregation and separation in public parks and swimming pools, churches, courthouses, and public hospitals, and particularly in "inferior Mexican schools," were stratagems to "keep the 'Mexican' in his place" and sources of anger that sought revenge in violence against others. "The so-called 'Mexican Problem' is not in fact a Mexican problem. It is a problem foisted by American mercenary interests upon the

American people. It is an American problem made in the USA."[29] In 1949, Ernesto Galarza wrote: "In many communities, Mexicans are still excluded from parks, from motion picture theatres, from swimming pools and from other public places."[30] In some important towns they are excluded from barbershops and stores. The exclusion produces northward migration. "Closely tied to this problem," Galarza adds, "is that of segregation. The location of the hundreds of Mexican colonies—invariably marked by the railroad tracks, cactus patch, city dump, and employment bureau signs—is in itself one huge, ubiquitous case of segregation."[31]

In the struggle for desegregation, one of the most interesting landmarks was the Supreme Court decision in *Cisneros* v. *Corpus Christi*, by which Mexican Americans were recognized as an "identifiable ethnic minority group" for purposes of school integration with Anglos. Since Mexican Americans are technically white or Caucasians, school districts used this as rationalization to pair or integrate predominantly Mexican American schools with predominantly black schools. Large school districts, such as Houston, appealed to this rationalization to bring together race and ethnicity without touching Anglo children. The court decision did not stop discriminatory practice on this basis, and states continue to maintain an "ethnic imbalance" that is clearly discriminatory. Only California, of the five southwestern states, has done anything significant to discontinue discriminatory practices.

Although less obvious, discrimination against Mexican Americans in employment has been rampant. Private as well as government investigations have verified this fact.[32] Discrimination is related to various societal conditions. Mexican Americans are seldom found in high-wage occupations. They are almost totally absent in university presidencies and seldom present in deanships. No Mexican American has been president or member of the board of any large corporation. There are few Mexican Americans in any of the professions. Typically, Mexican Americans crowd the low-wage occupations.

> Mexican Americans are most likely to be chosen to serve on police advisory commissions, welfare advisory councils, and employment advisory committees. Very rarely are they admitted to public utilities or highway commissions, or executive bodies of public commerce, finance, and city planning. Nor do the Mexican Americans fare much better with respect to public roles in federal agencies. They are more acceptable, it would appear, as the recipients of protection services than as administrators and technicians.[33]

Despite the myths of lack of ability and ambition,[34] the proportionate underrepresentation of Mexican Americans in positions of power and prestige can be attributed to structural discrimination.[35] The deliberate efforts of the federal government to establish "affirmative action" programs throughout government and industry have borne fruits—not enough to satisfy the needs, but enough to indicate progress.

Investigators of the Civil Rights Commission visited the Southwest in the late 1960s, gathering documentation of discriminatory practices by law-enforcement officers. Hearings indicated that Mexican Americans have been discriminated against in the administration of justice in various degrees, ranging from very little discrimination in urban areas to a high degree of discrimination in villages and small towns, especially in Texas. The commission gathered complaints leveled against law-enforcement officers of "excessive and discriminatory use of force," "unequal treatment of juveniles," "lack of courtesy," "inequalities in treatment of traffic violations," "frequency of arrests for 'investigation' and 'stop and frisk' practices in Mexican American neighborhoods," and "harrassment of narcotics addicts in Mexican American communities." In addition, the commission found that Mexican Americans are given "inadequate police protection" and are interfered with in their efforts to organize. Local remedies are frequently inadequate in transacting internal and external complaints, removing obstacles to litigation, and controlling "retaliation by police officers against complainants." The commission recommended that the national government, from which most redress must be expected, make "more intensive Federal investigations" and the processing of complaints more effective.[36] The commission also found that the judicial process is defective in the selection of jurors, in the use of bail, and in assigning adequate representation for indigents in both criminal and civil cases. In turn, Mexican Americans distrust the courts and the judicial process and complain about the insensitivity of law-enforcement officials.[37]

Community Organizations and Mobilization

Community mobilization, in the sense of collective action to correct social evils or to improve living conditions, is a very old concern among Mexican Americans. It has taken the form of: (1) church-connected activities; (2) mutual aid and socioeconomic organizations; (3) marches, strikes, and moratoria; and (4) neighborhood centers of cultural awareness and social services.

CHURCH-CONNECTED ACTIVITIES

For generations the church has played a significant role in the life of the Mexican American community. Labeled "Catholic Action" by Pope

Pius XI in the 1930s, Catholic parishes have long organized communities for the building of schools, orphanages, health clinics, and hospitals. Mexican Americans, as well as other ethnic Catholics, became a part of these organizations.

Although frequently the church took a neutral attitude, individual parishioners of Mexican American descent would be invited to participate in the organizational action. In recent times, and under the pressure of the Chicano movement, the church granted the ministry to mestizos. There are now bishops of Mexican American extraction who are more sensitive to the needs of the Mexican American community, as Bishop Patrick Flores of San Antonio has so skillfully demonstrated. In New Mexico, the participation of the laity in the affairs of the church and in the affairs of the community has been due mostly to the characteristics of village life.

MUTUAL AID AND SOCIOECONOMIC ORGANIZATIONS

Mutual aid societies have existed in Mexican communities everywhere in the country. These *mutualistas* have been the forerunners of labor unions and of contemporary community action programs. Typically, they began as burial and survivor benefit organizations. Many *mutualistas* can trace their ideological and structural characteristics to similar societies in Mexico. Credit unions, literary clubs, masonic and fraternal lodges, and consumers cooperatives have proliferated in town and country. In New Mexico, most popular and useful were the irrigation associations.[38]

After World War II some old organizations became very powerful, many died out, and new ones emerged. Some have already been mentioned in another context. Three others that deserve special reference are the Council of Inter-American Affairs, the Council of Mexican American Affairs, and the Community Service Organization. The first was a government office established during World War I to develop good neighbor relations with Latin American nations in support of the war effort. The council immediately became a symbol of Mexican American recovery and a possible instrument for improving Hispano-Anglo relations. The Council of Mexican American Affairs, founded in 1953, was more community oriented and conscious of local need. It was tailored after the fashion of the Council of Inter-American Affairs. The Community Service Organization was founded in 1947. In the early 1960s it evolved into a large, comprehensive, and grass-roots poverty program with federal funds. During this period similar organizations mushroomed from Saginaw, Michigan, to San Diego, from Seattle to Brownsville, and from Eagle Pass to Milwaukee.[39]

MARCHES, STRIKES, AND MORATORIA

The heterogeneity of the Mexican Americans as a minority category, and the fact that village studies of New Mexico rural life have portrayed a submissive and gentle picture of *raza* people, have obscured the reality of the struggle for rights and opportunities. Strikes occurred in the gold and silver mines, in the sugar beet fields, along the railroad tracks, in the cotton fields, in lumber operations, in vineyards, and in factories. The best-known strikes in this century have been the cantaloupe strike of 1928 in the Imperial Valley; the berry strike of 1933 in El Monte, California; the San Joaquin cotton strike of 1932; the pecan shellers strike of 1938 in San Antonio; the Brownsville, Texas, strike of 1965; and the strike in Delano (La Huelga) organized by Cesar Chavez in 1965.[40]

In contrast to strikes that make the news, few marches have reached a level of public awareness, although there have been thousands of them. The most famous marches have been the South Texas farm workers march to Austin in 1966; the march to Sacramento under Cesar Chavez in 1966; and the *Marcha de La Reconquista* of the Brown Berets that took place at various times at the turn of the 1970s.

During the early 1970s moratoria were organized in Mexican American communities to protest American involvement in Vietnam. In one such march and moratorium considerable police-initiated violence erupted, resulting in the death of Mexican American journalist Ruben Salazar in Los Angeles in 1970. The moratorium focused upon antiwar protest, in part because many Chicanos have come to see themselves as Third World peoples, allied with liberation movements such as the one in Vietnam, and compared with Anglos, Chicanos were proportionately more often drafted to fight in Vietnam and more often killed in the war. Some Chicanos came to see the draft as a way of exerting Anglo control over the Mexican American and of stifling Mexican American protest over social, political, and economic discrimination.

NEIGHBORHOOD CENTERS

Neighborhood centers have become foci of cultural rivalism. Here artists of all sorts gather to create symbols of *La Raza* in its multifaceted complexity. The centers produce paintings, posters, and plastic art, teach mural-building techniques, organize recitals, present plays and poetry contests, and disseminate literature with the ideological content of the movement. Nahuatl language[41] and art is frequently studied, and of course contemporary Mexican arts and letters are kept before the eyes and mind. Outstanding among these centers are those in East Los Angeles, San Diego, Berkeley, San Antonio, El Paso, and Denver.

Political Participation

According to some activists, every type of organized activity that is aimed at or results in community mobilization is political in character. I use political action in a more narrow sense to mean action in the electoral process and in running the government at any level. The historical record indicates that Mexican Americans have participated actively in this process, although this participation has varied by area and by social class identification. Literacy in English has been a barrier to political participation in the Southwest. In addition, many Mexican Americans either are resident aliens or refuse to register to vote, thinking that their influence in the political process is relatively insignificant. For many years the poll tax kept them from voting.

The history of Mexican American political organizations dates back to the close of the nineteenth century. These organizations have met with mixed success. The Political Association of Spanish Speaking Organizations (PASSO) and the Mexican American Political Association (MAPA) represent two recent groups which have achieved some distinct gains. The first started in Texas and was the vehicle for winning the election of city officials in Crystal City in 1963. Its success in other parts of Texas and the Southwest was rather limited and PASSO has experienced a decline. MAPA, on the other hand, has been active since its 1958 inception in California, and ironically it became the most vulnerable target of attack by more radical organizations because of its more traditional and middle-class politics.

A third political group of major import in recent years has been *La Raza Unida* party. Two simultaneous developments prepared the road for the emergence of *La Raza Unida*. First, Chicanos gained greater access to higher education during the civil rights movement of the 1960s, and like so many other minority peoples, these students participated in the black movement. In a reversal of past experiences, the Chicano students of the 1960s did not relinquish their barrio loyalties. On the contrary, they showed pride in their origins. Student organizations mushroomed in several parts of the country, and eventually merged.

Second, the barrio youth also were inspired by the civil rights movement. They became more sensitized to their own social, economic, and political conditions, while simultaneously becoming aware of their potential electoral force. These individuals, left in the barrios, united to establish organizations and community centers.

La Raza Unida represents a coalition between college-educated Mexican American youths and their age-peers in the barrios. What emerged was not another middle-class-dominated political group, but a "revolutionary" organization with Third World identifications. The party has achieved greatest success in the border counties of southern Texas. Here, Mexican Americans represent a clear plurality of the population, yet poverty and lack of education had prohibited them from mobilizing their political potential. Since the conditions of southern Texas are unique, the party has not prospered elsewhere.

The Chicano Movement[42]

The ideological basis of *La Raza Unida* and similar organizations has been the Chicano movement. The movement erupted in the middle 1960s from the socioeconomic and political conditions of the barrios and the cotton and sugar beet fields, and from general farming workers' conditions in California and Texas. At first it was a quiet revolution, but then it became massive and boisterous. The peaceful, almost religious, marches to Sacramento (1965) and to Austin (1966) were just manifestations of latent suffering and incipient organized farm labor. But by 1969 and 1970 the suffering was exploding in anger everywhere, resulting in moratoria and confrontations with representatives of Anglo-America. Soon it moved from the fields and the barrios to school grounds and university campuses.

The Chicano movement has manifested itself in many ways. Through community action programs, political parties, marches, strikes, moratoria, and lawsuits, activist Mexican Americans have been demanding respect for the civil rights of their minority group. The Chicano movement is both a political and a cultural revolution.[43] As a political revolution the movement has four facets: the internationalistic, the nationalistic, the pluralistic, and the communalistic. As cultural revolution, the Chicano movement has two major streams: the revivalistic and the apostolic.

POLITICAL FACETS

The internationalistic facet of the political revolution is based on the following premises. The United States-Mexico border is an artificial line separating people otherwise united by language and traditions. Kinship bonds surviving for generations cross the dividing line and cannot legitimately be broken by the border. Legality does not create legitimacy. Thus the Chicano movement affects persons and families on both sides of the border.

The nationalistic facet of the movement is identified with Reies Lopez Tijerina and Rodolfo "Corky" Gonzalez. Tijerina has postulated a literal concept of land return to its original heirs in compliance with the Treaty of Guadalupe-Hidalgo. Gonzalez has postulated a symbolic possession of the Southwest, identified now as *Aztlán*, the place of the origin of the Aztecs. Both have called for mestizo unification to create power by establishing parallel institutions. "Chicano power" has been their cry.

The third facet, typified by *La Raza Unida*, maintains the necessity for political pluralism. The traditional parties, in this view, do not and cannot meet the needs of the Chicanos. This facet of the movement tends to be more middle-class oriented than the others. The attack on the establishment is strictly on the basis of access to positions of power, not with the intent of changing its structure.

In contrast with the pluralistic, the communalistic facet of the movement is probably the deepest rooted in the traditions of Mexican American heritage, and is perhaps the most revolutionary. One could say that it constitutes the foundation of the other three facets. It is exteriorized in such expressions as *la familia* and *carnalismo*,[44] and is probably the most penetrating meaning of *la raza*. Communalism can be traced in the two traditions that came together to make the mestizo. It was practiced in northern Spain even before the launching of Columbus' expedition. The Aztecs had independently developed it into a well-established system of land tenancy and cooperative agricultural production that kept all levels of the community well fed. The contemporary Mexican *ejido* is a reflection of these two traditions. People work the soil together, and share tools, labor, and profits. The emphasis is on communal work activities woven by family networks. However, although aware of the practice, the Chicano movement has paid only lip service to it. *Carnalismo* has replaced communal ownership of land with a spiritual brotherhood that leads to small sharing, such as quarters or lodging with travelers. No one particular group has made this facet of the movement its cause. Even Cesar Chavez, who has come so close to communalistic ideas, has not adopted this part of the ideology into his own. Thus it remains an ideal frequently expressed, but seldom realized.

CULTURAL STREAMS

The political revolution of the Chicano movement cannot be separated from its cultural revolution. The two interact in such a way that one cannot be understood without the other. Analytically, two streams have been differentiated within the Chicano cultural revolution: the revivalistic and the apostolic. These, in turn, interlock and interpenetrate so intimately that distinctions in given situations are matters of emphasis.

The revivalistic facet involves cultural renovating efforts. For generations Mexican Americans have maintained their cultural heritage by a variety of means, such as mutual aid societies, literary clubs, fraternal lodges, credit unions, local newspapers, patriotic celebrations, visits and pilgrimages to ancestral lands and shrines, Spanish publications and radio stations, and Mexican movies. Often invisible to the outsider, the traditions were nevertheless kept in force. The people are reminded of them in graffiti, murals, posters, art centers, and more recently in public schools, Chicano schools, workshops, conferences, conventions, marches, and moratoria. Chicano studies programs now established in more than a hundred colleges and universities in the West, Southwest, and Midwest are keeping the fire burning. Theater groups, both in universities and in the barrios, add to the revivalistic effort. Two high-quality journals in the social sciences and the humanities—*Aztlán* and *El Grito*—are dedicated to cultivation of the Mexican American heritage and renovation of its spirit.

The apostolic facet of the Chicano cultural revolution has deliberately tried to communicate with the larger society at all levels and in all tones. The content of this communication is not only the plight of *raza* people, but advocacy for a reconsideration of their culture. Targets of the apostolic action have been schools and universities, the federal government, private employers, and the total society. Since the 1920s the emphasis had been on the recognition and respect of cultural differences between Mexican and Anglo, and the means to facilitate integration of the former into American society through the normal educational process. It was part of an accommodation and assimilation effort. The emphasis now is not only on recognition of and respect for cultural differences, but on their maintenance in a culturally pluralistic society in which the "melting pot" utopia has obviously failed. The real America, the ideology continues, is not simple but complex. To this goal, student organizations have mushroomed throughout the land. The most common, persistent, and articulate have been *Movimiento Estudiantil Chicano de Aztlán* (MECHA), Mexican American Youth Organization (MAYO), and United Mexican American Students (UMAS). They have been able to establish study programs to reevaluate teaching materials related to the Mexican American history, contributions to society, and identity.

The special target of the apostolic effort has been the federal government's discriminatory practices in employment of Mexican Americans. The Johnson administration responded to the effort by creating the Cabinet Committee for Spanish-Speaking People. The Nixon administration pushed farther yet with its "sixteen-point program" and the establishment of an office within the Civil Service Commission to enforce it. By 1973 these efforts had produced an increase to 3 percent of Spanish surnames in the federal payroll—still below their percentage

(6 percent) in the total population, but a gain nevertheless. State and local governments and private industry have been penetrated with less zeal. Such attempts have been relatively fruitful, although there is much to be done, according to reports emanating from the Equal Employment Opportunity Commission.[45]

Conclusion

The Mexican American problem is certainly an American problem. It is also a Mexican and a Mexican American problem. This is not just a play on words; it encompasses a very complex reality having no simple solutions. Mexican Americans constitute a problem for the United States and Mexico, just as Mexico and the United States constitute a problem for the Mexican Americans.

AN AMERICAN PROBLEM

Discrimination is built into American society; employment and unemployment are seasonal and completely dependent on the requirements of the corporate economy, not on the needs of the laborers; education is open to wealth and ability, which in turn is predicated on family sociocultural conditions. Thus the problems faced by Mexican Americans are generally similar to those faced by other minority groups. The origin of these problems is not found in the nature of the minority groups themselves, but in the values, attitudes, behaviors, and structures of the American majority society.

In the face of these obstacles, Mexican Americans must pursue well-defined strategies in their local, regional, and national organizations to achieve their goals.

A MEXICAN PROBLEM

Mexico is also a source of difficulties for Mexican Americans. Under current conditions the Mexican economy cannot support its rapid population growth. Since family relations determine migration patterns, an outlet for this pressure is the United States. The social and psychological consequences of drastic, restrictive immigration policies disturb many in the Mexican American community. Many feel that Mexican aliens, whether legal or not, are true brothers under the skin. How can one turn an illegal immigrant in to the border patrol or immigration officials? One must feed and shelter one's kin when they arrive. Others in the Mexican American community argue otherwise. The illegal immigrant is seen as unfair competition on the labor market; thus the "wetback" is seen by some not as a true brother, but as a burden.

A MEXICAN AMERICAN PROBLEM

Finally, the Mexican American is a problem to himself. He is caught between the economies of two societies; he is between two cultures and two loyalties. Internally he is also caught between at least two ideologies and two strategies for action. The key to successful civil rights action has been in tight organization, which has been used effectively by well-educated, middle-class groups. It has been less effective among the poor, who lack the education, time, and energy needed for such organization. And yet without the poor, any movement of this type will fail. The answer to this predicament lies in a coalition of workers, students, and the poor. However, the workers have come to mistrust students, and students are being coopted by corporate employment and are losing their interest in the poor.

The splintering of activist groups and the accompanying disorganization has been a serious internal problem that has weakened the Mexican American campaign for full civil and political rights in this society. Without coalitions and unification, Mexican American power will remain disparate and relatively ineffectual.

NOTES

1. *Encomienda* was a land grant.
2. Frank Tannenbaum, *Mexico, the Struggle for Peace and Bread* (New York: Knopf, 1956), p. 34.
3. Charles C. Cumberland, *Mexico, the Struggle for Modernity* (New York: Oxford University Press, 1968), p. 141.
4. In 1804, thirteen Americans entered the territory, according to Rupert Narval Richardson and Carl Coke Rister, *The Greater Southwest* (Glendale, Calif.: Arthur Clark, 1935), p. 71.
5. Ibid., p. 58.
6. Paul S. Taylor, *An American-Mexican Frontier* (Chapel Hill: University of North Carolina Press, 1934), p. 294.
7. David J. Weber, *Foreigners in Their Native Land: Historical Roots of the Mexican Americans* (Albuquerque: University of New Mexico Press, 1973), p. 98.
8. Harold G. Halcrow, *Agricultural Policy in the United States* (New York: Prentice-Hall, 1953), p. 151.
9. Matt Meier and Feliciano Rivera, *The Chicanos: A History of the Mexican American* (New York: Hill & Wang, 1972), p. 124.
10. Carey McWilliams, *North From Mexico* (New York: Lippincott, 1949), p. 184.
11. Ibid., p. 193–94.
12. See Meier and Rivera, *The Chicanos*, p. 162, and Abraham Hoffman, *Unwanted Mexican Americans in the Great Depression* (Tucson: University of Arizona Press, 1974).
13. Meier and Rivera, *The Chicanos*, p. 195.
14. Julian Samora, *Los Mojados: The Wetback Story* (Notre Dame, Ind.: University of Notre Dame Press 1971), p. 81.
15. Anthony Gary Dworkin, "The Peoples of *La Raza*: The Mexican Americans of

The Reports

Los Angeles," in *The Blending of Races*, ed. Noel P. Gist and Anthony Gary Dworkin, (New York: Wiley, 1972), pp. 170–71.
16. This is now known as the "zoot suit riots."
17. United States Commission on Civil Rights, *Counting the Forgotten. The 1970 Census Count of Persons of Spanish-Speaking Background in the United States, April, 1974* (Washington, D.C.: Government Printing Office, 1974).
18. *Texas Observer*, July 26, 1974, p. 14.
19. United States Bureau of the Census, *Census of Population 1970: Subject Reports*, Final Report PC(2)-1A, *National Origin and Language* (Washington D.C.: Government Printing Office, 1973).
20. United States Bureau of the Census, *Current Population Reports, Population Characteristics, Persons of Spanish Origin in the United States March 1973*, Series P-20, No. 264 (Washington, D.C.: Government Printing Office, 1974).
21. The reader is referred to Table 3–1 (p. 42) for the relative percentages of black, white, and Spanish individuals distributed by occupational categories. As can be seen in this table, the distribution of Spanish-surname individuals in occupational groups more closely resembles that of blacks than of whites.
22. Fred H. Schmidt, *Spanish Surnamed American Employment in the Southwest* (Washington, D.C.: Government Printing Office, 1970), passim.
23. U.S. Bureau of the Census, *Current Population Reports*.
24. Roberta V. McKay, "Employment and Unemployment Among Americans of Spanish Origin," *Monthly Labor Review* 97 (April 1974) : 15.
25. For Cubans, the median income was $9,237, while for Central and South Americans it was $11,069. Puerto Ricans, however, tended to suppress the median as their median was $6,379. See U.S. Bureau of the Census, *Census of Population, Final Reports PC(2)-1A and PC(2)-1E, Puerto Ricans*.
26. Some 51 percent of the Mexican Americans own homes, compared with 15 percent of the Puerto Ricans.
27. On early discrimination see Weber, *Foreigners in their Native Land*; on some court battles see Manuel P. Servin, *The Mexican Americans: An Awakened Minority* (Beverly Hills, Calif.: Glencoe Press, 1970), pp. 174–87.
28. Meier and Rivera, *The Chicanos*, pp. 190, 245.
29. Wayne Moquin and Charles Van Doren, *A Documentary History of the Mexican Americans* (New York: Praeger, 1972), p. 318 and passim.
30. Ibid., p. 338.
31. Ibid.
32. See Leo Grebler, Joan W. Moore, and Ralph C. Guzmán, *The Mexican American People: The Nation's Second Largest Minority* (New York: Free Press, 1970), p. 232; Lawrence B. Glick, "The Right to Equal Opportunity," in *La Raza: Forgotten Americans*, ed. Julian Samora (Notre Dame, Ind.: University of Notre Dame Press, 1966), p. 100; Guadalupe Salinas, "Mexican Americans and the Desegregation of Schools in the Southwest," *Houston Law Review* 9, 1971, p. 933; and Equal Employment Opportunity Commission, *Houston Hearings*, June 1970, passim.
33. Ernesto Galarza et al., *Mexicans in the Southwest* (Santa Barbara, Calif.: McNally and Loftin, 1969), pp. 53–54.
34. James S. Coleman and Ernest Q. Campbell, *Equality of Educational Opportunity* (Washington, D.C.: Government Printing Office, 1966), and Grebler, Moore, and Guzmán, *Mexican American People*.
35. See Glick, "Right to Equal Opportunity," and Schmidt, *Spanish Surnamed American Employment*.
36. United States Commission on Civil Rights, *Mexican Americans and the Administration of Justice in the Southwest* (Washington, D.C.: Government Printing Office, 1970), pt. 1.
37. Ibid., p. 60.
38. Charles P. Loomis and Olen Leonard, *Culture of a Contemporary Rural Community: El Cerrito, New Mexico*, Rural Life Series, no. 1 (Washington, D.C.: Department of Agriculture, 1941).

39. See McWilliams, *North from Mexico*; Samora, *La Raza*; and Julian Nava, *Viva La Raza* (New York: Van Nostrand, 1973).

40. See Rodolfo Acuna, *Occupied America* (New York: Harper, 1972); John Gregory Dunne, *Delano: The Story of the Grape Strike* (New York: Farrar, Straus, 1967); and Ed Ludwig and James Santibanez, *The Chicanos* (Baltimore, Md.: Penguin Books, 1971).

41. The Aztec language.

42. Throughout the Southwest, different terms have been used by Mexican Americans to describe themselves. "Latin Americans" was the preferred term in Texas; "Spanish Americans" was most often used in Arizona, New Mexico, and Colorado; in California the preference was toward "Mexican Americans." The word "Chicano" is gaing acceptance, especially among the young and students. The term stresses the mestizo heritage of Mexican Americans.

43. Julius Rivera, "Power and Symbol in the Chicano Movement," unpublished manuscript, 1973.

44. *La familia*—the family—means a Chicano group dedicated to the movement. *Carnalismo*, from carnal (*carne*—flesh, blood relative), means the bond between those so dedicated.

45. Equal Employment Opportunity Commission, *Houston Hearings*, pp. 585 ff.

Suggested Readings

Burma, John H., ed. *Mexican-Americans in the United States.* Cambridge, Mass.: Schenkman, 1970.

Dunne, John Gregory. *Delano: The Story of the Grape Strike.* New York: Farrar, Straus, 1967.

Gonzáles, Nancie. *The Spanish Americans of New Mexico: A Heritage of Pride.* Albuquerque: University of New Mexico Press, 1969.

Grebler, Leo, Joan W. Moore, and Ralph C. Guzmán. *The Mexican-American People: The Nation's Second Largest Minority.* New York: Free Press, 1970.

Madsen, William. *The Mexican Americans of South Texas.* New York: Holt, 1964.

McWilliams, Carey. *North From Mexico.* New York: Lippincott, 1949.

Moore, Joan W., with Alfredo Cuellar. *Mexican Americans.* Englewood Cliffs, N.J.: Prentice-Hall, 1970.

Rendon, Armando. *Chicano Manifesto.* New York: Macmillan, 1971.

Samora, Julian, ed. *La Raza: Forgotten Americans.* Notre Dame, Ind.: University of Notre Dame Press, 1966.

Servín, Manual P. *The Mexican Americans: An Awakening Minority.* Beverly Hills, Calif.: Glencoe Press, 1970.

Wagner, Nathaniel N., and Marsha J. Haug, eds. *Chicanos: Social and Psychological Perspectives.* St. Louis, Mo.: Mosby, 1971.

INEKE CUNNINGHAM
AND ANIBAL MOLINA

PUERTO RICAN AMERICANS

A Study in Diversity

History: Progress Toward an Ambiguous Status

Although Puerto Rico has been part of "the United States of America, its territories and possessions"[1] (although now neither a territory nor a possession) for all of this century, its history has for the most part been ignored or, perhaps, misrepresented in the American history textbooks available in most schools and universities.[2] Therefore a brief survey of Puerto Rican history is in order here. This kind of survey is perhaps of more importance for the understanding of Puerto Ricans on the mainland than for other migrant groups in the United States. In the first place, their history has led them to American citizenship, and they may both enter and leave the country freely, with no regard to quotas. Second, although Puerto Rico is a geographically distinct area, it has had difficulty in defining its political identity, first with regard to Spain, and more recently with regard to the United States, so that some confusion and uncertainty remain in this area.

SPAIN AND PUERTO RICO

The island of Puerto Rico was "discovered" by the Western world in the first decade of the sixteenth century when Juan Ponce de León established a colony under the flag of Spain. At the time the island was already inhabited by Arawak Indians who, being a relatively peaceful people, offered little resistance to the Spanish colonizers. Some fled to other islands, many were killed by the Spaniards' weapons or their diseases, and some were assimilated by the colonists. By the nineteenth century their culture had disappeared to a large extent, although the Hispanic culture which survived contained many elements of Indian influence.[3] A few slaves were brought by these first colonists, but many more were later imported to work on the coastal sugar plantations.[4] As in other Spanish colonies, many of the colonists did not bring wives, so the practice of keeping African or, more commonly, Indian mistresses was not frowned upon. Thus by 1800 Puerto Rico was inhabited by people exhibiting all shades of color from darkest black to palest white, but all were Spanish in language, culture, and political orientation.[5] However, in competing for attention from the mother country, the Puerto Ricans tended to be overshadowed by Cuba and the city of Santo Domingo.

It was in about 1800 that the people of Puerto Rico began to think of themselves primarily as Puerto Ricans rather than Spanish, and to consider how they might influence their own destiny.[6] In 1812 a new Spanish constitution provided Puerto Ricans with full citizenship status; they were no longer to be merely colonial subjects. They also were given a voice in the legislature of Spain. Although the constitution was revoked after three years, it was reinstated off and on over the next thirty years, and for the rest of the century the island's leaders attempted, with more or less success, to obtain greater control over Puerto Rican affairs. Finally in July 1898 Puerto Ricans, for the first time in their history, elected a completely autonomous legislature and president. Although not an independent country, Puerto Rico had total control over her own affairs and over her territory. Two weeks later troops from the United States of America occupied Puerto Rico, and shortly thereafter Spain, in the Treaty of Paris, ceded the island to the United States as part of the settlement of the Spanish-American War.

THE UNITED STATES AND PUERTO RICO

The autonomy was lost immediately. For twenty years the island was governed by military governors who not only knew and seemed to care little about Puerto Rico but, unlike the Spanish governors of previous decades, could not even speak the people's language. Through the Jones Act of 1917 Puerto Ricans became American citizens, but the American-appointed governors, although now civilians, maintained the same level of knowledge, concern, and language. The people and their problems were largely ignored. The country was exploited economically like any other colony.[7] Puerto Rican leaders argued whether they should regain their own destiny as a state or as an independent country, but in reality they had no powers to effect either.

In 1940 Luis Muñoz Marin formed the Popular Democratic Party, the first political party to declare the island's political status an issue of lesser importance and to focus instead on improving the welfare and economy of the Puerto Rican people. With the slogan *"Pan, Tierra, y Libertad"* (Bread, Land, and Liberty), and a focus on the *jibaro,* or farmer, the new party rapidly gained widespread support. Within ten years enormous political gains had been achieved. The status question, too, was at least temporarily settled. In 1947 the Jones Act was amended to enable Puerto Ricans to elect their own governor. The Puerto Rican Federal Relations Act of 1950 authorized the people of Puerto Rico to draft their own constitution and reorganize the government. Following this, on July 25, 1952, the Commonwealth of Puerto Rico[8] was officially constituted. The present commonwealth relationship with the United States is based on common citizenship, common defense, a common market, and a common currency.

Thus the political identity of the island has been solved, but the solution seems temporary, even if long-term. There is still much discussion regarding both complete independence and full statehood, and some agitation for either final solution.

MIGRATION NUMBERS

Puerto Ricans had begun to migrate to the United States almost as soon as Puerto Rico became American territory. The census of 1910, taken only twelve years after Puerto Rico came under American administration, identified 1,513 individuals of Puerto Rican birth residing in the United States. Already New York City had become a target for Puerto Rican migration, as one-third of these had settled there.[9]

It should be noted that counting Puerto Rican migrants presents difficulties for several reasons. First, immigration records cannot be used, for since Puerto Ricans hold American citizenship they cannot be considered immigrants, so neither their entry into the mainland nor their return to the island, if made, are specifically recorded. Second, there is frequent movement back and forth between the island and the mainland, with return to Puerto Rico for holidays and frequently longer periods. A census count in the United States is therefore likely to miss some Puerto Rican Americans who are back on the island during the counting period, although it might pick up some Puerto Ricans visiting the United States temporarily. Finally, census techniques in the United States have been found to underestimate the Spanish-speaking population by as much as 10 percent.[10]

These difficulties in counting accurately the number of Puerto Ricans who have migrated to the United States should not deter the sociologist from the study of Puerto Rican migration. The numbers are relatively small in any case. In 1970 there were approximately 1.5 million Puerto Ricans living in the United States[11] compared to, for example, Italians, with over five million immigrants between 1820 and 1970, as well as their descendants,[12] and blacks with a population of 22.5 million in 1970.[13] Puerto Rican Americans represent more than one-third of all Puerto Ricans, as the population of the island is about 2.7 million.[14] However, the small size of the Puerto Rican American minority as compared to some other American minorities is more relevant to the life chances and life styles of Puerto Rican Americans than is the large proportion of Puerto Ricans living in the United States.

MIGRATION TRENDS

The exact numbers of Puerto Rican migrants are less important than certain trends which can be identified in Puerto Rican migration. Two trends are of particular import to the Puerto Rican American. These are the geographic trend, or where Puerto Rican migrants have settled, and the chronological trend, or when Puerto Ricans have migrated.

The geographic trend can be noted from data presented in Table 1. The chief target for Puerto Ricans moving to the United States, as noted earlier, has been New York City. But beyond that Puerto Ricans have, for the most part, settled in the populous states of the Northeast and Midwest. Probably the primary reason for this has been that Puerto Ricans, coming from the Caribbean, tend to enter the United States from the east, and New York City is the main entry gate to all migrants and immigrants arriving from the East. In addition, many industries which can offer jobs to incoming migrants are located in these states.

The significance of this trend toward settlement in the Northeast and Midwest, with concentration in the urban areas, is that Puerto Ricans have had to compete with other, larger minorities for available jobs. Several large European immigrant categories, such as the Irish, Polish, and Italians, have shown a similar geographic trend, as have the blacks, who in this century has migrated North from southern states. All of these minorities are much more numerous than the Puerto Rican migrants, which has put the latter at somewhat of a disadvantage. For example, with fewer numbers, Puerto Rican Americans are not as able to organize and demand jobs as are larger minorities.

Figure 1 illustrates the chronological trend of migration to and within the United States. It can be seen that all of the large categories of European immigrants settling in the same geographic areas as the Puerto Ricans arrived many years earlier. Their peak migration years were between 1880 and 1920. Only Americans of African descent are recent

193

The Reports

TABLE 1

STATES WITH LARGEST POPULATION OF PUERTO RICANS
AND PERCENTAGE OF URBAN POPULATION, 1970*

State	Puerto Rican Population	Percentage of Total Puerto Rican Population in the U.S.	Percentage of State Puerto Rican Population Located in Urban Centers
1. New York	878,980	63.2	99.2
2. New Jersey	136,937	9.8	95.9
3. Illinois	88,244	6.3	99.2
4. California	46,955	3.4	96.1
5. Pennsylvania	44,947	3.2	93.6
6. Connecticut	38,493	2.8	97.2
7. Florida	29,588	2.1	92.0
8. Massachusetts	24,561	1.8	96.9
9. Ohio	21,147	1.5	97.2
10. Indiana	9,457	0.7	94.6
TOTAL	1,319,309 1,391,463†		94.8

* Calculated from data in U.S. Bureau of the Census, *U.S. Census of the Population, 1970, Subject Reports, Puerto Ricans in the United States,* Final Report (Washington, D.C.: Government Printing Office, 1973), Table 1.
† Total U.S. population of persons of Puerto Rican birth or parentage.

migrants and can be found in large numbers where Puerto Ricans have settled.

CAUSE OF MIGRATION

According to Lee,[15] factors relating to the cause of migration can be discussed under four headings: (1) factors associated with the area of origin, frequently named "push" factors; (2) factors associated with the area of destination, or "pull" factors; (3) intervening obstacles; and (4) personal factors. In any given migration, factors in all of these areas are probably relevant to a varying degree.[16]

Puerto Rican migration to the mainland has frequently been explained by noting that it has tended to correspond with fluctuations in American business cycles.[17] The causal factors are more complicated than this, however, as Macisco also acknowledges. Another factor was perceived labor shortages in the United States, especially during the Korean War of 1951–1953. An intervening obstacle which was made less burdensome was transportation. Prior to World War II most traffic

194

FIGURE 1

PERCENTAGE OF TOTAL IMMIGRANTS OR MIGRANTS TO THE UNITED STATES
FROM SELECTED COUNTRIES ARRIVING DURING EACH TWENTY-YEAR
PERIOD FROM 1820 TO 1960

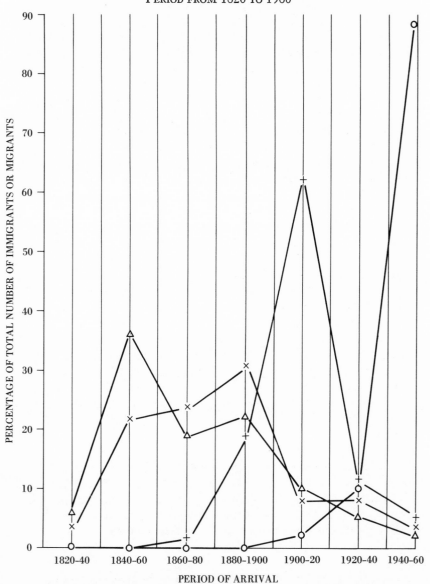

Irish are represented by the symbol (△), Germans by (×), Italians by (+), and Puerto Ricans by (○). The data in this figure are calculated from a compilation of data from U.S. Bureau of the Census, *Historical Statistics of the United States, Colonial Times to 1957* (Washington, D.C.: Government Printing Office, 1960); idem., *Statistical Abstracts of the United States, 1973* (Washington, D.C.: Government Printing Office, 1973).

between the mainland and the island had been by ship, taking several days and resulting in a limitation in the numbers of people who could find passage. During the war this means of transportation stopped almost totally, but after the war it was supplanted by air travel. This took much less time, many flights were made available, and cost was relatively low. Thus an economic lure, whether real or perceived, provided a pull factor, and the availability of low-cost transportation facilitated the migration of Puerto Ricans to the mainland.

Personal factors undoubtedly contribute to Puerto Rican migration as well. Examples of such factors are the young man from the countryside who has heard from others that New York City offers excitement, which may be a sufficient inducement for him, or the young woman who goes to New Jersey to live with or near her older sister, who has previously migrated. It is difficult to distinguish clear patterns of such personal preferences, but they are not insignificant. This may be a fertile area for future research.

Factors relating to conditions on the island have been perhaps even more important in pushing migrants from Puerto Rico toward the potential jobs in the United States. Several characteristics of the migrants themselves are indicative of this.[18] For example, migrants from Puerto Rico tend to be better educated than the Puerto Rican population as a whole, even though they are less well educated than the American population. Half of them have completed at least eight years of schooling, as compared to a median of six years for the population of Puerto Rico in general. The migrants are also relatively young, 83 percent being between the ages of fourteen and forty-four. Nearly two-thirds of them originate from the rural areas of the island. Industrialization in Puerto Rico since World War II has been characterized by a decline in the agricultural sector and a substitution of capital-intensive industries for labor-intensive industries. This has led to a relative stabilization of the participation rate in the labor force. Thus many younger Puerto Ricans, predominantly from rural areas, have found jobs difficult to secure, even if they have obtained an education. These frequently have become migrants. As both these "push" factors and the "pull" factors mentioned above have become operative since the 1940s, Puerto Ricans are relatively recent migrants in the United States.

LATE ARRIVALS

Their late arrival put the Puerto Ricans at a disadvantage, particularly as compared to the European minorities previously mentioned, in that these minorities already had established themselves. The Germans, Irish, Polish, Italians, and others were for the most part of peasant stock and came to the United States with little education at a time when the country was in the process of industrializing. Thus they were able to fill the many unskilled and semi-skilled occupations which were becoming available. As industrial development continued, more skilled and white-collar jobs as well as managerial occupations became available. The immigrants who had taken the unskilled and semiskilled jobs could thus move into these new positions as they received training and experience in their new country. Meanwhile new waves of immigrants kept entering the country, and they in turn could take the positions opening up at the unskilled and semiskilled levels. Thus, because industrialization and immigration were occurring simultaneously, upward mobility became a reality for many of these minorities.

The Immigration Act of 1924, in which quotas were established, put an end to the seemingly limitless immigration from many countries to the United States. Therefore, the more recent migrants, blacks from the South and Puerto Ricans, took the lower-skilled occupations. Many of these assumed that in the North there were opportunities for advancement, as there had been for other minorities previously. However, several variables were not the same.

Puerto Rican migrants, as noted above, have been relatively well-educated Puerto Ricans. Black migrants also have tended to have more years of education than the immigrants who entered the United States around the turn of the century. But both migrant categories still have less education than the native white population. Puerto Rican males and females of age fourteen and over, for example, had a median of 9.5 years of education, or 2.7 years less than the median education for the native white population.[19] Furthermore, years of education may not be a strictly comparable variable between migrants and white native Americans. Certainly the quality of education obtained by blacks as compared to whites, year by year, is open to question. Similarly, many Puerto Rican migrants suffered from poor-quality education. Part of the early policy of the United States government toward administering the territory of Puerto Rico was to "prepare the Puerto Ricans for Statehood as rapidly as possible."[20] The various commissioners of education for Puerto Rico appointed by American presidents understood this to mean that Puerto Rico should become a bilingual territory, if not an English-speaking one, as rapidly as possible. This led to various policies, from making English the primary medium of instruction in all grades in Puerto Rican schools, to making English the language of grades six and beyond.[21] These policies were interchanged and varied every few years until 1937, when Spanish was established as the primary language of the Puerto Rican school system.

During these years teachers were frequently attempting to instruct students in a language neither of them knew, with predictable results.

Therefore, many Puerto Rican migrants to the United States received their "years of education" in a system unable to give the same quality of education provided by many other school systems. Their education accorded them no advantage over earlier immigrants in competing for higher-skilled and higher-paid jobs.

Another factor helped to deny the advantages which the Immigration Act of 1924 had seemed to imply for the Puerto Ricans. After the 1930s the American economy changed rapidly, making the structural conditions for social mobility more difficult to overcome. Automation resulted in the creation of comparatively more skilled and white-collar occupations for which a fairly high level of education became a prerequisite, and those who had taken the unskilled jobs could not move into these occupations on the basis of experience and on-the-job training. Although the European immigrant also brought to the United States a rural background and even less education than the later migrants, his opportunities for social mobility were superior because at the time of his arrival the industrial structure was expanding at all levels. The "last men in," the blacks and the Puerto Ricans, have entered the labor force of a postindustrial mechanized society where advancement to higher positions is more difficult, and no later migrant group is arriving to take their place at the bottom rung of the ladder.

LANGUAGE AND RACE

Still other factors have added to the disadvantages faced by the Puerto Rican migrant attempting to advance in American society. The burdens which changing language policies placed upon the Puerto Rican educational system were noted above. These policies failed to teach much English to the majority of Puerto Ricans, and most of the migrants thus have added difficulty in adjusting to the United States, for language is one of the keys to understanding a new culture. Nonfluency in English also has become a stigma which has kept individuals out of many occupations and prevented them from acquiring higher education. Earlier immigrants had the same language problem, but at that time all the competing immigrant groups lacked fluency in English. The "late arrivals" who provide the major competition for Puerto Ricans are the southern blacks. Language is therefore proportionately a greater handicap for Puerto Ricans in the United States than it had been for other minorities.

Spanish has not been the only factor which has been used as a basis for discrimination against Puerto Ricans. Many are physically distinct from the white majority population in terms of skin color, facial structure, and so on, so racial prejudices contribute to discrimination. Racial differences do not mean the same thing to a Puerto Rican as to a member of American society, as will be noted in more detail. Nonetheless, visibility is another difficulty many of the Puerto Ricans have to face as they attempt to assimilate into the American social structure. For these Puerto Ricans the language handicap, if present, is clearly defined; the visibility handicap is less so, since degrees of visibility are perceived differently by the Puerto Ricans and by the white majority. This difficulty in definition may make race even more of a problem than language for some migrants, as it is harder to confront.

Previously it was noted that Puerto Ricans, as a whole, make up a rather small minority in this country, compared to many of the others. In a democracy where individual votes are counted, paucity in numbers comprises another handicap. Puerto Ricans have been able to generate very little political power and influence outside of their own communities.

The Puerto Rican, therefore, has arrived in numbers and at a time which put him in a position of disadvantage with regard to other minorities in several respects. Although the other minorities have shared some of the characteristics which give the Puerto Ricans this handicap, the combination of these characteristics as they affect him make his adjustment to the social structure of the United States particularly difficult in certain ways.

Adjustment: Trying to Fit Two Cultures Together

Minorities in the United States frequently have unique cultural values which they either brought with them as immigrants from the culture of "the old country," or developed through generations of existence as a minority in this country. The Puerto Ricans are no exception to this, and certain of the cultural values they hold differ from the cultural values of the white majority of the United States.

Not all cultural differences produce conflict. However, some cultural differences held by minorities present handicaps to advancement in the social structure fabricated for the most part by the majority. Certain cultural values brought by the Puerto Rican migrants may be considered such handicaps, to some degree. These values are neither right nor wrong, or rather may be either right or wrong depending upon one's perspective. However, their chief relevance to the Puerto Rican minority rests in whether or not they provide assistance or obstruction to adjustment and social advancement in American society. We shall look at certain important values held by Puerto Ricans which may provide added handicaps to the migrant seeking improvement in his way of life in a new society.

RESPECT

A major value which is noted in most of the literature regarding Puerto Rican culture, and in fact Hispanic or Latin culture in general, is that of *dignidad*, or dignity. This concept has frequently been identified, or perhaps misidentified, usually by non-Puerto Rican or non-Spanish observers, as "a pride which is almost an obsession and which leads frequently to the substitution of fancy for fact."[22] In this light it has been seen as a residual trait of a Spanish culture which was able to create and maintain a vast colonial empire, and has been equated with the stereotype of British arrogance.

In actuality, *dignidad* is closely linked with *respeto*, or respect. This is best described by Lauria,[23] who considers it a ceremonial idiom. Through consideration of respect all Puerto Ricans, regardless of social class or status, are able to display their own sense of human worth and to acknowledge another's. *Respeto* in Puerto Rico is a characteristic of encounters among all people, not just a characteristic of certain individuals. *Una falta de respeto*, a failure to respect, is a serious fault. When quarrels arise between two persons, leading to fighting and even serious violence, one or both of the participants usually place the fault on *una falta de respeto* on the part of the other. Every Puerto Rican has worth as an individual, or *dignidad*, whatever his social standing, and everyone who interacts with him even in the most casual manner must acknowledge this through *respeto*.

As *respeto* consists of a ritual to display honor in social situations, so is there a ritualization of defamation.[24] This is embodied in the word *relajo*, which means joking or kidding. Through *relajo* one may insult another without committing *una falta de respeto*. This situation, however, is always carefully defined. One may never insult another until prior mutual respect has been established. Initiating kidding with another implies taking him into one's confidence, since he may kid back without disrespect. In its most elaborate form this leads to a contest of insults in which each participant uses stronger and stronger insults until one of them withdraws. By withdrawing one loses, but maintains his respect. *Una falta de respeto* occurs only if the loser withdraws with hostility, or the winner persists with insults after the other's withdrawal.

With these ritualizations the Puerto Rican is able to maintain his sense of self-worth in all social situations. These concepts are carried with him when he migrates, and are functional to some degree within the Puerto Rican American community. This is illustrated by two passages in Piri Thomas' autobiography of the son of Puerto Rican migrants growing up on the streets of New York City. The first of these concerns his meeting with a street gang when his family had moved to a new neighborhood during his early adolescence. When he realized he would have to fight he quickly brought up a question of personal dignity, in the knowledge that the leader of the gang would fight him fairly and single-handedly before the rest of the gang, all being Puerto Ricans, or commit *una falta de respeto*.[25] In the second instance, Thomas at age seventeen pushes a black acquaintance into a "joking contest," termed "dozens" on the streets of New York, to see how far he may safely go before questioning the other seriously regarding problems of race. He is confident that the other will indicate his limits prior to terminating the discussion completely.[26]

This cultural value of respect may work the wrong way for the Puerto Rican in American society in certain situations. Respect in Puerto Rico is a quality accredited to every individual, whatever his position or accomplishments. In American society, however, respect is much more closely linked to achievement and esteem. One must earn the respect of others before one is entitled to it. Therefore many Americans often act toward strangers in a manner which would be considered by a Puerto Rican *una falta de respeto*. Similarly, joking and kidding by Americans need not follow a clearly indicated mutual sharing of respect, and this, too, could be misinterpreted by the migrant. The rituals of *respeto* and *relajo* permit the individual to demonstrate his self-worth and maintain his dignity. If these rituals are violated and no substitution is offered, dignity is impaired and one's self-esteem may be damaged. Therefore these cultural values may have psychological consequences for the migrant.

FAMILY SIZE

Attitudes toward the family form an important part of Puerto Rican culture. Several aspects of these attitudes are also relevant to the success or failure of migrants in adjusting to American society. One example of this relevance is illustrated in attitudes regarding family size. Puerto Ricans, both in the United States and Puerto Rico, tend to have large families. Census data for 1970 shows that the average family size among Puerto Ricans living in the United States at that time was 4.1, as compared to the national average of 3.5.[27] This increased family size is a significant economic burden.

The reasons for large family size among Puerto Ricans are not known for certain. The Roman Catholic church is the predominant institution in Puerto Rico as in other Spanish societies, but the degree of influence wielded by the church on the attitudes of the people is probably less here than in many other Catholic societies, such as the Irish or the Italian. Studies in Puerto Rico have led to the conclusion that church influence on family size is minimal.[28] *Machismo*, the Latin male ideal of masculinity, has also been proposed as an explanation for this phenomenon, and there is some data which indirectly supports this possibility. However, Stycos,[29] who has studied the question in Puerto Rico in detail, concludes that the major problem is lack of communication between husband and wife. The wife bears more children, assuming this is what the husband wants but never questioning directly, with the frequent result that a larger family is produced than either intended. Whatever the reason for them, larger families may well be an economic handicap for the Puerto Rican American.

FAMILY RELATIONSHIPS

Three themes regarding family interrelationships which appear to be prevalent in Spanish and Latin cultures may be a source for conflicts arising later in the lives of children raised in these cultures. In a study among college students in Puerto Rico[30] it was found that these themes are still strongly held in Puerto Rican culture.[31] The themes are as follows: (1) the mother is so much the family affectional figure that later in life the son's devotion to his mother may interfere with the devotion shown to his own wife; (2) the father is the authority figure, and strong emphasis is placed upon children learning to be submissive and obedient to his dictates; and (3) there is a sexually based dichotomous set of cultural expectations with regard to children, boys being accorded higher status and given more freedom than girls.

The first of these values is unlikely to have a different effect upon migrant families or Puerto Ricans living in the United States than it does upon families living in Puerto Rico. There are no studies on the impact of migration upon this theme. It could be assumed that all values which are part of the Latin culture would weaken with successive generations of the descendants of migrants as they accept more of the cultural values of the host society over those of their parents. However, the specific effect of the first of these three themes on new migrants probably does not impose any additional psychological handicap.

Consideration of the father as an almost absolute authority figure within the family structure does have an effect on the Puerto Rican migrant. The male Puerto Rican adult must maintain his authority in demonstrable fashion by providing for his family. If his ability to do this is impaired, his ability to assert his authority is also impaired. There are two factors which might well weaken the ability of the Puerto Rican American man to maintain his authority. First, if his wife or children refuse to accept his authority, there are fewer sanctions against them in the society in which they now live than there would be if they lived in Puerto Rico.[32] This is particularly true regarding personnel connected with social services, since these personnel are more likely to be non-Puerto Rican and therefore to have less understanding for Latin cultural values. The second factor lies in the different employment opportunities open for men and women in the United States. Unemployment figures for Puerto Ricans in New York City have consistently been higher than for other minority groups in the city, and for female Puerto Ricans they are slightly higher than for males. Yet since 1950 there has been a trend of increasing improvement in the status of women's occupations relative to men of the same age.[33] As women are able to find positions of higher status than their husbands, it becomes more and more difficult for their husbands to maintain absolute authority in the house. These two factors make it increasingly arduous for the Puerto Rican male migrant to maintain the cultural role assigned to him, adding possible stresses to his efforts to adjust to a new society.

The third of these themes found in family relationships consists of the double standards applied to the raising of children. In Puerto Rico boys are given great freedom. They are taught to respect and obey their fathers and *machismo* (masculinity) is frequently stressed, but their upbringing is reasonably unrestricted. Girls, on the other hand, are quite closely supervised. Virginity is highly prized, so when girls are out of the house they are chaperoned, and their upbringing is rather restricted.

These patterns of socialization frequently cause problems for both parents and their children when the family migrates. Boys in the majority culture of the United States are taught values such as self-reliance, aggression, and competition. These values are reinforced by the *machismo* value in the Latin culture, but there is little emphasis on the other Latin values of parental obedience and devotion toward one's mother. Therefore Puerto Rican boys on the streets of large cities in the United States tend to be excessively oriented to *machismo* and less inclined to give their parents what the parents consider to be proper deference.[34] This leads to two frequent reactions on the part of the parents.[35] One is to attempt to place the responsibility for the child's care on the state, claiming that the government prevents proper disciplining. More frequently. however, parents respond by oversupervising and overprotecting their sons, which leads to increasing psychological problems for these sons as they reach adulthood.[36]

To supervise his daughters in the way his cultural value dictates recommend, the Puerto Rican parent must virtually keep them in the house when they are not at school, as he cannot trust non-Puerto Rican members of the community to chaperone them properly. This excessive restriction causes stress for the daughters. In Puerto Rico girls tend to marry early, as this is one of the ways in which they can escape the restrictions of their upbringing. For girls of migrant families, however, the strict supervision tends to make early marriages less frequent, and girls stay with their parents for longer periods.[37] Of the six girls interviewed by Cooper,[38] none had married before the age of twenty, although a majority are married by this age in Puerto Rico.

Family structure is also disturbed by migration to the United States, and this, too, can have consequences for the Puerto Rican migrant. In Puerto Rico family relationships are very close, and the family will often function as an extended family even if they do not live in the same house. Usually there are several female family members available to help care for the children, since male family members participate very little in child care. After migration, however, other family members are not always nearby and the mother usually has to raise her children alone.[39] Puerto Rican women in the United States have less of a tendency to seek work than women of other minority groups.[40] Whether or not this is a consequence of their need to spend more time on child care is not known.

One cultural value related to the extended family which affects adjustment of the Puerto Rican to American society is the concept of *personalismo*, or personalism, most thoroughly analyzed by Cochran.[41] He points out that since life is organized among Puerto Ricans on a family basis, they prefer informal arrangements and personal contacts to formal channels and group decisions.[42] These preferences are a handicap to the Puerto Rican in the more formal, impersonal American industrial society.

RACIAL ATTITUDES

One area which represents a marked contrast between Puerto Rican cultural values and those of the United States is that of race. The population of Puerto Rico is racially mixed, but the marked racial discrimination evident in the United States is not present on the island, or at least is not manifested in the same form. It has been fashionable to claim the Puerto Rican has no color problem, but that is not so. Puerto Ricans are very aware of shades of color among themselves, and racial discrimination, although very mild, is widespread throughout island culture.[43] Padilla[44] has noted eight different terms which Puerto Ricans use to denote color. As shown in Table 2, when Puerto Ricans were separated by mainlanders into three categories, white, mixed, and Negro, and then asked the terms they would use to refer to themselves and to other members of the groups, three terms were applied to some individuals from each of the categories. Three were used to denote individuals from both the mixed and Negro categories, and only two were used specifically for members of a single category, the white. Therefore, it can be seen that racial categories are blurred for the Puerto Rican. As Fitzpatrick[45] describes it, "In the United States, a man's color deter-

TABLE 2
TERMS USED BY PUERTO RICANS TO DENOTE COLOR

References of Outgroup	References of Ingroup	References of Individuals Describing Self
White	White	White
	Trigueño Hispano	Hispano
	Grifo	Trigueño
*INTERMEDIATES**		
Puerto Rican or "Mixed"	Negro	De Color (of color)
	Trigueño	Trigueño
	Indio	Hispano
	Grifo	Indio
	Hispano	
Negro	Negro	De Color (of color)
	Trigueño	Trigueño
	Indio	Hispano
	Grifo	Indio
	Hispano	

SOURCE: Elena Padilla, *Up from Puerto Rico* (New York: Columbia University Press, 1958), p. 76.

* A category to include the numerous racial terms used by Puerto Ricans introduced by C. Wright Mills, Clarence Senior, and Rose K. Golden, *The Puerto Rican Journey* (New York: Harper & Row, 1950).

mines what class he belongs to; in Puerto Rico, a man's class determines what color he is."

Racial attitudes in the United States cause marked problems for the Puerto Rican migrant. The plight of the black American is quickly observed by him, and so he does not want to be identified as black. The race problem poses one of the most difficult adjustments for the Puerto Rican. In an early study[46] it was recognized that this burden was particularly severe on the brown or mixed Puerto Rican, as he felt a strong need to prove in a black-or-white society that he was not black. Therefore he emphasized instead that he was Puerto Rican, and delayed adjustment to American society. That this situation is still prevalent is illustrated again in Piri Thomas' autobiography,[47] for he was mixed, and experienced these same problems. The black Puerto Ricans and the white Puerto Ricans have an easier adjustment.

IDENTITY

Does the Puerto Rican migrant identify himself as a Puerto Rican? Few studies have attempted to answer this question in a very scientific, systematic fashion. Padilla[48] made some systematic observations regarding New York Puerto Ricans. Most other studies of Puerto Rican identity tend to be descriptive and rather politically oriented, so they are less concerned with how Puerto Rican Americans identify themselves than with how various authors think Puerto Rican Americans should identify themselves.

Padilla[49] notes that Puerto Ricans in the United States identify strongly as a Spanish group, referring to themselves as "Hispanos." This identity buffers the change faced by the migrants; they don't have to become "Americans"[50] immediately, but can continue to identify with the culture they have left. On the other hand this delays, if not hinders, assimilation into their new society.

Perhaps the most interesting of Padilla's observations are those regarding the Puerto Rican migrants' evaluations of other peoples in the United States, as well as the evaluations of Puerto Ricans by these peoples. The author, who studied Puerto Ricans in New York, reports that white Anglo-Saxons and Italian immigrants are accorded high status by all Puerto Ricans; other European immigrants, Jews, and Cubans are accorded high status by Puerto Ricans raised in New York and low status by recent migrants; and blacks are given a low status by recent migrants, and a slightly higher status by second-generation Puerto Rican Americans. All these categories except the Cubans accorded the recent Puerto Rican migrants low status, but accorded high status to second-generation Puerto Rican Americans.

Several facts should be kept in mind while considering these results. The data for this study were gathered in the mid-1950s, and many events which have occurred since then may have changed the attitudes reported by Padilla. For example, the Cubans and Puerto Ricans view each other differently than they did before the Cuban revolution, as many upper- and middle-class Cubans emigrated from their country for political or other reasons, changing the character and size of Cuban immigrant minorities elsewhere. Second, the major Puerto Rican migration occurred since World War II, thereby increasing greatly the size of the Puerto Rican minority in the United States. Third, there has been a change in the way minorities see themselves in the United States since the 1950s, or at least there has been agitation for such change. Therefore the generally negative identity which Puerto Rican Americans tend to give themselves, as Padilla's results were interpreted to show a decade later,[51] may be inaccurate. Several writers have indicated reasons for such a negative identity. Some claim it to be the result of a long period of submission to colonization on the part of the Puerto Ricans, first to Spain and then to the United States.[52] As was pointed out earlier, however, the status of Puerto Rico is somewhat ambiguous. Though it manifests some characteristics of a colony, to equate it with such and to thus equate attitudes, identities, and stereotypes of Puerto Ricans with the characterizing colonized peoples is probably somewhat simplistic and would not apply to the minority as a whole. Hernandez Alvarez[53] suggests that Puerto Rican migrants may accept a chronically inferior position in American society in return for the immediate benefits this society awards through welfare for the poor.

Such conclusions are hardly justified at the present time, however, for many Puerto Rican migrants. The negativity of their self-assessment is increasingly open to question. As no recent study has been made, we can only note certain generalizations and leave specific conclusions to future studies.

Puerto Rican Americans identify themselves as Puerto Ricans, as distinct from Americans, Latins, blacks, whites, and so on. As was pointed out in the previous section, for some Puerto Ricans this is an alternative to racial identity. It does not take a migrant long to realize that it is not advantageous to be identified as nonwhite, and since, particularly for recent arrivals, racial distinction is blurred, identity as a Puerto Rican is more real, less problematic, and more acceptable. When they are forced into a racial identity, as in the United States Census, where no provision in the questionnaire permits them to identify as Puerto Ricans, more and more are identifying as white. In 1970, 93 percent of all Puerto Rican Americans did so.[54]

Movements have developed and progressed during the past several years to encourage minority members, especially younger individuals, to identify themselves and learn more about their particular history and culture. Programs of Puerto Rican studies, such as those offered at the City Colleges of New York and Rutgers University, provide a Puerto Rican orientation. The Puerto Rican American can learn about Puerto Rican culture and history and be better able to identify himself as a Puerto Rican because it is his heritage, not only because it offers him an escape from racial identification.

Results: Evidence for Success or Survival in the New Society

For the most part, increasing socioeconomic status is the desirable result of migration, so success, in this context, means socioeconomic success. Three commonly used parameters of such success are educational achievement, occupational skill level, and income. These are the measurements by which we shall judge the success of the Puerto Rican migrants.

Occupational skill and income should correlate with the length of time migrants have been in the United States. Supporting data, however, are very difficult to find, since studies obtaining the parameters have not included length of stay. Such data have been collected for migrants who returned to Puerto Rico to live,[55] but since these are return migrants the data do not necessarily apply to Puerto Ricans on the mainland.

All three parameters should increase with each successive generation of Puerto Ricans in the United States. There are data to measure this increase, with two limitations. It is difficult to identify third-generation Puerto Rican Americans (children of United States-born Puerto Ricans) because, since their parents were born in the United States as well, they frequently identify themselves as Americans. Second, Puerto Ricans have been arriving in large numbers just since World War II, so many of the second generation have not yet entered the labor market, and numbers of persons measured are therefore low for these parameters. However, even within these limitations, data can be found which allow an examination of the question of whether the Puerto Rican Americans are succeeding socioeconomically.

EDUCATION

Educational achievement for the Puerto Rican in the United States gives a baseline for assessing performance. One of the most comprehensive studies of the educational achievement of American minorities is the "Coleman Report."[56] No distinction is made in the report among generations or among birthplaces, so no conclusions can be reached as to whether a given minority is improving or not, but the basic educational achievement of each minority studied can be examined. For the Puerto Rican American the picture is not good. In achievement testing, Puerto Ricans scored lower than all other minority groups, except for blacks. However, Puerto Ricans are most plentiful in the Northeast and Midwest, and when the blacks of these regions are studied separately from other blacks, their achievement test scores are also higher than those of Puerto Ricans.[57] On the verbal ability and reading comprehension portions of the tests Puerto Rican Americans scored significantly lower than any other minority, including the other Spanish-speaking one, the Chicanos.[58] Puerto Rican students showed the greatest differences in performance in between-school comparisons of any minority, suggesting that they were the most poorly prepared students of any minority when they entered school.[59] But perhaps the grimmest statistic of all concerned motivation, which was illustrated by answers to two questions. Sixteen percent of the twelfth-grade Puerto Rican students stated they would quit before finishing high school if a family problem arose, three times as many as the next closest category, the Chicanos, and 13 percent indicated that they were totally unconcerned with how well they performed scholastically, as compared to 5 percent of the Chicanos, who were again the closest group.[60]

What do these statistics mean? It is simple to blame the Puerto Ricans' poor performances in the achievement tests on Spanish, but the performances of the Chicanos, with a similar language background, lead to the conclusion that this explanation is not sufficient. Achievement tests are sometimes criticized for not being culture-free. But the fact that they are culture-bound makes them better estimators of the degree to which the tested minority students are succeeding in the host culture. Judging by achievement test results, the Puerto Ricans are not succeeding too well. Perhaps this is related to the fact that they are the least prepared for school of any minority students. For the most part they have arrived in the country more recently than have Mexican Americans. This combination of recent arrival and nonfluency in English may explain both the poor results in achievement testing and lack of preparedness for school.

The questions regarding motivation suggest that the Puerto Rican students vary markedly from other minority groups in their low concern about their performance. These responses reflect a greater orientation toward the family and informal group interactions as compared to formal organizations. However, they display a motivational handicap in a society where success and competition are valued highly.

The data from the "Coleman Report" refer to students from various minorities, but make no attempt to differentiate between first and second-generation migrants, so no information is provided as to whether successive generations are improving, or at what rate. Two studies have been made which provide such information. Macisco[61] has compared Puerto Ricans born in Puerto Rico (first generation) with those born in the United States (second generation), and then compared both of these categories with the total American population. Kantrowitz[62] has compared Puerto Ricans born and raised in New York with the non-Puerto Rican white population of New York City, studying these groups in 1950 and also in 1960 to note rates of change over time. Therefore we have two perspectives on the success of Puerto Rican migrants in moving upward in American society.

Educationally, the Puerto Ricans appear to be improving. Macisco[63] has found that the median years of education completed for first-generation Puerto Rican migrants between ages twenty-five and thirty-four are 8.0 for males and 7.2 for females. For second-generation migrants the median figures for these same age groups are 10.0 for the males and 10.3 for the females. The median for the American population of these ages is 12.2 for both sexes. Thus Puerto Rican migrants are progressing, but they have not yet achieved the educational levels of the host population. The data presented by Kantrowitz[64] support this conclusion. He notes that the percentage increase in 1960 over 1950 in numbers of students completing any given level of education is similar in both New York Puerto Ricans and non-Puerto Rican whites. However, the actual percentage of New York Puerto Ricans completing any given level of schooling is much less in either year than the percentage of whites. Therefore, although the Puerto Ricans are becoming better educated, it is at the same rate as the white majority, so they are improving without really catching up.

SKILLS

Regarding occupational skills, the unemployment rate for first-generation Puerto Ricans is approximately twice that for the general population among both males and females.[65] For second-generation migrants it is about midway between the general population and first generation for the males, but the unemployment rate for second-generation females is much closer to that of the general population than that of first-generation females. Kantrowitz[66] has studied this issue from a different perspective. In white collar jobs in 1950, he notes that Puerto Ricans held fewer managerial positions with regard to their educational levels than other whites but the same or more professional and clerical positions. In the blue-collar jobs they held fewer foremen's positions but more service positions. The percentage increase of Puerto Ricans in each of these categories in 1960 over 1950 was approximately the same for Puerto Ricans as for whites, but by 1960 the differences between Puerto Ricans and whites in absolute numbers had been magnified. Again, data regarding employment rates and occupational skill levels suggest that the Puerto Rican migrants are improving, with females perhaps improving their positions at a greater rate than males. However, their rate of improvement is insufficient to enable them to catch up with the majority population.

INCOME

Data regarding income show that, as with education, Puerto Rican migrants are behind most other minorities in the United States.[67] The median income of all American families in 1973 was $12,050, for all of the American Spanish-speaking population $8,720, and for Puerto Rican American families $6,780. The impact of these figures is magnified when it is remembered that Puerto Rican families are larger than average, so the differences in per capita income are even larger. Macisco[68] has again found an increase in income of second-generation Puerto Rican wage earners as compared to the first generation, but the national average is higher than either. Kantrowitz[69] has only limited data on income, but his conclusions are again that, although Puerto Ricans showed some improvement between 1950 and 1960, non-Puerto Rican whites have increased their incomes at the same or more rapid rates.

Socioeconomically, therefore, migrants from Puerto Rico have been improving their positions over time, but they are not catching up to the general population. If they have "succeeded" as migrants, their success is qualified.

Solutions: Four Alternatives to Assimilation

The evidence just presented leads to the conclusion that a large percentage of the Puerto Rican minority is not succeeding in the attempt to assimilate to the host culture. Those who are successful become indistinguishable from the majority and cannot be identified as members of the minority. Others are actively seeking alternatives to assimilation, either because they do not think assimilation will be successful, or because they are unwilling to make the changes necessary for assimilation. Some of these alternatives will be discussed in this section, but those who are seeking them are perhaps only a small portion of all Puerto Rican Americans. Many of the migrants are probably not trying to assimilate and are not actively seeking an alternative, but instead have given up, leaving any success to be found by a later generation. It is difficult to determine what segment of the population shares this characteristic. The only behavioral characteristic specifically representative of giving up is return migration to Puerto Rico, but probably a large number of Puerto Ricans who have given up do not return to the island. In any event, the alternatives discussed below cannot be assumed to be relevant to all Puerto Rican Americans.

POLITICAL SOLUTIONS

Through political power members of a minority can improve their status by influencing policy decisions which will favor them. Because Puerto Ricans are American citizens by birth, they can vote as soon as they establish residence on the mainland, so it could be assumed that they would attain political power in proportion to their population more quickly than immigrants from other countries have done. This, however, has not been the case. Part of the problem has been that the migrants have scattered to small communities in many urban areas, and the communities themselves are not of sufficient size to confer political power. Even in New York City, where the largest Puerto Rican population is located, the migrants are underrepresented. As recently as 1970 they had no elected representatives in the city government, despite the fact that they made up more than one-tenth of the population.[70] Gerrymandering at all levels can succeed in keeping minority representation low, but Puerto Rican representation is even lower than would be expected from gerrymandering. The Puerto Rican population is younger on the average than other minority groups, but even so, it is estimated that fewer than 35 percent of eligible Puerto Ricans in New York were registered to vote in 1970.[71] Although this political alternative is theoretically open to them, Puerto Rican Americans do not appear to be taking advantage of it.

REVOLUTIONARY SOLUTIONS

One alternative is prompted by the lack of success of other means. During the 1960s several minority political action groups arose, perhaps the best known being the Black Panther party. Some of these groups emanated from what essentially had been street gangs in the cities. Among these was the Young Lords party, an organization which arose in Chicago from the Young Lords gang, and made up largely of Puerto Ricans from the local community. In 1969 the Young Lords Organization, New York State Chapter, was formed from the merging of several small groups of Puerto Rican youth. Both youth from the streets and Puerto Rican students were represented in the organization.[72]

The Young Lords Organization has been active in programs such as free breakfasts, TB and lead-poisoning detection, and free health clinics, aimed to provide needed services for Puerto Rican Americans. Many programs of a more political nature have also been instituted, such as rallies, marches, political education classes, and taking over a church and a hospital. The Young Lords Organization is primarily revolutionary, with a political platform calling for Puerto Rican independence and socialism. It cannot help the Puerto Rican to assimilate into and succeed in American society, as its political energies are aimed toward radically changing the society. Yet revolution is one approach toward changing a system which cannot be overcome. However, such revolutionary organizations do not at present appear to have widespread support among Puerto Rican Americans, and are unlikely to be successful, at least in the near future.

VOLUNTARY ORGANIZATIONS

Voluntary organizations have arisen among many minority peoples as a way for them to help each other and to provide services which are not otherwise easy for them to obtain. These organizations come into being in response to specific needs within the various minorities, and survive to the extent that they answer to the needs they were conceived to fulfill. Such organizations have been of benefit to the Puerto Rican minority.

That such action groups arise among Puerto Ricans in the United States is somewhat surprising. Rogler[73] notes several reasons for this surprise. First, Puerto Rican culture has little tradition of civic involvement through organized groups. Second, political machines in most cities attempt to subvert such organizations for political purposes. Third, unassimilated migrants tend to hold to the belief that partisan politics minutely governs the structure of local agencies. In other words, Puerto Rican Americans tend to see formal organizational assistance as controlled by the established political system, and look for personal assistance to more personal, less formal systems, such as extended family connections or patrons. In a detailed study of the formation of one such action group, Rogler[74] noted two primary reasons for its success: its members kept out of any established political structure and rightly refused to permit the organization to perform any political functions, and the organization was not used to give specific help in individual cases, but instead worked with established services to make them more adaptable to Puerto Rican needs and more sensitive to Puerto Rican outlooks. By maintaining a separation from the established political power systems, and utilizing a more formal, impersonal approach, these organizations are able to be of service to Puerto Rican migrants. If they joined the political structure, they would probably be controlled or dominated by nonminority interests; if they tried to offer specific, personal help, their resources would soon be exhausted.

Not all of these organizations are small, community-based action groups. Some large organizations service Puerto Rican communities in many locations in the United States. Examples are the Puerto Rican Family Institute, which attempts to make available professional social services, and perhaps the most successful one, ASPIRA, which promotes higher education for Puerto Rican Americans. These organizations, while operating on a much larger scale, still maintain the characteristics of the small community organizations: they remain nonpolitical and they seek to help Puerto Rican migrants acquire more benefits from already established educational and social services, rather than attempting to provide these specific services.

The existence and success of these organizations are in themselves evidence of the inability of Puerto Ricans to assimilate to American society. They have only been successful to the extent that they have remained separated from the established power structures and have focused on Puerto Rican problems and the Puerto Rican communities.

If Puerto Ricans were indistinguishable from the rest of the society in which they live, they would not have use for organizations characterized by these particular distinctions.

RETURN MIGRATION

The fourth alternative to assimilation is to give up and go home. That this alternative is chosen by a significant number of Puerto Rican migrants is shown by the rate of return migration to Puerto Rico from the United States. Certainly the number is large, although return migrants to Puerto Rico are as difficult to count as Puerto Rican migrants to the United States. Surveys of all passengers arriving and leaving Puerto Rico by plane have shown that in 1969, 1972, and 1973 more passengers arrived than left; the figure in 1972 was almost forty-two thousand excess arrivals.[75] This suggests considerable return migration. In April 1972 the Puerto Rican Planning Board[76] surveyed all persons living in Puerto Rico who were born there. Return migrants were considered to be persons who had lived in the United States for at least three consecutive months at some time in the past. By these criteria it was discovered that almost 30 percent of all males between the ages of twenty and fifty-four were return migrants, as were almost 20 percent of all females between the same ages. Although these figures attest to the numerical significance of return migration, they do not tell us what percentage of Puerto Rican Americans return to the island to live, nor do they include information about second-generation Puerto Rican Americans who may migrate to Puerto Rico. These figures also include Puerto Rican Americans who might have been visiting Puerto Rico briefly in April 1972 but had no intention of staying, and therefore can hardly be classified as return migrants. Between 1952 and 1961, 31 percent as many children were transferred from schools in the United States to Puerto Rican schools as were transferred in the opposite direction.[77] This suggests that perhaps nearly a third of Puerto Rican migrants returned, although since most of the migrants are single males (or males without their families) data regarding school transfers are somewhat indirect and may not give an accurate representation of true return migration.

Return migration does not necessarily represent only those Puerto Rican Americans who have either given up on or rejected assimilation to American society. Many return migrants have improved their education and skills with relation to the overall island population. Hernandez Alvarez[78] has observed that "return migration is selective of the occupational elite of the Puerto Rican migrant population." Many migrants perhaps return for reasons similar to those for which they originally migrated—economic opportunities now appear better on the island.

Others may return to their families after having improved their education and increased their savings.

However, although education and skills of the return migrant may be higher than those for the nonmigrant, his job level in the Puerto Rican labor force is not higher, and unemployment rates for return migrants are significantly higher than for the general population.[79] Occupational level increases and unemployment rates decrease the longer the return migrant remains in Puerto Rico. This phenomenon has been explained by the finding that many return migrants display a "voluntary job instability," not taking a job in Puerto Rico or taking one temporarily of low skill because they remigrate to the United States shortly after they have returned.[80] Most return migrants to Puerto Rico, therefore, remigrate.

This finding suggests an intriguing possibility. Return migration may not be a manifestation of giving up on assimilation. It may instead be a manifestation of back-and-forth migration made possible by the ease of obtaining transportation between Puerto Rico and the United States and the absence of a national border to be crossed.

Studies of migration patterns in West Africa have shown evidence of a similar situation there.[81] Most rural households in northern Ghana have sent at least one of their members as a migrant to a large town in the south. The migrants send back money and gifts to their relatives who remain in the rural areas, and frequently return for visits. These rural-urban migrants do not assimilate fully to urban society, but remain an extension of the rural family, although they must take on some of the characteristics of the urban dweller. This pattern of migration is so prevalent in West Africa that 80 percent of income tax paid in the western Niger territories is paid from money sent back by migrants to the towns of Ghana and the Ivory Coast.[82]

A FIFTH ALTERNATIVE

This may then be a fifth alternative to assimilation for the Puerto Rican American. Most Puerto Ricans have relatives living in the United States, and most Puerto Rican Americans have relatives on the island. Many Puerto Rican American communities have social organizations formed by people originating from a given town on the island, and links between these groups and their town of origin remain strong. Some migrants may therefore represent extensions of their extended families or Puerto Rican communities migrating temporarily, seasonally, or intermittently to the United States. For these migrants the goal would be transplantation rather than assimilation; they represent an attempt by some segment of Puerto Rican society to share directly in the economic advantages of American society.

215

Whether this pattern accounts for a significant proportion of Puerto Rican migration requires further research to discover. The possibility is only suggested by the data presently available, but the implications of such a possibility are widespread. Migrants whose purpose is to act as an extension of their family or community, rather than reestablish themselves in a society with greater opportunities, must be judged on a different scale than we have been using. The longer such migrants remain in the United States, the more likely they would be to take on characteristics of American society. But their goal would not be assimilation, so success for them cannot be measured with regard to whether and to what degree they have assimilated. Their achievement should be measured against the norm for the society to which they belong, that of Puerto Rico, rather than the norm for the society in which they live, that of the United States. It is probably more relevant to compare them with Puerto Rican nonmigrants than with New York blacks.

Migrants or immigrants to or within the United States have been popularly considered to be in search of fulfillment of the "American dream," whatever that is, and their success or failure in this achievement has been measured in comparison with the national average or with competing migrants or immigrants. As we have seen, such comparative statistics paint a rather grim picture for the Puerto Rican, and it does not appear to be improving over time. But perhaps we are using the wrong statistics. The Puerto Rican who returns to the island is more skilled and better educated than the one who never leaves. Therefore the Puerto Rican American may be attempting not to fulfill the "American dream," but rather to extend a Puerto Rican experience beyond the boundaries of his island. With respect to this goal, he may well be successful.

NOTES

1. This designation was used publicly by President Ford as recently as August 24, 1974, one week after he received a letter from Puerto Rican Resident Commissioner Benitez protesting his earlier use of the phrase. The letter had been publicized to Puerto Ricans.

2. An example of this is the distinguished text by Samuel Eliot Morrison, *Oxford History of the American People* (New York: Oxford University Press, 1965), which equates the present relationship between the United States and Puerto Rico to that between Great Britain and Canada.

3. Lidio Cruz Monclova, "The Puerto Rican Political Movement in the 19th Century," in *Status of Puerto Rico: Selected Background Studies Prepared for the United States-Puerto Rico Commission on the Status of Puerto Rico* (Washington, D.C.: Government Printing Office 1966), p. 12.

4. Steward et al., *The People of Puerto Rico* (Urban: University of Illinois Press, 1956), pp. 41–42, note that the Spanish colonists used many Indians and even a few white slaves in the West Indies, as well as Africans. This practice contributed to the eventual broad racial mix on the island.

5. Cruz Monclova, "Puerto Rican Political Movement."

6. This concept is supported in detail in ibid., pp. 15–17.

7. Steward et al., *People of Puerto Rico*, pp. 62–78, discuss the degree to which Puerto Rican agriculture was controlled by absentee owners living in the United States, and the dependence of the Puerto Rican economy on the American economy.

8. The official title in Spanish is *Estado Libre Asociado*, or Free Associated States. The relationship between Puerto Rico and the United States is closer than that among members of the British Commonwealth, and more free than for the Commonwealths of Massachusetts or Pennsylvania, for example.

9. These figures were taken from U.S. Bureau of the Census, *U.S. Census of the Population, 1960, Subject Reports, Puerto Ricans in the United States, Final Report* (Washington, D.C.: Government Printing Office, 1963), p. viii, Table A.

10. U.S. Commission on Civil Rights, *Counting the Forgotten: The 1970 Census. Count of Persons of Spanish-Speaking Background in the United States* (Washington, D.C.: Government Printing Office, 1974).

11. U.S. Bureau of the Census, *Statistical Abstracts of the United States 1973* (Washington, D.C.: Government Printing Office, 1973).

12. This figure was compiled from data given in U.S. Bureau of the Census, *Historical Statistics of the United States, Colonial Times to 1957* (Washington, D.C.: Government Printing Office, 1960), and U.S. Bureau of the Census, *Statistical Abstracts*, Table 143, p. 95.

13. U.S. Bureau of the Census, *Statistical Abstracts*.

14. Ibid., p. 792.

15. Everett S. Lee, "A Theory of Migration," *Demography* 3 (1966): 47–57.

16. A similar "push-pull" migration factor is reported for black Americans by Jackson in his report on Afro-Americans in this book (pp. 133–64). There, of course, the migration is between the North and the South.

17. John J. Macisco, Jr., "Assimilation of Puerto Ricans on the Mainland: A Socio-Demographic Approach," *International Migration Review* 2 (1968): 21–39.

18. This conclusion is proposed in "Puerto Rican Migration: A Preliminary Report," mimeographed report prepared for the U.S. Civil Rights Commission by the Puerto Rican Research and Resources Center, Inc., on January 31, 1972. The figures presented are quoted by them from the *Report on Human Resources to the Governor, 1970,* by the Puerto Rican Planning Board.

19. U.S. Commission on Civil Rights, *Counting the Forgotten*, and U.S. Bureau of the Census, *Statistical Abstracts*, p. 115.

20. Ismael Rodriguez Bou, "Significant Factors in the Development of Education in Puerto Rico," in *Status of Puerto Rico*, pp. 147–314.

21. The nature of the impact of these policies are outlined in ibid. and discussed in much fuller detail by Aida Negron de Montilla, *Americanization in Puerto Rico and the Public School System 1900–1930* (Rio Piedras: Editorial Edil, 1970).

22. Regford Guy Tugwell, *The Stricken Land; The Story of Puerto Rico* (Garden City, N.Y.: Doubleday, 1947).

23. Anthony Lauria, Jr., " 'Respeto,' 'Relajo,' and Inter-Personal Relations in Puerto Rico," *Anthropological Quarterly* 37 (1964): 53–67.

24. Ibid.

25. Piri Thomas, *Down These Mean Streets* (New York: Knopf, 1967), pp. 57–58.

26. Ibid., p. 123.

27. U.S. Bureau of the Census, *Statistical Abstracts*.

28. J. Mayone Stycos, "Family and Fertility in Puerto Rico," *American Sociological Review* 17 (1952): 572–80.

29. Ibid.

30. Ramon Fernández-Marina et al., "Three Basic Themes in Mexican and Puerto Rican Family Values," *Journal of Social Psychology* 48 (1958): 167–81.

31. It should be noted that the study referred to was of the students of two freshman courses at the University of Puerto Rico, so the sample can hardly be considered representative of the population of Puerto Rico as a whole. These themes are dis-

The Reports

cussed here, however, because some variation of them is discussed in practically all the general literature regarding Puerto Rican Americans, even though there are very few available studies which document them specifically. Similar characterizations of familial interrelationships can be found in other cultures, and many investigators consider them to be more closely related to socioeconomic level than to a specific culture. See Oscar Lewis, *La Vida: A Puerto Rican Family in the Culture of Poverty— San Juan and New York* (New York: Random House, 1965). These cultural values may therefore be more relevant to lower-class migrants than to a specifically "Puerto Rican" or even "Latin" culture.

32. Nathan Glazer and Daniel Patrick Moynihan, *Beyond the Melting Pot: The Negros, Puerto Ricans, Jews, Italians and Irish of New York City* (Cambridge Mass.: M.I.T. Press, 1963).

33. This is documented in the previously cited mimeographed report, "Puerto Rican Migration: A Preliminary Report," p. 39.

34. The degree of this orientation is illustrated by Paulette Cooper, *Growing Up Puerto Rican* (New York: Arbor House, 1972). She interviewed seventeen young Puerto Ricans from New York City. Of the eleven boys four claim they were having complete and frequent heterosexual experiences before they were ten years of age. One claimed he had started at six. Much is probably more bragging than truth, but a relatively high percentage of boys apparently feel the need to demonstrate their *machismo*.

35. Glazer and Moynihan, *Beyond the Melting Pot*, pp. 124–25, discuss the various parental reactions to these problems, citing, primarily, student projects from the New York University School of Social Work.

36. Ibid., p. 124.

37. Ibid., p. 125.

38. Cooper, *Growing Up Puerto Rican.*

39. Glazer and Moynihan, *Beyond the Melting Pot*, p. 126.

40. U.S. Department of Labor, *Working Age Non-Participants. Regional Reports*, No. 22 (New York: U.S. Department of Labor Statistics, Middle Atlantic Regional Office, 1971).

41. Thomas C. Cochran, *The Puerto Rican Businessman* (Philadelphia: University of Pennsylvania Press, 1959).

42. Ibid., p. 158.

43. E. Seda Bonilla, "Social Structure and Race Relations," *Social Forces* 40 (1961): 141–48.

44. Elena Padilla, *Up From Puerto Rico* (New York: Columbia University Press, 1958).

45. Joseph P. Fitzpatrick, *Puerto Rican American: The Meaning of Migration to the Mainland* (Englewood Cliffs, N.J.: Prentice-Hall, 1971), p. 103.

46. C. Wright Mills, Clarence Senior, and Rose K. Golden, *The Puerto Rican Journey* (New York: Harper, 1950), p. 152.

47. Thomas, *Down These Mean Streets.*

48. Padilla, *Up From Puerto Rico.*

49. Ibid., pp. 44–95.

50. Puerto Ricans are of course, Americans, as are all Western Hemisphere peoples. They are even citizens of the United States, as was mentioned before. But they use the term most commonly to denote members of the society of the United States, and usually more specifically the white majority members of that society.

51. Patricia Cayo Sexton, *Spanish Harlem* (New York: Harper, 1965), p. 18.

52. Manuel Maldonado-Denis, "Puerto Ricans: Protest or Submission," *Annals of the American Academy of Political Science* 382 (1969): 26–31.

53. José Hernandez Alvarez, "The Post-Development Crossroads of Puerto Rican Migration," mimeographed (University of Arizona, 1971).

54. U.S. Bureau of the Census, *U.S. Census of the Population, 1970, Subject Reports, Puerto Ricans in the United States, Final Report* (Washington, D.C.: Government Printing Office, 1973).

218

55. Puerto Rican Planning Board, A *Comparative Study of the Labor Market Characteristics of Return Migrants and Non-Migrants in Puerto Rico* (San Juan: Commonwealth of Puerto Rico, 1973), p. 1.
56. James C. Coleman et al., *Equality of Educational Opportunity* (Washington, D.C.: Government Printing Office, 1966).
57. Ibid., pp. 219–20.
58. Ibid., p. 274.
59. Ibid., p. 297.
60. Ibid., pp. 278–79.
61. Macisco, "Assimilation of Puerto Ricans."
62. Nathan Kantrowitz, "Social Mobility of Puerto Ricans: Education, Occupation, and Income Changes among Children of Migrants, New York, 1950–1960," *International Migration Review* 2 (1968): 53–72.
63. Macisco "Assimilation of Puerto Ricans."
64. Kantrowitz, "Social Mobility."
65. Macisco, "Assimilation of Puerto Ricans."
66. Kantrowitz, "Social Mobility."
67. This information was taken from the 1970 census and reported in an article under the headline "1.5 Million Mainland Islanders Are Poorest of Hispanic Units" in *The San Juan Star*, August 7, 1974.
68. Macisco, "Assimilation of Puerto Ricans."
69. Kantrowitz, "Social Mobility."
70. Fitzpatrick, *Puerto Rican Americans*, p. 58.
71. Ibid.
72. Ibid., pp. 71–72.
73. Lloyd H. Rogler. "The Changing Role of a Political Boss in a Puerto Rican Migrant Community," *American Sociological Review* 39 (1974): 57–67.
74. Lloyd H. Rogler. "The Growth of an Action Group: The Case of a Puerto Rican Migrant Voluntary Organization," *International Journal of Comparative Sociology* 9 (1969): 223–24.
75. Puerto Rican Planning Board, A *Comparative Study*, p. 257.
76. Ibid.
77. This figure is calculated from data presented by Alvarez, "Post-Development Crossroads."
78. Ibid., p. 91.
79. Puerto Rican Planning Board, A *Comparative Study*, p. 228.
80. Ibid., pp. 240–44.
81. John C. Caldwell, *African Rural-Urban Migration: The Movement to Ghana's Towns* (New York: Columbia University Press 1969).
82. Jean Rouch, "Second Generation Migrants in Ghana and the Ivory Coast," in *Social Change in Modern Africa*, ed. Aidan Southall (London: Oxford University Press, 1961), pp. 300–304.

Suggested Readings

Cooper, Paulette. *Growing Up Puerto Rican*. New York: Arbor House, 1972.
Fitzpatrick, Joseph P. *Puerto Rican Americans: The Meaning of Migration to the Mainland*. Englewood Cliffs, N.J.: Prentice-Hall, 1971.
Glazer, Nathan, and Daniel Patrick Moynihan. *Beyond the Melting Pot*. Cambridge, Mass.: M.I.T. Press, 1963.
Lewis, Oscar. *La Vida: A Puerto Rican Family in the Culture of Poverty— San Juan and New York*. New York: Random House, 1965.

Padilla, Elena. *Up From Puerto Rico*. New York: Columbia University Press, 1958.

Senior, Clarence. *The Puerto Ricans: Strangers—Then Neighbors*. Chicago: Quadrangle Books, 1965.

Sexton, Patricia Cayo. *Spanish Harlem: Anatomy of Poverty*. New York: Harper, 1966.

JOSEPH STAUSS, BRUCE A. CHADWICK,
AND HOWARD M. BAHR

INDIAN AMERICANS

The First Is Last

Indian American history has been written primarily by non-Indians who popularized the taming of the American frontier. The well-worn themes of Indian cunning and cavalry heroism still dominate the accounts of the white man's struggle to subdue and civilize the savage. The military conquest of various tribal groups has been endlessly repeated in books, on the radio, and on the movie and television screens. And while the details of encounters between the whites and their red foes often stretch historical reality, the outcomes are accurate: the military subjugation of tribal groups and their forced removal to reservations.

The last major "battle" between the United States Army and American Indians was the mass slaughter of approximately three hundred Minniconjou and Hunkpapas at Wounded Knee Creek, shortly after Christmas, 1890. When the Indians stopped overt resistance and military force was no longer necessary, bureaucratic control of "Indian affairs" passed to the Department of the Interior. Decades of Indian acquiescence were marked by continued dominance by the whites. Only rarely was there legitimate Indian influence, much less control, in matters of federal Indian policy. Periodic visits by government officials, and occasional task force reports, have masked general official inactivity or, less charitably, mismanagement and exploitation. The result for Indian people was general poverty, unemployment, educational failure, alienation and low morale, and heavy alcohol abuse.

The period of Indian acquiescence seems to be over. Some might mark as its end the 1969 occupation of Alcatraz island by a coalition of angry Indians from many parts of the country. While others may define the Alcatraz occupation and more recent confrontation as the activities of a few militants and not an authentic indication of "Indian" feelings, the fact remains that there has been a significant increase of activism all over Indian country.[1] Indians young and old, from the reservation and the city, have emerged from former apathy with a new awareness of over two centuries of conquest, genocide, exploitation, discrimination, and neglect. The current cry is for Indians to be permitted to control their own affairs.

In this report we will not rehash the military conquests or the anthropological descriptions of the different tribes and language groups. Instead we shall concentrate upon the life styles and conditions of contemporary Indian Americans, touching upon history only as it provides essential context for explaining current conditions.

The First Sixty Years of War, 1830–1890

A review of the legislation about Indians passed by the United States Congress provides a revealing indication of how they have been defined and treated over the years. The major Indian legislation is summarized in Table 1. Initially the United States government dealt with the separate Indian nations by individual treaty, as specified in the Constitution. The intent of Congress to seek a military solution to the Indian problem is apparent in the initial creation of the Bureau of Indian Affairs (BIA) within the War Department.

In 1830 the Congress succumbed to pressures for opening up more Indian land for white colonization and ordered the BIA to relocate all Indians west of the Mississippi River. According to Congress, such removal was to take place *only* with the consent of the Indians themselves. Nevertheless, the Indian Removal Act was enforced without such approval and in direct conflict with a historic Supreme Court decision (*Worcester* v. *Georgia*) upholding the Cherokee nation's right to govern itself, which in effect meant they were exempt from the Removal Act. Indians who resisted relocation were forced to move by the military

Once removal was complete, Congress enacted the Trade and Intercourse Act of 1834, which regulated access to Indian lands west of the Mississippi. The pattern during the following sixty years, repeated again and again, was invasion of Indian land by whites, Indian resistance, and then "protective" action by the American military which allowed the

Indian Americans

TABLE 1

MAJOR LEGISLATIVE ACTION BY
UNITED STATES CONGRESS AFFECTING INDIAN AMERICANS

The First Sixty Years of War

1789	Federal Constitution specifying power to negotiate treaties with Indian nations
1824	Bureau of Indian Affairs (BIA) created within War Department
1830	Indian Removal Act
1834	Trade and Intercourse Act
1849	Department of the Interior created and BIA placed in it
1871	No further treaties/prior treaties valid
1887	General Allotment Act (Dawes Act)

The Eighty Years of Indian Affairs	
1924	Indian Citizenship Act
1934	Indian Reorganization Act (Wheeler-Howard Act)
1946	Indian Claims Commission
1953	House Concurrent Resolution 108 (termination)
1953	Public Law 280
1968	Indian Civil Rights Act

white settlers to consolidate and defend their holdings of Indian land. Several excellent historical accounts are available describing the numerous Indian wars of this period.[2] As the Indian nations were defeated and removed to reservations of less desirable land, Congress' attitude shifted from perceiving them as sovereign nations to viewing them as a national resource under the protection of the federal government. Accordingly, the BIA was transferred from the War Department to the Department of the Interior, a disastrous move for the Indians. Their so-called "advocate," charged with defending their rights and resources, was the same department seeking to make available additional Indian land and natural resources to an expanding industrial nation.

The policy of treaty negotiation with individual tribes continued until 1871, when Congress affirmed that no new treaties were to be made, although existing ones would be honored. Gradually the definition of the Indian nations as sovereign political units was replaced by an emphasis on assimilating them in the mainstream of American society. Accordingly, legislation was designed to hasten the desired process.

The stated objective of the Indian Allotment Act of 1887 was to make small farmers of Indians. Each family or individual was given from forty to one hundred sixty acres, depending on the fertility of the land. The theory was that the responsibilities and privileges of land ownership would make Indian people civilized, educated, and hard working, like whites. However much this explicit objective, if accomplished, would have damaged Indian morale and cultural integrity, the less obvious consequences of the act were far more costly, for its latent purpose was to make more Indian land available to whites.

After each Indian received his allotment, excess property was opened for homesteading or sale by the federal government. In addition, it was possible for individual Indians to sell their allotments. Initially each allotment was held in trust for twenty-five years before the owner could dispose of it, but public pressure forced Congress to pass legislature permitting the Secretary of the Interior to certify that a land owner was "competent" and thus could sell his land. The Allotment Act was not revoked until 1934, by which time Indian land had dwindled from one hundred thirty-eight million acres to only forty-seven million.[3]

The Eighty Years of Indian Affairs, 1890–1970

The military subjection of the American Indian and location of the survivors on reservations was followed by a period of "benign neglect." Periodically the nation was forced to acknowledge the exploitation or impoverishment of Indians, and occasionally there were attempts to pay at least partial indemnity. For example, over eight thousand Indian volunteers served in the armed services during World War I. Such a demonstration of patriotism motivated Congress to enact the Indian Citizenship Act of 1924, granting citizenship to all Indians. During World War II over twenty-five thousand Indian men and women served in the armed services and earned a distinguished record. One of the most famous Indian exploits was the transmission of vitally important military information in the Navaho language, thereby frustrating the Japanese cryptographers, who never were able to break the "code." Despite their demonstration of patriotism in wartime, the right to vote was not extended to all Indian citizens until 1948, when the Supreme Court declared unconstitutional the disenfranchisement clauses of the Arizona and New Mexico state constitutions.

Eventually Congress realized that the Allotment Act was destroying Indians' tribal identity and way of life and in 1934 passed the Indian Reorganization Act. The basic purpose of this act was to diminish governmental control of Indian affairs and to strengthen tribal authority by stopping the allotment of Indian lands and authorizing tribes to purchase new lands. It also encouraged self-government through the development of an "appropriate" written constitution. Approximately two hundred tribes took this option, while about seventy-five remained under federal jurisdiction.

In 1946 the Indian Claims Commission was created by Congress as a special tribunal to hear cases involving negligence and fraud by the United States in land transactions with Indians. By July 1969, 852 claims had been placed by different tribes before the commission; 304 cases had been heard. Of this number, 154 had been dismissed and 150 found in favor of various tribes, which had been awarded $330 million in settlements.

During the early 1950s the notion that Indians should be assimilated as rapidly as possible into American society again gained favor in Congress. The general intent was that they give up their special status as Indians and become subject to the same laws as other citizens. In 1953 the House of Representatives passed Concurrent Resolution 108 as a first step in taking the government out of "the Indian business." The intention of this administrative action was to terminate as soon as possible federal obligations guaranteed to Indians by treaty. Agreements with over one hundred tribes and bands, involving over thirteen thousand individuals and 1.3 million acres of land, were terminated. Two of the largest groups were the Klamath tribe in Oregon (2,000 tribal members), which lost over 860,000 acres, much of it prime timber land, and the Menominee of Wisconsin (3,270 persons), who lost 230,000 acres. Termination proceeded for several years despite its obvious consequences of increasing Indian unemployment and poverty, and further burdening already strained local and state tax structures.

Another approach to treating Indians the same as other citizens was Public Law 280 (1953), which authorized state law-enforcement agencies and courts to assume jurisdiction on Indian lands. This act was enforced in several states where the law and order function on reservations had been handled very well by tribal law enforced by tribal police and tribal courts. Again this legislation was enacted without any attempt to obtain the consent of the Indians affected. Today many tribes are attempting to regain legal jurisdiction (retrocession) on their reservations.

In 1967 an Indian omnibus bill was written, but before Congress acted, the bill was submitted to the various tribes for their comment. Certain aspects of it, particularly the proposal that tribes be allowed to mortgage Indian lands in order to generate working capital, made Indians fear more land losses. Because of this anxiety most tribes rejected the bill, and it was never enacted. The important thing to note is not that the legislature failed to pass, but that for the first time the federal government was making a serious attempt to permit Indians to direct the affairs of Indians.

The most recent general legislation enacted was the Indian Civil Rights Act of 1968. This bill extended the basic human rights guaranteed by the Bill of Rights to persons living on Indian lands. While Congress seems to have passed this bill with good intentions, it may have negative consequences for tribes which have developed their own judicial systems. Some of these are quite different from that of general society, and to enforce the Bill of Rights may weaken their means of (tribal) control. It is anticipated that cases of conflict between individual and tribal rights will eventually have to be decided by the Supreme Court.

The scale of the federal government's direction of the affairs of Indians is illustrated by the number of treaties, rules, and regulations that set forth Indian policy. The BIA manual which contains the procedures and rules directing the government's interaction with Indians amounts to thirty-three volumes and fills over six feet of bookcase space. In addition to this manual, BIA activities are influenced by 389 treaties, 2,000 regulations, 5,000 statutes, 2,000 federal trust decisions, and over 500 opinions by the United States Attorney General interpreting Indian law.

Contemporary Indians

One useful way of summarizing the effects of the sixty years of war and the eighty years of Indian affairs is to examine the degree of assimilation of Indian Americans into American society. A brief examination of assimilation and a recounting of persisting stereotypes and myths about the Indian will serve as a bridge from the past into the present.

ASSIMILATION

Assimilation refers to the absorption of a formerly autonomous group or society by another. It includes both *acculturation*, in which the values, beliefs, and behavior patterns of autonomous cultures converge, and *amalgamation*, which denotes the biological absorption of one human population by another. Because of the diversity of Indian cultures and groups, it is difficult to determine precisely the extent of their assimilation. However, utilizing basic indicators of assimilation such as degree of intermarriage, level of anti-Indian prejudice, and perception of Indians occupying political positions, it is possible to estimate their general level of assimilation into mainstream America.

Considerable acculturation is apparent in Indian people's acceptance of much of the life style of middle America, particularly the use of material or technological "advances," e.g., the automobile, the tape recorder, the television set. There has been acculturation in the other direction as well: Indian dress, jewelry, foods, and customs have been adopted by the dominant society. Considerable assimilation via intermarriage is also evident in the blood quanta records kept by various tribes and the BIA.[4] But the continued existence of anti-Indian prejudice and discrimination suggests that assimilation is far from complete, and a low level of assimilation is also indicated in the fact that relatively few Indians attain college degrees, occupy important positions in the corporate structure, or achieve high political office. Moreover, there seems to be a significant increase in the incidence of conflict between Indian groups and authorities representing white society (discussed in the section on "red power," pp. 245–51). In fact, whatever criteria of assimilation we use—acculturation, intermarriage, political participation, education, or rates of deviant behavior—the conclusion is that Indians are not fully assimilated into American society, and indications are that this condition will continue for a long time, if not indefinitely.

STEREOTYPES AND MYTHS

From the portrayal of Indian Americans by the mass media, several stereotypes and myths have developed that have interfered with sensible Indian policy. One important stereotype concerns the definition of "Indian." The BIA, Bureau of the Census, Indian Health Service, individual tribes, and the general public each have their own definitions. The stereotype perpetuated by the mass media is that all Indians look alike and thus can be identified by physical appearance. But all Indians do not look alike. Their skin color varies from very dark to white and their physical stature ranges from short to very tall. Another stereotype is that Indians live on reservations, yet over 40 percent of all Indians live in cities.

At least three major strategies have been employed by federal agencies to identify Indians. One strategy, based on a biological or genetic criterion, is utilized by the BIA and various tribes. It requires that persons designated as Indians be able to demonstrate a certain proportion, generally one-quarter, of Indian ancestry. Using this method of classification, the BIA identified 450,000 Indians as living on or near a reservation in 1970.

A second approach builds upon a psychological criterion, namely self-identification. This approach is currently used by the Bureau of the Census. Anyone may report himself as an Indian and be counted as such in the census. Using this method of definition, the 1970 census found 760,000 Indians in the nation.

A third technique of Indian identification involves the sociological criterion of acceptance by Indian people and participation in their social life. In other words, anyone recognized as a member of a tribal group or active in the urban Indian community is an Indian. We could not locate any national estimate of the Indian population using this technique, but given the disparity between census figures and estimates by Indian community leaders, the number would be substantially greater than that reported by the census. For example, the 1970 census for the Seattle metropolitan area reported 8,814, while urban Indian leaders place the number closer to 14,000. If such a disparity between census and community enumeration exists across the nation, then the Indian population as defined by this criterion is estimated at well over one million.

The problems of determining who is an Indian are very real and practical, as those so defined are eligible for BIA services, Indian Health Service care, special educational opportunities, land settlements, royalties, fishing and hunting rights, and other benefits guaranteed by treaty. Generally, the biological "degree of blood" is used by the BIA, Indian Health Service, and tribes which possess resources to be distributed. This very exact definition limits the number of individuals who qualify. On the other hand, those tribes which do not have reservations or trust land tend to be much more liberal in their definitions of tribal membership. Urban Indian groups place great emphasis on social and psychological identification. Those who perceive themselves as Indian and who are active in the community are usually accepted as being Indian.

A second myth that is a source of misunderstanding between whites and Indians is the notion that Indians do not have to pay taxes. This is simply not true. Generally Indians have to pay taxes just as do other citizens. The major tax benefit Indians are given is that the income derived from trust land by incorporated *tribes* is not subject to ordinary taxation. However, Indians living off-reservation pay income taxes, property taxes, sales taxes, and so on, and those living on trust land pay most taxes, with the exception of property tax.

The movie industry's portrayal of the oil royalties given to the Osage and other Oklahoma tribes has led many citizens to believe that *all* Indians receive periodic payments from the government. In reality, only a very small percentage of Indians receive payments from governmental funds. Generally these are members of the few tribes that have won settlements from the Indian Claims Commission for treaty violations and land encroachments. Usually the bulk of such payments goes into the tribal account for community projects such as education and housing programs, with only a limited portion distributed in per capita payments.

Another source of income for tribes and individual Indians is the leasing of grazing and mineral rights, and the sale of resources to private individuals or corporations. Frequently such income is handled by the

BIA, as they are responsible for the administration of trust land. Thus it may appear that the government is giving the Indian payments when in fact it is simply acting as financial agent in disbursing the payment.

Because of the publicity surrounding the recent fishing rights controversy in the state of Washington, many people believe that all Indians seek total freedom from fish and game regulations. On the contrary, the various tribes were guaranteed by treaty specific fishing and hunting rights in specific locations, and it is these treaty rights that most protest groups are trying to assert and retain.

In summary, many myths and stereotypes about Indians have interfered with the logical development of policies concerning Indian affairs. We have tried briefly to debunk a few, and trust that a further examination of contemporary Indians will lay other myths to rest.

SOCIOECONOMIC CHARACTERISTICS

Population Increase. Figures on the number of Indians living in the United States for the past eighty years, according to the Bureau of the Census, are presented in Table 2. Since 1890 the Indian population has nearly tripled, despite two major declines during this period. However, the general population of the United States has tripled during this time as well, so that Indians constituted only .39 percent of the American population in 1970, the same portion as in 1890. The most rapid growth in the Indian population has occurred during the last two decades covered in the table, and some predict that the proportion of Indians in the national population will increase. But a significant part of the apparent growth in Indian population in the 1960 census figures was accounted for by the change from enumeration identification to self-identification in the census definition of Indians. On the other hand, the dramatic increase between 1960 and 1970 cannot be accounted for in this way, and must reflect the high fertility of Indian people. Their crude birth rate (number of live births per one thousand population) is 37.4 for Indians and 17.8 for the total population.[5] One important factor holding down the growth of Indian population is their shorter life expectancy. The life expectancy of Indians is only 64.0 years, as compared to 70.5 for the total population. As medical care is improved on Indian reservations, a greater increase in population is anticipated.

Poverty. Much has been written about the poverty of American Indians. Statistics from the 1970 census presented in Table 3 document their severe economic disadvantage. Indians have significantly less education than the national average, which limits their employment potential. The lack of education combines with other factors, such as lack of jobs on reservations, to create a very high rate of unemployment. For the nation as a whole the male Indian's unemployment is three times greater than

The Reports

TABLE 2

INDIAN POPULATION CHANGE FROM
1890 TO 1970

Year	Population	Percent Change	Percentage of Total U.S. Population
1890	248,253	—	.39
1900	237,196	− 4.5	.31
1910	276,927	16.8	.30
1920	244,437	−11.7	.23
1930	343,352	40.5	.27
1940	345,252	0.6	.26
1950	357,499	3.5	.23
1960	523,591	46.5	.29
1970	792,730	51.4	.39

SOURCES: Public Information Office, Bureau of the Census, *We, the First Americans* (Washington, D.C.: Government Printing Office, 1973); United States Bureau of the Census, *Census of Population: 1970, Number of Inhabitants,* Final Report PC (1)-A1, *United States Summary* (Washington, D.C.: Government Printing Office, 1972).

the average. On several reservations the unemployment rate runs over 30 percent and would be much higher except that many individuals have never been employed or have given up looking for employment, and thus are not counted as being in the labor force.

Both the median family and individual income for Indians are only 60 percent of the national average. Indians living on reservations fare very poorly. The *highest* median family income for 1969 was only $6,115 on the Laguna reservations in New Mexico, while the lowest was $2,500 on the Papago in Arizona. Their impoverishment is even more pronounced if per capita income is taken as the standard. The highest per capita income for any reservation was $6,513 on the Flathead reservation in Montana; the lowest was only $588 on the Papago in Arizona. Finally, the percent of the Indian population living in poverty is three times that of the general population.

Education. Many Americans are convinced that education is the solution to the problems confronting contemporary Indian Americans. Education is seen as the key which will admit Indians to full participation in American society. The wishful thinking inherent in this position is exposed when the success and/or failure of Indian education is examined. In fact, much of the criticism of Indian education has dealt with its failure to achieve this goal of full Indian participation.

There have been three major national studies of the effectiveness of Indian education. The first was part of a large survey of the economic and social conditions of Indian Americans completed for the secretary of the interior.[6] This "Meriam report" was very critical of the BIA policy of transporting students to boarding schools long distances from their homes. It was discovered that the children, often at a very young age, were required to work four hours a day at heavy "production work" sup-

TABLE 3

SOCIOECONOMIC CHARACTERISTICS OF INDIANS AS COMPARED
TO THE TOTAL POPULATION

	Indian	U.S. Average
Education		
Median education for those over 25	9.8	12.1
Percent graduated from high school for those 25 and over	33	52
Unemployment		
Unemployment of males in civilian labor force 16 years and over	11.6	3.9
Unemployment of females in civilian labor force 16 years and over	10.2	5.2
Income		
Median family income	$5,832.00	$9,586.00
Per capita income	$1,573.00	$2,685.00
Percent persons whose income is less than the poverty level	38.3	13.7
Percent of family whose income is less than the poverty level	33.3	10.7
Housing		
Home ownership	49.5	63.0
Overcrowded	25.0	8.5

SOURCES: United States Bureau of the Census, *Census of Population: 1970, Detailed Characteristics,* Final Report PC(1)-D1, *United States Summary* (Washington, D.C.: Government Printing Office, 1972); idem, *Census of Population: 1970, Subject Reports,* Final Report PC(2)-1F, *American Indians* (Washington, D.C.: Government Printing Office, 1972).

porting the boarding school. The use of student labor to help support the schools was probably a violation of child labor laws and, more importantly, it interfered with academic achievement. The student who worked four hours each morning in the hayfields not only missed four hours of classroom experience but often was so tired in the afternoon that he could not give adequate attention to his schoolwork.

The second major study was authorized by the Civil Rights Act of 1964 and focused on the educational opportunities available to minority-group students as compared to white students.[7] The study was concerned with racial and ethnic segregation in schools; the quality of physical facilities, teachers, and curriculum; and ethnic variations in academic achievement. The findings relevant to Indian education are too varied and numerous to summarize here. In the main they reveal that Indian students do not receive an education comparable to that of their non-Indian peers.

The other major study of Indian education was the National Study of American Indian Education, conducted during 1967–1971 by Robert Havighurst. Over fifty technical papers and a volume for the general public[8] came out of this nationwide project.

There have also been periodic governmental hearings, such as the hearings before the Senate Subcommittee on Indian Education of the Committee on Labor and Public Welfare, chaired by Robert F. Kennedy (Special Subcommittee, 1968–1969). The first volume of the five-volume report of this committee is an excellent review of over eight hundred articles about educational research conducted by independent scholars over the past sixty years.[9] The conclusion of the majority of these studies is best summarized by the title of the report prepared by the Kennedy-directed committee: *The Failure of Indian Education—A National Tragedy.*[10]

Most people have assumed that once Indians started attending public school they would quickly be assimilated into society and their socioeconomic disadvantages would disappear. But as the Coleman report, the senate subcommittee hearings, and the Havighurst study so clearly demonstrate, Indian-white educational differences have persisted for at least fifty years. Table 4 presents national data collected in 1965 that demonstrate that even in the first grade Indian students are significantly behind in their academic development. These differences persist and in most cases increase with additional years of schooling. This trend is even more apparent when the test scores are converted into grade level placement (see Table 5). Compared to white students from the northeastern United States, Indian students continued to fall behind in verbal, reading, and math achievement as they progressed from the sixth through the twelfth grades. This means that when the average Indian student

TABLE 4

ACADEMIC TEST SCORES FOR INDIAN
AND WHITE STUDENTS FOR 1965

	Indian	White	Difference
First grade			
Nonverbal	49.2	54.1	4.9
Verbal	45.9	53.2	7.3
Twelfth grade			
Nonverbal	47.1	52.0	4.9
Verbal	43.7	52.1	8.4
Reading	44.3	51.9	7.6
Math	45.9	51.8	5.9
Average of all tests	45.1	52.0	6.9

SOURCE: James S. Coleman et al., *Equality of Educational Opportunity* (Washington, D.C.: Government Printing Office, 1966), p. 20.

graduates from high school, his ability in these three subjects approximates that of an eighth-grade white student.

In addition to their underachievement, the dropout rate for Indian students is twice the national average (52 percent versus 26 percent). About 10 percent of the appropriate-aged Indians have never been enrolled in school, and over half of those who do begin formal education drop out before high school graduation. Also, despite the fact that three-fourths of Indian students have repeated one or more grades, the competency of those who graduate is about four grades behind their white peers. Obviously education is not the panacea anticipated. It has opened up occupational and other social opportunities for some Indian

TABLE 5

CONVERSION OF INDIAN AMERICAN
TEST SCORES TO GRADE LEVEL PLACEMENT

		Test	
Grade	Verbal	Reading	Math
6	1.7	2.0	2.0
9	2.1	2.3	2.4
12	3.5	3.2	3.9

SOURCE: Adapted from James S. Coleman et al., *Equality of Educational Opportunity* (Washington, D.C.: Government Printing Office, 1966), Tables 3.121.1, 2,3, pp. 274–75.

people, but it has not resulted in complete assimilation or even in achievement levels comparable to those of the general population.

Where Indian people have taken control of the educational process and made it more responsive to their needs, there have been some notable exceptions to this dismal picture. For example, the Rough Rock Demonstration School and Navajo Community College are successful Indian-operated educational systems. In addition, national organizations like the National Indian Education Association and the Coalition of Indian-Controlled School Boards have emerged to influence educational policy.

URBAN MIGRATION

One important consequence of improving the Indians' educational achievements has been a significant migration from reservation to city in search of occupational opportunities. Many Indian leaders have lamented this "brain drain" from the reservations, as they feel it hampers reservation development. Because of the attractions of the city (more jobs, higher wages, better shopping facilities, better housing) and the oppressive poverty and unemployment on most reservations, at least 45 percent of all Indians now reside in an urban environment. Urban Indian communities are scattered across the nation; the ten cities with the largest Indian populations are listed in Table 6.

The BIA has accelerated the migration with the creation of relocation programs which have moved well over one hundred thousand Indians

TABLE 6

The Ten Standard Metropolitan Statistical Areas
with the Largest Indian Populations

Urban Area	Number of Indians
Los Angeles, California	23,908
Tulsa, Oklahoma	15,183
Oklahoma City, Oklahoma	12,951
San Francisco–Oakland, California	12,041
Phoenix, Arizona	10,127
New York, New York	9,984
Minneapolis-St. Paul, Minnesota	9,911
Seattle–Everett, Washington	8,814
Tucson, Arizona	8,704
Chicago, Illinois	8,203

SOURCE: United States Bureau of the Census, *Census of Population: 1970, Subject Reports,* Final Report PC (2)-1F, *American Indians* (Washington, D.C.: Government Printing Office, 1972), Table 11:138–141.

(nearly one out of every seven) to the city. There are over twenty different BIA-sponsored relocation programs. The main three are the Direct Employment Program, in which the individual is relocated and placed in a job; the On-the-Job Training Program, in which the individual is relocated and given on-the-job training leading to permanent employment; and the Adult Vocational Training Program, in which vocational training is given after relocation, thus preparing the participant for employment.

An examination of census data on residential patterns of urban Indians reveals that Indians tend to be widely dispersed and, unlike blacks and Mexican Americans, usually are not concentrated in certain low-income tracts or in identifiable ghettoes. Of the several factors that may account for the absence of Indian ghettoes, a very important one is the relatively small number of Indians. In order to create a ghetto similar to those of the blacks and Mexican Americans, almost all Indians would have to be next-door neighbors. Moreover, the Indians in any city come from many different tribes with different languages and cultures, and frequently do not feel a "consciousness of kind." This lack of ecological concentration has limited the Indians' participation in the war on poverty as they are not concentrated in a given area as a "target population." The Indians' dispersion throughout the city has also made communication and organization difficult. In a very real sense the Indian in the city is invisible.

One important consequence for Indians who migrate to the city is the loss of their right to many BIA services, including welfare payments and Indian Health Service care. The philosophy is that when the Indian enters the city he is assimilated into mainstream America and ceases to be an Indian. The impact of the loss of BIA services is frequently heightened by states which refuse Indian citizens services guaranteed other citizens. Several states refuse to provide public assistance to Indians if they own, either as individuals or as members of a tribe, reservation or trust land. Most states require a person applying for public assistance to sell his real property or mortgage it to the state. But reservation and trust land, especially if owned by the tribe, cannot be sold or mortgaged, and as a consequence Indian applicants are denied state aid. In some states pressure has been brought to bear by urban Indian groups, and in these areas trust and reservation land is now exempt from the real property provision of public assistance eligibility.

The ineligibility of urban Indians for BIA services is being challenged in the courts. A significant case, *Morton* v. *Ruiz*, was decided by the United States Supreme Court on February 20, 1974. Ruiz, a Papago Indian, left the Papago reservation to work in the mines at Ajo, Arizona, and was later put out of work because of a strike. The state refused him public assistance because his unemployment was a consequence of a strike and the BIA refused aid because he lived off the reservation. The court ruled in Ruiz's favor, forcing the BIA to provide him with services. This ruling was not a sweeping decision, as it specified certain conditions necessary for Indians living off the reservation to receive BIA services, but it represents a significant step in the right direction. It is anticipated that this ruling will encourage others, and eventually force the BIA to be more sensitive to the needs of urban Indians.

The urban Indians' fight for federal recognition has sometimes put them in conflict with reservation Indians. Reservation Indians, and tribal chairmen in particular, have perceived the BIA resources as limited, which means that any urban Indian gains are made at reservation Indians' expense. This conflict has been one factor preventing the national unity required if Indian people are successfully to initiate and foster social change.

A tactic of urban Indians to ease their adjustment to city life has been to develop an Indian center which provides the needed services. For example, the Indian Center in Seattle, Washington, maintains programs that provide emergency food and clothing, arrange temporary housing, assist in finding permanent housing, assist in finding employment, provide recreation for youth, teach cultural heritage classes and encourage students in the public schools, and provide alcoholism treatment, legal aid, and free medical care. The Seattle Indian Center had a very modest beginning and required years of diligent work by dedicated volunteers willing to overcome tribal factionalism in order to locate funds and operate the programs. Today the Indian Center is a stable ongoing enterprise staffed by approximately twenty full-time employees including secretaries, alcohol counselors, lawyers, and medical doctors. The characteristics of Indian centers in other cities have been described elsewhere.[11]

Monies were provided in 1971 by the Office of Economic Opportunity, Department of Health, Education, and Welfare, Department of Housing and Urban Development, and Department of Labor to create model Indian centers in seven cities to serve as examples for other communities. Only four—Los Angeles, Gallup, Fairbanks, and Minneapolis—were actually created. The results of these efforts are difficult to assess at this time, but hopefully reports of the model Indian centers' impact on the lives of Indians residing in these four cities will be forthcoming.

RESERVATION EXPANSION AND DEVELOPMENT

Many Indian spokesmen feel that reservation expansion and development are the means by which Indian ways can be maintained while at the same time improving the quality of life of reservation Indians. In this way, they feel, reservation life may eventually provide a viable alternative to urban migration. Reservation expansion is expected to increase the size of the Indian land base, and the development of agricultural, industrial, and recreational enterprises on reservations is expected to provide additional jobs and income.

Expansion. Indians have utilized several strategies to increase their land holdings. One approach has been to appeal to the courts or to Congress for corrections of mistakes which deprived various tribes of land. For example, a survey error in 1907 placed twenty thousand acres of Yakima reservation land in a national forest in the state of Washington. On May 20, 1972, President Nixon by executive order returned to the Yakima tribe their twenty thousand acres of choice timber land on Mount Adams. The Taos Pueblo tribe in New Mexico appealed to Congress for the return of the Blue Lake Mountain area on the grounds that this was sacred land and should be available for religious activity. After extremely bitter debate, in December 1970 Congress returned forty-eight thousand acres to the Taos.

A second strategy has been to reverse the termination process. As mentioned earlier, in 1953 congressional legislation provided for the termination of the Menominee tribe in Wisconsin. After considerable planning and preparation, termination was completed in 1961. Within a few years it was evident that a mistake had been made. Indian land passed into non-Indian hands, unemployment and poverty increased, and previously solvent tribal enterprises failed. The Menominee sought the assistance of the Wisconsin congressional delegation to introduce legislation repealing termination of federal supervision; reconstituting the Menominee as a federally recognized, sovereign tribe; and restoring federal services. This bill was passed in early 1974 and has tremendous implications for other tribes which have been terminated.

Even more significant have been attempts by nonrecognized tribes to obtain federal recognition and reservation land by appealing to general treaty rights and feelings of justice and fair play. Recently Congress *created* an eighty-five-acre reservation for the Payson Band of the Yauapai Apache in the Tonto National Forest in Arizona. The Yauapai Apache had traditionally lived in the Tonto Basin, but following the major Indian wars in the Southwest they were relocated to the San Carlos reservation a considerable distance away. In 1895 they bolted the reservation and settled on land near Payson, Arizona, that became a national forest in 1905. In 1909 the Forest Service gave the Yauapai a free special permit to use the land, and over the years they also used land beyond the boundary of the national forest. In 1954 land developers discovered that Yauapai did not have legal title to the land. The developers quickly moved to acquire such title, and immediately evicted the Indian residents. It is said that bulldozers destroyed an Indian family's home as they tried to rescue their belongings from it.

The Yauapai were forced back onto the national forest land, but in 1968 their special use permit was revoked, leaving them homeless. The BIA and the Department of the Interior refused to assist the Yauapai because they had left the San Carlos reservation. Finally the Yauapai appealed to Congress, and on October 7, 1972, Congress created the Payson Band of the Yauapai Apache reservation. This action sets a far-reaching precedent, as there are over fifty tribes which are federally recognized but have no trust land.

Let us cite a final example. Recently Senator Barry Goldwater sponsored legislation to give the Havasupai land on the rim of the Grand Canyon. Until January 1975 the Havasupai possessed a small, limited reservation in the bottom of the Grand Canyon which was not capable of supporting the tribal population in anything but extreme poverty. On January 4, 1975, President Ford signed into law a bill providing the Havasupai with 185,000 acres of land on top of the canyon, in the Grand Canyon National Park area.

Development. Many experts contend that factors such as capital, training, and experience can increase significantly the agricultural and industrial development of Indian reservations, and thereby raise the residents' standard of living. The extent of agricultural use of reservation land by Indians and non-Indians is presented in Table 7. Over thirty-five million acres are in use, with the major portion (thirty-two million acres) devoted to grazing.

Indians themselves are utilizing 80 percent of their total agricultural land. But a majority of the farm land, both dry and irrigated, is farmed by white farmers who have leased it from the Indian owners. The effects of leasing are obvious when it is noted that in 1968 gross agricultural production from reservation land was valued at $300 million, but only

TABLE 7

AGRICULTURAL UTILIZATION OF RESERVATION LAND

Land Use	Acres Utilized		Percentage of Indian Utilization
	Indian	Non-Indian	
Grazing	27,809,358	5,530,941	83
Dry farming	415,335	1,296,703	24
Irrigated farming	139,887	232,917	38
Total	28,364,580	7,060,561	80

SOURCE: Alan L. Sorkin, *American Indians and Federal Aid* (Washington, D.C.: Brookings Institution, 1971), p. 66.

one-third of this—$114 million—was accounted for by Indians. Thus Indians farm 80 percent of the land but reap only 38 percent of the agricultural income. Not only are Indians leasing the best land to non-Indians, but in general they are less efficient at production. For example, in a study of the Blackfeet Irrigation Project in Montana, Indian barley production per acre was 25 percent below that for non-Indian farmers on similar land, and Indian wheat and alfalfa production were 56 and 61 percent, respectively, below the production of non-Indians.[12]

Several strategies could be employed to increase agricultural development on Indian land. One would be to encourage such development on a tribal level so that large tracts of land could be consolidated and sufficient capital obtained to compete successfully in the "big business" of modern agriculture. Another tactic would be to arrange the best agricultural, land management, and business training available for Indian people interested in farming. Technical assistance should also be made available by the Department of Agriculture to assist in more efficient utilization of agricultural land.

Industrial development on reservations has been a recent phenomenon. The availability of inexpensive land, abundant natural resources, a cheap labor force, and tax benefits have encouraged manufacturers and processors to locate on reservations. By 1968, 137 manufacturing plants had been established on reservation land (see Table 8). But several characteristics of these plants should be pointed out in assessing the extent of potential future industrial development. First, they tend to be fairly small, averaging about eighty employees per plant. Second, it should be noted that industrial development on reservations provides only 4,375 jobs. Thus the impact of industrial development on the quality of life of reservation Indians at this point is very slight.

While there are many attractions for industries to locate on reservations, there are also serious problems, as shown by the fact that one of every five businesses established on reservations has failed. It is estimated that inexperienced management accounted for about half of the failures. A second factor associated with failure is the problem of finding an adequate market, as reservations tend to be in remote areas and manufactured goods have to be shipped to a distant urban center. This factor was credited with accounting for 30 percent of the failures. The other 20 percent of the failures were attributed to undercapitalization, or situations in which business did not have sufficient resources to weather tough periods of low productivity or economic slumps.

From the experiences of the industrial plants that have located on the reservations, both those that failed and those that survived, several problems have been identified which must be solved if there is to be greater industrial growth. First, ease of transportation is critical. Lack of roads

TABLE 8

INDUSTRIAL DEVELOPMENT ON RESERVATION LAND

| Fiscal Year | Number of Plants | | | Labor Force | | | |
| | | | | Indian | | Non-Indian | |
Year	Established	Closed	Operating	Number	Percent	Number	Percent
1957–59	4	1	3	391	70	171	30
1960	3	0	6	525	67	256	33
1961	4	0	10	702	58	505	42
1962	5	1	14	887	60	600	40
1963	6	2	18	1,395	45	1,719	55
1964	14	7	25	1,668	42	2,286	58
1965	21	6	40	2,011	45	2,479	55
1966	21	4	57	3,044	49	3,224	51
1967	23	3	77	3,730	50	3,666	50
1968	36	3	110	4,112	48	4,375	52
Total	137	27	110	4,112	48	4,375	52

Source: Alan L. Sorkin, *American Indians and Federal Aid* (Washington, D.C.: Brookings Institution, 1971), p. 81.

on reservations makes it difficult to transport needed raw materials and to move the finished product to market. On the typical reservation the average number of miles of road per one thousand square miles of land is fifty-five, as compared to one hundred fifty miles in surrounding rural communities. Not only do reservations have fewer miles of road, but the roads are of inferior quality. For example, in 1964 the BIA spent $206 per mile to maintain roads on Indian land, while surrounding rural county systems spent double this amount ($415 per mile).

Another problem limiting industrial development on reservations is the quality of the available work force. While there is a large, cheap labor force, as indicated by the high unemployment rates and low rates of pay on reservations (usually half as high as salaries in the surrounding community), this labor force has a fairly low level of education, training, and wage-work experience. Frequently vocational training is required to bring the skill level of the population to a minimum level. Finally, there have not been adequate feasibility studies estimating the prospects for survival of a proposed reservation industry. What is needed is for the BIA to do reliable feasibility studies so that before a tribe, corporation, or individual embarks upon a particular type of industrialization they understand the factors involved and the probability of success.

The Omnibus Bill of 1967 contained several features to encourage economic development. It authorized Indian tribes to form corporations which could issue tax-exempt bonds to raise needed capital. The bill also provided for federal guarantees of loans made to Indian enterprises. However, the provision permitting tribes to mortgage trust land as a means of obtaining additional capital resulted in the Indian community's rejection of the total bill because of a fear of loss of Indian land through foreclosures on mortgages. It is apparent that past measures, while well meaning, have not resulted in enough industrial development of reservations, and that assistance such as that contained in the Omnibus Bill of 1967, with the exception of the mortgage provision, is badly needed.

PREJUDICE AND DISCRIMINATION

The belief that Indians are subhuman, with limited intellectual and moral development, has influenced whites' behavior toward them. Negative stereotypes have influenced not only those with limited contact with Indians but also those responsible for administering government Indian policy. For example, in 1874 the agent at the Keshena, Wisconsin, agency wrote in his annual report that the Indians under his jurisdiction "are like boys sixteen or seventeen years old; they know too much to be Indians and too little to be white people."[13]

While the belief that all Indians are an inferior human species is rejected by most Americans today, there are too many who hold the stereotype that Indians are intellectually inferior, unsuitable for supervisory occupations, and potential alcoholics. While the wars of extermination have ended, Indians continue to be excluded from certain educational and occupational opportunities and from certain social relationships with whites.

In surveys of both rural and urban communities in the Pacific Northwest the authors have discovered considerable stereotyping of Indians. In Pendleton, Oregon, a community of fifteen thousand near a reservation, 81 percent of a sample of white adults agreed that "the average Indian gets drunk more frequently than the average white," and 44 percent agreed that "Indians don't get good jobs because they don't want to work." The same general trend, while not as strong, was discovered in Seattle, Washington, as 35 percent agreed, and only 25 percent disagreed, that the average Indian gets drunk more often than the average white. The other 44 percent indicated they didn't know whether the statement was true or not. The item about work from the Pendleton study was not included in the Seattle survey, but in response to a related item 22 percent of the Seattle residents agreed that "Indians don't have much ambition or drive for hard work."

Such stereotypes are perpetuated by the treatment of Indians in history books used in public schools.[14] Bowker[15] compared the treatment of Indians and blacks in sixty-seven contemporary American history texts published during the 1960s. The number of mentions, total size of mentions, and nature of adjectives used to describe Indians and blacks were determined for each text. He discovered that entire periods of Indian and black history were neglected, not even mentioned in the history texts. One surprising finding was that as the number of mentions of blacks in American history increased during the 1960s, the coverage of Indians actually *decreased*. A positive note is that public pressure in California, Michigan, and New York has forced abandonment of texts which grossly distorted the role of Indians and blacks in American history.

Evidence documenting racial discrimination is extremely difficult to obtain. One strategy is to utilize official records to compare the levels of education, income, home ownership, occupational status, arrest rates, and so on, between Indians and the general population. Some of this type of information has already been presented in this report. Compared to the general population, the Indian has significantly less education and income, is less likely to own his home, and has lower occupational status. The problem with this type of evidence of discrimination is that the Indian-white differentials may result from causes other than discrimination. For example, high unemployment rates among Indians reflect their values (e.g., the unsuitability of certain jobs), lack of education, or lack of appropriate work experience as well as direct discrimination.

A study of misdemeanor arrests, trials, and convictions in King County (Seattle), Washington, found that while Indians were arrested more frequently than non-Indians, the difference could not be positively attributed to discrimination.[16] The police contended that Indians committed more crimes, and thus were arrested more often. But it was possible to show that discrimination did occur in pretrial release on personal recognizance. When nature of offense and social class differences were accounted for, Indians were refused release significantly more often than whites. Moreover, although Indians were no more likely to be found guilty, the sentences imposed upon them, including both fines and time in jail, were significantly different from those for whites. Generally Indians were given smaller fines but had to serve more time in jail.

Another way to document discrimination against Indians is by systematic observation. Luebben[17] observed the treatment of Navahos who sought employment in the mines at "Carbonate City," Colorado. From his observations he concluded that Anglos were hired in preference to Indians; that Anglos obtained the better jobs; that Anglos received higher wages, even when Anglo and Indian both held the same job; and that Anglos were promoted much more quickly than Navahos.

Anti-Indian discrimination may also be documented from personal reports of the Indians themselves. A random sample of Indian adults in Seattle, Washington, were interviewed in 1972 and asked to report instances of discrimination they had personally experienced during the previous two years. The results (presented in Table 9) show the most frequently reported type of discrimination to be limited access to housing. One-third of the Indians said they had been refused housing because they were Indian. Here is an example of housing discrimination tape-recorded during the interview:

> Well, we were looking for a home awhile back—that's when we were still together—it was $150 and up and he was making good money, and they'd have vacancy signs and as soon as they'd see us, they'd say "Oh, I'm sorry, I forgot to take the sign down." We'd drive by two days later and the sign would still be up there. We tried about fifteen places all over Seattle.[18]

The second most frequently reported type of discrimination involved employment. One-fifth of the Indians said they had been deprived of employment solely on account of their Indianness. For example:

> I also had talked to another person who dwelled on the fact that I was an Indian and asked me if I drank and he was very polite but I knew that his

primary concern was that I very possibly wouldn't be a very good employee because I was an Indian and might drink excessively.[19]

Related to refusal to hire, 6 percent of the sample said they had been refused raises or promotions because of their Indianness:

They were up for a new foreman job and they wanted to go to a minority group, and they asked various blacks in our department and they turned it down and they asked one Indian besides myself in the department. And they asked me about it and one foreman said because I was an Indian, I was lazy just like all the other members of my race. So this came up later on as they reviewed my work record and this was a black mark against me, and thusly, I didn't get the job. But, as I said, later on, apologies were made and I should be up for the next foreman's job.[20]

TABLE 9

PROPORTIONS OF SEATTLE INDIANS REPORTING PERSONAL
EXPERIENCE WITH SEVERAL TYPES OF
ANTI-INDIAN DISCRIMINATION

	Percent Agreed (N = 119)
Have you ever been turned down when looking for a house or apartment and felt it was because you are an Indian?	32
Have you ever been refused a job and felt that it was because you are an Indian?	21
Have you ever been refused welfare benefits or given a hard time about them and felt it was because you are an Indian? (For persons who had applied for welfare benefits N = 69.)	19
Have you ever been arrested and felt that a big part of the reason was that you are an Indian?	18
Have you ever had trouble getting medical care and felt it was because you are an Indian?	14
Have you ever been deprived of the use of recreational facilities and felt that it was because you are an Indian?	8
Have you ever been turned down for a raise or promotion when you felt it was because you are an Indian?	6

SOURCE: Howard Bahr, Bruce A. Chadwick, and Joseph H. Stauss, "Discrimination Against Urban Indians in Seattle," *Indian Historian* 5 (1972): 10–11.

Of the Indians in the sample who had applied for public assistance, nearly 20 percent reported being the target of discrimination. Almost as frequent was the report of having been arrested primarily because one was Indian—18 percent felt they had experienced such discrimination at the hands of the police. Said one:

> I went over to a policeman and told him that I was bleeding internally and to take me to the hospital, but instead he took me to jail because he thought I was drunk, I was sick. I thought they were the kind of people, that when you ask for help, they would be humanitarian. So I asked him to take me to the hospital and instead they took me to jail, and said, "Where we're taking you, you'll have a very good doctor."[21]

Finally, a sizable proportion (14 percent) of the Indian respondents indicated they had been discriminated against by health care professionals:

> The nurse at the desk told me to go to Harborview Hospital. She just said I was an Indian and this was a white person's hospital. They said they just didn't get along with Indians. I just went to Harborview Hospital and got my rib taped up.[22]

We recognize that self-reporting of discrimination reflects only one side of the story, and that there may have been other factors involved which the respondent has neglected to tell, has forgotten, or did not know. Nevertheless these accounts reveal that Indians believe they suffer discrimination and are denied their civil rights. Even if many of the accounts are not literally true, they are circulated among the Indian community and influence Indians' behavior toward employers, police, landlords, social workers, and so on. The qualified Indian may not seek available employment because he is convinced that he will be discriminated against, and thus the economic deprivation is perpetuated. The person who needs health care may not seek it for the same reason.

The combined evidence obtained from official records, observations, and self-reported experiences indicates that considerable discrimination is presently practiced against Indian Americans. The various civil rights acts passed and amended during the past fifteen years have undoubtedly reduced the level of overt discrimination. The protest activities discussed below have also had an impact on discrimination, especially institutional discrimination.

RED POWER

The term "red power" means different things to different people. To many it means militant protest. To a newly elected tribal chairman it may mean economic development for the tribe. For non-Indians it is frequently associated with radical activism and the Indian counterpart of the black power movement. But all of these are oversimplifications. The spirit of red power has always been with Indian people. Its essence is the resolve of a people to control their own destiny; it is Indian determination of the affairs of Indians.

The term "red power" was introduced at the 1966 convention of the National Congress of American Indians (NCAI). In the past three decades at least three major national organizations have articulated the red power message. These are the NCAI, the National Indian Youth Council (NIYC), and the American Indian Movement (AIM).

Pan-Indian Organizations. The history of national Indian organizations is lengthy, dating back to the "Tepee Order" or "Society of American Indians" of the early 1900s.[23] "Pan-Indianism" emerged more strongly in the early 1940s with the development of the NCAI, founded in Denver in 1944. While membership is restricted to persons of Indian ancestry who are members of tribes, bands, or groups recognized by the federal government, NCAI attempts to focus on the broad issues facing all Indians. Today NCAI is a major "watchdog" and lobbyist for Indian legislation in Washington, D.C. Financial support has sometimes been a problem, mainly because NCAI is viewed by many Indians as a conservative body concerned only with reservation problems. There has been pressure on NCAI from excluded groups, such as urban Indians and nonreservation rural tribes, to change its membership restrictions so that members of all tribes may be included.

The NIYC developed out of the "Chicago Conference" of national Indian representatives held in June 1964 to review Indian policies. A number of Indian college students were dissatisfied with the meeting and met that August to set up their own national organization. They stressed using Anglo political tactics to reach their goals. One of their major areas of interest was education. NIYC assumed sponsorship until 1969, when it became independent, of the United Scholarship Service, which grants scholarships to Indian and Spanish American students. NIYC also organized a series of illegal fish-in protests in the state of Washington in 1964.[24]

Although the leaders of AIM have received national publicity as professional demonstrators and agitators, the early history of AIM reveals a much wider range of activities. AIM was started in Minneapolis during the summer of 1968 by Dennis Banks and George Mitchell. It emerged from a volunteer citizen patrol created in response to the Indian community's perceptions that police in Indian neighborhoods were guilty of harassment and brutality. On weekends members of the citizen's patrol walked through the neighborhood recording the arrests of Indians. Red jackets were worn to identify members and communication was provided by walkie-talkies. The patrol existed for about a year, during which time there was a noticeable reduction in the number of arrests of Indians. The police cooperated by turning over intoxicated Indians to members of the patrol. From the organization created to maintain the citizen patrol a national movement began. By 1971 AIM reported eighteen organized chapters across the nation, with twelve in urban areas and six on reservations.

These three national organizations have been deeply involved in organizing red power activities. Other groups, sometimes viable only briefly, have emerged in response to unique local circumstances.[25] Here our attention will be limited to a few events that have generated national interest.

Protest Activity. In 1964 a two-man occupation team claimed Alcatraz as Indian land under the Sioux treaty of 1868, which included a provision that surplus federal property be given to the Sioux. The claim was quickly rejected by the federal courts and the case was dropped. In late October 1969 the San Francisco Indian Center burned down, destroying the work of several decades. A method being needed to attract support and contributions for rebuilding the center, the occupation of Alcatraz was seen as a means of achieving national attention and attracting financial contributions. Therefore, early in November a small Indian force landed on Alcatraz. They were promptly removed by the guards. In the next landing, on November 19, 1969, two hundred fifty Indians arrived and claimed the island as Indian land. The stated objective was to turn Alcatraz into an Indian cultural and educational center. A support system was developed to provide the supplies needed to sustain the contingent on the island.

The federal government merely "waited out" the occupation force, many of whom eventually had to return to school, jobs, families, and other obligations. The occupation came to an end during the summer of 1971 when federal marshals surprised the twenty remaining occupants and escorted them off the rock. While the island was not turned over to Indians, the occupation of Alcatraz was definitely not a failure. It solidified Indian determination not to surrender additional land and was the source of inspiration for other invasions of federal lands.

In 1970 the federal government declared as surplus a portion of Fort Lawton, an eleven hundred-acre military reservation in Seattle, Washington. A group of urban and reservation Indians banded together in an organization called United Indians of all Tribes (UIAT) to claim the property. The objective of UIAT was to use the land for a national Indian cultural and educational center, with an emphasis on tribes of the Pacific Northwest. The city of Seattle contested the Indian claim,

The Reports

and sought federal authorization to develop Fort Lawton as a city park. On March 8, 1970, one hundred twenty Indians ranging in age from two to seventy-eight took part in the first of three occupations of the fort. The struggles of UIAT came to the attention of the regional offices of the Department of Health, Education, and Welfare, which stepped forward to make application for the surplus property in UIAT's behalf, thus putting the Indian claim on an equal basis with that of the city. After a two-year period of negotiations, the city of Seattle obtained a three hundred ninety-acre park, and a seventeen-acre plot was awarded to UIAT on a long-term lease. While the acreage is only a small percentage, it is adequate for the cultural center plans and also represents a symbolic victory over city and federal governments. The Fort Lawton case is extremely important for two reasons. First, the Indians won and land was secured. Second, a claim by urban Indians from many different tribes was recognized by the federal government.

The "Trail of Broken Treaties" which occurred in November 1972 has been described to the public as the "BIA office occupation." Most observers were given the impression that the occupation of the BIA office in Washington was the Trail's primary objective. On the contrary, evidence suggests that the organizers had planned peaceful demonstrations, but that three events which occurred after the caravans arrived in Washington, D.C., precipitated the siege of the BIA offices.

The caravans were planned in the summer of 1972 by a coalition of eight national Indian organizations: The National Indian Brotherhood (of Canada), the Native American Rights Fund, AIM, NIYC, the National American Indian Council, the National Council on Indian Work, the National Indian Leadership Training, and the American Indian Committee on Alcohol and Drug Abuse. In addition, four other national groups, the Native American Women's Action Council, the United Native Americans, the National Indian Lutheran Board, and the Coalition of Indian-Controlled School Boards, endorsed the idea of converging on Washington in an effort to influence congressmen and the impending national elections.

The organizers hoped to attract as many as one hundred fifty thousand Indians. The first four-mile long caravan arrived early in the morning on November 2, 1972, and the first precipitating event happened. St. Stephen's Episcopal Church, which had been scheduled as a place of lodging for the participants, was found to be infested with rats, and many of the participants were upset.

Next there was an encounter with the United States Army. The caravan members had planned to hold memorials at the Arlington Cemetery; their request was refused by the Army on the grounds that it violated regulations banning "partisan" activities.

The final precipitant was a confrontation with guards at the federal General Services Administration. While negotiations for new lodging were underway upstairs in the BIA office building, several hundred Indians waited on the ground floor. A shift change in the guards took place at 4.00 P.M. and for some reason the new guards proceeded to clear an area with force. There was a struggle, guards and BIA officials were evicted from the building, and barricades were set up. The occupation had commenced.

At first lodging was the primary issue. The government did not respond adequately to the lodging issue and the Indians added the new demand that several top BIA officials be fired. A federal court order was issued demanding that the building be cleared. The deadline was ignored, negotiations continued, and additional demands were added (to a total of twenty) as new deadlines were set and then extended.

On November 8 the Indians finally left the building. The White House promised that a high-level task force would be created to review Indian policy in general and the twenty specific demands in particular. Those demands did not receive much press coverage. Instead, the millions of dollars of damage to BIA headquarters held the spotlight. The twenty points were:

1. Restoration of constitutional treaty-making authority.
2. Establishment of a treaty commission to make new treaties.
3. Allowing selected Indian Americans to address a joint session of Congress.
4. Creation of a commission to review treaty commitments.
5. Review of treaty violations.
6. Resubmission of nonratified treaties to the Senate.
7. Enactment of a congressional resolution that as a matter of public policy all Indians will be governed by treaty relations.
8. Assurance of land reform.
9. Restoration of a one hundred ten million-acre native land base.
10. Restoration of rights to Indians terminated by enrollment.
11. Revocation of prohibitions against "dual benefits."
12. Repeal of state laws enacted under Public Law 280.
13. Resumption of federal protective jurisdiction for offenses against Indians.
14. Abolition of the BIA by 1976.
15. Creation of an Office of Federal Indian Relations and Community Reconstruction.
16. Allowance of immunities for Indian commerce.
17. Allowance of Indian tax immunities.
18. Protection of Indians' religious freedom.

19. Protection of Indians' cultural integrity.
20. Elimination of competition for funds by non-Indian-directed "Indian agencies."

The twenty points and the White House's written agreement to set up a task force were lost in the aftermath of the occupation. A large number of government documents were taken from the building during the occupation. Leaders of the group claimed these papers documented the mishandling of Indian affairs by the BIA. These claims were supported by columnist Jack Anderson, who was permitted to review some of the documents. With the BIA occupation, AIM emerged as one of the most powerful and influential national Indian organizations.

The most dramatic of the national Indian protests was the seventy-day occupation of the hamlet of Wounded Knee, South Dakota. A heightened awareness of the 1890 Wounded Knee massacre had been generated by Dee Brown's history of the Indian wars, *Bury My Heart at Wounded Knee*.[26] On the evening of February 27, 1973, approximately three hundred Indians supported by AIM quietly slipped into Wounded Knee. For a time eleven local residents were held as hostages. The demonstrators claimed they represented the Sioux people, on whose reservation Wounded Knee is located. They demanded suspension of the BIA-imposed tribal constitution and government, withdrawal of the BIA police force from the reservation, and an investigation of the loss of sovereign rights guaranteed by treaty.

The purpose of the demonstration was lost in the controversy and sensationalism surrounding the occupation. A force of federal marshals eventually numbering between three hundred and five hundred sealed off the area, and multitudes of curious speculators, supporters, anti-protestors, and reporters gathered.

Press coverage was widely criticized. Those opposed to the occupation, particularly the supporters of Richard Wilson, the elected tribal chairman of the Oglala Sioux nation, felt that the sympathetic news coverage prolonged the occupation. Government negotiators contended that many of the activities were staged for television coverage and interfered with serious negotiations. Eventually reporters were banned from the negotiations. The demonstrators themselves argued that too much attention was focused on weapons, shots fired, woundings, and other sensational events, rather than on the real bases for the protest.

After nearly a month Assistant United States Attorney General Kent Frizzell and AIM attorney Raymond Roubidauax started serious negotiations. These discussions looked beyond the problem of disarmament and included the issue of legitimate tribal government. On April 5, 1973, a settlement was announced and the siege was to be lifted. A six-point agreement was to go into effect: (1) a disarmament program was to begin; (2) Russell Means, an AIM official and principle organizer, was to submit to arrest; (3) a federal investigation of the current tribal government was to be conducted; (4) the Justice Department was to protect the civil rights of Indians who had defied the tribal government; (5) a presidential treaty commission was to reexamine the treaties between the United States and the Sioux nation; and (6) the input of the Sioux nation to the presidential commission was guaranteed. A few days later, Russell Means traveled to Washington, D.C., for meetings with governmental officials to work out the details of implementing the truce. For some unknown reason the meetings were postponed, and never were held.

On April 17 a government helicopter flying over the village became involved in a shooting match with the protestors. A dispute continues as to who fired the first shots, but once the shooting began the federal marshals opened fire and a battle raged for ninety minutes. Frank Clearwater, a newly arrived protestor, was killed. During the next ten days sporadic shooting continued and on April 27 there was a second fatality. This death prompted both sides to begin serious negotiations. Three elders from the Oglala Sioux nation joined the discussion and assisted in hammering out a disengagement formula.

The occupation ended on May 8, when one hundred fifty Indians surrendered themselves and their arms to the federal marshals. Most were indicted on charges associated with the occupation, but many of the charges were later dropped. The trial of the major participants resulted in one bloody confrontation between court officials and Indian supporters. All of the principle actors were eventually acquitted on the grounds that the government had utilized unconstitutional means in constructing its case.

The Future

Some Indians seem to think that the whites and their automated society will eventually disappear. In the words of an old Papago Indian to Vine Deloria:

The Papagos didn't really need the NCAI. They were like, he told me, the old Mountain in the distance. The Spanish had come and dominated them for 300 years and then left. The Mexicans had come and ruled them for a century but they also left. "The Americans," he said, "have been here only about 80 years. They too, will vanish, but the Papagos and the Mountain will always be here."[27]

In this view, perhaps the best strategy for Indians is to wait for the whites to disappear and the Indian cultures to be restored. Among those who accept this line of thought, the "apathy" that has characterized many Indians and tribal groups may continue.

Other Indians believe that the future of Indian affairs rests in the hands of Congress, and that the best tactics are activities to pressure Congress to protect Indian lands, cultures, and sovereignty. Congress, it is argued, protects the rights and privileges of vested interest groups. Given their small numbers, Indians must seek public sympathy and support, which can then be applied to members of Congress. This is a continuing battle, congressmen come and go, and new legislation reverses the policies of earlier legislation. Most Indian groups have learned to live with these transitory conditions by striving to take advantage of the current trends and not taking current promises too seriously.

On the positive side, there is evidence that Congress is taking its responsibility in directing Indian affairs more seriously. Presently a Senate subcommittee led by James Abourezk of South Dakota is investigating treaty violations. In any case, we may expect an increase in the frequency of protest activities as Indian organizations work for their causes.

In addition, it may be anticipated that the courts will frequently be asked to protect the rights that have been denied Indians by the legislative and executive branches of the United States government. It appears probable that the Supreme Court, in particular, will have to decide many cases of violated treaty rights.

NOTES

1. Robert C. Day, "The Emergence of Activism as a Social Movement" in *Native Americans Today: Sociological Perspectives,* ed. Howard M. Bahr, Bruce A. Chadwick, and Robert C. Day (New York: Harper, 1972), pp. 506–31.

2. Edward H. Spicer, *A Short History of the Indians of the United States* (New York: Van Nostrand Reinhold, 1969), and Dee Brown, *Bury My Heart at Wounded Knee* (New York: Holt, Rinehart, 1970).

3. An excellent discussion of this land loss appears in *Kirke Kickingbird and Karen Ducheneaux, One Hundred Million Acres* (New York: Macmillan, 1973).

4. Deward Walker, "Measures of Nez Perce Outbreeding and the Analysis of Culture Change," *Southwestern Journal of Anthropology* 23 (1967): 141–58.

5. Estelle Fuchs and Robert J. Havighurst, *To Live on This Earth* (Garden City N.Y.: Doubleday, 1972), p. 32.

6. Lewis Meriam, *The Problem of Indian Administration* (Baltimore: Johns Hopkins, 1928).

7. James S. Coleman et al., *Equality of Educational Opportunity* (Washington, D.C.: Government Printing Office, 1966).

8. Fuchs and Havighurst, *To Live on This Earth.*

9. Brewton Berry, *The Education of American Indians: Survey of the Literature,*

prepared for the Subcommittee on Indian Education of the Senate Committee on Labor and Public Welfare, 90th Cong., pt. 1, 1968.

10. Hearings Before the Special Subcommittee on Indian Education of the Committee on Labor and Public Welfare, United States Senate, 90th Congress, 1st and 2d sess., on the Study of the Education of Indian Children, 5 vols., 1968. Washington, D.C.: Government Printing Office, 1968.

11. John W. Olson, "Epilogue: The Urban Indian as Viewed by an Indian Caseworker," in *The American Indian in Urban Society*, ed. Jack O. Waddell and O. Michael Watson (Boston: Little, Brown, 1971), pp. 398–408, and Merwyn S. Garbarino "Life in the City: Chicago," in ibid., pp. 168–205.

12. William A. Brophy and Sophie D. Aberle, *The Indian: America's Unfinished Business* (Norman, Okla.: University of Oklahoma Press, 1966).

13. Commissioner of Indian Affairs, *Annual Report to the Secretary of the Interior* (Washington, D.C.: Government Printing Office, 1874), pp. 185–86.

14. Rupert Costo and Jeannette Henry, eds., *Textbooks and the American Indian* (San Francisco: Indian Historian Press, 1970).

15. Lee H. Bowker, "Red and Black in Contemporary American Indian Texts: A Content Analysis," in *Native Americans Today*, ed. Bahr, Chadwick, and Day, pp. 101–9.

16. Darlene Korfhage, "Differential Treatment in the Municipal Court System" (Master's thesis, Department of Sociology, Washington State University, 1972).

17. Ralph A. Luebben, "Prejudice and Discrimination Against Navahos in a Mining Community," *KIVA* 30 (1964): 1–17.

18. Howard Bahr, Bruce A. Chadwick, and Joseph H. Stauss, "Discrimination Against Urban Indians in Seattle," *Indian Historian* 5 (1972): 5.

19. Ibid., p. 6.

20. Ibid.

21. Ibid., p. 8.

22. Ibid.

23. Hazel W. Hertzberg, *The Search for Indian Identity* (Syracuse, N.Y.: Syracuse University Press, 1971).

24. American Friends Service Committee, *Uncommon Controversy: Fishing Rights of Muckleshoots, Puyallup, and Nisqually Indians* (Seattle, Wash.: University of Washington Press, 1970).

25. For a detailed account of many of the significant protest events of the past decade, see Day, "Emergence of Activism."

26. Brown, *Bury My Heart at Wounded Knee*.

27. Vine Deloria, Jr., "This Country Was a Lot Better Off When the Indians Were Running It," *New York Times Magazine*, March 8, 1970.

Suggested Readings

Bahr, Howard M., Bruce A. Chadwick, and Robert C. Day, eds. *Native Americans Today: Sociological Perspectives.* New York: Harper, 1972.

Brown, Dee. *Bury My Heart at Wounded Knee.* New York: Holt, Rinehart, 1970.

Deloria, Vine, Jr. *Custer Died for Your Sins.* New York: Macmillan, 1969.
————. *Of Utmost Good Faith.* New York: Bantam, 1971.

Waddell, Jack O., and O. Michael Watson, eds. *The American Indian in Urban Society.* Boston: Little, Brown, 1971.

Wax, Murray L. *Indian Americans.* Englewood Cliffs, N.J.; Prentice-Hall, 1971.

KENJI IMA

JAPANESE AMERICANS

The Making of "Good" People

Are Japanese Americans a minority group? Though most Americans know little about them, recent depictions of them are positive—they are "good" people, self-sufficient, cause little trouble to the rest of society, and so on. These views are supported by evidence of educational, occupational, and economic successes, as well as low incidence of social and personal pathologies which seem to plague many minorities. In many instances Japanese Americans are not labeled a minority because they seem to have "made it":

> By any criterion of good citizenship that we choose the Japanese-Americans are better than any other group in our society. . . . They have established this remarkable record, moreover, by their own almost totally unaided effort. Every attempt to hamper their progress resulted only in enhancing their determination to succeed. Even in a country whose patron saint is the Horatio Alger hero, there is no parallel to this success story.[1]

> The immigrants from Japan who settled in this country raised civic-minded, law-abiding families, and became doers and leaders in our communities. They have enriched our way of life more than any of us can ever say.[2]

This report examines Japanese Americans as "good" people because they stand out as a model minority.

They have not always been good people. The history of racism in this country against Japanese is filled with stories of unwarranted prejudice and negative treatment. There was a time when Japanese Americans were just plain "Japs," or "god damned Japs":

A Jap's a Jap. They are a dangerous element, whether loyal or not. There is no way to determine their loyalty. . . . It makes no difference whether he is American; theoretically he is still a Japanese and you can't change him. . . . You can't change him by giving him a piece of paper.[3]

The Japanese are less assimilable and more dangerous as residents in this country than any other of the peoples ineligible under our laws. . . . With great pride of race, they have no idea of assimilating in the sense of amalgamation. They do not come here with any desire or any intent to lose their racial or national identity. They come here specifically and professedly for the purpose of colonizing and establishing here permanently the proud Yamato race. They never cease being Japanese.[4]

Whenever the Japanese have settled their nests pollute the communities like the running sores of leprosy. They exist like the yellowed, smoldering discarded butts in an over-full ashtray vilifying the air with their loathsome smells, filling all who have misfortunes to look upon them with a wholesome disgust and a desire to wash.[5]

Japanese are immoral people . . . (who lead) California toward mongrelization and degeneracy.[6]

Though these statements may come from undeniably racist sources, others less associated with racism have also spoken against the Japanese, such as Earl Warren, some members of the American Civil Liberties Union, and many traditionally liberal persons. It is painful to read these statements, but in retrospect they document the view that the "good" people were not always "good."

The transformation of Japanese Americans into acceptable people results in part from their successful performance, which is treated as a validation of American ideology of individualism, self-help, hard work, deferred gratification, and so on. The success story takes on a more dramatic accent in light of a context of oppression and racism. Even official Japanese American organizations have cooperated in creating and sustaining this success image. However, recent misgivings among some Japanese have suggested both a reinterpretation of the success story and a changing ethnic identity.

The present report explores the above issues of racism against Japanese, the success story, and recent reevaluations of racism and success.

Background

MIGRATION

The first recorded visits of Japanese to the New World occurred in 1610, a decade before the Pilgrim migration. But it was not until the late nineteenth century that a significant Japanese migration occurred. In that period Japan experienced population changes which resulted in an oversupply of people who were moved off rural lands for cities and overseas migration. Although Japanese began immigrating in 1861, the bulk of immigration occurred between 1900 and 1924. In 1924 United States immigration policy prohibited further immigration. According to Daniels,[7] about 89 percent of the 275,000 Japanese immigrants entered in the twenty-four-year period.

The migration can be divided into two periods: (1) pre-1908; and (2) 1908 to 1924. The significance of these dates is political as well as social.

The United States Immigration Act of 1907, resulting from strong exclusionist forces in California, authorized the President to refuse admission to certain persons if he were satisfied that they were detrimental to labor interests. Later President Theodore Roosevelt proclaimed "that all Japanese and Korean laborers, skilled or unskilled, who had received passports to go to Mexico, Canada, or Hawaii and come therefrom" were prohibited from entering the continental United States.[8] Up to that time, many Japanese who had visas to Canada, Hawaii, and Mexico eventually entered this country.

In 1908 the United States and Japanese governments concluded a "gentlemen's agreement" whereby Japan would issue passports to United States-bound Japanese nationals only if they were former residents; parents, children, or wives of residents; or intending "to assume active control of an already possessed interest in a farming enterprise in this country."[9]

The significance of these steps is the beginning of Japanese exclusion on a national level, where previously only local and state governments passed measures restricting Japanese rights. Although these measures were aimed at the Japanese people, they occurred in a generally anti-Asian climate which included the Exclusion Act of 1882 prohibiting Chinese migration—the Japanese inherited a condition of racism against the Chinese.

The Omnibus Act of 1924 brought a logical conclusion to prior exclusionary moves: the prohibition of further Japanese immigration. Specifically the act denied admission to aliens ineligible for citizenship, which included those who were not free white persons (including Japanese), and aliens of African descent. Thus the two dates, 1908 and 1924, involved political actions which shaped Japanese migration to the United States.

During the first migration period, the typical newcomer was a young unmarried male who regarded himself as a sojourner planning to return home after making his fortune. He entered the economy as a labor replacement for Chinese workers who held jobs unwanted by whites in such areas as railroading, mining, and migratory farm work. Few from this first migration period intended to stay permanently.

The second period, on the other hand, found an increasing number establishing semipermanent residence on farms and in Japanese ghettos. Associated with the second period is the arrival of "picture brides." Wives were permitted to enter the United States after 1908. Under this arrangement, a single man could form a family by exchanging photographs with his prospective bride. This was an extension of the prevailing Japanese custom of arranged marriages. Most migrants retained plans to return home, but felt they were becoming too old to put off having a family—many were over forty.

These men did not see themselves becoming Americans, nor did they have any hopes of acquiring citizenship in the face of existing laws. However, as Modell suggests, these migrants "came for considerably circumscribed reasons, but caught up in the exigencies of life, they stayed, sustained spiritually as well as mechanically unassimilated."[10]

POSTMIGRATION

The years following migration can be divided into three periods: (1) prewar, 1924–1941; (2) war, 1942–1945; and (3) postwar, 1946 to the present. As with the migration period, the postmigration periods are shaped by developments external to the Japanese American community, such as World War II. These periods are directly related to the generational structure of the ethnic community. The migration years belong solely to the *Issei*, or first generation; the prewar and war periods mark the emergence of the *Nisei*, or second generation; and the last period marks the introduction of the *Sansei*, or third generation. The fourth generation, or *Yonsei*, have yet to become a significant element of the community. The wider American society entertains notions of generations, but not in the formalized sense as found in this ethnic group.

Issei. The Japanese have a proclivity toward marking persons and groups by specific social and historical references. For example, among the Hawaiian Japanese, members of the first group of Japanese laborers are called *Gan-nen-mono,* or "first year men," because they arrived in the first year of the *Meiji* era (1868).[11]

A moment's reflection will connect Japanese generational labels to history. The bulk of Japanese immigration occurred within only two decades, forming a group of homogeneous people. They were similar in regard to age, social position, province of birth, and common treatment by Americans. These immigrants shared mutual interests and identity, and when offspring began increasing it became clear that a separate grouping was forming—the Nisei. Issei and Nisei are distinctly separated both socially and historically. According to Mannheim, a generation shares "a common location in the social and historical process, and [it] thereby limit[s] them to a specific range of potential experience, predisposing them for a certain characteristic mode of thought and experience, and a characteristic type of historically relevant action."[12]

A literal definition of Issei would include persons born in Japan who migrated to this country; however, in practice, not all such persons are included. For instance, the "new" Issei, the post–World War II Japanese immigrant, is rarely called Issei. Between 1924 and 1942 a few immigrants such as ministers and students entered this country, but they did not share the same history as prior immigrants. One such person was Rev. Daisuke Kitagawa, who entered this country as a theological student and remained as a pastor of Japanese farmers; he was not thought of as Issei, but as an outsider.[13] His case documents the historical and sociological character of generational labels among this minority.

Nisei and Sansei. The other terms, Nisei and Sansei, are also associated with history and social structure. In spite of the successes of the Nisei in the postwar years, they tend to identify with the prewar and war years. They remember the hard times and struggles, especially the camp experiences. In California, when two Nisei strangers encounter each other, they often begin conversation with, "What camp were you in?" Whether they choose to emphasize the negative or the positive, it seems important for them to establish a mutuality of background through the recitation of camp experiences. Persons who weren't in the camps, including most Sansei, are often excluded from further conversation. Thus camp years are a feature of being a Nisei.

Two other features, among others, identify the Nisei: the hard times of the prewar years and the Nisei character. Chris Kato, a prominent Nisei educator in Seattle, identifies hard times as a feature of the Nisei:

> The kids of the Nisei generation were more serious about things such as education than the Sansei. Today there is so much more to attract young people away from studying. The parents of the Nisei were a lot stricter. The Sansei generation are more fortunate to have the financially secure state they are in today. They are mainly a part of the middle class whereas the Nisei had to cope with the depression, etc. No doubt the Sansei live a much better life but they must not lose sight of the credit that is due to their parents and Asian forefathers. It is they who sacrificed and buckled

down to give the young people what they have today. The older generations have done an outstanding job.[14]

Underlying Kato's comments are notions about the Nisei's character of resilience and "toughness." Lyman[15] identifies these traits as a balance between the "American" and the "Japanese." The emphasis on character involves a control over one's presentation of body, mind, and feelings.

Whereas the Nisei were preoccupied with "making the grade," Sansei are preoccupied with assimilation (pro and con) and with identity. Whereas previous generations lived in an atmosphere glorifying the melting pot notion, the Sansei live in a time when ethnicity and pluralist notions are encouraged, if not demanded; simultaneously, they live at a time when unprecedented assimilation opportunities have developed in occupation, residence, marriage, and so on. While no definitive analysis of the Sansei exists, they are clearly seen by other Japanese Americans as a generation set apart.

Generation and Social Organization. The importance of these generations for Japanese American social organization is threefold—authority, interaction, and association. Traditionally, Japanese are preoccupied with status and authority, whereby most descriptions of Japanese social organization place heavy emphasis on formal power or authority relations. Among Japanese Americans, generational status reflects authority, as manifested in the themes of power and power succession within the community. The Issei seldom could or would say anything favorable about the Nisei, whom they considered "unworthy." If you will reread Kato's comments above, there is a similar tone by a Nisei toward the "unworthy" quality of Sansei. These remarks reflect the problem of who holds power and how it is to be handed down. For example, a frequent interpretation of the impact of World War II on the Japanese American community is that the war precipitated the transfer of power from the Issei to the Nisei. Prior to the apparent power transfer there was continual derogation of the Nisei as having little right to power.

Another importance of generational count is the relevance for social interaction; generational count indicates common experiences unique to a set of people. Therefore, if one knows the generation of another person, one can guess that person's background and attitudes. Among Japanese Americans there is reliance on being able to read each other's situation without having to ask about it directly.[16] Knowing generation provides interactants with a device for anticipating the attitudes and behaviors of other Japanese Americans. The indirectness which characterizes Japanese interaction reinforces the "demand" for status information as found in generational identity.

259

Associations and other types of organizations are based on generation. Issei dominated the Japanese associations; Nisei dominate the Japanese American Citizens League; and Sansei now dominate newly emerging associations. Japanese churches are divided between Issei and Nisei, as found in separate services, boards, ministers, and so on, within the same churches. These illustrations document the pervasiveness of generation as a feature of social organizations within the community.

WHO ARE THE JAPANESE AMERICANS?

Notions of race are based on common-sense reasoning concerning biological descent, which is accepted as a self-evident fact of life. Sociologists, among others, find the biological descent criterion overly simple, since it does not address the complexities of history and social organization associated with racial classification. Although the Japanese Americans are relatively homogeneous compared with other ethnic groups, they are not identical with each other in terms of biography, attitudes, social status, and so on. Most attempts to characterize them unavoidably oversimplify the diversity of types and social experiences within this ethnic group.

The United States Bureau of the Census classifies Japanese Americans as those respondents who identify themselves as "Japanese American," "Japanese," "Nipponese," and "Oriental," but our concern is with identifying those persons who are meaningfully associated with the ethnic community. Thus, it is problematic whether or not to include Japanese war brides, postwar immigrants, and offspring of Japanese-white marriages. Based on members' notion of ethnic status, most of the latter are excluded from discussion.[17]

This report refers to Japanese Americans as those people who immigrated from Japan prior to World War II (probably before 1924) and their descendants who remain in this country (Nisei, Sansei, and Yonsei). Furthermore, remarks shall be confined to those Japanese in the continental western states, principally California, Oregon, and Washington, thus deemphasizing Hawaii and nonwestern states. The deemphasis is based on the differing conditions which separate the continental western states Japanese from those residing in other regions.

In Hawaii, since the turn of the century the Japanese have been the largest nationality group, which results in completely different power relations between the Japanese and other resident ethnic groups. For example, unlike those living on the mainland, Hawaiian Japanese have dominated the political scene (such as holding one of the two Senate positions and both House of Representatives positions). Unlike the mainland Japanese, they were not "relocated" during World War II.

The rest of the United States, excluding the western states, did not share an awareness of, or a concern with, the "Japanese problem." In the first place, the number of Japanese was small. When Arkansas was considering legislation against Japanese ownership of land, only two farms were owned by Japanese. Second, the nonwestern states were most likely *second* points of entry for Japanese migration rather than *first*. Japanese movement to those parts is more likely to have occurred mainly after World War II, which meant that they were more Americanized, spoke English as a first language, had higher socioeconomic position, and were college educated. Third, and associated with the above two factors, the non-West Coast states do not share the fervor of anti-Asian racism. In short, significant contextual conditions separate the experiences of the continental western states Japanese from other Japanese Americans.

Population and Socioeconomic Characteristics

The amount of literature on the "Japanese problem" earlier in this century might lead the reader to imagine a sizable number of Japanese Americans. When compared with the total number of all immigrants, the Japanese constituted a small percentage; for example, during the 1915–1924 period, when European migration was at a low due to World War I, the Japanese were only 2.16 percent of the total immigration number.[18] In 1970 the United States had 591,290 Japanese among a 203 million-plus population, proportionally less than three per thousand.

At one time most Japanese lived in rural areas (e.g., in 1920 over 51 percent lived in rural areas, but by 1970, 90 percent lived in metropolitan areas, compared with 73 percent of the entire American population). Though they began moving from farm areas before 1940, relocation during the war years resulted in a sudden increase of urban Japanese—in 1940, 55 percent were urban, but by 1950 the proportion jumped to 71 percent.

In spite of this shift to urban places, a great majority of Japanese remained in the western states. Of the mainland Japanese during 1940, 95 percent lived in western states. By 1950 the percentage dropped to 80 percent (reflecting the wartime government encouragement to leave the West Coast), with the greatest concentrations in California—respectively about 36 percent of all Japanese Americans. Within these states, the vast majority reside in cities—Los Angeles-Long Beach (103,944), San Francisco-Oakland (33,270), San Jose (15,945), and Sacramento (12,015). There are no mainland cities with more than 2 percent Japanese; Los Angeles-Long Beach, with the largest concentration of mainland Japanese, has only a little over one percent Japanese population.

Perhaps the most striking demographic characteristic is the sex-age distribution reflecting Japanese American migration history. In a stable and typical population, such as that of the United States as a whole, one finds a continuous age distribution from young to old. However, since most Japanese migrants arrived at about the same time, with similar ages and family formation stages, the resulting age distribution shows a gap between the Issei and Nisei. In 1940 the median age of Issei males was fifty-five and of the Nisei males it was seventeen—a thirty-eight-year age gap! Since Issei females were on the average eight years younger than Issei males, mothers were generally thirty years older than their children. This age gap reinforced the social organization of generation. Recent figures continue to reflect discontinuous age distributions resulting in demographic correlates of social organization—Issei, Nisei, and Sansei.[19]

Traditional measures of socioeconomic position—education, occupation, and income—document the upward social mobility and well-being of the Japanese Americans. Since 1940 they have had the highest level of education among all racial groups, including whites; the 1970 figures on median years of education uphold this pattern—Japanese (12.5 years), whites (12.2 years), blacks (9.9 years). Other educational measures reinforce this interpretation, such as the fact that 30 percent Japanese versus 22 percent white have had at least some college. Schmid and Nobbe,[20] using a measure of occupational level, found the Japanese consistently higher than all racial groups except whites in 1940 and 1950. But in 1960 they surpassed even whites. In 1940 only 3.8 percent of all employed Japanese males (fourteen years and older, living in California) were classified as professionals; by 1950 the percentage rose to 4.4 percent; by 1960 it shot up to 15 percent; and by 1970 it was 23.8 percent. Income-wise, they surpass all racial groups except whites. In short, these figures document the Japanese American success.

Community and Society

This section deals with the internal (community) and external (society) facets of the Japanese American world. The study of community deals with the internal features, such as values and norms, as well as the more traditional institutions, such as the family. The investigation of society concentrates on the public face of the community, or the relations with the external world. Included will be the themes of racism, success, and assimilation/acculturation. We will examine the articulation between the two sections, particularly the ways observers have traditionally examined the community, in order to explain its manifestation in society.

COMMUNITY

Students of the community have concentrated on two interrelated facets—culture and social organization. Culture often refers to values and norms, and sometimes to a member's ways of describing behavior and of constructing motives for action. Social organization, on the other hand, refers to "actual" social patterns. Though there are other ways of organizing materials on the community, we will adhere to this traditional distinction. Furthermore, again following precedent, the discussion will emphasize those components which are used to "explain" the success image. Since the Sansei are only in the early adult stage and have not been intensely studied, most of the following discussions pertain to Issei and Nisei. The success theme is about the Issei and the Nisei and, furthermore, the Sansei are primarily of interest under the themes of assimilation and acculturation.

Culture. Most Issei were born and reared during the Meiji era (1868–1912), a time of rapid Japanese industrialization and nationalism. Although Japan had formally abandoned the feudal order, it retained and emphasized fixed hierarchical positions and predictability of speech and action. Parent-child, employer-employee, ruler-subject, and superior-inferior are examples of fixed hierarchical positions. The major emphases in such relations are upon subservience of the inferior, particularism of the relation, and collectivity orientation. Thus from a Western view inferiors appear deferent and highly obsequious, while superiors appear paternal and arrogant. Other qualities of the inferior are adaptive, conformist, dependent, and compromising.

The other theme, predictability of speech and action, is exemplified by this Confucian quote:

> In all things success depends on the previous preparation and without such preparation there is sure to be failure. If what is to be spoken is previously determined, there will not be stumbling. If affairs be previously determined there will be no difficulty with them. If one's actions have been previously determined there will be no sorrow in connection with them.[21]

This emphasis is contrary to Western ideals about initiative and spontaneity.

Clearly these are ideals and are not actualized in any literal sense, but they provide themes used by Japanese for characterizing behaviors. Though some writers will attribute to these ideals a causal power, we will refrain from such projections unless some cited author does so.

A focus on ideals overlooks historical and social circumstances in which these ideals are actualized. For example, although Japanese Americans can be related to Japanese culture, any analysis does not automatically apply to all of them. Some studies show Japanese Americans adhering more strongly to traditional Japanese ideals than do current-day Japanese from Japan.[22] Perhaps the most important social fact differentiating Japanese from Japan from those residing in America is the inferior-superior position of the latter to the white population. Japanese Americans seem even more subservient than those of the old country.

Kitano[23] suggests that the *enryo* ideal is most appropriate for Japanese Americans. The generalized term means reserve, diffidence, restraint, deference, and obsequiousness. The ideal within the American context was expanded to fit a variety of situations—rules for interaction with whites, how to handle ambiguous relations, how to deal with confusion, embarrassment, and anxiety. It reveals itself in diverse manners, including hesitancy in speaking out in public settings, refusal of favors or invitations (especially the first time), refusal of second helpings, refusal to ask questions or assert oneself, and refusal to ask for salary raises. Kitano also recognizes two components of *enryo*: (1) *hazukashi*, which means a fear of how others will react, resulting in shame or feeling foolish (manifested embarrassment and reticence); and (2) *hige*, which means denigrating oneself and one's family in public. The behavior of Japanese Americans manifesting *enryo* gives the appearance of high conformity, nonaggressiveness, cooperation, and even docility in the eyes of other Americans. Schoolteachers often reacted favorably to Nisei children because they honored authority, complied with directives, and rarely caused trouble.

Psychological studies of Nisei and Sansei tend to confirm this characterization. Meredith and Meredith[24] found Sansei males more reserved, humble, conscientious, shy, and regulated by external realities than a comparable white group. They also found the Sansei to be more inhibited, introspective, less socially outgoing, and poorer social contacts. Arkoff[25] found them to be more deferring, self-abasing, inhibited, and less dominant than a "normal" sample. Hutchinson and associates,[26] in a study of classroom participation, found that they participated less often than whites.

Most Japanese American organizations are not known for being radical, nor do they push ideologies except those which are currently available and considered desirable by most people. They reflect a strategy of low profile or a "don't rock the boat" attitude. It is a strategy of accommodation to a superior which involves a deemphasis on ideology and an emphasis on situationalism and conformity. All of these features are consonant with ideals of a Meiji inferior.

The second component, predictability of speech and action, is reflected in the notion of "face." One's performance, including behavior and manifestations of one's feelings, is treated as consequential. From an American standpoint, the Japanese seem to take it too seriously. For instance, Caudill[27] observes the Issei to be very vulnerable to insult from the outside world, consciously placing great emphasis on the need to control himself. Lyman observes, "Nisei character at its best is exhibited in cathectic management and by control over, and suppression of, spontaneity, emotionalism, and inappropriate expressiveness."[28] Not only does Lyman state this characterization, but he also points out that such traits result in the appearance of patience, cleanliness, courtesy, and "minding one's own business," which have, in part, accounted for the acceptability of Japanese Americans to white middle classes.

A third and related ideal is achievement, but it is not of the variety found in American ideals, with their focus on the individual. Numerous studies of Japanese Americans have identified the achievement orientation,[29] which is derived from one's social identity. According to this view, achievement of some honor is a repayment to one's social collective, such as the family. Achievement brings honors to the collective, but failure raises the prospects that one has failed to reciprocate one's obligation:

> If a Japanese child failed to achieve or to meet societal expectations, the mother reproached herself for raising her children inadequately. As a result the child felt guilt for the pain he was causing his mother and shame for not meeting set standards. He learned that by achieving he could assuage his guilt feelings, atone for previous bad behavior and bring honor and praise to his family.[30]

In summation, previous research has identified the enryo syndrome, face management, and achievement as three ideals held by Japanese Americans. Although these characterizations oversimplify the Japanese American experience, they nevertheless seem useful for understanding the experience. Our previous discussion on generation is reinforced by these characterizations, because generations are sociological entities which embody the inferior-superior relationship.

Social Organization. Although Meiji Japan had the state, the extended kinship system, village and work organizations (with their *oya-bun-kobun* structure—a fictive parent-child relation), as well as other established institutions, the Issei entered a country in which they had to establish some variations of these institutional orders from scratch. Even before the turn of the century, the Issei began establishing institutions (e.g., Japanese Associations, *kenjinkai* or associations of persons from the same province) which developed into a network of cross-cutting organizations, reaching its peak of solidarity and strength just before World War II. As we shall see, that system of interdependent institutions was strongly modified and continues to change as societal changes develop.

The Issei, motivated by both inclination (due to common language, culture, and identity) and rejection by the wider society, sought each other out for companionship, financial help, jobs, socialization into ways of local situations, protection, and so on. As a result, the developing bonds of social organization created a place for the migrant and a strong sense of collectivity, with an associated system of effective social controls. The intersecting social organizations were businesses, family, church, school, associations, and a network of obligations which we will call the informal system. Although each organization had some independence from each other, and considerable factionalism existed within and among them, the system of organizations tended to present a portrait of high cohesiveness and singularity to outsiders. As we shall see, this portrayal stems largely from the Japanese preoccupation with order and harmony as ritually required images for public presentation.

The economics of the community was critical because it reinforced the system of mutual obligation and thus solidarity. Jobs in the wider community were restricted, resulting in two options: to work in the most menial positions, or to try one's hand in business. Many continued in menial positions, but most tried their hands in a diversity of self-employed jobs. Although a large number failed, they learned that certain businesses were more likely than others to succeed, such as marginal service businesses, services to whites in areas of little competition from whites (e.g., gardening), and ethnically related enterprises (e.g., produce). An indication of the small business predominance is found in Miyamoto's[31] study recording nine hundred separate Japanese establishments in Seattle during 1930, or about one business for every nine Japanese persons.

A 1937 study of Los Angeles Nisei indicated the continuation of the second generation into a similar job structure (e.g., approximately 70 percent were employed in retail fruit and vegetable establishments).[32] Even where nonfamily members were employed, a common pattern of employee-employer relation was a fictive parent-child relation (*oyabun-kobun*) which reinforced ethnic notions of morality and commitments to the community. Union organizers frequently had difficulty recruiting Japanese to join because they felt a loyalty to their employer which would be weakened by union activities. Thus businesses were part of an extended system of mutual obligation which involved not only employer-employee relations, but also special considerations with ethnic business associates. A Japanese farmer would give special prices to a Japanese produce man; a gas station dealer would give an "ethnic rebate." As a general practice, special prices and services were extended to other ethnics, which helped to sustain a sense of community.

The Japanese extended kinship was a major integrative institution in Japan, but the move to the United States curtailed the continuation of that system in its old form—the system is basically a corporate entity built around mutual economic exchange between the Main (*honke*) and the family branch (*bunke*).

As we have witnessed, other ethnic organizations such as prefecture groups substituted for this deficit. However, the family maintained a major role in socialization and social control over individuals through the formal maintenance of hierarchical authority and male dominance. Although the actual day-to-day operation of such families was often at variance with these ideals, such as frequent dominance of the mother in a decision-making role, in public family members exhibited ritual compliance with them. If divorce rate is used as a measure of family stability, Japanese families were highly stable, showing a rate among all generations of 1.6 percent.[33]

Perhaps the most important feature of the family was the transmission of values which, in spite of communication problems, and in conjunction with other Japanese social organizations (e.g., church), continued to socialize individuals who responded to the community's mechanisms of social control. The child's social identity was connected at two levels of collectivity to which he was obligated—the family itself, and the ethnic community. Public deviance was treated not as an individual matter, but as having implications of failure for both family and the ethnic community. Whether or not outsiders viewed them as such, members of the community were preoccupied with these considerations.

All of the above organizations, including Japanese Associations, churches, and other unmentioned social groups, dovetailed to achieve cohesion and control. However, the informal system was underplayed, since the community provided formal and ritually prescribed features to outsiders. Those formal systems did not function without the informal structures, which were located in face-to-face contacts and community reputation. Those watching from outside rarely saw the backbiting, gossiping, nitpicking, and factionalism which lies behind the walls of solidarity and social order. The contrast between the formal civility and the backstage "dirt" gave outsiders an inaccurate perception of the community.

The informal system provided the mechanism of social control as well as a means of communicating good deeds and fortunes, which were rarely directly relayed. An important component of the informal system were rules of reciprocity. A study by Johnson[34] involved an unspoken exchange whereby each party was expected to understand the exchange without having to explicate the grounds for reciprocity. For example, *koden* was a funeral gift, usually money, which was expected from members of the neighborhood, who in turn expect a *kōden* when some member of their family dies. The amount was carefully regulated depending on the *kōden* previously received from the family of the deceased, and on the relation to the deceased. Those who did not reciprocate are punished by not getting a *kōden* when it was their turn, or by gossip attacking their reputation; in the extreme, they could be ostracized. All of the above ethnic social structures involved expressions of solidarity, which resulted in a strong sense of community—them and us.

The foundational conditions supporting these organizations, and the associated solidarity, changed in the postwar years. Since much of the community was based on a separate ethnic economy, its change was inevitable with the movement of Nisei away from small ethnic businesses and into professional and other white-collar employment in nonethnic enterprises. The initial postwar years saw the temporary reestablishment of the prewar ethnic community, but the gradual and even sudden shifts in occupational choices no longer provided the past structural basis. There are few, if any, studies which provide as detailed a portrait of the postwar community as of the prewar period.

Assimilation and the consequent weakening of ethnic solidarity and social control are topics for further investigation. Miyamoto[35] suggests the emergence of a "dual-like" structure in which the world of work and the world of sociability are parallel but unconnected, except for the warm bodies that oscillate between them. The separation of the Japanese into two parts—the white world and the ethnic world—suggests the continuing viability of the ethnic community, albeit in reduced form.

SOCIETY

What kind of society did the Japanese Americans face? How have they responded to it? We gave some ideas above, but we will now elaborate on their experience. Two Issei poets give a glimpse of what happened to them:

When wintertime comes
I still wonder what it was
That made me endure
Those deep-abiding sorrows
Which wrung my very bowels.[36]

A wasted grassland
Turned to fertile fields by sweat

Of cultivation:
But I, made dry and fallow
By tolerating insults.[37]

Most Americans are unaware of racial oppression of the Japanese, and even among those who know about it, few are aware of the impact on Japanese as persons. For the most part the Japanese seem to endure this hardship without expression of sorrow or anguish, leaving many to believe the inconsequential impact upon a "stoic" people, and yet the dimensions of human suffering and uncertainties cannot be overstated. Their experience stems from a society which placed restrictions and showered abuse upon them from all levels, from the ordinary face-to-face encounter to the highest steps of legal process. As we have seen, the exclusion movement began by restricting immigration and ended by the prohibition of any immigration through the 1924 immigration act.

It is interesting to note parallels between the Japanese immigrant and the European immigrant. Both existed on the margin of society, but the second generation of both seemed driven to equal or outdo the "real Americans," and both spawned a third generation that looked back with pride to the first generation—the Hansen thesis on immigrants.[38] Many non-Japanese will find parallels between immigrant groups, but few experienced the extensive legal and social exclusion based on race. While it is true that the same 1925 legislation restricting entry into the United States affected both Japanese and non-Anglo-Saxon origin white persons, the Japanese were excluded altogether, whereas others were permitted limited, but continued, immigration: Japanese quota—0, Italian quota: five thousand, British quota—sixty-five thousand.

We have commented on racist policies, but we haven't emphasized that the fabric of racism included many foreigners other than colored peoples. Kenneth Roberts, a novelist, wrote: "If a few million members of the Alpine, Mediterranean, and Semitic races are poured among us, the result must inevitably be a hybrid race of people as worthless as the good-for-nothing mongrels of Central America and south-eastern Europe."[39] We cannot minimize the impact of racist policies toward "Alpine, Mediterranean, and Semitic" peoples, but they have been recruited into the same racist mentality as employed against them. During the latter part of the nineteenth century, Italian immigrants formed quasi-military organizations specifically for the exclusion of Asians.[40] After World War II, Italian immigrants attempted to prevent American-born Japanese from returning to Oregon by boycotting them through denial of business transactions, such as purchases of goods and services and distribution of farm products.[41] Certainly the experience of racism does not necessarily create an understanding of such policies toward

269

another group. Underlying these observations is not only the support of racist policies by those who suffered similar prejudices, but the stronger sentiment against people of different color. Persons of Italian and German descent were not incarcerated during World War II as were Japanese Americans, in spite of the same state of war between the United States and their countries of origin.[42] Though those people of non-Anglo-Saxon white descent can often be identified, the Japanese remain a race apart.

The multifaceted character of racism can be traced to the originators of our political system—the founding fathers. They had no conception of the possibility of Japanese immigration when they wrote the first naturalization act in 1790 which permitted citizenship rights only to free whites, intended to exclude Negroes and Indians. When the Chinese began sojourning in this land, white legalists saw that the founding fathers had not made provisions for Asians and therefore interpreted this absence to mean that Chinese were ineligible. This interpretation, expanded to include Japanese, separated even those "inferior" whites of "Alpine, Mediterranean, and Semitic" backgrounds from Asians. The history of Asian exclusion turns on this interpretation of naturalization rights.

In 1922 Takao Ozawa, an Issei with years of residence in the United States and commitments toward Americanization, was refused citizenship by the Supreme Court on the grounds that he was not a free white man. Though the definition of white man was not explicated by the early lawmakers, the presiding justice used the technical decision that Ozawa was not Caucasian. This may seem legally sound, but the racist ground for this decision was revealed when the same justice denied citizenship to an East Indian, not on the grounds that he was not Caucasian (Indians are technically classified as Caucasian), but on the grounds that the founding fathers of 1790 meant "color" when they referred to nonwhites.[43]

This issue on citizenship affected Japanese economic opportunities. In that same year (1922) two naturalized Issei were denied rights to incorporate a real estate firm because they did not have the right to be naturalized.[44] In other instances, many Japanese were denied licenses to fish, to own business, and so on, because of their alien and ineligible status. For example, the Seattle city government prohibited Japanese from running employment offices, second-hand shops, billiard halls, dance halls, and detective agencies.[45]

Many labor unions, the source of the strongest and most pervasive anti-Japanese sentiment, prohibited union membership to Japanese. Samuel Gompers, president of the American Federation of Labor (AFL), frequently denounced them and refused alliances with all-Japanese unions. The Asiatic Exclusion League included in its membership over two hundred labor unions. Other entities overtly working against Japanese included the press, American Legion, farmers' organizations, and numerous nativist organizations such as The Native Sons of the Golden West, which sought to save California from the "Yellow-Japs." They often worked side by side with politicians who saw the anti-Japanese stance as an expedient strategy, such as Senator Phelan, who ran on slogans of saving California from the "Yellow menace."[46]

Perhaps the most celebrated cases of legal racism, related to the above developments, are the alien land laws. Beginning with California's passage of the Webb-Heney Act of 1913, which prohibited land ownership and limited leasing rights of aliens ineligible for citizenship (thus retaining those privileges for white aliens), fifteen states adopted some form of such laws: Arizona, Arkansas, California, Delaware, Idaho, Kansas, Louisiana, Montana, Nevada, New Mexico, Oregon, Texas, Utah, Washington, and Wyoming. Although Oregon had enacted its first anti-Japanese land law in 1923, it passed a further restriction in 1945 which prohibited aliens from working on farms, living on farms, and even stepping onto farm fields. Though the law was declared unconstitutional in 1949, it reflects the persistence of racial forces. Even though many of these laws were rescinded after World War II, some remained in force as late as 1966.

Many Japanese took evasive measures to circumvent these laws, such as leasing lands from "trusted" citizens who held nominal ownership of them, as well as from American-born Japanese. In spite of these practices, the laws had important consequences: restricted Japanese farm activity, reinforcement of Japanese segregation, and many personal hardships. Although some white commentators[47] suggest the relative ineffectiveness of these laws, Japanese writers[48] stress the importance of the restrictions. The almost unmeasurable dimensions of anxiety, anger, and heightened awareness of subordination cannot be easily dismissed. Even though few Japanese lost lands to state governments, many experienced those expropriations as personal attacks which reinforced their alienation from this society. As one Issei states:

> For the average Issei there were just jobs for the lower class people, and consequently, changing one's employment was very difficult. There were about eight Japanese farmers in our town and most of them owned their land. After Alien Land Law was passed, they made arrangements with their children or friends who were citizens, and obtained white sponsors in order to run their farms legally. In other words, they obeyed the letter of the law but evaded its spirit. A couple of them were exposed for violation of the Land Law and their land was confiscated by the State. Really, every

farmer lived in fear and trembling. Since at any time the Prosecutor's office could pick up violators at will, anyone might be apprehended as a violator. So actually we were all walking a tightrope.[49]

Though many of the prior activities were directed against the Issei, the Nisei inherited this same racist tradition. Although few segregated schools existed, not many were able to find employment in non-Japanese enterprises commensurate with their training. For example, few, if any, teacher-trained Nisei were employed in public schools. The litany of racial maltreatment only confirms the experiences of other colored minorities: frequent physical and verbal abuses; exclusion from hotels, barbershops, restaurants, and other service enterprises; residential segregation; Jim Crowism in theaters and other entertainment places—some theaters had a "nigger heaven" for Japanese; occasional arson and bombings; boycotting of Japanese businesses; "Jap quotas" in professional schools; and so on.

The crowning act of this list is the incarceration of over one hundred ten thousand Japanese (of which 64 *percent were American citizens*) during World War II. This number included about 88 percent of all mainland Japanese. From December 7, 1941, to February 19, 1942, a little more than two months transpired between Pearl Harbor and the president's signing of Executive Order No. 9066, which legalized the removal of Japanese Americans from the West Coast. A comparable number of Japanese in Hawaii, several thousand miles closer to the war zone, were not incarcerated at the insistence of the United States Army, which needed them for labor to sustain the Hawaiian war efforts. The same organization, the Army, insisted that the mainland Japanese were a military threat in spite of no evidence of sabotage and other evidence to the contrary which was available for official inspection (e.g., FBI reports). The technical grounds of military necessity was the official reason, but there is little doubt about the prevailing anti-Japanese sentiment resulting from the history of anti-Asian and anti-colored attitudes, the dramatic events of the war, opportunists (political leaders such as Earl Warren, newspaper writers, and competing farmers and businessmen), and racial attitudes of civil and military leaders.[50]

The term "relocation camp" has a neutral bureaucratic tone, as do the various other terms referring to concentration camps—assembly center, internment camp, relocation center, and segregation center. With the years these terms have been increasingly abandoned for the more emotional one of "concentration camp." We have come to associate that term with Buchenwald, Dachau, and Auschwitz—all notorious places of death, with images of bodies stacked like cords of wood. America's concentration camps did not match the physical tortures and abuses of those camps. However, the American government did take both aliens and citizens out of their homes, with little regard to property and existing lives, and placed them under armed guards in isolated, barbwired camps. The Supreme Court, after the fact, legitimized this unprecedented violation of rights in a country which prided itself on slogans of freedom and humanitarian principles.

During the war, the governmental agency in charge of incarcerated Japanese Americans was the War Relocation Authority (WRA). The WRA decided, even prior to completion of the last camp structure, that the relocation was unnecessary for military reasons. Therefore, in conjunction with the Endo case, which involved the illegality of the WRA detaining a loyal American citizen,[51] and the combat sacrifices of the Japanese American 442nd Infantry Battalion, among others, government policy was directed toward dissolution of the camps and reintegration of these people. In this case the government was acting as an advocate for the rights of Japanese Americans, contrary to the public sentiments which favored continued incarceration and even worse treatment.[52]

Though the immediate postwar years saw the continuation of blatant anti-Japanese actions (e.g., shooting, arson, threats, and dynamiting), the war years were a turning point in the long years of racial oppression. With the conclusion of the war and the American occupation of Japan, sentiment toward Japan began its transformation from enemy to friend. This turnabout in conjunction with the realization of unjust treatment of Japanese Americans, as well as their well-publicized loyalty, changed the wider society's feelings toward them. On the legal front, the Oyama case, concerning the rights of land ownership, led to the abolishment in 1946 of the California Alien Land Laws.[53] In 1952 the Issei were permitted citizenship rights and new Japanese immigration was allowed after twenty-eight years of exclusion. Residential restrictions were relaxed and channels of occupational mobility were opened.

The current state of Japanese Americans seems idyllic in contrast to the prior history of maltreatment. However, they remain a race apart, encountering such discriminatory practices as: continued lack of housing in some areas; reluctance to hire and promote Japanese in white organizations; discourtesies, slights, and stereotypes in face-to-face interaction; continued downgrading of Asians as people; omission of Japanese American experiences from educational curricula; stereotyping in the public media; and denial of governmental services and monies to the Japanese American community.

To other minorities, this recitation of woes presents no new information except for the specifics of the maltreatment of yet another minority, for even the relocation experience is no news to Indian Americans, who have had repeated "relocations." To majority peoples the recitation may be news. Many non-Japanese react with disbelief about the incarceration, as if such an act would not be repeated. An underlying assumption is that American society has come a long way toward racial harmony. However, many Japanese Americans continue to feel suspicious about this assumption, for even the most dramatic act, the relocation episode, was and continues to be supported: in 1943 Bloom and Riemer[54] found approval of Japanese incarceration among 63 percent of West Coast college students, and 73 percent approval among Midwest college students; a 1969 survey reveals that over 48 percent of California respondents continue to feel the same way.[55] The latter report probably reflects a lack of concern rather than an active interest in Japanese Americans as persons with rights and feelings.

Aside from those with concerns involving issues of legal principles, why should the average person be asked to read about a people whose numbers barely reach three in one thousand? As we have stated, the litany of woes is no news. The answer lies in the successful performances of a minority who suffered the maltreatment dispensed to people of color. They stand as a "model" to all other minority proples. Before we get carried away with a good success story, let us examine the specifics of Japanese American response to racial subordination: (1) they exhibited a low profile with surprisingly little evidence of overt counteraggression; (2) they showed little evidence of social and personal pathologies commonly found among colored minorities; and (3) they showed high levels of occupational, educational, and economic success. After examining these points, we will introduce some theoretical explanations.

The Low Profile. Throughout the early exclusion treatment, the Japanese Americans showed restraint. From their perspective they practiced *gaman*, which means suppressing and internalizing one's emotion and anger, a norm related to *enyro* ideals.[56] The two Issei poets quoted earlier practiced *gaman*. Another Issei, who ran a hotel, reflects this same spirit:

> In Portland, where the air of exclusion was comparatively weak, yet from time to time white guests came in, looked at our faces, said, "Jap!" and left. But even though we were insulted, we kept on working silently.[57]

"Quiet people" indeed. In spite of recorded instances of counteraggression, the *gaman* attitude prevailed, perhaps reflecting the image of an inferior subject of colonialist overlords.

Modell[58] reports an absence of Issei affirmation of questions ascertaining whether they felt bothered, hindered, or even noticed opposition from Caucasians. Though the respondents were interviewed in the early 1960s about their prior half-century life, a time span which might reduce the sharp edges of rebuffs, the response seems paradoxical in light of the documented history of racial opposition. In contrast, respondents from Ito's social history[59] freely discuss their strong feelings about racial opposition, as illustrated by previous quotations from that source. How do we juxtapose Modell's observations with Ito's observations of ostensibly the same population? Among Japanese there are conventions of politeness which affect what will be said. Thus Japanese respondents will often give replies which they think the interviewer desires. If they are asked about racial prejudice by strangers or persons representing some official agency, they are prone to give positive or noncommittal responses. Often the interviewer asks questions expecting strictly dichotomous responses—yes or no. Thus the Japanese are often queried over whether or not they like America. In reality, respondents possess many attitudes and feelings (sometimes conflicting), and therefore their replies depend upon circumstances of interviewing, relationship with interviewers, and the specific questions. These are not new insights, but they provide a context within which to examine Modell's paradox. He suggests, "In retrospect the Issei define the rebuffs they have in fact received as not serious, because they have never adopted . . . a view of their stay here conforming to the assimilationist ideal."[60] Although Modell's observation has virtue, it is too simplistic, in light of Ito's materials. We feel the Japanese respondents continue to sustain their self-conception as being Meiji-like subordinates in a social structure which placed the Japanese in the lower ranks. Their continued silence to outsiders concerning racial oppression is but a ritual affirmation of existing social stratification.

Though the above commentaries refer largely to Issei, they have relevance for Nisei. The Nisei were not socialized in Meiji Japan, but they have acquired and sustained a subordinate role as "inferiors." During the immediate postwar years Nisei consciously sustained a low profile in order to avoid suspicion, clearly the role of subordinate people; for example, in Chicago they avoided being in crowds of more than three Nisei on public streets or five in restaurants. Kitano[61] points out how self-conscious Nisei are about appearing ostentatious—they avoid loud talking, loud clothes, big cars, and fancy houses. Perhaps the most striking instance of subordination, the acquiescence during World War II, remains a reluctant topic for most Nisei. Many Sansei claim their parents rarely mention the camp years, and outsiders are startled to hear this period dealt with as just "water under the bridge" (e.g., Kato, a Nisei, says, "The Nisei and Issei were willing to forgive and forget the incidents during W. W. II. . .").[62] Kikuchi, a Nisei diarist, wrote that the Japanese were not "too damaged" by the war experience, but in fact gained from it.[63]

Though the camp experience remains for many an "unspoken" topic, or is even treated as an ordinary affair, it remains the most important event for many Nisei. Some say they had delayed reactions, such as one Nisei who claims that he became angry only ten years after; others treat those years as a major chronological marker of their lives, using phrases like "before the war" and "after the war." For some there is no "after the war" because they feel emotionally buried in those camps, as if they have not been able to pass through a mourning period for a lost one.[64] Fujimoto,[65] who spent his early childhood in a camp, feels it is his most important life experience, having consequences even to this day; whenever he meets other Japanese, he inquires into their camp experiences. As mentioned earlier, in spite of Nisei silence with Sansei and outsiders, a favorite topic whenever Nisei get together is "camp." Although no systematic research exists on the impact of camp life, these comments support the importance of that experience in spite of silence and trivialization by Nisei.

Are Nisei exhibiting *gaman* or *enryo*? Definitive research on this topic remains to be done; however, there is no reason to doubt the continuity of the Meiji-era inferior role among Nisei. In short, the Japanese American response to the oppressions of society has not been one of challenge, but of silent affirmation of racial domination, a policy conducive to favorable societal reaction; e.g., "You Japanese have done a splendid job without making a fuss like other minority groups."

A Law and Order People. Migration is typically associated with social and personal pathologies, such as crime, poverty, ignorance, and physical and mental ill-health, which result from the uprooting process that destroys social organizations and places migrants at the bottom of the social stratification. Japanese migrants were not the worst elements of Japanese society, nor were they the poorest peasants. Among all American immigrants of the day, they were not only the most literate, but also brought the most money. After the turn of the century the Japanese government, fearing damage to their image, screened out undesirable persons, such as those of ill repute.

Consistent with this selection process, the Japanese were among the most law-abiding citizens, as indicated by traditional measures of pathologies. This pattern carries to this day. For example, Japanese Americans have among the lowest arrest rates since their arrival—in 1960 their arrest rate (per 100,000 population) was 187, compared with 1,461 for whites and 5,642 for blacks; their juvenile delinquency rate (per 100,000) was 450, compared with 1,481 for non-Japanese. Studies of inner cities frequently shows high rates of delinquency among all ethnic groups; however, the Japanese are an exception.[66]

Only 1.6 percent of Japanese American marriages end in divorce, indicating a high degree of family stability. Furthermore, few Japanese show up on welfare rolls, and generally they have lower unemployment rates than other groups; in 1960, 2.8 percent were unemployed, while 5.5 percent whites and 12.7 percent blacks were unemployed. In short, all of these traditional measures indicate a law-abiding, self-sufficient, and compliant people.[67]

Success and Assimilation. As previous discussions reveal, Japanese Americans achieved higher levels of education and occupation than whites, and lagged behind the latter only in income. Although the Levine and Montero study[68] of socioeconomic mobility oversamples the better-off sector of this group, its indications of continued upward movement are consistent with other research. Among their Issei sample, 35 percent had attained white-collar positions (5 percent professional, 28 percent managerial, and 2 percent clerical) and, as one might suspect, a large percentage were self-employed small businessmen. Forty-five percent were occupied with farm positions, and the remaining 20 percent were blue-collar workers. Social mobility among Nisei reveals two trends: movement away from farm to white-collar occupations, and from managerial to professional roles. Among Nisei males, 71 percent are white-collar, 12 percent are farm, and 17 percent are blue-collar workers.

Education figures from the same study show 57 percent of Nisei respondents having at least some college, and 88 percent of Sansei with comparable education. At the time of this survey, the majority of those with some college were still in the process of finishing a degree. About seven in ten Sansei seek a professional position, in comparison with 5 percent of Issei and 32 percent of Nisei who have actually achieved such a position. These figures show a continuing high rate of occupational and educational mobility.[69]

An expected corollary to success is assimilation, which implies an eventual disappearance of Japanese Americans as separate from mainstream America. Though the ethnic community remains separate and identifiable, current trends seem to indicate its eventual demise.

Levine and Montero[70] find white-collar Nisei more assimilated than blue-collar Nisei, as reflected by residence in primarily white neighborhoods, greater acceptance of children marrying outsiders, lesser involvement with the ethnic community, and lesser fluency in the Japanese language. These observations, in conjunction with earlier remarks on a rising proportion of Japanese moving into white-collar positions, suggest increasing assimilation for the entire ethnic community. Numerous studies of attitudes and behaviors document a growing similarity of each succeeding generation with white Americans.[71] For instance, the Kitano study shows a decreasing level of ethnic identity with each succeeding generation. Based on data collected in 1966 and 1967, the Japanese American Research Project shows numerous indicators of assimilation: 32 percent of Nisei want their offspring to associate exclusively with other Japanese, versus 9 percent of Sansei; one-half of Nisei have at least one non-Japanese friend, versus three-quarters of Sansei; each succeeding generation is less likely to be Buddhist (Issei—65 percent; Nisei—37 percent; Sansei—24 percent); each succeeding generation is more likely to live in non-Japanese areas (Issei—45 percent; Nisei—58 percent; Sansei—67 percent); and among those who belong to a voluntary organization, 60 percent of Nisei belong to an all-Japanese group, versus 49 percent of Sansei.[72]

Perhaps out-marriage is the most sensitive indicator of assimilation. Very few Issei or Nisei married outsiders, reflecting both internal community pressures and disapproval from the wider society as found in antimiscegenation laws (California declared them unconstitutional in 1948, when the out-marriage rate for Los Angeles County was 11 percent). By the 1970s the rate of out-marriage averaged 50 percent.[73] The Montero and Levine study[74] indicates, among married Japanese, 10 percent of Nisei and 40 percent of Sansei married outsiders in 1967. Since 70 percent of Sansei were unmarried at that time, it is important to note that 55 percent of single Sansei were either going steady with or intending to marry an outsider. In brief, reports on attitudes, residence, friendship, religion, voluntary organization membership, and marriage indicate increasing assimilation.

COMMUNITY AND SOCIETY

How did the Japanese American community survive their adversities and succeed so well? How did a previously maligned group become "good" people? We have documented not only the adversities, but the success and "imminent" disappearance of this ethnic minority. Two factors are generally used to explain this phenomenon: (1) the ethnic culture; and (2) the cohesive ethnic community. We discussed both factors above and have all but stated their causal power. Hosokawa, a Nisei newspaperman, asks, "What is there about my cultural heritage that sustained me in the time of trial?"[75] A chorus responds: "Japanese cultural values."[76] Caudill and DeVos[77] suggest the compatability of Japanese cultural values and norms with the American setting. The ethnic culture seemed to produce people who caused little trouble, as indicated by low rates of pathology and acquiescence to white domination, and who have been strongly achievement oriented.

The second explanation, not necessarily contradictory to the first, proposes the force of ethnic group solidarity in providing materials and moral support for success:

The achievement . . . can be explained by the high degree of community organization which this group established, the opportunities for advancement which the organization created, and the controls over the population which the organization made possible.[78]

Each person, each family, each locality has owed the community allegiance: nothing is done without fully considering its effect on "the Japanese image." In return, the community has bolstered every such part with material and moral support. Each family, each institution has been more effectively working within a context of accord.[79]

Kitano uses the same explanation when accounting for differences between deviant and nondeviant Japanese. Deviant Japanese are more likely than nondeviant Japanese to be marginal to the ethnic community —greater likelihood of coming from broken homes, less involved in ethnic social circles, less identified with the community, and less likely to appear Japanese (dress, speech, and physical demeanor). Among the relatively few Japanese in institutions for the mentally ill, the disproportionate number are marginal to the ethnic community, e.g., the elderly, single, lower-class male. Kitano suggests the low rates of deviancy can be explained by the community provision of an alternative, legitimate opportunity structure to satisfy economic, social, psychological, and political needs within the community when such opportunities are restricted in the wider society.[80] In summary, both values and community solidarity are frequent explanations for Japanese American motives for achievement and acceptability to American middle classes, which in turn explain their successes.

This section traced the major preoccupation with the success story, but before the reader can settle on this characterization important questions must be addressed. The next section reflects on those questions.

Reflections

Ferment of social change often makes prevailing images and questions obsolete. The topics of success, assimilation, and explanations of success are sensitive to societal changes because they are part of the mechanics of describing, explaining, and legitimizing social order. Thus instead of being detached from the society, they are thoroughly embedded within the world views of participants, including both subjects and observers. Consequently, those changing images and questions are sensitive reflections of predominating social thought and pressures. The following reflections will examine these questions: (1) are they really successful? (2) will they assimilate? and (3) how are those explanations of success limited?

WHAT MEASURE SUCCESS?

A generation ago the success story would have been an adequate characterization of the Japanese American minority, but changing expectations and viewpoints have rendered it obsolete. The measures of occupation, education, and income have obscured the qualified success, which includes both narrowly limited occupational fields and confinement in the middle and lower ranks of organizations. Japanese are stereotyped as unqualified for leadership, lacking assertiveness and ability to reach out toward others. Kitano[81] observes few Japanese Americans (in contrast to Japanese from Japan) in upper ranks of organizations, and a reluctance among whites to view them as anything but high-class subordinates. Casual observations of Japanese on college campuses often lead to the imagery of them as engineers, scientists, accountants, and in associated areas involving technical and instrumental skill; these observations are confirmed by studies showing large percentages of Japanese enrolled in areas requiring a minimum of self-expression. For example, Watanabe[82] reports 68.2 percent of them on one college campus majoring in engineering, physical sciences, and associated fields. Parallel to complaints by women liberationists about the limitations imposed on them, Japanese Americans are experiencing limitations imposed on them, of choice, through the process of stereotyping by the wider society and the heritage of accommodation of prior generations.

Related to these observations are numerous psychologically oriented studies which document correlates of the historic Japanese subordinate status—as individuals they seem to lack spontaneity, creativity, expressiveness, leadership potential, "normal" resolution of emotional problems, and so on.[83] Arkoff and Weaver[84] and Maykovich[85] report on ambivalent self-acceptance of their Japanese bodies in light of white physical standards of white skin, tall stature, deep-set eyes, and wavy hair of a color other than black. Associated problems of self-concept and identity are also reported.

What about Japanese Americans who have not realized the "American Dream"? The 1970 census lists 43,356 individual Japanese living at or below the poverty level. They constitute about 7.5 percent of all Japanese, and among them 20.8 percent are sixty-five or older. These figures, relative to other groups, are small and, given the preoccupation with success, such small proportions cause little or no concern. However, to deny their existence is to overlook that undesirable side which inhabits all ethnic communities. The sizable percentage among that group identifies a neglected sector—the poor and elderly Issei.[86]

The recurrent portrayal of well-being reflects the community's concern with ethnic image since the earliest days. One consequence of this concern is the low rate of officially recorded pathologies. For example, refusal to receive welfare assistance stems from anticipated loss of face for both individual and family. Extension of this preoccupation to mental health, delinquency, crime, and all areas of deviation creates a possible disjuncture between official recognition and experienced pathologies. From the ethnic community member's view, troubles are best contained within; e.g., special drug programs have been organized within the ethnic community. Kitano[87] records an instance in which a Japanese family sent two troublesome males to Japan in order to prevent harm to the community's image. Hence statistics on well-being are probably inflated, obscuring many instances of individual suffering.

Recent observations of Japanese Americans in small businesses do not confirm expectations of success. According to Tsutomu Uchida, executive director of the Asian American Business Alliance in Los Angeles,[88] ethnic businesses are "mom and pop" operations which seem destined for marginal existence because the owners lack aggressiveness required for success. He further notes that recent Asian immigrants show greater aggressiveness than American-born ethnic entrepreneurs. We know that the Issei were very daring and willing to take chances, whereas succeeding generations seem to have acquired a more subordinate attitude of low profile and acquiescence. This points to the problem of accommodation, a practice which may have worked in the past, but seems to have less payoff today. The observation also raises questions about our previous interpretation of Japanese Americans as following the *enryo* norms. Rather than interpreting their behavior as a result of these norms, one might claim the norms validated or normalized the colonial-subject status of the group. Recent Japanese immigrants have not had the experience of a lifetime of inferior status vis-à-vis another ethnic group, and therefore they are less likely to acquiesce and melt into anonymity.

Though these commentaries dwell on success as desirable, the changing emphasis lies not in being required to be successful, but in creating options compatible with individual inclination. Surely this is a sentiment compatible with the feelings of most Americans, as against prescription of adult roles.

Stereotyping persists in the public's mind, and social institutions seem destined to perpetuate it. Kane's study of forty-five textbooks reveals Japanese being "frequently treated in a manner implying they were racially inferior. Offensive generalizations were applied . . . and positive materials about their correct status and contributions were omitted. . . ."[89] As Ogawa[90] suggests, "Japs" have become Japanese, but nevertheless they remain less than human. Perhaps it is a feature of our

The Reports

society to desire treatment as a person rather than a category. To the extent that Japanese Americans accept this sentiment, they continue to feel separate from the society.

An outsider might react with puzzlement over this questioning of success—perhaps with an attitude of "What more do you want?" Previous goals of education, occupation, and income are seen as inadequate, with rising expectations directed toward less tangible goals of full equality, freedom to break out of narrowly defined pigeonholes, dignity, and so on. An exchange of commentaries between a Nisei and Sansei illustrates the changing expectations and values. Hisashi Kobayashi, a Nisei, states:

> Though they have been spat upon, ridiculed, denied citizenship, and incarcerated in prison camps, the Japanese have persevered. They have survived the white racist society and revealed how evil it can be. At the same time they did not show outright hostility toward the white society responsible for these acts. . . . The old Japanese character attributes instilled in them made them decide to suffer the indignities and hardships and hopefully, through perseverance survive and make the white majority realize its error.
> . . . The Asian-American is accused of losing his identity in pursuit of the betterment of life for his family. However, his great adaptability enables him to assimilate himself while maintaining his racial identity. These attributes of hard work, quietness, and ambition are being attacked as an "Asian Uncle Tomism."[91]

Ken Tanaka writes in reply:

> Mr. Kobayashi subscribes to the school of thought which upholds the attainment of "good life" (usually meaning a life imbued with sufficient prestige and material possession to elicit approval of others and to satisfy much of one's desires), however often at the expense of losing and suppressing what the younger Asian-American considers to be human right. . . .[92]

Tanaka's reference to "human right" includes democratic rights and human respect. Their talk and the underlying moralities separate these two writers, reflecting different world views.

ASSIMILATION AND LOSS OF IDENTITY?

Many observers anticipate the eventual disappearance of Japanese Americans because assimilation is expected to destroy ethnic group identity. For example, Americans of German descent treat their "ethnicity" as incidental to other, more important identities, such as occupation. Although the influence of the ethnic community has eroded, some see prospects for its survival in a new synthetic form. Some studies indicate the continuing viability of the ethnic community for identity, sociability, and support functions.[93]

Reported studies on assimilation are frequently based on questionable assumptions and ill-conceived instruments, such as the use of Christian membership as indicative of assimilation, thus overlooking membership in predominantly ethnic churches—a feature of continuing ethnic social organization.

Matsumoto, Meredith, and Masuda[94] speculate about the paradoxical finding of a greater degree of ethnic identity among Seattle Japanese than among those in Honolulu. The paradox follows from the observation of a continuing high degree of ethnic organization among Honolulu Japanese. They reflect on the ethnic identity questionnaire, which is largely based on Meiji values rather than the apparent emergence in Honolulu of a neo-Meiji value system which nevertheless supports continuing ethnic solidarity. In other words, a focus on traditional Japanese values as a measure of ethnic social organization may obscure continued ethnic group solidarity which has evolved a new set of values.

A basic flaw in these studies has been an inability to relate their measures to the day-to-day lives of Japanese Americans and how they remain wedded to communal obligations. In addition, they ask questions which are insensitive to the interview situation (and the implied social obligations and vicissitudes of interactions), as if interviews could occur in a vacuum. In short, many of the studies on assimilation using traditional measures of in-group orientation and behavior fail to articulate with the actual behaviors and meanings accorded by group members. The studies, while attempting to use objective measures of assimilation, fail to ground them in an adequate ethnography of Japanese Americans.

Takagi[95] and Kagiwada[96] have reacted to the underlying racism of many American sociological works such as the writings of Robert Park, a pioneer in assimilation studies. Both react to the usage of the assimilation concept, which seems to support: (1) Anglo-American culture as the most desirable standard: (2) assimilation necessarily involving acceptance of Anglo-American culture; (3) foreign cultures threatening this civilized culture; and (4) assimilation as the goal of all colored minorities. Both researchers advocate an alternative view, including: (1) Anglo-American culture as not necessarily the most desirable; and (2) alternative cultures being fostered within the society.

Takagi[97] claims a racist bias in American social science, particularly those culture and personality theories which explain Japanese American success on the basis of compatibility of Japanese and Anglo-American values, e.g., deferred gratification—supposedly values of high objective virtue. Alternative to this view on the intrinsic virtues of Anglo-American values is their extrinsic function—persons who display those values are rewarded by gatekeepers of the society, e.g., teachers. In short, the notion of assimilation, instead of being a purely objective concept, has had a questionable racist and political background. Historically, Robert Park and other American sociologists were skeptical about the assimilation of the Japanese because they were very foreign and seemed unlikely to accept American ways. Succeeding social scientists reinterpret them as already possessing, if not identical values, values highly compatible with the American setting. This turnabout reveals as much about outsiders who have labeled them as it does about the people themselves. The term "assimilation" has been used to justify the existing social order as much as to describe the well-being of colored minorities.

These comments are not meant as arguments against a possible factual disappearance of Japanese Americans, but as reflections on the ways commentators have chosen to characterize the possible demise. Pressures within the past generation have given rise to the possibility of a renewed ethnic identity, but whether it will involve a rejection of previous notions of assimilation and acculturation remains problematic. Current efforts at reconstituting ethnic groups, both academically and in the community, reflect the success of Afro-Americans in claiming the right to determine their destiny, including an in-group revision of their place in society. In the past academics were concerned with assimilation and acculturation because they reflected the common concern of the larger society, i.e., "How does it adapt a minority to the society?" The failure of the melting pot thesis has led to its opposite, pluralist thesis. There is pressure by majority members on minority groups to pursue ethnic consciousness—"Do your own thing." Paradoxically, while sociologists anticipate the eventual assimilation of Japanese Americans, younger Japanese seem to be advocating the affirmation of a separate ethnic group, partially reflecting the sentiment of the anti-melting pot thesis current among most minorities. In conjunction with the legitimacy of blacks demanding to represent themselves and not have their images created by white experts, many Japanese assert that they have been inaccurately depicted. The issues of bias and cultural relativity raise questions about the adequacy of white social scientists in dealing with minority groups, or even of minority researchers who have accepted white perspectives.

White Americans remain unwilling to distinguish among different Asians, and consequently they tend to treat Asians as a homogeneous category. Each Asian group has a different background culture, history of relations between country of origin and the United States, and migration pattern, resulting in different interests and problems. In spite of these real differences, there may emerge an Asian American or Pan-Asian identity, reflecting common colonial subject-like status.

The American Indians have not always thought of themselves as a single people, but their identification and treatment by the society as a single people has created "native Americans." Similarly, Asians of various backgrounds may see themselves as single people. On several West Coast college campuses Asian American programs have emerged, in many instances on the initiative of college administrators (e.g., Asian American Studies Center at UCLA). Recently the National Institute of Mental Health (NIMH) has initiated and funded an Asian American mental health organization reflecting both political and bureaucratic pressures toward the creation of an Asian American community. This proposed community includes the "leftover" among colored peoples (the major groups being black, Chicano, and native American), including East Indian, Pakistani, Guamanian, Samoan, Indonesian, Filipino, Vietnamese, Thai, Burmese, Chinese, Korean, Japanese, and all people who are both racially Asian and whose ancestors come from Eastern Asia and the Pacific Rim. Bureaucratically, it is simpler for government agencies to deal with these hodgepodge groups (the total American population of which is less than two million) as a single entity. They are also being encouraged to consolidate for political reasons—more power in unity than in separateness.

We are cautious in predicting the development of a viable Asian American identity and political organization, but the single issue which unites them is their common experience of racism, parallel with the Third World on the international scene. In short, Japanese Americans facing assimilation, however defined, also face prospects of new identities resulting from societal changes. Any consideration of these possible changes requires a reflexive analysis of the grounds upon which assessments are made.

REVISIONIST VIEWS ON THE MAKING
OF GOOD PEOPLE

Are the "good" Japanese people really the product of a cultural background compatible with middle-class virtues? What about the cohesiveness of their social organization? Revisionists reexamine these questions with an emphasis on redirecting attention to the societal context as explanation. Formal features of Japanese culture emphasize maintenance of proper hierarchical relations or social order. Changes in social order are legitimized through the vocabulary of traditional norms. This insistence on the appearance of order accounts for the look of continuity in Japanese society in spite of the tensions, struggles, and conflicts which are ubiquitous in its history. The danger in analyzing Japanese society or Japanese American organizations lies in overlooking the day-to-day and covert actions which seem contrary to public presentations. For example, little mention has been made of socialist and left-wing activities among early Japanese Americans. Those aspects of any subordinate group which threaten existing relations are often suppressed. Thus the traditional Japanese normative view of honoring authority and power is quite compatible with prevailing dominant group sentiments, which raises questions about the usual depictions of Japanese American compliance.

An examination of Japanese American history reveals instances of insubordination such as labor strikes. Lind[98] points out that the history of Hawaiian plantation difficulties, especially in 1909 and 1920, when workers demanded higher wages, involved Japanese in the forefront. Yoneda[99] and Ichioka[100] write about the buried past of an "unquiet" people—those not of the same mold as people who stereotypically are guided by *enryo* norms. How do we deal with these opposing views? A suggestive lead is found in Tong's article[101] on Chinese Americans. The docility of the Chinese, similar to the Japanese quiet character, is attributed to their culture. However, Tong suggests the early Chinese immigrants were not strongly imbued with a culture of docility and, in fact, exhibited an undeniable assertiveness. The docility, Tong argues, results from years of racial oppression rather than cultural background; e.g., at one time on the American West Coast the Chinese were killed freely, as if they were not human. Uyematsu[102] concurs with Tong's analysis as applied to the Japanese. Hence the traditional characterization of the Japanese as quiet and subordinate, although descriptive of many contemporary Japanese Americans, is explained by two opposing views—either as a result of Japanese culture or of racial oppression. Although compelling evidence for either argument remains to be gathered, the phenomenon can be treated as an interaction between culture and societal context—the traditional framework was used to organize an already existing racist nexus. Further research is needed to illuminate how the traditional framework was used within this context.

Others also observe the inadequacy of culture and group solidarity explanations of success. The postwar shift in race relations, and the associated upward social mobility of this ethnic group, cannot be explained sufficiently by those factors or by the public's recognition of injustice and the combat sacrifices of Japanese Americans. Those explanations of success overlook the Japanese possession of middle-class virtues long before the postwar period. The period after World War II was one of general prosperity, which meant the Japanese were not seen as a threat to the laboring classes as they had been in the post-World War I period. The latter period was one of economic hardships associated with high levels of racism, as previously experienced by the Chinese during times of economic hardships.

Most researchers on Japanese Americans focus on the ethnic group itself, leaving an impression that racism is a constant force without a sociological or historical context. Racism is a shorthand means of describing ill treatment of a racial minority, but a full characterization requires a description of the racial context. Miyamoto,[103] citing McWilliams' work,[104] traces California politics to the large stream of migrants who sought easy wealth but, finding themselves exploited by the few who made it big, developed early recognition of power in organization, such as labor unions. Thus a significant part of California history is the struggle between laboring people and the owning class. Asians were often used to break strikes and keep wages low. Asians also seem to become independent farmers and small business entrepreneurs:

> The underlying racial prejudice . . . came from the psychology of persons who themselves largely were "outsiders" and who, confronted by the absence of a well-established social organization, had constantly to keep an eye on the "other fellow" to guard against the loss of values won by hard struggle.[105]

The Japanese did not inherit only anti-Asian prejudice, but also the economic and social conditions which fostered it.

Finally, after World War II, problems with other racial minorities (e.g., blacks and Mexican Americans) became more prominent. In fact, the Japanese were diminishing as a proportion of the population relative to other racial groups. Both blacks and Japanese were less than 3 percent of the Los Angeles County population before World War II (respectively 2.7 percent and 1.3 percent), but after the war blacks increased significantly and Japanese decreased in proportion (1960: black—7.6 percent, Japanese—1.3 percent).[106] Associated with the diminishing proportion was an increasing reference to Japanese Americans as a model for other minorities. In short, the success of Japanese Americans results from a variety of factors other than cultural heritage—economic conditions, history of California politics, international relations, relative numbers.

The social and historic context affects not only a racial minority; it also affects the questions and preoccupations with the minority. The earlier preoccupation with the success story stems from our country's traditionally lower tolerance of ethnic differences and a desire to foster structural assimilation of minorities. In Brazil, where higher tolerance of ethnic diversity exists, studies of Japanese migrants and their descendants focus on social class, clearly a traditional Brazilian preoccupation. In contrast, American studies of Japanese focus on their social problems as a disadvantaged minority group. This difference between Brazil and the United States suggests how our concern over minorities reflects the wider society's ideologies.[107]

Recent trends in race relations dwell less on accommodation and more on a pluralist solution. Regarding Japanese Americans, the image of acquiescence and a demand to be "oneself" are both highly non-Japanese because they deemphasize social relations and obligations and emphasize the individual.

The previous quotes illustrating general differences (the Kobayashi-Tanaka confrontation) document a shift in viewpoint accounting for the conflict of interpretation on the role of Japanese Americans, such as whether or not they have dignity. The shift from accommodation to confrontation involves a shift from collectivity to individual orientation, and from rituals of social order to the assertion of one's inner feelings. Paradoxically, the older values led to public affirmation of assimilation and acculturation, and the newer values led to a surface display of ethnic separation which nevertheless shows closer affinity to contemporary American values.

Conclusions

"Japs are now good people. They are successful because they have worked hard and they ought to be a model for other minorities." This crude characterization has been increasingly attacked by Japanese Americans, reflecting changes in minority relations. The emphasis on success in occupation as well as in areas of citizenship seems to be, in retrospect, the majority's preoccupation with Asian minority people. An alternative viewpoint suggests that the emphasis distorts the feelings and perspectives of Japanese Americans, and that new themes ought to be developed.

Whether or not we choose to look at the revisionist outlook as temporary and superficial, we are faced with the political and moral problems resulting from attempts to characterize. For what end are we creating images of this group? The images are as much a reflection of the creator as they are of the subject. Some readers may feel dissatisfied with our qualified answers and views of Japanese Americans—perhaps some still have questions, such as: "Are they, or are they not, successful?" "Aren't they basically middle class, and therefore assimilation is only a matter of time?" "Assuming they are successful, isn't the best explanation still their cultural values?" As we have suggested, the interpretation of success, assimilation, and other descriptions depends on one's criteria and more generally on one's ideological and social purchase.

These considerations speak to questions of truth. Implicitly, we have treated the success theme as defective and therefore of questionable

288

truth value. However, we have alluded to the circumstantial features of accounts, which alerts us to the particular truth as a reflection of the context. Therefore, on some occasions the Horatio Alger–like characterization of Japanese Americans has some utility, while on other occasions it fails miserably. By the same token, revisionist views have their role in some contexts, such as attempts to revitalize the ethnic community. Thus truth is tied to a context of usage.

One approach is the examination of how various accounts of Japanese Americans are generated and sustained. Although previous remarks contain allusions to this perspective, systematic discussions remain beyond this report. Further studies ought to consider exploring this perspective. Silverman states:

> We take the objective character of social reality to reside in socially organized acts of interpretation and maintain that social relations and institutions have no inherent meaning or nature. . . . The problem for sociology arises in discovering what routines of interpretation and action constitute, for members, what *they* come to regard (for all practical purposes) as a "family" and as "typical" family life, and how these interpretive schemes (background expectancies) rely on *their* sense of social structure.[108]

Substitute for "family" any social structure such as ethnic group or generation. In effect, Silverman suggests we need to examine social experiences in more detail, paying particular attention to the practices utilized by both the researcher and his subject. These remarks apply to all of our characterizations of Japanese American social organization, such as how Japanese norms were used to organize ethnic activities, how notions of generation are used on a day-to-day basis for organizing activities, and how Japanese Americans became "good" people.

Researchers on Japanese Americans often overreify notions of generation. Although demographic data correlate with generational labels, when generation is treated as a technical, and not necessarily social, matter, troubles arise for researchers. Numerous studies discover exceptions and find it necessary to use arbitrary judgments in classifying individuals. For example, the Japanese American Research Project at UCLA came across individuals whose fathers were Issei but whose mothers were Nisei; since they had no socially identified "two and one-half" generation, they choose to classify those individuals as Nisei rather than Sansei.[109] In contrast, Nakanishi,[110] while comparing generations, classified "mixed" generation respondents as Sansei (one had a Nisei mother and an Issei father, another had a Nisei father and a mother who was an Italian native). How do we reconcile these instances of ambiguity and arbitrary classification with technical and analytic ideals? Lyman offers these reflections:

> Age and situation may modify the strictness of membership in these generational group, but while persons might be informally reassigned to a group to which they do not belong by virtue of geographical or generational criteria, the *idea* of the groups remains intact as a working conception of social reality. . . . In practice they (offspring of mixed parentage) tend to demonstrate the sociological rule that status is as status does; that is, they enjoy the classification which social relations and personal behavior assign to them and which they assign to themselves.[111]

In short, generation is not an analytic device independent of members' usage. Research remains to be done on how members use generation to organize their everyday life. Our characterization of Japanese American social organization is largely, therefore, a member's characterization through and through. Parallel with this use of a generational label are Berreman's observations of Indian social identities: "Clearly, social identity cannot be understood without understanding the variation in peoples' knowledge and use of categorical terms and the individual and circumstantial sources of that variation."[112]

The general theme of this report—the making of "good" people—not only involves attempts to explain *why* they achieved success, but also involves *how* such a transformation took place. Though there is some debate about the reality of success, the society now treats the Japanese as socially acceptable. From the early migration period through World War II, the Japanese were seen and treated as a defective people; how were they transformed into good people?

Garfinkel's[113] study of degradation provides an excellent model for understanding the upgrading process. Garfinkel studied the process of degradation, or the transformation of persons from higher to lower status. For example, court procedures ending in guilty judgments involve a ritual whereby a previously "innocent" person is transformed into a "guilty" person. A retrospective reading of the person's guilt includes a charge that the person was guilty *all the while*, rather than his guilt being the result of the arbitrary judgment of the court proceedings. The accent of guilt seems to rest on the belief of "real" guilt which somehow exists as an invariant truth, independent of any process of discovery.

Similarly, Japanese Americans are not treated as having been "bad" in the first place, but rather that the truth of their moral character had yet to be discovered. The upgrading process is the reverse of degradation—a previously suspect people are later seen as having been virtuous all along, in spite of the society's blindness to that character. Although this process of status transformation remains to be researched, particularly the documentation on how it was done, this example illustrates theoretical questions which articulate Japanese American studies with sociology in general.

In effect, this example of societal rituals of status transformation, as well as the various practices of the community in producing social organization, are topics for deeper and further analysis. Many of the paradoxical findings, conflicting interpretations, and ambiguities displayed in extant materials will be clarified by examining the practices producing facts about Japanese Americans.

Finally, let us examine our frequent reference to racism. It is not a monolithic and abstract evil that hovers over Japanese Americans during their every waking moment. Not all whites have had the opportunity or desire to practice racism against this minority, and many whites have aided and abetted them through bad times, even at personal self-sacrifice, such as losing jobs. If provided with the facts, most persons today will agree that this country's Japanese were maltreated. A former political proponent of Japanese evacuation stated after the war, "Well, personally, I thought it was the right thing to do at the time, in the light of after events, I think it was wrong, now."[114]

Are we to infer some progress in American morals and humanity toward this minority? A "yes" answer is overly optimistic and overlooks social and economic conditions associated with racism. We are creatures of our times and we are overly prone to moralize about evil at a distance.

Most Americans may find difficulty in locating wrongdoing against this minority; however, in large part, their reflections occur as if racism could be treated in the abstract. The concreteness of racism need not manifest itself in such obvious guises as incarceration, but frequently exists in unspoken attitudes which lie beyond a curtain of kind and ingratiating remarks. Overt expressions of hostility are muted, given the polite demeanor of most persons and the world-wide success of Japanese. Thus the easy denial of racism against Japanese Americans exists because most persons are not faced with dramatic circumstances requiring awareness of it; rather it continues in mundane forms without reflection—it is the unthinking stereotyping and processing of Japanese Americans as something other than human.

NOTES

1. W. Petersen, "Success Story: Japanese American Style," *New York Times*, January 9, 1966, p. 20.
2. Richard Nixon quoted in W. Hosokawa, *Nisei: The Quiet Americans* (New York: Morrow, 1969), p. 493.

3. Ibid., p. 492.

4. V. S. McClatchy before the Senate, 1924. Quoted in R. Daniels, "The Issei Generation," in Roots: An Asian American Reader, ed. A. Tachiki et al. (Los Angeles: UCLA Asian American Studies Center, 1971), p. 99.

5. American Defender, April 27, 1935. Quoted in D. Ogawa, From Japs to Japanese (Berkeley, Calif.: McCutchan, 1971), p. 13.

6. Senator Phelan before the Senate Committee on Immigration and Naturalization, 1920. Quoted in C. McWilliams, California: The Great Expectation (New York: A. A. Wyn, 1949), p. 19.

7. Daniels, "Issei Generation."

8. S. Lyman, The Asian in the West (Reno: University of Nevada Press, 1970), p. 66.

9. Y. Ichihashi, Japanese in the United States (Stanford, Calif.: Stanford University Press, 1932), p. 62.

10. J. Modell, "The Japanese American Family," Pacific Historical Review 37 (1968): 78.

11. M. Marumoto, "First Year Immigrants to Hawaii," in East Across the Pacific, ed. H. Conroy and T. S. Miyakawa (Santa Barbara, Calif.: ABC CLIO Press, 1972), p. 5.

12. K. Mannheim, "The Problem of Generation," Psychoanalytic Review 57 (1970): 381.

13. Hosokawa, Nisei, p. 187.

14. E. Ko and A. Ohashi, "Interview with Chris Kato," Asian Family Affairs, 1973.

15. Lyman, Asian in the West, pp. 81–97.

16. Ibid.

17. Members' notion or view refers to how bona fide group members classify and judge something, such as who belongs to the minority group. Generally we try to present the member's viewpoints, but for a variety of reasons this is not always possible. For example, our use of "Japanese American" includes the Issei even though they may not have seen themselves as 'American." This deviation is made because it is stylistically more convenient. Our shortcomings in the use of members' notion results, in part, from the lack of sufficient research and theoretical developments on this critical concept. For a significant statement on this issue see H. Garfinkel, Studies in Ethnomethodology (Englewood Cliffs, N.J.: Prentice-Hall, 1967).

18. W. Petersen, Japanese Americans (New York: Random House, 1971), p. 15.

19. Ibid., pp. 72–81.

20. Calvin Schmid and Charles Nobbe, "Socio-economic Differentials among Non-White Races," American Sociological Review 30 (1965): 909–22.

21. Confucious, quoted by M. K. Maykovich, Japanese American Identity Dilemma (Tokyo: Waseda University Press, 1972), p. 32.

22. A. Arkoff, G. Meredith, and S. Iwahara, "Male Dominant and Equalitarian Attitudes in Japanese, Japanese-Americans, and Caucasian-American Students," Journal of Social Psychology 64 (1964): 225–29.

23. Harry Kitano, Japanese Americans (Englewood Cliffs, N.J.: Prentice-Hall 1969), pp. 103–5.

24. G. M. Meredith and C. Meredith, "Acculturation and Personality Among Japanese American College Students in Hawaii," Journal of Social Psychology 68 (1966): 175–82.

25. A. Arkoff, "Need Patterns in Two Generations of Japanese Americans in Hawaii," Journal of Social Psychology 50 (1959): 75–79.

26. S. Hutchinson et al., "Ethnic and Sex Factors in Classroom Responsiveness," Journal of Social Psychology 69 (1966): 321–25.

27. W. Caudill, "Japanese American Personality and Acculturation," Genetic Psychology Monograph 45 (1952): 3–102.

28. Lyman, Asian in the West, p. 85.

29. W. Caudill and G. De Vos, "Achievement, Culture, and Personality: The Case of the Japanese Americans," American Anthropologist 58 (1956): 1102–26.

30. Maykovich, *Japanese American Identity Dilemma*, pp. 35–36.
31. S. F. Miyamoto, "An Immigrant Community in America," in *East Across the Pacific*, ed. Conroy and Miyakawa, pp. 214–43.
32. I. Nodera "Second-generation Japanese and Vocations," *Sociology and Social Research* 21 (1937): 464–66.
33. Kitano, *Japanese Americans*, p. 156.
34. C. L. Johnson, *The Japanese-American Family and Community in Honolulu: Generational Continuities in Ethnic Affiliation*. Ph.D. diss., Syracuse University, 1972.
35. Miyamoto, "An Immigrant Community," p. 240.
36. Yukari Tomita, in K. Ito, *Issei: A History of Japanese Immigrants in North America*, trans. S. Nakamura and J.S. Gerard (Seattle, Wash.: Executive Committee for the Publication of *Issei*, 1973).
37. Katsuko Hirata, in ibid.
38. M. L. Hansen, *The Immigrant in American History* (Cambridge, Mass.: Harvard University Press, 1940).
39. Quoted in Max Lerner, *America as a Civilization* (New York: Simon and Schuster, 1957).
40. Andrew Rolle, *The Immigrant Upraised* (Norman, Okla.: University of Oklahoma Press, 1968), p. 259.
41. M. Pursinger, "Oregon's Japanese in World War II: A History of Compulsory Relocation" (Ph.D. diss., University of Southern California, 1961).
42. Incredible as this seems, the United States government, in a policy of racism consistent with these acts, incarcerated about two thousand Japanese-Peruvians (who were not under the legal jurisdiction of the United States in the first place), many Peruvian-born and married to native Peruvians. The government intended to use these Japanese as exchange hostages. Some persons in government circles even contemplated using Japanese Americans for the same purposes (Paul Jacobs, Saul Landau, and Eve Pell. *To Serve the Devil* [New York: Vintage Books, 1971]). As if this weren't the ultimate in violation of people's rights, in 1943 the American Legion convention proposed to send all Japanese Americans to Japan after the war as a nucleus for the "democratic" reorganization of Japan! Ostensibly Japanese Americans were to exhibit loyalty to the United States by complying with this charade. Fortunately this proposal did not materialize (Pursinger, "Oregon's Japanese," pp. 331 ff.). We were not the only country to incarcerate Japanese. Canada, like the United States, put its own citizens in concentration camps, but it also approved plans to ship all Japanese Canadians to Japan; only upon the strong objection of a small libertarian minority was the plan scrapped (Conroy and Miyakawa, eds., *East Across the Pacific*, p. 142).
43. Petersen, *Japanese Americans*, pp. 47–48.
44. Ibid., p. 51.
45. Ito, *Issei*, p. 155.
46. Petersen, op. cit., p. 32.
47. Daniels, "Issei Generation," p. 88; McWilliams, *California*, pp. 64–66; and J. Modell, 'On Being an Issei: Orientations Toward America' (Paper presented at 67th Annual Meeting of the American Anthropological Association, San Diego, Calif., 1970).
48. Kitano, *Japanese Americans*, p. 26, and M. Iwata, "The Japanese Immigrants in California Agriculture," *Agricultural History* 34 (1962): 25–37.
49. Ito, *Issei*, p. 165.
50. Petersen, *op. cit.*, pp. 66–94.
51. J. ten Broek, E. Barnhart, and F. Mason, *Prejudice, War, and the Constitution* (Berkeley, Calif.: University of California Press, 1968), pp. 225–260.
52. Petersen, *op. cit.*, pp. 88–94.
53. Hosokawa, *Nisei*, p. 448.
54. Leonard Bloom and R. Riemer, "Attitudes of College Students Towards Japanese Americans," *Sociometry* 8 (1945).
55. Harry Kitano, *Race Relations* (Englewood Cliffs, N.J.: Prentice-Hall, 1974), pp. 213–31.
56. Kitano, *Japanese Americans*, p. 109.

The Reports

57. Ito, *Issei*, p. 527.
58. Modell, "Japanese American Family," pp. 78–79.
59. Ito, *Issei*.
60. Modell, "Japanese American Family."
61. Kitano, "Japanese Americans," p. 220.
62. Ko and Ohasi, "Interview with Chris Kato."
63. J. Modell, *The Kikuchi Diary* (Urbana: University of Illinois Press, 1973).
64. Maykovich, *Japanese American Identity Dilemma*, pp. 74–75.
65. I. Fujimoto, "The Failure of Democracy in a Time of Crisis" in *Roots*, ed. A. Tachiki et al., pp. 207–14.
66. N. S. Hayner, "Delinquency Areas in the Puget Sound Region," *American Journal of Sociology* 39 (1934): 314–28.
67. Kitano, *Japanese Americans*, pp. 156, 158, 159.
68. G. Levine and D. Montero, "Socioeconomic Mobility Among Three Generations of Japanese Americans," *Journal of Social Issues* 29 (1973): 33–48.
69. Ibid.
70. Ibid.
71. H. Kitano, "Inter and Intra-generational Differences in Maternal Attitudes Towards Child Rearing," *Journal of Social Psychology* 63 (1964): 215–20, and J. Feagin and N. Fujitaki, "On the Assimilation of Japanese Americans," *Amerasia Journal* 1 (1972): 13–30.
72. D. Montero and G. Levine, "Third Generation Japanese Americans: Prospects and Portents" (Paper presented at the Annual Meeting of the Pacific Sociological Association, San Jose, Calif., 1974).
73. J. Tinker, "Intermarriage and Ethnic Boundaries: The Japanese American Case," *Journal of Social Issues* 29 (1973): 49–66, and A. Kikumura and H. Kitano, "Interracial Marriage: A Picture of the Japanese Americans," *Journal of Social Issues* 29 (1973): 67–81.
74. Montero and Levine, "Third Generation Japanese Americans."
75. Hosokawa, *Nisei*, p. 494.
76. Lyman, *Asian in the West*; Caudill, "Japanese American Personality"; and Kitano, "Japanese Americans."
77. Caudill and De Vos, "Achievement, Culture, and Personality."
78. Miyamoto, "An Immigrant Community," p. 241.
79. Petersen, *Japanese Americans*, p. 232.
80. H. Kitano, "Japanese-American Crime and Delinquency," in *Asian-Americans: Psychological Perspectives*, ed. S. Sue and N. Wagner (Ben Lomond, Calif.: Science and Behavior Books, 1973), pp. 161–70.
81. Kitano, *Japanese Americans*.
82. C. Watanabe, "Self-Expression and the Asian-American Experience," *Personnel and Guidance Journal* 51 (1973): 390–96.
83. Caudill and De Vos, "Achievement, Culture, and Personality."
84. A. Arkoff and B. Weaver, "Body Image and Body Dissatisfaction in Japanese Americans," *Journal of Social Psychology* 68 (1966): 323–30.
85. Maykovich, *Japanese American Identity Dilemma*, pp. 68–70.
86. R. A. Kalish and S. Moriwaki, "The World of the Elderly Asian American," *Journal of Social Issues* 29 (1973): 187–209.
87. H. Kitano "Japanese-American Mental Illness," in *Asian-Americans*, ed. Sue and Wagner, pp. 161–70.
88. *Los Angeles Times*, July 26, 1974, pp. 16–17.
89. M. B. Kane, *Minorities in Textbooks* (Chicago: Quadrangle Books, 1970), pp. 122, 129.
90. Ogawa, *From Japs to Japanese*.
91. Maykovich, *Japanese American Identity Dilemma*, p. 76.
92. Ibid., p. 75.
93. F. Hosokawa, "Social Interation and Ethnic Identification Among Third Generation Japanese" (Ph.D. diss., UCLA, 1973), and C. L. Johnson, "The Japanese-

American Family and Community in Honolulu: Generational Continuities in Ethnic Affiliation" (Ph.D. diss., Syracuse University, 1972).

94. G. M. Matsumoto, G. M. Meredith and M. Masuda, "Ethnic Identity: Honolulu and Seattle Japanese-Americans," in *Asian-Americans*, ed. Sue and Wagner, pp. 65–74.

95. P. Takagi, "The Myth of 'Assimilation in American Life,'" *Amerasia* 2 (1973): 149–58.

96. G. Kigiwada, "Confessions of a Misguided Sociologist," *Amerasia* 2 (1973): 159–64.

97. Takagi, "Myth of 'Assimilation.'"

98. Andrew Lind, *Hawaii's Japanese: An Experiment in Democracy* (Princeton, N.J.: Princeton University Press, 1946).

99. K. Yoneda, "One Hundred Years of Japanese Labor in the USA," in *Roots*, ed. Tachiki, pp. 150–58.

100. Y. Ichioka, "A Buried Past: Early Issei Socialists and the Japanese Community," *Amerasia Journal* 1 no. 2 (1971): 1–25.

101. B. Tong, "The Ghetto of the Mind: Notes on the Historical Psychology of Chinese-Americans," *Amerasia Journal* 1 no. 3 (1971): 1–31.

102. M. Uyematsu, "The Emergence of Yellow Power in America," in *Roots*, ed. Tachiki, pp. 9–13.

103. S. F. Miyamoto, "The Forced Evacuation of the Japanese Minority During World War II," *Journal of Social Issues* 29 (1973): 11–31.

104. McWilliams, *California*.

105. Miyamoto, "The Forced Evacuation of the Japanese Minority During World War II," p. 18.

106. Kitano, *Japanese Americans*, p. 166.

107. J. B. Cornell and R. J. Smith, "Japanese Immigrants Abroad" (Paper presented at 67th Annual Meeting of the American Anthropological Association, San Diego, Calif., 1970).

108. D. Silverman, "Introductory Comments," in *New Directions in Sociological Theory*, ed. P. Filmer et al. (Cambridge Mass: MIT Press, 1972), pp. 1–14.

109. G. Levine, personal communication, 1974.

110. D. Nakanishi, "The Visual Panacea: Japanese Americans in the City of Smog," *Amerasia Journal* 2 (1973): 82–129.

111. Lyman, *Asian in the West*, p. 84.

112. G. D. Berreman, "Social Identity and Social Interaction in India," unpublished manuscript, 1970.

113. Harold Garfinkel, "Conditions of Successful Degradation Ceremonies," *American Journal of Sociology* 61 (1956): 420–24.

114. Hosokawa, *op. cit.*, p. 492.

Suggested Readings

Hosokawa, W. *Nisei: The Quiet Americans*. New York: Morrow, 1969.

Jacobs, P., S. Landau, and E. Pell. *To Serve the Devil*, New York: Vintage Books, 1971, pp. 166–270.

Kitano, Harry. *Japanese Americans*. Englewood Cliffs, N.J.: Prentice-Hall, 1969.

Light, Ivan. *Ethnic Enterprise in America: Business and Welfare among Chinese, Japanese, and Blacks*. Berkeley, Calif.: University of California Press, 1972.

Lyman, Stanford. *Asian in the West*. Reno: University of Nevada Press, 1970.

Petersen, William. *Japanese Americans*. New York: Random House, 1971.

Sue, Sidney, and Harry H. L. Kitano, eds. *Asian Americans: A Success Story? Journal of Social Issues* 29 (1973): entire issue.

Sue, Sidney, and Nathaniel Wagner, eds. *Asian-Americans: Psychological Perspectives*. Ben Lomond, Calif.: Science and Behavior Books, 1973.

ten Broek, J., E. Barnhart, and F. Matson. *Prejudice, War, and the Constitution*. Berkeley, Calif.: University of California Press, 1968.

WEN LANG LI

CHINESE AMERICANS

Exclusion from the Melting Pot

The history of Chinese Americans reflects the development and extent of American racism. The Chinese were the only immigrants barred by law and by name from entering the United States. Until they appeared on the Pacific Coast, the traditional American policy of open immigration remained inviolate. Most free men could enter the United States and, after a short waiting period, become citizens fully equal to the native-born. The Chinese Exclusion Act of 1882 was the first departure from official American policy of laissez-faire immigration to be made on solely ethnocultural grounds. The decision to exclude the Chinese sharply challenged the prevailing assumption about the melting pot nature of America.

Under such extremely hostile circumstances, the social lives of early Chinese Americans were understandably isolated and miserable. They encountered continual discrimination and harassments, and even occasional lynchings.[1] Partly voluntarily and partly involuntarily, they confined themselves to ghetto areas, which were often called "Chinatowns." Nevertheless, despite hostile and unaccommodating conditions, Chinese Americans did not succumb to total despair and frustration. Chinese Americans have broken through the barriers of prejudice and have surpassed the average educational and income levels of native-born whites.

For these reasons an investigation of Chinese Americans as a racial and ethnic group is worthwhile. Study of this group should enhance understanding of how race relations developed in the United States. The body of the report will begin with an historical description of Chinese immigration and the tribulations experienced by the ethnic minority. The examination will focus on sociological variables that created the interracial conflicts. Changes in the minority group's conditions will also be discussed: Their occupational roles, for instance, have evolved from those of miners, to railroad workers, to domestic service workers, and finally many to professionals; the racial perceptions of the dominant group have changed concomitantly. A final point to be made is that the decline of racial discrimination should not be equated with the total assimilation or integration of Chinese Americans. Unsolvable problems, such as identity problems, especially among the young, remain to confront present-day Chinese Americans.

The Unwelcome Immigrants

Chinese immigration to the United States began in around 1850. The discovery of gold in California served as a magnet, drawing the people of southern China and those of eastern America together on the Pacific Coast. At this time there was no railway transportation across the American continent, so the journey from the East Coast usually took months. The two tides of immigration, East and West, met at a point which was as far removed from New York as it was from Hong Kong.

For a short time peaceful coexistence prevailed between the races. The Chinese performed the tasks that the western gold speculators willingly left to them. Most white miners, having worked in one area, left to hunt for richer territory elsewhere; the Chinese returned to work out low-yield diggings and comb over abandoned tailings, since even second-hand stakes were sometimes profitable. The rewards were especially attractive to the southern Chinese, whose economic lives had been ravaged by the Taiping Rebellion (1850–1864).

Several waves of Chinese immigrants came to the United States, which they called *Kim Shan*, or the Mountain of Gold. The gold rush movement did not spread too far inside China, partly because the Ching Dynasty prohibited any Chinese from leaving the Empire. Most of the immigrants came from Sze Yap, or the Four Districts located about one hundred miles east of Hong Kong and south of Canton. Most were men whose intention was to dig enough gold to improve the lives of their families at home.

But the sojourner attitude soon proved distasteful to native Americans. The hard-working habits of the Chinese also became too much competition for the natives. An eminent sociologist has observed:

> That the Chinese would be at once important productive units and serious competitors is indicated by their low standard of living and their industrious habits. The Chinese peasant and farm laborer is accustomed to the hardest kind of work and the most careful avoidance of all waste. . . . These habits spell intense competition and undercutting of native labor, if the two groups are engaged in the same occupations.[2]

Thus the peaceful coexistence was only temporary. Its demise was evidenced in a special Foreign Mining License tax passed by the California legislature. The tax was usually imposed exclusively on the Chinese. Although they earned their livings only from old mining claims that white men had abandoned, tax officers descended on them once a month with an exorbitant swindle.[3] Yet compared with subsequent anti-Chinese measures, the tax was a minor imposition. As the Chinese population in California increased, the feeling against the Chinese became more intense. By 1860 they represented nearly 10 percent of all Californians. By the end of the century fear of the "yellow peril" was rampant, and the Chinese immigrants became convenient scapegoats for any social malfunctions.

As the gold rush tapered off in the early 1860s, a new employment opportunity emerged for the Chinese. The federal government, after much debate, resistance, and hesitation, decided to build a transcontinental railroad. The Central Pacific Company was in charge of laying tracks from the West, and the Union Pacific Company from the East. Rougher terrain made construction of the western section more difficult, and the labor shortage was rather keen. A contractor for the Central Pacific Company, Charles Crocker, decided to use Chinese labor, despite the objection of his associates that "Chinese were physically incapable to handle the job."[4] After a trial use of Chinese workers, Crocker became totally dependent on them. Nearly twelve hundred Chinese men, often scornfully referred to as "Crocker's pets," were hired for the construction.

The construction lasted about five years, 1864–1869. When it ended nearly twenty-five hundred workers were out of jobs. Many of them were Irishmen who had been employed by the Union Pacific Company, competitor of the Central Pacific. Nearly a million people had also moved to California on the transcontinental railroad, with a labor surplus an inevitable result of the in-migration. During the 1870s the California labor market was characterized by a series of management-labor disputes. Hostility toward the Chinese was well developed, showing a curious mixture of class and race conflicts. As an example, one writer reported the following resolution passed at a miner's meeting:

> Be it resolved: That it is the duty of the miners to take the matter into our own hands . . . to erect such barriers as shall be sufficient to check this Asiatic inundation. . . . That the Capitalists, ship-owners and merchants and others who are encouraging or engaged in the importation of these burlesques on humanity would crowd their ships with the long-tailed, horned, and cloven-hoofed inhabitants of the infernal regions.[5]

The hostility was more than verbal; first in the mining districts and then in the cities, Chinese were robbed, beaten, and murdered. These crimes were rarely punished, due to the notorious laxity of law enforcement in California at the time, and to a court ruling that no Chinese person could testify against a white man. Mark Twain made the following observation: "Any white man can swear a Chinaman's life away in the courts, but no Chinaman can testify against a white man. Ours is the 'land of the free'—nobody denies that—nobody challenges it."[6]

In the 1870s and 1880s whites occasionally burned and pillaged Chinatowns, wantonly slaying the wretched inhabitants. On "China steamer days" San Francisco hoodlums made a sport of welcoming to Chinatown the disembarking sojourners. This "sport" took the form of taunts, beatings, brickbats, and the hurling of overripened fruit in an atmosphere of drunken hilarity.[7] Anti-Chinese agitation ultimately forced passage of the Chinese Exclusion Act in 1882. Mary Coolidge commented on the passage of the act as follows:

> The clamor of an alien class [Irish] in a single State—taken up by politicians for their own ends—was sufficient to change the policy of a nation and to commit the United States to a race discrimination at variance with our professed theories of government, and this so irrevocably that it has become an established tradition.[8]

Chinese immigration declined thereafter, but the hostility of white labor to the resident Chinese persisted. They were forced out of manufacturing employment in white-owned firms, and even Chinese-owned cigar and garment manufacturers experienced public pressure to cease operations that were in economic competition with white firms. These pressures left the resident Chinese with few opportunities. They were thus employed in "women's jobs," such as domestic service, laundry work, and work in restaurants and in small retail stores catering principally to other Chinese.[9]

The most serious consequence of the Exclusion Act for the Chinese was its effect on marriages and families. Restrictive immigration broke up natural human groups. Alien Chinese laborers were no longer permitted to bring their wives or children to the United States. The Immigration Act of 1924 further restricted the possibility of naturalization for Chinese Americans' spouses. An alien-born woman who married a citizen could no longer automatically assume his citizenship. Consequently, many American-Chinese couples as well as Chinese-born families became separated for long years.

The situation was not rectified until sixty years later, when the Chinese Exclusion Act was repealed in 1943. The following year an annual quota of one hundred five was established for persons of Chinese ancestry. In 1946 the Immigration Act was amended and alien wives of citizens were made admissible on a nonquota basis. Perhaps the most outstanding legislation, which affected the composition of the Chinese population as well as its course of acculturation, was the War Brides Act of 1947.[10] By permitting approximately five thousand Chinese women to enter the United States, this act helped to preserve family units. Legislative acts of the early 1950s also benefited about six thousand highly educated Chinese students in American colleges who were stranded on student visas when the Communists took control of mainland China. These students were permitted to remain, and a majority of them are now United States citizens.

The advent of Communist rule in China also caused thousands of persons to flee to Hong Kong. In 1962 President John F. Kennedy signed an executive order allowing their entry into the United States as alien parolees. After two years of residence the parolees were permitted to change their status to that of resident aliens. But the most progressive step in recognizing the equality of all races and nationalities came with the enactment of a new immigration law in 1965. It replaced the former quota system of allocating immigration, which had been heavily weighted in favor of Europeans. The new law permitted up to twenty thousand persons to be admitted annually from Taiwan and two hundred from Hong Kong. Likewise, up to twenty thousand persons from other Asian countries can be admitted annually. Regularly there are more applications than openings. Legislature and executive acts such as those mentioned above have gradually altered the demographic characteristics of the Chinese American population.

Changes in Demographic Structure

The demographic history of Chinese Americans clearly shows the effects of changing immigration legislation. Looking at the last hundred years, the size of the Chinese community increased greatly before 1880 but declined steadily after 1882, when the Exclusion Act was passed. Beginning with the 1920s the Chinese American population increased slightly, an increase possibly due to more births than deaths and illegal immigration, rather than to legal immigration. Only after World War II did large-scale immigration revive.

Despite all sinophobic arguments, the Chinese American population has never been overwhelmingly large. When anti-Chinese sentiment became prevalent in California in the 1860s, the Chinese population was only about thirty-five thousand. What the dominant group viewed as a threat, however, was the rate of growth in the Chinese American community. The population almost doubled itself every ten years. It was sixty-three thousand in 1870 and one hundred five thousand in 1880. This accelerating pace of increase seemed to aggravate the hostility of the dominant group. But this group failed to realize that the proportion of Chinese decreased as the population of California grew. In 1860 the Chinese represented nearly 10 percent of all California's population; ten years later the proportion had dropped to 8.6 percent, and in 1880 to 7.5 percent.

Hostile reactions and resentments, sanctioned by the Exclusion Act, contributed greatly to the decrease of the Chinese American population between 1890 and 1920. By 1920 only sixty-two thousand Chinese persons were left in the coterminous United States (see Figure 1). Most of the immigrants could not withstand the hostile environment and returned to their fatherland. The population decreased from one hundred seven thousand in 1890 to ninety thousand in 1900, to seventy-two thousand in 1910, and finally to sixty-two thousand in 1920. Nearly half the immigrants left during this thirty-year period.

Between 1920 and 1940 the slight increment in the Chinese American population from sixty-two thousand to seventy-seven thousand might simply have been due to natural increase. (The annual rate of growth for the Chinese-American population was only about 1 percent.) Not until the end of World War II did immigration again have a significant impact. By 1950 the Chinese population had increased to one hundred eighteen thousand, and during the next twenty years the decennial rate of growth was between 70 and 90 percent. In other words, from 1960 to 1970 the Chinese American population nearly doubled itself. Today the United States contains approximately half a million Chinese, who constitute a quarter of 1 percent of the total population.

Comparison between the patterns of Chinese immigration growth in the 1880s and in the 1970s shows a close resemblance. In both periods an accelerating pace of population increase is observable. But the dominant group's perception of the growth patterns are apparently different. Although it remains to be seen whether the recent growth will induce

FIGURE 1

POPULATION AND SEX RATIO OF CHINESE AMERICANS,
COTERMINOUS UNITED STATES, 1860-1970

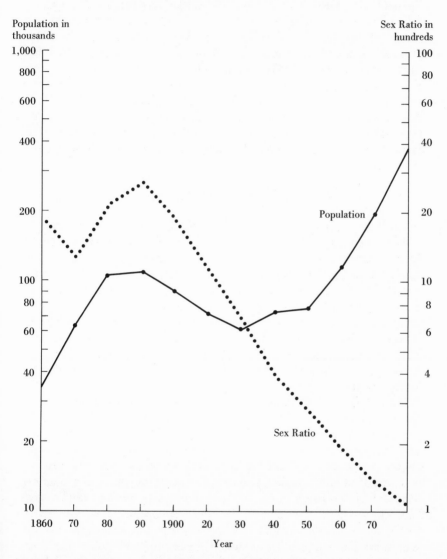

strong resentments and legislative restrictions on further immigration, one may safely assert that the present social climate differs entirely from that of the 1880s, when the Chinese were exploited by the whites on the frontier.

During the 1880s Social Darwinism represented a prevalent mode of human thinking: The fittest should survive and those who fail should be doomed. The Americans' view of the Opium War (1839–1842) was a clear example. When the Chinese were defeated in their resistance to the sale of opium, distinguished American statesman John Quincy Adams strongly condemned the Chinese as totally anticommercial and vehemently applauded England for rectifying an outrage upon the rights of nature; England was simply extending "her liberating arm to the farthest bound of Asia."[11] The popular Darwinian view of races as basic units in the struggle for control of a static supply of resources was clearly expounded by an eminent nineteenth-century sociologist, Edward A. Ross. He expressed the sinophobia of his time vividly: "Owing to its high Malthusian birth rate, the Orient is the land of cheap men. The coolie, though he cannot outdo the American, can underlive him."[12]

Sex Imbalance and Racial Slurs

The fear of "yellow peril" was not simply due to the increase in Chinese population. The sex composition and residential distribution of Chinese immigrants functioned equally to induce the resentments of the dominant group. The first Chinese immigrants in the United States intended to remain for only a short time and, in accordance with Cantonese tradition, left their wives in the homes of their parents. Understandably, the sex ratio of Chinese immigrants was extremely high. As shown in Figure 1, their sex ratio in 1860 was about two thousand, which means that for every female there were twenty male immigrants. As immigration increased, the sex ratio tended to increase, reaching its highest point of one female for twenty-seven males in 1890.

The imbalance in the sex ratio had stressful social implications. The almost womanless condition of the Chinese aroused concern and provoked condemnation by the dominant group. The few Chinese wives who did join their husbands in America were usually married to merchants. These women were kept in well-guarded seclusion and seldom ventured from their homes, which were generally the living quarters behind their husbands' stores.[13] The shortage of women might have been mitigated if the Chinese had had opportunities to intermarry within the American population. However, segregation, custom, and law kept most Chinese apart from other Americans and discouraged not only interracial marriages but also those intimate and primary relations that are prerequisite to nonarranged marriages. Until the Civil Rights Act in 1965, fourteen states specifically outlawed marriages between whites and Chinese or "mongolians."[14]

Prostitution was an inevitable sequel to the excess of males in Chinatowns. Other "recreations," such as gambling halls and dens where opium might be smoked, were also established. Control over these enterprises gradually shifted to the hands of several rival secret societies. The incidences of vices and evils in Chinatowns were perhaps not much different from those of any ghetto area, but they gave a good excuse for racial slurs and discriminations. Fear of perverted sexual proclivities on the part of the Chinese immigrants was by no means confined to California. A full-page report in the *New York Times* in 1873 illustrated the sexual fears on the East Coast, as Miller has meticulously documented:

> To the reporter's inquiry about a "handsome but squalidly dressed young white girl" present in an opium den, the owner replied with a horrible lear, "oh, hard time in New York. Young girl hungry. Plenty come here. Chinaman always have something to eat, and he like young white girl, He! He!"[15]

The racial slurs and discriminations culminated and were institutionalized in the Chinese Exclusion Act. After 1890 the disappearance of many Chinese immigrants reduced concomitantly the sex ratio imbalance, as well as the anti-Chinese movement. The overall sex ratio has decreased almost unidirectionally since then.

Reduction in the sex imbalance was nevertheless a slow process. Chinese males still far outnumbered females during the fifty years before World War II. The decline of the sex ratio was perhaps induced more by the high return migration of Chinese laborers than by the alleged illegal entry of Chinese women to the United States. Partly because of some female births, the sex ratio dropped to seven hundred, or seven males per female, in 1920. A decade later the United States census recorded fifteen thousand, five hundred Chinese females and sixty thousand males, a sex ratio of about four hundred. Not until the middle of the twentieth century did an approximate balance between the sexes begin to occur. The reports of 1950 indicate the effects of postwar relaxation of immigration restrictions and the increase in births among Chinese Americans: The sex ratio had reached its lowest point in a century—one hundred ninety, about two males for one female.

The postwar upsurge of Chinese immigration has not significantly increased the sex imbalance. The peculiar phenomenon which Sung[16] called "mutilated families" has not been at all prevalent among recent Chinese immigrants. Perhaps due to their relatively higher socioeconomic backgrounds, the recent immigrants have tended to move as family units. This pattern of migration is of course contrary to that of the early immigrants. Liberalized immigration laws have also helped to stabilize the sex structure. Many postwar Chinese immigrants to the United

States have remained bachelors until middle age, when they were financially able to go to Hong Kong in search of wives. Often these older men, accustomed to lives of hardship in the United States, married younger, more modernized Chinese women. After marriage the men returned with their wives to the crowded, dilapidated quarters of urban American Chinatowns. Sung[17] describes a number of marital failures that arose from clashing expectations. Lee[18] cited a divorce rate of 8.5 among the Chinese in San Francisco.

Chinatown in Transition

Changes in the Chinese immigrants' characteristics can perhaps be best discerned by examination of their residential distribution. The pattern of Chinese settlement offers good clues to other demographic and behavioral characteristics, such as: how long the group's cultural heritage can be maintained; where the strength of old-world social organizations is concentrated; and what the dominant group's reaction is to the immigrants' numerical size.

The pattern of Chinese settlement, according to Rose Hum Lee,[19] can be divided into three periods, roughly corresponding to the growth and decline of immigration movements: 1850 to 1880, the period of concentration of Chinese population; 1880 to 1910, the period of dispersion; and after 1910, the period of reconcentration. Early immigrants settled in California, and between 1850 and 1880 showed little inclination to move outside that state. Concentration probably helped to satisfy the psychological, social, and economic needs of the early immigrants as they attempted to adjust to a strange new environment. By 1880 the trend toward dispersion to urban areas outside California had begun, prompted by the increased size of the immigrant Chinese population and, concomitantly, the hostile environment. Hence New York, Chicago, Boston, and Philadelphia experienced an influx of Chinese immigrants. Several reasons may account for the fact that the Chinese tended to settle in the larger cities. A primary factor was the nature of their occupations and business undertakings after various laws were enacted to proscribe their participation in mining, the civil service, teaching, medicine, dentistry, and so on. The Chinese were also excluded from skilled occupations by the labor unions' concerted efforts. To mitigate discriminatory laws and employment practices, the Chinese had to find "soft spots" in the labor market. These were often located in a city or at a railroad junction, and involved doing the cooking, washing, and ironing in a predominantly male society. In several southern states the Chinese were recruited as agricultural laborers. They entered the plantation system at the bottom, as sharecroppers, to replace the "liberated" black laborers.[20]

During the first few decades of this century, the reconcentration of the Chinese in metropolitan cities perhaps reflected the rural toward urban movement of the total American population. In 1910, 57 percent of the Chinese were in cities of more than twenty-five thousand inhabitants. The proportion increased to 66 percent in 1920.[21] However, renewed immigration after the 1940s also seemed to enhance the process of reconcentration. Table I gives clues to the changes of Chinese regional distribution in the last three decades.

TABLE 1

TEN STATES WITH LARGEST CONCENTRATION
OF CHINESE AMERICANS, 1950–1970

Rank	1950	1960	1970
1	Calif. (38.8)	Calif. (40.3)	Calif. (39.5)
2	Hawaii (21.6)	Hawaii (16.1)	N.Y. (19.0)
3	N.Y. (13.4)	N.Y. (15.8)	Hawaii (12.2)
4	Ill. (2.8)	Ill. (3.0)	Ill. (3.3)
5	Mass. (2.4)	Mass. (2.8)	Mass. (3.2)
6	Wash. (2.3)	Wash. (2.3)	Wash. (2.2)
7	Texas (1.6)	Texas (1.8)	N.J. (2.0)
8	Penna. (1.5)	Penna. (1.6)	Texas (1.9)
9	Oregon (1.4)	N.J. (1.6)	Penna. (1.6)
10	Ariz. (1.3)	Mich. (1.4)	Mich. (1.5)
Total Chinese population	150,000	237,000	432,000

NOTE: The figures in parentheses are percentages of the total Chinese population.

California's proportion of the Chinese American population has always been the largest. In the last few decades its share remained in the neighborhood of 40 percent, but has appeared to decrease during recent years. New York has emerged as another major center of Chinese settlement. The proportional increase there has been remarkable: 13 percent in 1950, 16 percent in 1960, and 19 percent in 1970. In contrast, Hawaii's proportion of Chinese Americans has steadily declined: 22 percent in 1950, 16 percent in 1960, and 12 percent in 1970. Currently there are more Chinese in New York than in Hawaii. Some southern states formerly contained small, but nonetheless significant, proportions of the Chinese American population. The significance has disappeared recently. For instance, Texas' share of the Chinese population, ranked seventh in 1950, had dropped to eighth by 1970.

The reconcentration of the Chinese population in certain cities does not imply the revival of Chinatowns containing a diversity of social classes. The present function of Chinese communities is somewhat different from that of one hundred years ago. Previously, the emergence of Chinese communities often resulted from persecution of the entire ethnic group, whose presence was considered objectionable by the dominant group; the persecuted Chinese tended to seek safety within the ghetto, where mutual aid and protective organizations were available to mitigate outside hostilities. Thus far, the external environment seems differentially ameliorated. Residential segregation, though still existent, is less prevalent than it once was. Many recent immigrants, especially affluent individuals, do not *have* to reside in Chinatowns, as their predecessors did.

Chinatowns are no longer totally isolated residential communities for the Chinese. Their economic functions rival the diversification of many other communities. Rose Hum Lee described the composition of San Francisco's Chinatown:

> Within a quarter of a square mile are crowded some 16,000 inhabitants, whose lives in many instances, begin and end with the tourist crowd. For others, life is completely Chinese-centered; for another group, Chinatown is a place of residence, while their work is in uptown offices, agencies, or business. For a fourth group, their residence is away from Chinatown, across the Bay in Oakland or along the peninsula, where they return home at night after the day's work in Chinatown.[22]

Dispersion of the Chinese from the Chinatown is indirectly confirmed by the results of the 1970 census, which showed approximately 70 percent of the Chinese population residing within central cities. Interestingly, the proportion was almost linearly correlated with the life cycle. It was lowest, 65 percent, among the young adult population (twenty through thirty-four). Among the middle ages (thirty-five through forty-nine) the proportion increased to 68 percent, and it was even higher, 72 percent, among the old ages.

Where Chinatowns have declined, various mutual aid and protective organizations have been weakened. Traditionally, a Chinese community revolved around clans, groups of individuals stemming from a common ancestor and bearing the same surname. The clan relationships formed the basis for preferred social interactions, the extension of mutual aid and protection, and power interrelations. It is well known that a particular Chinatown often has been organized around a given clan. In addition, there developed in Chinatowns various types of organizations such as *tongs* (associations) and *hui kuans* (congregations). The most notable was the Chinese Six Companies, or Chinese Consolidated Benevolent Association. Whenever new immigrants arrived, the various associations served as caravansaries, credit and loan societies, and employment agencies. Undoubtedly some of them evolved into racketeering operations, including extortion and prostitution. But overall their functions have been positive. Some researchers have concluded[23] that an informal association, a *hui*, provided the organizational base for a rotating credit system that became the principal source of capital for entrepreneurship and business development in Chinatowns. Thus the decline of some Chinatowns has deprived some new immigrants of the benefits, and perhaps the tyrannies, of various social associations.

Racial Stereotypes: Old and New

The change of the Chinese community and the dominant group's perception of the Chinese are mutually interactive. In the early stages of immigration, prejudice and discrimination kept the Chinese in ghettos and confined them to a few selected manual occupations. These circumstances, in turn, reinforced the dominant group's prejudice and discrimination in subsequent years. But the changing structure of the Chinese community also caused racial images to change. Now the Chinese are viewed as one of the "model minorities," and the racial slurs that were used to describe them have disappeared. Thus a review of changes in the Chinese image may shed light on the evolution of a minority group.

The unfavorable American image of the Chinese developed gradually. No single event, person, or group can be isolated as being primarily responsible for it. Although the clamor of the working class in California helped promote anti-Chinese sentiments, the important point is that the Chinese Exclusion Act was overwhelmingly endorsed by the Congress of the United States. Research[24] has shown that a significant factor in establishing negative American attitudes toward the Chinese was the unfavorable image that preceded their immigration to the United States. Indeed, racial slurs against the Chinese were prevalent among American opinion makers long before the first Celestial gold seeker set foot upon California soil.

During the colonial period, Americans were generally ignorant of China. Their concepts of the Chinese were often legacies from sixteenth-century Europe, which were derived from the tales of Marco Polo or the exaggerated perceptions of Jesuit priests. For example, George Washington in 1785 expressed great surprise to learn that the Chinese were not white, although he had known that they were "droll in shape and appearance."[25] Americans' ignorance of China undoubtedly helped the opinion makers to influence their audience. Subsequent historical developments between the two countries unfortunately contributed to the negative image. As contacts were established, American traders, diplomats, and missionaries went to China to explore the myth of the "Middle Kingdom." The majority of American visitors regarded the Chinese as ridiculously clad, superstition-ridden, dishonest, cruel, marginal members of the human race who lacked the courage and intelligence to confront the oppressive despotism under which they lived. Few Americans showed esteem for the Chinese and their culture. The first Anglo-Chinese conflict in 1840 further exposed the fundamental weakness of the Chinese Empire. Contrasting their old ideas of her greatness with their sudden discovery of her weakness, Americans began to infer that China was decadent, dying, fallen greatly from her glorious past. The Opium War was, therefore, an important catalyst in popularizing the anti-Chinese theme which had been developed and polished over several decades by traders, diplomats, and missionaries.

Under this shadow the first Chinese immigrants arrived in the United States. From the beginning of their immigration every newspaper, whether or not it supported the use of Chinese workers under contract, referred to the Chinese as "coolies." The term was often used interchangeably with "Chinamen," though many of the Chinese immigrants were not contracted workers. Undoubtedly the coolie image became so imprinted on the public's mind that the Chinese were stereotyped as inferior, industrious, filthy, obedient, and cowardly. Such stereotypes were even confirmed by "social science" research. An anthropological study in 1877 stated:

It is true that ethnologists declare that a brain capacity of less than 85 cubic inches is unfit for free government, which is considerably above that of the coolie as it is below the Caucasian.[26]

Enactment of the Chinese Exclusion Act and subsequent discriminatory legislation reinforced the public's stereotypes of the Chinese. Journalism purportedly documented sensational stories of tong wars, opium dens, and white slave girls held by Chinese "opium fiends." The character of Fu Manchu, evincing "menace in every twitch of his finger and terror in each split second of his slanted eyes," instantly intensified the public's fear of "yellow peril."[27]

The negative Chinese image persisted until the end of the 1930s. In a classic 1933 study, Katz and Braly[28] reported that "superstitious" and "sly" were still the two major traits which Americans commonly ascribed to the Chinese. However, World War II seemed to mark a change in attitudes. After the war the traditional characterization of the superstitious, sly Chinese gave way to a more neutral or slightly positive stereotype. Negative perceptions faded; instead, the Chinese were most popularly characterized as "tradition-loving," "loyal to family," and "quiet." These stereotypes of the Chinese seem to have been rather persistent in the years since the war. Surveys in the last three decades have shown very little change, despite the prolonged build-up of international hostility following the Korean War.[29]

For the most part, Chinese are now considered a model minority, often described as patient, courteous, and Americanized. Daniels and Kitano[30] have suggested that the Chinese image is "whiter than white,' reflecting high achievement status by white middle-class standards. These new stereotypes point to the success of Chinese Americans by virtue of their hard work, thrift, and obedience.

But it is still too early to conclude that Chinese stereotypes are overwhelmingly and exceedingly favorable. The nature of the stereotypes often seems to depend upon the mood or condition of the dominant group. To some extent, increased friendliness between the People's Republic of China and the United States may give Chinese Americans more favorable stereotypes.[31] By the same token, any change in political relations could easily revive old stereotypes. Favorable stereotypes of the Chinese may also be only relative and temporary, resulting from the dominant group's unfortunate experiences with other minority groups. These experiences are reflected in assertions that the Asian Americans' successes should be used as a model by other minorities, and that America is not really racist since some nonwhite minorities have achieved the "American Dream."

Harold Issacs[32] has suggested that new perceptions of the Chinese rarely replace the older, contradictory stereotypes; these are simply filed away side by side. Although the overall stereotypes may be favorable, the public's perceptions of the Chinese are still ambivalent, combining admiration with contempt and affection with hostility. In general, the Chinese are "good, kind, highly civilized, vigorous, industrious, persevering, loyal and wise"; but Issacs cautions, "It takes a second sharper look at the Kaleidoscope screen to see more shadowy places where the less attractive images of the Chinese lurk, and where attitudes of dislike, antipathy, and hostility are to be found."[33]

Weiss[34] also notes a clear sex difference in the favorability of Chinese stereotypes. The Chinese male image of being honest, studious, and obedient does not connote masculinity, a desirable American cultural trait. On the other hand, the "Suzy Wong" image of Chinese females—slim, sexy, feminine, and charming—can be viewed as a more positive one. He sums up the observation as follows:

Although the Chinese male has also been popularly characterized as

311

"clean, honest, industrious, and studious," "a paragon of family virtue," "respectfully obedient to his elders" (traits acceptable in business and family success), he is still identified as "shy," "introverted," "withdrawing," and "tongue-tied" (traits unacceptable to current ideas of romanticism). . . . Furthermore, the occidental stage, screen and television image of the "hero" includes too few physical or cultural features of Oriental men.[35]

Whether such stereotypes are rooted in facts or in fancy requires independent investigation and separate assessment. But one thing remains clear: the perception truly affects the reality. As W. I. Thomas once stated, "If men define situations as real, they are real in their consequences."[36] In the 1860s Chinese males were perceived as being physically incapable of undertaking railroad construction work, and thus were initially barred from employment. One hundred years later, when asked to justify the exclusion of Chinese laborers and apprentices from working on a Chinese cultural project, a union official replied that the Chinese were "too small" for construction work.[37]

Bipolar Occupational Roles

The ambivalent stereotypes of the Chinese indicate more than historical-political complexities. Understandably, when a minority group begins to emerge as an equal competitor of the dominant group, the dominant perception of the minority tends to intermix old disdain with new respect. But it is also likely that the current occupational roles of Chinese Americans reinforce their ambivalent image. Social psychologists have suggested that racial stereotypes are affected by people's perceptions of the occupational roles associated with different races; for instance, slaves are thought to be lazy, coolies are considered industrious, and so on. Considering the bipolar occupational roles of Chinese Americans, such an explanation seems plausible.

The bipolarity of the Chinese occupational distribution is clearly shown in Table 2. The Chinese are very well represented in technical activities and independent professions, but not in managerial and proprietarial occupations. The Chinese seem to be underrepresented among skilled laborers and among craftsmen and foremen, but heavily represented in the low-skilled service occupations. The bipolar distribution becomes more striking when the Chinese labor force is compared with the white labor force. Only 15 percent of the white labor force are professional and technical workers, but 29 percent of Chinese are in this category. Only 7 percent of the whites, but 24 percent of the Chinese, are service workers, such as cooks and laundrymen. These two occupa-

TABLE 2

OCCUPATIONAL DIFFERENTIALS BETWEEN WHITE AND CHINESE
AMERICAN MALES AGES 16 AND OVER

Occupations	White	Chinese
Professional and technical workers	14.7%	29.6%
Managers and administrators	11.7	12.3
Sales workers	7.3	4.5
Clerical workers	7.5	9.4
Craftsmen and foremen	21.9	6.5
Operatives	19.2	9.9
Nonfarm laborers	5.9	2.7
Farm laborers and farmers	4.8	0.7
Service workers	7.0	24.4
Total	100.0	100.0

SOURCE: United States Bureau of the Census, *Census of Population: 1970* (Washington, D.C.: Government Printing Office, 1972), Tables 6, 13.

tional categories combined constitute more than 50 percent of the Chinese labor force.

The Chinese American occupational distribution undoubtedly reflects cumulative historical incidents and immigration patterns. Most "Chinatown" Chinese were forced to adapt their economic skills to the needs of western frontier environments. "Women's jobs" became the trademark of the Chinese. Among recent immigrants, however, are many scholars and professionals, including two Nobel Prize winners. They are predominantly non-Cantonese and are unable to communicate with the present-day "Chinatown" Chinese, who are of Kwangtung origin. These two groups are probably the major constituents of the bipolar occupational roles. A third group may be broadly labeled "Hawaiian Chinese." They are also of Kwangtung origin, but did not experience many of the discriminations and bigotries of the western frontiers. Having originally come to Hawaii as plantation laborers, not miners, they eventually shifted to other occupational roles, including grocers and independent tradesmen. These immigrants were upwardly mobile. Many of their descendants have become professional and technical workers.

The upward social mobility of Chinese Americans has been impressive, especially within the last two decades. Census reports show that the proportion of professional and technical workers in the Chinese labor force was only about 3 percent in 1940, but has steadily increased since then. The comparable figure in 1950 was 7 percent, and in 1960, 15 percent. By 1970 it reached as high as 28 percent. Compared to data on other ethnic groups (21 percent for Japanese, 8 percent for Spanish Americans, and 6 percent for blacks), the 1970 figure is exceedingly high.[38]

The dramatic rise in occupational status is not due simply to the recent immigration of Chinese scholars and professionals, though this factor is undeniably significant. The most important change has occurred within the old immigrant community, as suggested by the census data. Among the Chinese born in the United States, younger cohorts show a clear tendency to achieve higher social status than older cohorts. For example, the proportion of Chinese workers in the upper white-collar class is 29 percent for ages fifty-five to sixty-four; it monotonically increases to 42 percent for ages forty-five to fifty-four, 46 percent for ages thirty-five to forty-four, and 52 percent for ages twenty-five to thirty-four. In contrast, the proportion of Chinese workers in the manual class tends to be positively correlated with age: the older the generation, the higher the proportion of manual workers.[39]

Many explanations may be cited for the impressive upward mobility of Chinese Americans. Obviously their cultural value system is one important cause. The Chinese culture explicitly sanctions hard work as an efficient and honorable means of advancement. This attribute so permeates the Chinese value system that most Chinese persons, regardless of their country of residence, are known for being industrious. That they are sometimes labeled the "Jews of the Orient" indicates their strong drive for success. This factor is also one reason why they are often resented by the dominant group.

But "value system" is a grandiose and ambiguous term. Put more simply, the greatest facilitator of Chinese upward occupational mobility is probably the high level of Chinese educational attainment. Educational aspiration is the link between value system and occupational mobility. The traditional Chinese social structure promoted education and examinations as the only means by which a commoner's son would become a prime minister. Norms favoring education are, therefore, well integrated in the Chinese American community, and the immigrants have used education effectively to advance. Today the average Chinese American has at least one or two years of college training. An individual Chinese American's earnings may be lower than a white's when both persons have comparable educations and occupations. But considered as a group, the Chinese have higher average educational and occupational levels, which raise their average income above the whites'. In 1970 the Chinese Americans' median family income was slightly more than

$10,000, whereas the national median was $9,500. Unemployment of 3 percent for the Chinese in 1970 was also less than the rate for most other minority groups.

Resistance to Assimilation

Until recently, the Chinese family structure appeared to be one of the few cultural traits that resisted Americanization; in this characteristic, Chinese Americans were more Chinese than American. The Chinese family has often been called the basic, unalterable unit of their society, able to withstand social change, Westernization, and other crises. Whether this statement will remain true is uncertain. But one cannot deny that the family structures of immigrants from the Western hemisphere have adapted to America much faster than have Chinese families.

Clans, for example, may still be found among Chinese Americans. A clan is a group of individuals who are related because they have a common ancestor or because they bear the same surname. Among other functions, clan relationship forms the basis for preferred social interaction, and mutual aid and protection. Perhaps the most salient feature is that clans have provided their members with opportunities for commercial monopolies. Certain clans among Chinese Americans organized brotherhoods in trade, manufacturing, and types of labor.[40] The Dear clan tends to operate fruit and candy stores in San Francisco's Chinatown, and the Yee and Lee clans own better-class restaurants and supply most of the cooks for domestic service. In his study of Mississippi Chinese, James Loewen identified the tight clan structure as one of the most tangible assets possessed by the Chinese merchants:

After the initial entrance of Chinese in the late 1800's a new Chinese immigrant usually would have been sent for by a relative already successfully operating a Delta grocery. Upon arrival, he would be taken in and put to work in the relative's store, thus accumulating a priceless legacy of business experience, a legacy unavailable to at least the Negro sector of this potential competition. Then, after he had learned sufficient rudiments of English and store operation, he would be set up in his own business by a combination of savings, a loan from his relatives, and credit from wholesalers, with whom he had become acquainted during his "training period."[41]

Not only has the Chinese family structure had economic ramifications; it also has apparently contributed to low delinquency rates in the stable Chinese community. Parent-child relationships have been characterized by a formal, respectful expression of traditional role expectations. In the socialization process, children have been taught to place great value on family solidarity. Self-expression has been sacrificed to maintain harmonious relationships within the family.[42] Some essential differences between Chinese and American families have been noted by Betty Sung:

> [The Chinese] father never tries to be a friend to his son, nor the mother a big sister to her daughter. There is never the informal comradeship or intense emotional feelings between the Chinese parent and child as there is in American homes. A parent is the authority that demands obedience and authority must maintain dignity.[43]

Several studies have pointed out that such traditional parent-child relationships may have helped to keep delinquency rates low. Commenting on the way young Chinese children and adolescents get along with each other, Sollenberger[44] noted among the young a lack of aggressive behavior such as bickering, quarreling, or fighting. Traditionally oriented Chinese parents are much more strict about controlling their children's aggression than are American parents; they want their children to conform to the traditional way of gentleness, manners, and willingness to acquiesce. In addition, positive values of sharing and noncompetitiveness are stressed.

But recent social changes in Chinatowns have disrupted the former situation. Predatory delinquent gangs and political extremist groups can be found in many Chinatowns. The present delinquency rate in Chinatowns is no less than in other American metropolitan communities. The point has been made previously that Chinatown as a group center has been broken. The traditional family structure has lost its tight control over the young generation, perhaps as an unavoidable consequence of the assimilation process. When the young are permitted upward mobility by the open structure of American society, the formal, respectful attitudes toward their elders are difficult to maintain.[45] A Chinese parent begins to lose the authority and dignity which prevailed in his own parents' time.

Changing family structure may not be the only factor contributing to an increasing delinquency rate. Intergenerational conflict cannot fully explain the recent rise of juvenile delinquency in the Chinese community; another important element is found among the recently arrived immigrant youth who speak little or no English, have few salable skills, and are thus too handicapped to enter the occupational or social mainstream of American society. On the surface the conditions of these immigrants seem comparable to those of other oppressed and deprived groups, such as blacks, Chicanos, and Indian Americans. But more thorough examination of their backgrounds reveals that these recent cohorts of young immigrants differ significantly from previous cohorts. Most of the recent groups came from lower middle-class families in Hong Kong, where the delinquency rate is much higher than in the average Chinese metropolis. Thus gang wars in American Chinatowns apparently reflect the characteristics of the immigrants' original community. This explanation of delinquency among the recent immigrants gains credence in light of their predecessors' experiences. The well-publicized tong wars among Chinese Americans in the 1920s were partly related to the interlineage and intervillage fighting which were prevalent in South China. Villages in Kwangtung and Fukien were often at war with one another. The people were divided according to language and custom, as well as by descent. Conflicts were easily provoked when proprietary interests were strong.[46]

Delinquency is not the only phenomenon indicating the transition of Chinese American families. The elimination of traditional large family norms among all groups of Chinese in America is also evident. The same Western influence was felt in Hong Kong and Taiwan before immigrants from these regions settled in the United States. It is plausible that the higher the educational attainment of the immigrants, the smaller their family size; thus their family structure tends to be nuclear. Living with grandparents has become rare, almost like a cultural relic. Francis Hsu vividly describes the anachronistic situation of a large family structure in the United States:

A grandfather from Taiwan joined his son and daughter-in-law permanently. The young couple made him very welcome and showed every consideration, as a Chinese son and daughter-in-law should. After six months, their American-born six year old son could contain his curiosity no longer. He asked in front of the elder, "Why does Grandpa stay here all the time? Does he have no home of his own?"[47]

Another feature of the changing Chinese family in America is that marriage is no longer parentally arranged. Parents are consulted, and parental consent is still very important, but parents no longer have the entire responsibility. In this respect also the Chinese in America are like their educated counterparts in the land of their ancestors. However, other changes, such as intermarriage, are more peculiar to the Chinese in America. Quite a few Chinese Americans have intermarried with non-Chinese. Rates of intermarriage are highest among the highly educated and among Hawaiian Chinese. Research has shown that in the early 1960s, 55 percent of Chinese marriages in Hawaii involved a non-Chinese spouse.[48] But this figure seems questionably high. The 1970 census sources revealed that about 30 percent of Hawaiian Chinese married with other races; the rate of intermarriage was about 15 percent for the total Chinese American population.

Finally, the practice of ancestor worship is greatly modified among Chinese Americans. Ancestral altars in homes have nearly disappeared. Until 1950 some filial sons still carried the ashes of their dead parents to be buried in China; this ritual is no longer practiced. Taking advantage of a growing religious vacuum, the Presbyterian church began the first evangelical efforts among the Chinese immigrants. It has worked consistently in the Chinatowns for decades.[49] A number of other churches have followed suit. By the late 1950s approximately sixty-two Protestant and six Catholic churches were established in Chinatowns across the country. About 8 percent of Chinese Americans might be known as Christians.[50] The rise of Chinese Christian membership is a strong indication that the Chinese family system in no longer a social institution serving the traditional religious function. Chinese families in the United States are gradually becoming Americanized.

Problems of Integration

Assimilation is not synonymous with integration. Although Chinese Americans are unquestionably acculturated and assimilated, they are by no means integrated. That is, they are not wholly and unreservedly accepted as members of American society. Length of settlement is not always the crucial criterion of integration when members of a minority have physical characteristics that set them apart from the dominant group. The major racial problem currently facing Chinese Americans may not be overt discrimination, but a struggle for identity and a lack of acceptance as full members of American society.

Chinese Americans are often perceived as sojourners, although some have been in the United States for several generations. The marginality of their status is manifested almost daily in their experiences. Whereas the common expression for European travel is "going to," Asian Americans are somehow "going back," even if they are visiting Asia for the first time. The following is a Chinese college professor's observation:

> As a third-generation American, a Korean War G.I., a Stanford doctorate, I am typical of other Asian Americans who are outraged by statements such as: "How long have you been in the U.S.?" and "You speak English quite well."[51]

Marginal treatment by the dominant group has alienated many Chinese Americans. They are constantly reminded that they are "marginal men."

Some are prompted to ask themselves who they really are, and if they should retrieve their own cultural heritage in order to maintain racial identity. The term "banana," meaning white inside and yellow outside, has developed in recent years to characterize scornfully those Chinese who belittle their own ethnic roots to pursue full integration with the dominant group.

Many Chinese Americans can testify to their failures in pursuing full integration. Lacking a "proper" social origin, they can at most achieve middle-class status. An invisible ceiling prevents their further upward social mobility. In a sense, Chinese Americans have never generated a solid unified community structure which could provide clientele for a valuable profession. Chinese Americans are divided into various sub-groups, including Chinatown Chinese, recent immigrants, and Hawaiian Chinese. The differences in their cultural systems are greater than outsiders have perceived. Thus a solid Chinese clientele, which is very much needed by such high-prestige professions as law, may not be available. When Chinese lawyers turn to white clientele, they encounter further problems, as Lyman states:

> A Chinese American lawyer might not appeal to white clients because of his allegedly poor facility in English, supposedly lower status in the courts, and general lack of contacts and widespread experience. Hence, most Chinese who have studied law have entered city, state, or federal service, where most of these problems do not arise.[52]

Consequently, college-educated Chinese Americans exercise a high degree of selectivity in career and professional choices. Many are engaged in engineering, chemistry, optometry, pharmacy, and federal and state governmental occupations.[53] These professions tend to be practical, that is, conducive to a comfortable middle-class life style, but they do not facilitate high upward mobility, for they are too technical and specialized.

Chinese Americans' investment in education does yield reasonable payoffs; it facilitates their climbing up the social ladder, from service workers to professionals. Yet education has not helped the Chinese obtain the most prestigious and financially rewarding occupations, because these professions require more than merely education. Table 3 clearly shows the differential returns of education between whites and Chinese Americans.

As education increases, personal earnings tend to increase. This generalization applies to both whites and Chinese. But the effects of education on white incomes is much more dramatic than the effect on Chinese incomes. For instance, with a high school education a white worker can expect to earn approximately $10,000 per year; the compara-

TABLE 3

AVERAGE PERSONAL EARNINGS BY EDUCATIONAL
ATTAINMENT FOR WHITE AND CHINESE AMERICANS

Education	White	Chinese	Chinese/White Ratio
None	$10,693	$ 7,192	0.67
Elementary 1–4	12,990	11,624	0.89
Elementary 5–7	10,001	11,900	1.19
Elementary 8	10,175	12,541	1.23
High school 1–3	9,800	10,532	1.07
High school 4	10,069	11,496	1.14
College 1–3	11,940	10,415	0.87
College 4	14,093	13,107	0.93
College 5 or more	17,312	14,901	0.86
Total	11,511	12,292	1.07

SOURCE: Computed from 1 percent public use sample of the 1970 census.

ble figure for a Chinese worker is about $11,000. However, after completing four years of college, a white person earns about $14,000, and a Chinese person earns about $13,000. So the differential pattern is reversed. The higher the education, beyond the level of no education, the wider the differential gap. The Chinese tend to compete least successfully with whites at the most highly educated level.

Education is nevertheless the only avenue for upward Chinese mobility. Table 3 shows that the Chinese will experience the most severe financial deprivation with little or no education. The average income for a noneducated white is about $11,000, but only about $7,000 for the Chinese. If financial rewards for education can be used to indicate indirectly the extent of racial inequality, then it appears that at both ends of the educational spectrum, the least and the most educated, Chinese Americans encounter greater disadvantages. Their disadvantages may be due not to explicit, conscious discrimination, but to their own apprehensions and limitations. Nevertheless, the consequences at least partly result from the historical and sociological conditions experienced by Chinese Americans.

The climate of racial revolts and identity struggles has led many Chinese Americans to reexamine their ethnic roots and their relatively disadvantageous position. A significant development today is the overt and dynamic nature of ethnic concern. Most of the young Chinese involved have grandparents who were born in the United States, many of whom never learned to speak English and thus did not actually face the same bicultural problems as do their grandchildren. Whereas yesterday's proper road to success and acceptance was passive cultural separation, very assertive avenues are developing today. The open structure of American society has begun to be extended to such minority groups as Chinese Americans; differentials between races in cultures and life styles are tolerated and somewhat accepted. However, William Petersen calls attention to a trend that may make contraassimilation a new fashion:

> Under the Ethnic Heritage Studies Act, the federal government distributes a few million dollars annually for the many imitations of Black Studies. . . . Most colleges with any Asian students have been under pressure to follow the crowd, and may now have a course or two at an introductory level. . . . Like counterparts focused on other subnations, such courses and publications are often antischolarly in their basic premise.[54]

The antiassimilative movement is likely to prove only transitory and a part of the youth culture. Most Chinese Americans tend to dissociate themselves from this trend. Sandwiched between the racial conflicts of blacks and whites, the Chinese are cautious about playing the middleman role. Since the beginning of their immigration in the 1850s they have been caught in the struggles between capitalists and unionized workers, favored by the former and resented by the latter. Perhaps the Chinese are not eager to have the historical squeeze replayed. Chinese Americans have also learned lessons from their counterparts in Southeast Asia, who were once used by colonists to oppress the natives and eventually became targets for the natives' revenge. A similar incident is occurring among today's Mississippi Chinese, as Loewen has observed:

> Ironically, now that White Mississippi has begun to accept the Chinese more fully, the Chinese themselves are leaving. Occupationally oriented toward large Western cities, most will not remain much longer in the land of their youth. Segregation is slowly dying, but not without violence, and some of that violence is directed toward the race which for so many decades stood in the middle. And as segregation ends, the special place it created for the Chinese ends as well.[55]

Formerly, whenever the sojourners were subjected to harsh revolts and discrimination, they could return to China. Today they have little hope or desire of resettling in mainland China or in Taiwan or Hong Kong. The latter islands are not the homeland of most Chinese Americans, and certainly not of American-born Chinese. The marginality of Chinese Americans is probably not unique. Fitzgerald made similar observations about the Chinese in Southeast Asia:

The Reports

While there are still considerable differences between individual Overseas Chinese and between the situation of the Chinese in each country of Southeast Asia, the present generation of Overseas Chinese is far more inclined to regard itself as belonging to the countries of residence than to China. It may not be prepared to abandon its language and cultural traditions, but that does not mean that it regards itself as bound to China by nationality or political affiliation, or that it is prepared to serve the Chinese government. It may not be prepared to integrate, but that does not mean that it is not willing to identify completely with the countries of residence.[56]

What has been observed in Southeast Asia appears equally valid in the United States. Fitzgerald's conclusion is perhaps the proper one regarding the prospect for integration of Chinese Americans.

NOTES

1. San Ying Wu, *Mei Kuo Hua Chiau Pei Nan Chi Shih* (*One Hundred Years of Chinese in the United States and Canada*) (Hong Kong: Chia Lo, 1954).
2. Donald Taft, *Human Migration* (New York: Ronald, 1936), p. 480.
3. Rodman W. Paul, "The Origin of the Chinese Issue in California," in *The Aliens*, ed. L. Dinnerstein and F. C. Jaher (New York: Appleton-Century-Crofts, 1970), pp. 161–72.
4. Betty Lee Sung, *Mountain of Gold* (New York: Macmillan, 1967).
5. Edward Daniels and Harry Kitano, *American Racism* (Englewood Cliffs, N.J.: Prentice-Hall, 1970), p. 36.
6. Samuel Clemens (Mark Twain), *Roughing It* (Hartford, Conn.: American, 1880), p. 391.
7. Ivan H. Light, *Ethnic Enterprise in America* (Berkeley: University of California Press, 1972), p. 6.
8. Mary Roberts Coolidge, *Chinese Immigration* (New York: Henry Holt, 1909), p. 182.
9. Light, *Ethnic Enterprise*, p. 7.
10. Rose Hum Lee, *The Chinese in the United States of America* (Hong Kong: Hong Kong University Press, 1960), p. 18.
11. Stuart Creighton Miller, *The Unwelcome Immigrant* (Berkeley: University of California Press, 1969), p. 95.
12. F. H. Matthews, "Yellow Peril," in *The Aliens*, ed. Dinnerstein and Jaher, p. 270.
13. Hubert H. Bancroft, "Mongolianism in America," in his *Essays and Miscellany* (San Francisco, Calif.: San Francisco History Co., 1890), pp. 327–28.
14. Stanford M. Lyman, *Chinese Americans* (New York: Random House, 1974), p. 91.
15. Miller, *Unwelcome Immigrant*, p. 184.
16. Sung, *Mountain of Gold*.
17. Ibid.
18. Rose Hum Lee, "Established Chinese Families in the San Francisco Bay Area," *Midwest Sociologist* 19 (1957): 19–26.
19. Lee, *Chinese in the United States*.
20. James W. Loewen, *The Mississippi Chinese* (Cambridge, Mass.: Harvard University Press, 1971).
21. Lee, *Chinese in the United States*.

22. Ibid., p. 62.

23. For example, see Light, *Ethnic Enterprise.*

24. Miller, *Unwelcome Immigrant.*

25. Ibid., p. 14.

26. Ibid., p. 145.

27. Dorothy B. Jones, *The Portrayal of China and India on the American Screen,* *1896–1955* (Cambridge, Mass.: Harvard University Press, 1955), p. 31.

28. Daniel Katz and Kenneth Braly, "Racial Stereotypes of 100 College Students," *Journal of Abnormal and Social Psychology* 28 (1933): 280–90.

29. See M. Karlins, T. L. Coffman, and G. Walters, "On the Fading of Social Stereotypes," *Journal of Personality and Social Psychology* 13 (1969): 1–16, and Wen L. Li and Linda Yu, "Interpersonal Contact and Racial Prejudice," *Sociological Quarterly* 15 (1974): 559–66.

30. Daniels and Kitano, *American Racism.*

31. Wen L. Li and Shirley W. Liu, "Ethnocentrism Among American and Chinese Youth," *Journal of Social Psychology,* 1975.

32. Harold Issacs, *Scratches on Our Minds: American Images of China and India* (New York: Capricorn, 1958).

33. Ibid., pp. 72–73.

34. M. S. Weiss, "Selective Acculturation and the Dating Process: The Patterning of Chinese-Caucasian Interracial Dating," *Journal of Marriage and Family* 32 (1970): 273–78.

35. Ibid., p. 274. A notable exception is the Bruce Lee image in Kung Fu movies.

36. W. I. Thomas and F. Znaniecki, *The Polish Peasant in Europe and America* (2 vol. reprint ed., New York: Knopf, 1927). Originally published in 1918.

37. Lyman, *Chinese Americans,* p. 138.

38. U.S. Bureau of the Census, *Census of Population, 1970.* Subject Reports, Final Report PC(2)–1A. *National Origin and Language.* (Washington, D.C.: Government Printing Office, 1973), p. 36, Table 6.

39. Li and Lin, "Ethnocentrism."

40. Lyman, *Chinese Americans,* p. 31.

41. Loewen, *Mississippi Chinese,* p. 38.

42. Stanley L. M. Fong, "Assimilation and Changing Social Roles of Chinese Americans," *Journal of Social Issues* 29 (1973): 117.

43. Sung, *Mountain of Gold,* p. 171.

44. Richard T. Sollenberger, "Chinese-American Child-Rearing Practices and Juvenile Delinquency," *Journal of Social Psychology* 74 (1968): 12–23.

45. Robin M. Williams, *American Society,* 3rd ed. (New York: Knopf, 1970), pp. 84–85.

46. Kung-Chuan Hsiao, *Rural China: Imperial Control in the Nineteenth Century* (Seattle: University of Washington Press, 1960), pp. 418–33.

47. Francis L. K. Hsu, *The Challenge of the American Dream: The Chinese in the United States* (Belmont, Calif.: Wadsworth, 1971), p. 37.

48. Ibid., p. 31.

49. H. R. Cayton and A. O. Lively, *The Chinese in the United States and the Chinese Christian Churches* (New York: National Council of Churches of Christ in the United States of America, 1955), pp. 38–40.

50. Lee, *Chinese in the United States,* pp. 276–89.

51. Albert H. Yee, "Myopic Perceptions and Textbooks: Chinese American's Search for Identity," *Journal of Social Issues* 29 (1973): 105.

52. Lyman, *Chinese Americans,* p. 136.

53. Beulah Ong Kwoh, "The Occupational Status of American-born Chinese Male College Graduates," *American Journal of Sociology* 53 (1947): 192–200.

54. William Petersen, *Asian Americans* (Washington, D.C.: Urban Institute, 1974).

55. Loewin, *Mississippi Chinese,* p. 6.

56. Stephen Fitzgerald, *China and the Oversea Chinese* (New York: Cambridge University Press, 1973), p. 188.

Suggested Readings

Barth, Gunther. *Bitter Strength: A History of the Chinese in the United States, 1850–70.* Cambridge, Mass.: Harvard University Press, 1964.

Daniels, Edward, and Harry Kitano. *American Racism.* Englewood Cliffs, N.J.: Prentice-Hall, 1970.

Hill, Herbert. "Anti-Oriental Agitation and the Rise of Working-Class Racism." *Society* 10 (1973): 43–54.

Hsu, Francis L. K. *The Challenge of the American Dream: The Chinese in the United States.* Belmont, Calif.: Wadsworth, 1971.

Lee, Rose Hum. *The Chinese in the United States.* Hong Kong: Hong Kong University Press, 1960.

Light, Ivan. *Ethnic Enterprise in America.* Berkeley: University of California Press, 1972.

Lyman, Stanford. *Chinese Americans.* New York: Random House, 1974.

Miller, Stuart Creighton. *The Unwelcome Immigrant.* Berkeley: University of California Press, 1969.

Saxton, Alexander. *The Asian in the West.* Berkeley; University of California Press, 1971.

EUGEN SCHOENFELD

JEWISH AMERICANS

A Religio-Ethnic Community

Some time ago I asked a college professor who was a friend of mine, "Do you believe in God?" Although somewhat startled by the question he responded without hesitation: "No!" I probed further by asking: "What do you consider yourself to be?" Since the topic of conversation was religion, he responded with some hesitation, "I am a Jew." His hesitation expressed this apparent paradox: How can anyone be a Jew and not believe in God? Is not belief in God a necessary prerequisite for a religious identity? Yet this professor's dilemma is not an isolated case. Many individuals who call themselves Jews reject religious rituals and confess to being agnostics if not atheists.

The paradox dissolves once we realize that being Jewish encompasses a multiplicity of identities. One may, for instance, place primacy on religious identity, or see oneself as a member of an ethnic group, or as a member of a national political group (as in the case of the Israelis). Contrary to popular misconception, Jews do not constitute a race, if by "race" we mean a category of people who possess biologically inheritable traits. What, then, is the common feature of the people who are called Jews? The answer is that there is no one common feature. Religion is one of several, as are a common history and culture, a common way of life, and finally a collective concern with the state of Israel.

Variations within identity are as old as Judaism itself. Such differences already existed, for instance, in the times of the prophets: Some Jews, who followed the prophets rather than the priest, opposed the strict ritual emphasis of religion, and endeavored to substitute plain moral requirements for elaborate ceremony and formal creed. Since the destruction of the Second Temple in A.D. 70, and the Jewish exile from the homeland, Jewish identity has remained primarily within the domain of religion and ritualism. Only since the nineteenth century have Jews begun again to emphasize other aspects of Judaism, such as a philosophical and moral concern and a national-political identity known as Zionism. Similarly, in the United States, being Jewish has a different essence to different people. Some perceive themselves as adherents of a particular religion, while others see themselves primarily as an ethnic group. In this regard Gans writes:

> I must . . . distinguish between two aspects of Jewish life, *Judaism* and *Jewishness*. By Judaism, I mean the Jewish culture (using that word, again, in its anthropological sense). But the term Judaism itself has two applications; we speak of traditional or of a symbolic Judaism. Traditional Judaism embraces a great complex of sacred and secular, ceremonial and everyday codes of behavior patterns. . . . Jewishness, on the other hand, refers to one's sense of identity as a Jew, and the concomitant sense of identification with other members of the Jewish community. Primarily a feeling of belongingness, Jewishness has been an effect rather than a cause of cohesion of that community.[1]

The present trend, Gans feels, is toward "Judaization," a trend manifested by the lessening importance of Judaism as a religion and the substitution of an "objects culture" based on such items as Jewish candy, Jewish bacon, Jewish jokes, and stars of David.

Glazer is more explicit in his analysis of the source of Jewish identity. Viewing American Jewry from an historical perspective, he identifies the existence of what he calls "religious" and "secular" Judaism. Glazer claims these two aspects of Judaism are not only separate, but on occasion have been antagonistic. Glazer writes that in the 1920s and 1930s:

> The synagogue and religion offered but one center of life and interest among many on the American Jewish scene. Other specifically Jewish centers of activity, of equal or greater importance were constituted by philanthropic work by Jewish politics and by Jewish culture. The leading figures in these fields were often indifferent when actually not hostile to religion. And so one had a split between what one may call Judaism, the historic religion, and Jewishness; namely all the activities which Jews came to carry on without the auspices of religion.[2]

Melvin Tumin is another sociologist who has dealt with the question of Jewish identity in America, though in a peripheral manner. He observes that "Jews are concerned with the problem of their identity and consciously seek to come to terms with that problem at its most serious level."[3] This quest for identity, Tumin says, brings about a paradoxical situation. On the one hand there is an organizational reinvigoration; synagogues and day schools are ever increasing in numbers, a fact which would lead one to believe that there is a tendency toward increased Jewish identification. On the other hand, "Jews have been vocal and effective in their insistence . . . not to be identified as Jewish."[4] Thus, there are simultaneously "two opposing moves in Jewish life—[one] toward a Jewish center and [another] away from it. . . ."[5] What Tumin seems to observe is that there exists a duality in Jewish identification resulting from the divergence of religious and cultural aspects. Because of American values, the Jew seems constrained to return to his religious institutions. It is in regard to this point that Tumin writes:

> The return to the Jewish community and its center and its synagogue represents, as yet, nothing more . . . than a smooth fitting in of Jews into American life at its worst—and on precisely the same terms as the Presbyterians, Baptists, and all others.[6]

This constraint toward a religious identification is further evidenced by the Jew's quest for status and a desire to be a hundred-percent-American. Tumin writes:

> In duplicating this 100 percent [*sic*] community-cum-church posture of the non-Jewish American, the Jew vouchsafes himself as an allrightnik in the American host community operating with the morally dubious notion that one's neighbors will respect one more if one is religious, the Jew seeks to insure that acceptance. . . .[7]

Other scholars who have examined the nature of Jewish identity have found it to contain many component parts. A closer examination of the various subidentities, however, will show this multiplicity constitutes only two major dimensions: Judaism and Jewishness. Lazerwitz,[8] for instance, identified nine components of Jewish identity, but a subsequent factor analysis of his data showed that these components are not independent identities but form two identity clusters, which he designated as "religio-pietistic" and "Jewish organizational."

Although we are stressing the duality of Jewish identity, we must hasten to add that these identities are not completely independent. A commitment to Jewish ethnic culture does not preclude one's commitment to religion, nor does commitment to religion preclude commitment to ethnic culture. Lazerwitz[9] notes that Jews who are highly involved in the Jewish community are strikingly more religiously observant than those having a low involvement. Of what importance is this difference in the content of personal identity? Is it not sufficient that one should perceive oneself a Jew and thereby align oneself with the Jewish community? The answer is no. Differences in the content of one's identity entail a different reference group, and consequently different values, norms, and outlook.

Jews in America: An Historical Perspective

An historical approach to the understanding of Jewish Americans—their identity, religion, and life—is imperative, for Jews are products of different countries and varied historical conditions which have affected them in different ways. As a result, Jewish identity, world view, and attitude toward the Gentile community is by no means unilateral.

American Jews consist of an admixture of three groups of immigrants who came to this country at three different periods of its history from three different geographical areas. The oldest residents are the Spanish-speaking Jews (Sephardim), whose roots in this country are almost as old as those of the pilgrims. In 1654 twenty-three Jewish families, in an attempt to escape Portuguese persecution, left the occupied Dutch colony of Racife in eastern Brazil and came to New Amsterdam, the present New York, another Dutch colony. The hospitality and freedom which the Jews enjoyed in the Dutch colonies in South America was not extended to them by Peter Stuyvesant, governor of New Amsterdam, who would have preferred to expel the new emigrants. However, the Dutch East India Company, proprietor of the colony, overruled the governor and permitted the new settlers to remain.

Although these Jews came from South America, their original home was the Iberian peninsula. After the Roman destruction of the Jewish homeland in Judea, Jewish cultural life shifted to Babylon, where a great Jewish civilization flourished for approximately seven centuries. But as the great Jewish schools in Babylon began to be closed, Jewish cultural life in Spain, which was now under Arab rule, was growing. In 1492, the year which marked the discovery of the American continents, Jews were being expelled from their homes in Spain. They carried with them into their new homes their old heritage of a love for learning and grace. Soon after the first twenty-three Sephardic settlers arrived in New Amsterdam, others of similar background came to join them, and Jewish communities were established in Newport, Rhode Island, Savannah, Georgia, Philadelphia, Pennsylvania, and Richmond, Virginia.

From 1840 until imposition of the quota system in 1924, Jewish emigration, primarily from Germany, Russia, Poland, and Hungary, was relatively heavy. Social conditions in the countries from which these Jews emigrated differed appreciably, and hence their attitudes toward religion and politics and their perception of the non-Jewish world also differed. Let us now turn to the earlier emigrants—the German Jews. Jewish life in Germany until the nineteenth century was marked by the dominance of the yellow star, the badge of shame, and above all by the high walls of the ghetto. Jewish association with the "outside world" was very limited, and as a result life within the walls of the ghetto was governed by age-old traditions and the strict letter of religious law. Sachar writes:

> Limited intellectually, ground down economically, despised socially, disinherited politically, the Jews were also decried and persecuted for race and religion. It was not astonishing that, with no hope for participation in the life of the country, Jews swaddled themselves in their own traditions. . . .[10]

The rise of the enlightenment, with its idealism, and the subsequent revolutions of the eighteenth century also affected the freedom of the Jews, for the concepts of liberty and equality applied in some measure to the Jewish population of Western Europe. The walls of the ghettos, like those of Jericho, were falling, and with their destruction new trends in assimilation and acculturation gathered force.[11]

The authority of the Talmud, which for centuries had been the foundation of the Jewish religion, was now challenged; proponents of this challenge pointed out that the ancient doctrines and practices had too long resisted the natural process of change and evolution. Perhaps more significant than the changes in religious ritual was rejection of the nationalistic element in Judaism; the universal aspect, rather than restoration of Zion and return to the homeland, was emphasized. Religious acculturation accompanied general assimilation. The prayers were shortened and recited for the most part in the native language, new hymns in the vernacular were introduced, and the sermon, as in Protestant religious groups, became the most important part of the worship service. In short, the Western Jews started to shed their national and cultural identity and to assume the identity of their host. They now began to think of themselves as Germans, Frenchmen, or Englishmen who practiced a Jewish (Mosaic) religion, rather than as Jews bearing a separate ethnic or national identity.[12]

As Western Jews began to identify themselves culturally with Europe while maintaining their Jewish religion (although greatly reformed), Eastern Jews took an exactly opposite course—they began to minimize their religious affiliation, while simultaneously stressing the national and cultural elements of Judaism. This difference in the evolutions of the Western and Eastern Jew was directly related to the differences in their political and social situations. In the West Jews found themselves becoming politically free and possessing increased educational and economic opportunities; in the East the Jews' situation was just the opposite. Not only were they subjected to the confinement of the ghetto and to the restrictions of anti-Jewish laws, but they also had to endure the cruelties of the pogroms.

In 1791, at the order of Catherine the Great, Jews in Russia were confined to a small district in the Ukraine known as the "pale of settlement." While their ghettos in Western Europe were being opened and the Jews were being granted greater freedom, in Russia the Jewish lot was worsening steadily, aggravated still further by the conscription law of Nicholas I.[13] The spring of 1881 saw the beginning of an outburst of hostilities against Russian Jews; these violent outbreaks were not random occurrences, but seemed rather to have been well planned and directed. In addition to this series of attacks, which the government seemed unable to control, the Jews also had to contend with the infamous "May laws" of 1882 which restricted their travel, business, and education. Needless to say, this hostile attitude of the host did not encourage Jewish assimilation, but instead turned them away from the path of integration. The budding "Haskalah," the movement of enlightenment, "changed its orientation; instead of worshipping the Shrine of European culture, it placed itself at the service of the national regeneration of the Jewish people."[14] This trend to nationalism, later known as Zionism, was political rather than religious, for the religious belief that suffering is the natural lot of Jews and a prerequisite for the coming of the Messiah became unacceptable to the leaders of the Haskalah. The doctrines of the Messiah, i.e., the patient wait, submission to temporary difficulties, and postponement of retribution, lost ground to the desire for an immediate solution of the Jewish difficulties. If religion taught that the Messiah was the only legitimate leader who might return the "exiles" to their national land, then this new movement was nonreligious, and in fact sometimes antireligious. Its imminent goal became self-determination and not God-determination.[15]

When we turn our attention to the Jewish Americans of today we discover that their identity is rooted in the orientations brought over by the Jewish migrants from both West and East. They are products of the cultural heritage of the German as well as the Russian Jews. It therefore becomes imperative that we now consider, even though briefly, how these influences were transmitted.[16]

The first wave of German Jewish migration into the United States began in the 1840s. Of the two million Germans who entered this country between 1850 and 1860, about 5 percent were Jews.[17] The social climate they found in America, together with their liberal tendencies, facilitated their acceptance of the American culture. The German Jews became an integral part of the "Westward Ho" movement, and with other American pioneers they crossed the great mountains and rivers, conquering the prairies and the forests of the new American frontier. Since there was as yet no concentration in urban areas, the German Jews did not form the voluntary ghettos characteristic of Russian Jews; American social conditions encouraged integration, and the German Jews responded. "The German Jews," writes Glazer, "were not only peddlers and merchants, but also manufacturers, intellectuals, politicians, and even workers, active in every sphere of American life."[18] This tendency to acculturate lessened the specialization of areas of interest, and consequently there was little to mark the German Jews apart from the rest of the population.

Unlike the background of the German Jews, which emphasized assimilation, the Russian Jews' background was one of national and religious separatism. While the German Jews came mostly from urban centers, the Russian Jews came from the isolated *shtetl*.[19] While the German Jews looked upon America as their country, the Russian Jews saw it as just another *galuth*[20] where, God willing, they might make a better income. Unlike the Western Jews, who settled in America at the time of frontier expansion and thus spread westward themselves, the Eastern Jews came at the time of urban expansion. Their future lay in the cities, where they rapidly formed a proletariat.[21] While the German Jews in America maintained their religious identity, though changing the form and content of their ancient religion, the Russian Jewry was divided between those who continued the Orthodox religion in the same manner as they had in Russia, and those who became irreligious or antireligious.

When the Russian Jews began their migration into the United States, their voluntary mode of settlement was the ghetto. This self-isolation, together with the isolationist ideology that provided the mainstay of the *shtetl* existence, acted as a forceful prophylactic against changes in the orthodox religion. The ghetto synagogues came to possess a geographical identity, some bearing the name of the country from which the members had migrated, others the name of the province or town in which they were located.

The consequence of ghetto existence upon Jewish religion in America has been paradoxical. On the one hand, the ghetto, in its isolation from the rest of the population, made possible a continual religious orthodoxy by providing the physical means, such as synagogues, kosher food, and proper garments,[22] as well as the moral atmosphere. On the other hand, the ghetto also provided an opportunity for generating "nonreligious" Jews, that is, those who accepted and maintained the Jewish cultural heritage without following Jewish religious precepts. Regarding this point Glazer remarks:

> The relationship to Judaism of these almost totally Jewish residential districts was an ambiguous one. While they made it possible for every variant of Judaism to find a minimal number of adherents, they also made possible a varied social life that was utterly indifferent—in many cases even hostile to Judaism. There were organizations that carried some kind of Jewish activity, but were formally anti- or a-religious like Zionist and the Yiddishist groups.[23]

The antireligious Jewish movements in America are also associated with the rise of Jewish social organization and the development of the Zionist and socialist movements. Jewish social organizations such as the Jewish centers and the B'nai B'rith provided Jews with means for nonreligious identification. Glazer notes that:

> In the twenties and thirties, the center suggested to a number of people that it might be the nucleus for a new type of Jewish community. Its focus would not be religion but something we may call "Jewishness."[24]

The Zionist movement, begun in Russia and brought from there to America, provided a further means to nonreligious Jewish identification. More often than not, Orthodox rabbis opposed this movement; their opposition stemmed from a disagreement regarding the settlement of the Land of Israel. While the Zionists advocated immediate reestablishment of a homeland in Palestine, the rabbis contended that the only legitimate return to the "Holy Land" would come through the leadership of the Messiah, at a time to be decided by the Providence.[25] Nor were the Orthodox rabbis the only opponents of Zionism: The antinational and antitraditional position of the Reform rabbis was also in diametric opposition to Zionist aims. Prinz writes:

> The liberal branch of the rabbinate was openly hostile and attacked the new [Zionist] movement violently. The German rabbis prevented the holding of the first Zionist Congress in Munich. The American Reform Rabbis adopted resolutions which rejected Zionism with unmitigated violence.[26]

Finally, the Jewish socialist movement, brought to the United States by Russian Jewish migrants, presented another mode for nonreligious Jewish identification. It represented a movement in Russia the primary aim of which was political change, as one response to totalitarian government. Many Jewish youths, as members of an oppressed minority, joined leftwing organizations and selected socialist parties and their aims as a means by which they hoped to shed their minority status. Through such association with socialist political parties, Jews became involved with economic as well as political issues. They became concerned not only with the lack of political freedom and with Czarist totalitarianism, but also with the economic position of labor.[27] When they migrated to America the Jewish socialists of Russia brought along their views concerning labor and politics, but political freedom, which once had been perhaps their main concern, lost its great significance to them. Instead, they found in America a new phenomenon to which they could transfer their socialist interests, namely, the Jewish proletariat.

In 1900 the majority of the Russian Jewish migrants were engaged in clothing manufacturing, and most of them were laborers.[28] Youths who in Russia had been members of the socialist organizations transferred their area of activity from the political sphere to the economic sphere of socialism, and began to organize the Jewish proletariat into unions. The Bund, the Jewish socialist movement which followed the Jews from Russia to America, became the central point around which the Jewish proletariat rallied. Because of its progressive nature, the Bund broke away from religion and from religious organizations which stressed conservatism, orthodoxy, and an antiprogressive orientation, for change was interpreted as a departure from the ancient ideals, and the religious standpoint was thus viewed with suspicion.

With the help of the news media, the socialist ideologies of the Bund spread and became prevalent among the Jewish proletariat. During the first part of the twentieth century it was not uncommon for Jewish workers to read antireligious Yiddish newspapers, to vote socialist, and to join socialist-oriented unions. One such popular paper was the Jewish *Daily Forward*, whose editor was Abraham Cahan.[29]

In addition to organizing unions, the socialist groups also organized Yiddish schools which reflected the irreligious orientation of the socialist movement. Glazer describes these schools as follows:

Many of the schools that Jewish children attended after public school were not only neutral toward religion but were in principle atheistic and anti-religious. This was the case with a good part of the very active Yiddish school movement. Just as the passage of time, the arrival of new immigrants, and growing competence in adapting to the American scene had strengthened the institutions of Judaism, so had it strengthened the institutions of Jewish socialism, which were particularly attached to Yiddish, the language of the Jewish masses.[30]

333

The socialists were not the only Jews who wanted to minimize religion while maintaining the Jewish culture; there were also nonpolitical groups that wanted to minimize, even eliminate, the religious facet of Judaism, while maintaining its values and ideologies in order to maintain a culture which was Jewish in content. These groups established the Sholom Aleichem Yiddish schools, parochial schools whose purpose was to teach nonreligious Judaism.[31] The importance of this nonreligious cultural school is made clear by the fact that during the mid-1930s, seven thousand Jewish children in New York City alone attended them.[32]

The attitudes the first-generation Jews brought to the United States can be briefly summarized as follows: The German Jews stressed religious reforms while accepting the American cultural ethos, the Russian Jews brought both religious orthodoxy and nonreligiosity, but in both cases there was a strong inclination to maintain the Jewish culture. At this point it becomes necessary to view the impact which the above outlined heritages have had on second-generation Jews in America.

Hansen points out that second-generation ethnic groups, in their desire to acculturate, tend deliberately to slough off behavioral characteristics and values associated with their immigrant background. In its briefest form Hansen's law states: "What the son wishes to forget the grandson wishes to remember."[33] This process of forgetting among the Jewish Americans was not an omnipresent phenomenon. It occurred only among the Russian Jews; the second-generation German Jew had fewer such characteristics to slough off, since his parents had already accomplished this for him back in Germany.

The second-generation Russian Jews, "desperately anxious to become unequivocally American, were resentful of the immigrant culture to which the older generation seemed so eager to submit."[34] But for the most part Jewish religion and the Jewish culture were almost inextricably fused, and seemed so inseparable to the second-generation Eastern Jew that in his desire to dissociate himself from Jewish culture, he also dissociated himself from Jewish religion. Warner and Srole vividly depict the second generation's dissociation from the synagogue in Yankee City; there was such a drop in the synagogue attendance, they point out, that an elder Jew in Yankee City declared, "Sometimes we haven't even got enough men for a minyon [quorum of ten men needed for a religious service]. . . ."[35]

In addition to dissociation from the synagogue, the second generation's process of Americanization included a breaking away from the self-imposed ghetto of their parents and settling in the suburbs instead. They left the area in which identification as a Jew could have continued even without observation of the Jewish religion. In the ghetto one heard and spoke Yiddish; there one could eat a kosher meal and partake of all the varieties of Jewish dishes, take part in the Jewish social movements, and read the Yiddish newspapers and novels.[36]

It was precisely the second generation's sloughing off of Jewishness and Judaism which paved the way for the third generation's desire to reenter Jewish life. Their parents having moved out of the ghetto into "better neighborhoods" and suburban areas, the children of second-generation Jews now "played with Gentile ones on a level of middle-class respectability that does not generally countenance the simple name-calling and fist-fighting of the old slum. . . ."[37] Through their association with Gentile children and the lack of symbols of their identity around them, the third generation posed the question, "Why am I a Jew?" as a central theme of self-inquiry, and made the question of identity a central problem of their intellectual life.[38]

Gans,[39] like Glazer, points out an increased consciousness of and concern with Judaism in America, and attributes it to the fact that since society was labeling Jews anyway, most parents of third-generation children decided to train their children in Judaism. This new concern with Judaism was but a manifestation of a new symbolic Judaism, which consisted in the possession and the display of Jewish "objects of culture."[40]

Jewish "objects of culture" are artifacts of Jewish significance used as religious symbols; their purpose is to tie the Jew to his religious past. The rise of symbolic Judaism, argues Gans, was stimulated by the third-generation children's need for religion, but this need does not explain why these "objects of culture" have become the means of Jewish religious expression. If the third generation does have a need for religious experience, one would expect that attendance at religious services and worship rituals would have increased, yet this has not occurred. Attendance at religious services in the United States is now just as poor as it was in Yankee City,[41] and many synagogues with a large membership still have difficulties forming a minyon.[42] But if the third-generation Jews do not need religion personally as a "psychological cushion" to help avert their fears, whence the use of the religious symbols?

Herberg says that one explanation for the return to religion is the fact that religious association satisfies one's needs for identity. "The third generation began to remember the religion of its ancestors to the degree at least of affirming itself Jewish in a religious sense. . . ."[43] The religious objects can thus be interpreted as symbols around which the Jews in America center their religious identity; these "objects of culture" have become their flags.

Another explanation for the mushrooming of these "objects of culture" is the desire to display one's religious associations. This need among Jews to exhibit their relationship with their religion has been noted by other investigators. Warner and Srole, for instance, discovered this phenomenon among Yankee City Jews:

> It is noteworthy that the movement of the P[2] Jews, who had been so markedly dissociated from the orthodox synagogue, into the synagogue structure was justified by their relations to the American social system. For example, a P[2] upper-middle-class Jew, a leader in the campaign, after discussing how the younger Jews had thrown over their Jewishness, said: "The young men have found out that even to have the Christians like us, we should go to the synagogue. A Jew who is an honest Jew and takes an interest in his synagogue, that is, in his community, is really liked better by the Gentiles. A Christian who is a customer of mine told me that he would have more faith in one who was an "observing Jew" than in one who denied his religion.[44]

Jewish Americans today find themselves in a dilemma—how to maintain a religious identity while not practicing the ritualistic aspects of religion. How can they forego the traditional religious behavior, such as synagogue attendance, keeping holidays and the sabbath as days of rest, and keeping the *Khasruth*,[45] and identify themselves as Jews without the inconvenience of ritual laws? In what way can they symbolize their attachment to a religion without using the traditional means, which demand self-denial? This is where the religious "objects of culture" have a significant function. Instead of religious practice, present-day Jewish Americans publicly proclaim their Jewishness by wearing *mezuzahs* and "stars of David," displaying *menorahs* and *kiddish-cups*, placing upon the table doilies and tablecloths with Jewish symbols, and displaying pictures and books on Jewish topics; this mode of identification seems to agree with the American ideal of properly displayed property.

The constraint toward a Jewish religious identification in the United States was observed long ago by Weber; its importance increased tremendously with the anticommunist concerns of the McCarthy era. To be a nonbeliever then was tantamount to a profession of communism, and one's display of "faith in a deity" was essential to one's "Americanism." In addition to this pressure to be "religious," increased commitment to one's Jewish identity was also facilitated by two factors: the aftermath of the Nazi atrocities and the rise of the state of Israel. In 1934 Hitler came to power in Germany during a period of social and economic disorganization; by blaming the Jews for the postwar economic chaos Hitler attempted to integrate German society as a first step to world supremacy. Not only did he legislate anti-Semitic regulations, but he also developed concentration camps as a means to solve the "Jewish question." The holocaust began in 1938 with a purge lasting several days and nights: Jews were killed, synagogues burned, millions of dollars worth of property was destroyed. In addition, German Jews were ordered to pay $400 million, the sum of fines assessed on Jews who possessed more than $2,000. During World War II both German Jews and Jews from countries occupied by the Germans were herded into concentration camps, where they were systematically killed either by gas or through overwork and starvation. By the end of the war in 1945 over six million Jews, or about one-third of the Jewish population of the world, had been killed. Such extinction was to have been, as Eichmann declared, the solution to the Jewish question.

Obviously, this threat to Jewish existence heightened Jewish consciousness and helped to develop stronger ties among Jews on both the social and political levels. With the defeat of Germany, some half-million Jews were left homeless, living in displaced persons' camps. Some of these emigrated to the United States with the help of organizations like the American Joint Distribution Committee (AJDC), Hebrew Immigrant Aid Society (HIAS), and the Organization for Rehabilitation through Training (ORT). Unlike the time of the mass immigration of East European Jews during the previous century, the Jewish communities in America were far better organized and hence able to help these new immigrants to settle, provide them with occupational opportunities, and integrate them into the mainstream of American life.

The second major event which heightened Jewish consciousness in the United States was the development of the state of Israel. In light of the tragic events which befell the Jewish people during World War II, the United Nations voted to establish the state of Israel in the ancient homeland of the Jews. This realization of a two-thousand-year-old dream has since electrified the imaginations of Jews and non-Jews throughout the world. However, the cost of developing the land, the absorption of immigrants from Europe and North Africa, and the expenditure for defense that has been necessary for its survival have been enormous. The Jewish people in America have contributed both financial and moral support, resulting in a heightened Jewish identity among Jewish Americans. Moreover, the establishment of Israel has not only created a center for perpetuation of Jewish culture, but has also become a symbol of security. No longer will Jews in any country be faced, as they were in Germany, with the problem of having to flee one country and yet having no other willing to accept them. The doors of Israel are open to any Jew, and when anti-Semitism becomes rampant in his home country he now knows of a place open for emigration.

337

The Jewish Religion

Textbooks dealing with Jewish religion often begin by describing the three sects of Orthodox, Conservative, and Reformed Judaism. Differences among these three sects lie primarily in the degree of their acceptance of traditional rituals. However, the underlying moral conceptions and religious philosophy of all three divisions are remarkably similar, and therefore we shall treat the Jewish religion as a single entity.

The Jewish religion is based on the Torah, i.e., the first five books of the Bible (the Pentateuch). Depending on the degree of one's orthodoxy, Jewish religious life is also influenced and determined by the Talmud, i.e., the rabbinic literature which developed during the first century B.C. and second century A.D. While faith is an essential component of all religions, the primary emphasis of Jewish religion is placed not on faith but on the performance of commandments (*Mtizvoth*), and on rationalism rather than on emotionalism. (This is not to say that emotional involvement is totally absent.) Such emphasis on the obedience to Jewish law produced a "religious system [which] is in reality nothing but a contract between Jehovah and His . . . people, a contract with all its consequences and all its duties."[46]

THE SYNAGOGUE AND THE TEMPLE

The structure of Jewish communal worship is congregationalist; each place of worship determines its own existence. The rabbi is hired by the congregation and his future is determined by it. While the primary function of the synagogue is to be a place of worship, it has many other purposes as well, some of which are traditional and historical while others are of more recent origin. The Hebrew words for the synagogue are: (1) house of worship (*Beth T'filoh*); (2) house of study (*Beth Hamidrosh*); and (3) house of gathering (*Beth Haknesseth*). Hence the synagogue has traditionally been a place of worship as well as a place where rabbinical students and lay people came to study, and a community center for various activities such as charitable work. Many of its activities have today been taken over by special community organizations, yet the synagogues and temples have not completely abrogated their functions. In addition to religious services, a synagogue today also provides for instruction of religion and Jewish history. Most synagogues and temples have Sunday Schools where Jewish history is taught, as well as afternoon classes for the instruction of the Hebrew language, which is both the language spoken in Israel and the language of the prayers.

In the past, when Jews settled in a new community, the first communal activities were the erection of a synagogue and a cemetery. Today cemeteries are still part of the synagogue organization, and in many instances membership in a synagogue also assures burial in a Jewish cemetery. Obviously, the synagogue and the temple are centers for the rituals which are part of the Jew's life cycle (e.g., circumcision, Bar Mitzvoh, weddings). In addition to these activities, present-day synagogues have also become social centers sponsoring various types of youth organizations, men's clubs, and women's auxiliaries.

The Rabbi. The word "rabbi" means teacher, which indicates that the rabbi's earlier function was not primarily religious (that is, his activity was not necessary for the attainment of salvation, as is the case with a priest or minister), nor was he essential to the performance of religious rituals. In Judaism any knowledgeable person can perform any essential ritual from birth to death.[47] However, since most Jews lack the proper knowledge, this function has been taken over by a specially trained individual—the rabbi.

Among the Orthodox the rabbi serves the additional function of judge and ritual arbiter. In many Jewish communities there are Jewish civil courts, which have no legal standing but which are available to those Jews who wish to present cases of tort for arbitration to a rabbinical court. Such cases are decided on the bases of the religious-civil laws found in the Talmud. Obviously the rabbinical court's decisions have no legal authority and hence cannot be legally enforced, but are binding to the extent that the parties to the tort have accepted them to be binding.

Orthodox Jewish life is very complex. Daily life is guided by a great many rituals which define what a person may or may not wear, do, eat, and so on. When an Orthodox Jew has questions about the specifics of a given ritual, the permissibility of foods, or behavior during religious holidays, he directs such questions to the rabbi for interpretation and decision. Traditionally, the rabbi has had two main functions—to learn and to teach; today, however, he has become a quasi minister whose role is similar to that of the Christian minister. Hence he is also expected to perform public relations and to help create a good Jewish image in the community. Moreover, he is the leader of a religious service in which the sermon has become central. Finally, similar to the minister, the rabbi is expected to counsel his flock, visit the sick, and provide for the general welfare of his congregation.

Rituals. Although we most often think of rituals in a purely religious context, they often have important communal consequences. Rituals in the Jewish religion, in addition to defining appropriate behavior vis-à-vis the deity, also serve as a vehicle for identity formation and hence for perpetuation of the ethnic group. To be a Jew one not only must perceive oneself as a Jew, but also perform acts motivated by the desire to be perceived as a Jew by others. In other words, rituals serve as means of integrating the Jewish community.

The Reports

Jewish life in general, then, is governed by many rituals, and the extent to which those rituals are observed provides the major criterion for differentiation among Orthodox, Conservative, and Reformed Judaism. For Orthodox Jews, all ritual laws are binding; Reformed Jews, on the other hand, have eliminated many of the traditional rituals. It would be impossible to examine all the various proscribed rituals in the space of this report, but we shall examine a few of the major ones.

Dietary ritual (Kashruth). Almost everyone has encountered the term "kosher." It refers to dietary laws which determine what animals may be eaten and in what manner the meats of such animals should be prepared. For instance, only those mammals that chew the cud and have cloven hoofs may be used as meat. In addition, these animals must be slaughtered ritually; the meat must be voided of blood; and the mixing of meat and dairy products must be avoided. Finally, only the meat of the front half of the animal is usable, unless the hind quarters are specially cleaned and certain veins and tendons removed.

Holidays. Jewish holidays are considered days of rest, and as such forbid work. Restrictions on activity vary with religious orientation: Orthodox Jews may not work or cook, and are further restricted with regard to the distance they may walk and the transportation of objects in public areas, while Reformed Jews limit these restrictions primarily to the pursuit of economically gainful employment. Most important, however, is the function of holidays as family days. The Sabbath, for instance, was traditionally the day in which the father examined his son about his studies, the family took leisurely walks, and kinsmen visited each other.

JUDAISM IN AMERICA

While most Eastern European Jews who settled in America were Orthodox Jews, this religious division soon gave way to the Conservative and Reformed branches of Judaism. This change may be attributed to economic conditions and social mobility.

The constraints which orthodoxy imposed on Jewish life were difficult to observe. In the Eastern European small town (often known as the *shtetl*) Jews were primarily tailors and keepers of small shops, and these activities were subservient to religious demands. In the United States Jewish immigrants settled primarily in the large cities of the Northeast, where they became the proletariat of the garment business. The twelve-hour, six-day work week did not permit for the observance of the Sabbath and holidays, the latter of which often fell on weekdays.

Although Jewish religion stresses intellectualism in preference to emotionalism, Jewish life in Russian villages was not particularly conducive to the pursuit of knowledge. Life was difficult at best, most hours were spent in making a living, and there was hardly time for the leisure required for study. Prayer, emotion, and communal associations became a main feature of synagogue activities and were accompanied by increased emotionalism and conversation—features often associated in the United States with the behavioral patterns of the lower class. As the Eastern European Jewish immigrants began to achieve financial success, they also sought middle-class respectability. To achieve the latter they needed not only to belong to a religion (which, according to Weber, is in itself a symbol of respectability), but to a religion in which decorum was central—a need fulfilled by the Conservative and Reformed branches of Judaism. The latter not only lowered ritual requirements, but also provided a worship service in which appropriate middle-class behavior was essential.

In addition to changes induced by mobility, synagogues and temples were also affected by the assimilating force of the majority religion. Instead of remaining a participatory religion in the tradition of Orthodox worship, Reformed Judaism became an audience religion. No longer do the worshipers in the Reformed temples surround the cantor in loud prayer; instead they face the performing rabbi quietly and with little participation. English, rather than Hebrew, has become the primary language of prayer, with the sermon as the dominant feature of the service. The meanings of holidays and their ritual observance have also acquired features of the dominant Christian religion. Chanukah, a minor holiday commemorating the Maccabean revolt against Rome, has now, because of its proximity to Christmas, assumed dominance. In fact, it is viewed by Christians as the Jewish Christmas, and with it Jews have incorporated the practices of giving gifts, sending cards, and occasionally decorating a "Chanukah bush."

Social Values

Of the many values which are part of the Jewish culture, the three most dominant are justice, charity, and communality.

In contrast to Christianity, in which the dominant value is love, Judaism stresses above all the ideal of justice. This is not to say that love as a value is absent from Judaism nor justice from Christianity, but rather that if we examine the various components of the Christian and Jewish value systems, we will find that love supersedes all other values in Christianity as justice does in Judaism. Justice in Judaism is perceived as the foundation of life: "Justice, justice shall thou pursue that thou mayest live. . . ."[48] As a value in Judaism, it seeks to prescribe equity in asymmetrical power relationships; its concern for the use and abuse of power and privilege is manifest in the Jewish practice of questioning and critically examining political systems. Perhaps this concern for justice may be related to the Jewish propensity to vote for liberal causes and to be predominantly associated with the Democratic party, a party most often associated with liberal causes.

Closely associated with the ideal of justice is that of charity. The Hebrew word for charity, *Tzedokoh*, is derived from the same root (*Tzadok*) as the Hebrew word for justice, *Tzedek*. In other words, charity as an activity is related to maintenance of justice, of equity between the weak and the powerful. As a result, an act of charity for Jews is a normative act and not an act of free will—a duty, not a choice; it is part of the Jewish legal structure and hence part of the communal structure. It is not surprising that the Jewish American community has created many organizations designed to provide various types of aid to those in need.

Finally, Jews place primacy on community orientation as opposed to self-orientation. Rejection of the community is tantamount to apostasy: it is the wicked son, parents are told, who removes himself from the collectivity. To Jews, life, as Zbarowski and Herzog wrote, is with people.[49]

THE JEWISH COMMUNITY

Jews, like any other ethnic group in the United States, live within two communal organizations. First they are part of the larger communities in which they reside, and second they are part of their own ethnic subgroups, which provide emotional security and ethnic needs. In the larger communities they earn their living, participate in politics, receive the greater part of their education, and seek to achieve their social status; it is here that they are sanctioned if they violate the law or social norms. To this extent their membership and participation in the community is almost the same as that of any other member of the community in a similar socioeconomic position. Yet membership in an ethnic-religious group still presents constraints for social mobility, particularly in the status order. Faced with the need to stratify among themselves in terms of honor and prestige, Jews have in the past created status structures which parallel those of the majority group, by means of the same criteria prevalent in the status organization in the community at large. These status groups, moreover, represent distinct endogamous groups. The content of the status order of the Jewish community does not differ appreciably from that of the larger community, with the exception of the importance of education as a determinant of status position. In the Jewish cultural system education is considered paramount and has great bearing in allocation of status honor. A college professor, although having a lower income than most professionals, will nevertheless be accorded greater honor than members of other occupations with greater incomes.

The "separate but equal" type of social organization, though representative of the first-generation immigrant community, still exists in urban areas. This is because second- and third-generation descendants, having been socialized in America, began shedding the minority characteristics of their parents and attempted to enter the status organizations of the majority group. Their attempts have met with different degrees of success. Kramer and Leventman point out:

> Jews have been more successful in gaining entry into organizations based on the norm of inclusiveness than those based on exclusiveness. That is, more Jews belong to service organizations with civic functions (North State Centennial Committee or North City Aquacentennial Committee) than the more "social" organizations in which members are recruited by special invitation.[50]

An important difference between organizations based on inclusiveness and those based on exclusiveness is the degree of intimacy among the associating members. Association in inclusive groups is more often businesslike and confined to specific roles. (For instance, when an association is devoted to the promotion of a civic activity, each member of the group is assigned a task and interaction is most often associated with that member's task performance.) This is not to say that members of an inclusive group will not develop informal ties, but simply that the primary reason for such a group's existence is not social. In such organizations as country clubs and athletic clubs, on the other hand, intimate association is more frequent; in the steam room and swimming pool the last vestige of formality is lost. Given these conditions, exclusiveness as a value for selecting members becomes most important. In other words, under conditions in which individuals do not have symbols (such as clothes) to define their social positions and to serve as a guard against intimacy, the right to select one's associates becomes imperative.

The need for a status hierarchy, however, is in itself not a sufficient reason for the development of a minority community. It is therefore important that we examine what other needs the subcommunity satisfies. Obviously, existence of the subcommunity can be attributed to the integrative nature of cultural similarity; it is understandable that people who share similar historical experiences, language, and so on, will seek each other's companionship. Although cultural similarity is an important explanation for association, development of the Jewish community and its continual existence is more attributable to the fact that it provides the means for fulfilling esoteric needs which cannot be sat-

isfied by the larger community. These needs center around: (1) produc-
tion-distribution-consumption; (2) socialization; (3) social control; (4)
social participation; and (5) mutual support.[51]

PRODUCTION-DISTRIBUTION-CONSUMPTION

The economic life of American Jews is, as we said, centered in the
general community. But it is the Jewish community that makes available
to him the commodities necessary for his religious life. Observance of
the dietary laws, for instance, would be impossible without the services
of the subcommunity, and dietary needs are but one of many rituals
that require special products. Other such products are prayer shawls,
books, and so on.

SOCIALIZATION

The Jewish religion, as we have indicated before, places emphasis on
knowledge and study. In a section of the Bible which Jews have traditionally recited daily, Jews are instructed to "teach them [the laws] dili-
gently unto thy children, and shalt talk of them when thou sittest in
thine house, and when thou walkest by the way and when thou liest
down, and when thou risest up."[52] Even before the birth of Christ,
Jewish communities which had more than twenty-five children were
instructed to provide public education. Although the injunction on
learning is related to religious subjects, it was instrumental in developing
a favorable attitude to learning in general[53] and a high esteem for the
learned. Thus the rabbi, the learned teacher, is always seated at the head
of the table, given the honorable seat in the synagogue, and generally
treated with deference. This respect for the learned man has become
generalized to include secular as well as religious learning.

Another reason for the importance of education is to be found in the
history of Jewish experience. Because of frequent persecutions, money
and possessions were seldom a source of security; possessions were often
taken away or left behind when Jews were forced to leave the country of
their residence. Only education, knowledge, and skills were commodities
which could never be taken away, and therefore they were seen as the
foundation for security. A related consequence of the concern for education is that Jews generally seek to reside in parts of the cities and suburbs which have the best educational systems.

In addition to secular education, Jews also seek to provide their children with religious education, which is seen as the mechanism for the
continuation of Jewish existence. Most Jewish children start their religious education at about the age of six and complete it at thirteen, when
they become Bar or Bat Mitzvoh, literally a son or daughter of the commandments, signifying their having gone through the rite of passage

that marks entry into adulthood. These schools are most often part of a synagogue or temple, although there are several educational institutions directed and supported by the Jewish Board of Education. The latter aims to be nonsectarian by providing a curriculum acceptable to Orthodox, Conservative, and Reformed Jews. The last ten years have seen a revival of religious parochial schools where, in addition to general subjects, Hebrew language is taught as a secondary language, and a concentration in religious and historical studies is offered. Next to the home, Jewish schools were and are the most important institutions for developing ethnic consciousness and identity; hence the Jewish community places primacy on the support and development of the educational system.[54]

SOCIAL CONTROL

Social interaction founded upon a normative structure is essential to all communities. It is the nature of the norm that violations of norms will be sanctioned. In other words, in all social and patterned relationships there are elements of control, and to the extent that Jewish association is communal, it also includes mechanisms of control.

Social control can be either formal or informal. Formal control is constituted by the legal system and the sanctions imposed for violations of it. In the case of informal control, sanctions are imposed most often by breaking off associations and by withholding services and resources.

Formal social control is vested in the *Beth Din* (house of judgment), the Jewish court composed of three rabbis acting as judges. As we mentioned earlier, such a court has no legal status and is not legally empowered to implement its decisions. It serves only for those individuals who, out of their own volition, seek this court's arbitration, mostly in cases of torts and violation of contracts (which includes divorce as a process of contract dissolution). Judgment is rendered on the basis of Talmudic laws—a set of legal codes which includes the explanations and amendments to the laws found in the first five books of the Bible. The most severe punishment this court can render is excommunication, which is reserved for those acts which undermine the continual existence of Jews as a people. One such act is intermarriage. Traditionally, the parents of an exogamous Jew have declared their son or daughter dead and have followed all laws and customs associated with mourning. However, with the continual increase in the rate of intermarriage, these severe sanctions have become less used, and generally persons who intermarry today are neither declared dead nor cut off from all communal relations.[55]

External pressures for conformity to ethnic and religious norms are becoming weaker. The Jewish community, the existence of which depends greatly on voluntary financial contributions, can no longer afford to isolate and sanction those whose conformity is marginal. Consequently, in the face of ever-increasing deviance, a reinterpretation and reevaluation of traditional norms has evolved. For example, the norm of "compulsory endogamy" has changed to "preferred endogamy," exemplified by the following statement: "I would prefer that my son marry a Jewish girl, but it is his choice, and as long as she is a good girl it will be all right."

Social control based on the individual's fear of the subcommunity's retaliatory capability is declining. Similarly, fear of social isolation and ostracism is also declining. Being Jewish is no longer a necessary or sufficient, although often preferable, reason for friendship with another Jew. Without a sanctioning capability, then, what mechanism binds the Jew to this subcommunity? The primary reason is the individual's felt need for maintaining his identity. He adheres to Jewish values and norms because he wishes to be identified as a Jew and to derive both psychological and social benefit from such identification. He can maintain a sense of euphoria and, by identifying himself as a religious person, also be identified as a respectable person.

SOCIAL PARTICIPATION

Association among Jews is facilitated both by place of worship and by social and cultural centers. In addition to religious worship, synagogues have long served as centers for the development of personal associations. Presently, however, worship attendance among Jews is very low, perhaps lowest among all major religions in the United States. Lazerwitz[56] reports that only 28 percent of New York Jews attend services once a month or more frequently. Yet the synagogue or temple remains an important mechanism for initiating and maintaining social relationships among Jews. More importantly, ritual participation in such events as Bar or Bat Mitzvoh, weddings, and other celebrations functions to reinforce Jewish identity, since such participation allows Jews to develop a sense of euphoria about being Jewish.

Religion is not the only activity that brings Jews together. Horace M. Kallen, editor of the nonreligious Jewish newspaper *Forward*, has often suggested that Jewish life in this country should be built on a variety of Jewish experiences—political, social, and philosophical as well as religious. In Russia, for example, during the period of Jewish Enlightenment (1860–1900), a nonreligious expression of Jewish identity already existed: the Yiddish movement[57] encouraged the development of nonreligious literature based on the life experiences of Jews in the *shtetl* in Russia. Jewish centers in the United States became popular during the 1920s as places where Jews could not only learn English and prepare themselves for citizenship, but which also furthered the development of Jewish literature and plays.[58]

MUTUAL SUPPORT

"All Jews are responsible for each other": so goes the Talmudic statement. This responsibility encompasses all facets of life which affect the welfare of Jews on both the individual and the community levels.

Since they have always comprised a community within a community, Jews have long been concerned with the image they project to the larger community, and particularly with its effect on anti-Semitism—a prejudice which is unfortunately still widely prevalent. Glock and Stark report that in a national sample one-third of the respondents scored in the highest category on the Anti-Semitic Belief Index, while another 40 percent scored medium high. Thus 73 percent of the American public showed a considerable propensity for anti-Semitic beliefs.[59] Two national Jewish agencies, the Jewish Committee and the Anti-Defamation League of B'nai B'rith, have been concerned with organized intolerance to Jews in general, and particularly with the prevalence of anti-Semitism. Through the legal system these organizations have fought against discrimination in employment and residence, and have been successful in destroying restrictive covenants which specify that homes in certain areas will not be sold to minorities.

The Jewish community also provides extensive support for individuals, primarily in the areas of health, the aged, youth services, immigration, and employment.

Concern with health dates back to the period of mass immigration in the 1890s, when living conditions in the crowded rooms in the lower east side of New York and other Jewish ghettos helped create a high incidence of tuberculosis. These conditions helped to bring about the creation of the first three Jewish hospitals and sanatoriums for tuberculosis victims, which became the forerunners of present-day Jewish hospitals. Later development of general hospitals has been related to Jewish dietary considerations; these hospitals, although nonsectarian, provided kosher meals as well as other ritual considerations for the practicing Jew. At the present time in the United States, fifteen of the sixteen cities with a Jewish population of over forty thousand, and half of those cities with a Jewish population between sixteen and forty thousand, have a Jewish hospital.

Closely tied with health care facilities are the Jewish homes for the aged, which now care for nineteen thousand elderly persons. In addition to health care and social and personal services, these homes also provide for various religious considerations. (It is interesting that the

Hebrew word for "home for the aged" is *Beth Avoth*, meaning literally "home of our fathers.")

Beginning in the 1880s, Jewish mass immigration from Eastern Europe included many Jews fleeing from Czarist persecution. These Jews left almost all their possessions behind and came to this country poor and often ill-equipped to survive the rigors of urban life. To help these people a number of agencies came into existence such as HIAS, ADJC, and ORT. A precedent for helping immigrants is found as early as 1828, with the foundation in New York of the Hebrew Benevolent Society. In 1845 the B'nai B'rith (sons of the covenant) was organized, and has concerned itself with philanthropic activities ever since. Immigration between the two world wars declined drastically, primarily because of the quota system which limited the number of immigrants from each European country. Since World War II, however, Jewish immigration has again increased, and has consisted primarily of displaced persons from German concentration camps. The abovementioned organizations, together with Jewish family services in particular communities, have provided financial, moral, and personal help in resettling the new immigrants.

Most Jewish communities, through the Jewish Federation or the community center, now provide various youth services. These include summer camps where, in addition to recreation, there are courses in Jewish history and language. Other services include employment counseling and placement and family counseling and adoption services.

FUTURE PROSPECTS

It is difficult to predict the future of a people. If one may assume that the past record is a good indication of the future, we may say with fair certainty that Jews as a people will maintain their existence. It is now two thousand years since Jews were first driven from their homeland, and in spite of various difficulties they have been able to maintain their identity and sense of community. However, the extent of their integration into the majority society, or their maintenance of separatism, is primarily a function of social conditions. Historically, self-segregation has not always been voluntary. The negative attitude of a majority community and its legal restrictions have tended to keep Jews and Gentiles apart and to prevent active integration. When such restrictions have not been imposed, Jews have integrated and ethnocentrism as a philosophy has diminished.

At present in the United States—at least within the last ten years—the integration of Jews into the larger society has increased and has been manifested by a high rate of intermarriage. Generally when language, customs, and national prejudices are maintained and the socioeconomic status of a group remains low, endogamy is most prevalent. Since Jewish Americans have long ago shed many of their traditional customs and language and have moved into higher-status positions, one may expect increased integration and decreased endogamy among them. At the same time, however, other conditions are reinforcing Jewish consciousness and heightening Jewish identity as an ethnic group—namely, the state of Israel and continued world anti-Semitism. Establishment of the state of Israel provided an important link for Jews to their historical past; to a great extent, the life and identity of world Jewry is tied to the cultural life of the people of Israel. The positive accomplishments of that state have helped to maintain pride in Jewishness as well as to change the image of the Jews from an acquiescent martyr-like people to that of a people who can actively determine their life fate. In other words, Israel has helped to strengthen the Jews' pride in being Jewish, and the constant threat to this state's continued existence acts as an additional force for heightened Jewish consciousness and identity.

NOTES

1. Herbert J. Gans, "American Jewry: Present and Future," *Commentary* 21 (1956): 424–25.
2. Nathan Glazer, "The Jewish Revival in America: I," *Commentary* 20 (1955): 493.
3. Melvin Tumin, "Conservative Trends in American Jewish Life," *Judaism: A Quarterly Journal of Jewish Life and Thought* 17 (1964): 133.
4. Ibid., p. 135.
5. Ibid.
6. Ibid., p. 137.
7. Ibid.
8. Bernard Lazerwitz, "The Ethical Impact of Jewish Identification," *Judaism: A Quarterly Journal of Jewish Life and Thought* 18 (1969): 421.
9. Ibid.
10. Abram L Sacher, *A History of Jews* (New York: Knopf, 1930), p. 260.
11. Cecil Roth, "The Jews of Western Europe," in *The Jews: Their History, Culture, and Religion*, ed. Louis Finkelstein (New York: Harper and Brothers, 1949), pp. 250–83.
12. Sachar, *History of Jews*, pp. 273–98.
13. Under this law, Jews in a community were obliged, by fair means or foul, to fill a given quota for the Russian armed forces. In many communities bands of "Cathers" kidnapped Jewish children as one of the means to satisfy the ever-increasing demand for soldiers. Life in the *shtetls* of the Pale are described in the works of Shalom Aleichem, J. L. Perez, Mendele Mocher S'forim, and J. Fichman.
14. Rufus Learsi, *The Jews in America: A History* (New York: World, 1954).
15. We will omit for our purposes the migration of the Spanish Jews—Sephardim—and will begin with the massive migration of the German Jews.
16. Excellent presentations of the Jew's struggle in Russia are Louis Greenberg, *The Jews in Russia: The Struggle for Emancipation* (New Haven, Conn.: Yale University Press, 1944), and S. M. Dubnow, *The History of the Jews in Russia and Poland from the Earliest Times to the Present Day*, trans. I. Friedlander (Philadelphia: Jewish Publication Society of America, 1916).

The Reports

17. Learsi, *Jews in America*.

18. Glazer, "Jewish Revival" p. 16.

19. M. Zabrowski and E. Herzog, *Life Is With People: The Culture of the Shtetl* (New York: Schocken Books, 1962), p. 12. *Shtetl* are "small towns and enclaves within the area stretching from the eastern borders of Germany to the western regions of . . . Russia (embracing Poland, Galicia, Lithuania, White Russia, the Ukraine, Berserubia, Slovakia, and northeastern regions of Hungary)."

20. Refers to a diaspora or all lands outside Israel.

21. Glazer, "Jewish Revival."

22. Garments which are "shatnez" free, i.e., certified not to contain a mixture of wool and linen.

23. Glazer, "Jewish Revival," p. 494.

24. Nathan Glazer, *American Judaism* (Chicago: University of Chicago Press, 1957), p. 91.

25. In Mukacevo (the author's home town) in Czechoslovakia there were frequent fights between the Zionist and the Orthodox youth, and the chief rabbi of the community excommunicated the faculty of the local Zionist Hebrew School because they rejected the messianic concept.

26. Joachim Prinz, *The Dilemma of the Modern Jew* (Boston: Little, Brown, 1962).

27. Howard M. Schaar, *The Course of Modern Jewish History* (New York: World, 1958), pp. 323–46.

28. C. Bezalel Sherman, *The Jew Within American Society: A Study in Ethnic Individuality* (Detroit: Wayne State University Press, 1965), p. 87.

29. Sachar, *History of Jews*, pp. 327–28, notes that the Yiddish dailies represented definite political and economic views, and that those of the *Daily Forward* were socialist. "The *Forward*," he writes, "became the representative voice of American Jewish socialism. . . . The 'light' category . . . [the]so-called human interest happenings, [were] retold and interpreted from the 'Socialist-Jewish point of view.'" By 1902, this newspaper became very popular and achieved a circulation of 200,000.

30. Glazer, *American Judaism*, p. 87.

31. The roots of Yiddish orientation can be traced to the influences of such writers as Mendele, Sholem, and Peretz. For a more extensive discussion see Yudel Mark, "Yiddish Literature," in *The Jews*, ed. Finkelstein, p. 859.

32. Glazer, *American Judaism*.

33. Ibid.

34. Ibid.

35. W. Lloyd Warner and Leo Srole, "Assimilation or Survival: A Crisis in the Jewish Community of Yankee City" in *The Jews: Social Patterns of an American Group*, ed. Marshall Sklare (Glencoe Ill.: Free Press, 1958).

36. Glazer, *American Judaism*, pp. 72–105.

37. Glazer, "Jewish Revival," p. 493.

38. Ibid.

39. Gans, "American Jewry," pp. 422–30.

40. Bernard Lazerwitz, "Jews In and Out of New York City, *Jewish Journal of Sociology* 3 (1961): 254–60.

41. Bernard Lazerwitz, "Religion and Social Structure in the United States," in *Religion, Culture, and Society*, ed. Louis Schneider (New York: Wiley, 1964), p. 641.

42. The author is acquainted with many synagogues in St. Louis and Memphis, and in the small towns of southern Illinois, where members are assigned dates so that a "minyon," the necessary ten men for public service, is assured.

43. Will Herberg, *Protestant-Catholic-Jew* (Garden City, N.Y.: Doubleday, 1955), p. 190.

44. Warner and Srole, "Assimilation," p. 355.

45. The dietary laws, which specify what Jews may and may not eat.

Jewish Americans

46. Werner Sombart, *The Jews and Modern Capitalism*, trans. H. Epstein (Glencoe, Ill.: Free Press, 1951).

47. There is one ritual for which a *Kohen* (hereditary priest) is necessary: the "redemption of the first born." If a woman's first child is a male, he is ritually redeemed from the diety who proclaimed in the Bible, "Sanctify unto me all the firstborn . . ." (Exod. 13:2).

48. *Deut.* 16:20.

49. Zbarowski and Herzog, *Life Is With People*.

50. Judith Kramer and Seymour Leventman, *Children of the Gilded Ghetto* (New Haven, Conn.: Yale University Press, 1961), p. 98: "For reasons of service to the community, or humanitarian or democratic ideals, organizations based upon the norms of inclusiveness attempt to recruit as many members as possible, regardless of socio-economic background. In contrast, organizations based upon norm of exclusiveness represent status communities and select their members according to specific social and economic qualifications."

51. Roland Warren, *The Community in America* (Chicago: Rand McNally, 1963), p. 208.

52. *Deut.* 6:7.

53. The importance of education among Jews can be evidenced from the following statistics: In Providence, R.I., for instance, in 1960, 8.2 percent of its total population, 25 years and older (including Jews), have had graduate or postgraduate training, compared with 33.8 percent of its Jewish population. Similar differences were found in New York, where in 1964, 15.9 percent of its population held graduate or postgraduate degrees compared with 27.4 percent of its Jewish population (Marshall Sklare, *America's Jews* [New York: Random House, 1971], pp. 51–60).

54. Of all the monies collected by the Jewish Federation, one-fourth is allocated to Jewish education (*The American Jewish Yearbook* [New York: American Jewish Committee, 1972]).

55. Of all marriages between 1966 and 1972, 31.7 percent were intermarriages (Fred Massarik, *Intermarriages: Facts for Planning* [New York: Council of Jewish Federation n.d.]).

56. Lazerwitz, "Jews In and Out of New York City."

57. Yiddish is jargon based on the German language, with an admixture of Hebrew and the language of the country.

58. For further discussion, see Glazer, *American Judaism*.

59. It is interesting to note that anti-Semitic attitudes are related to belief systems. Members of conservative religions are more likely to be anti-Semitic than members of liberal religions. For instance, it is lowest among Unitarians (11 percent) and highest among Baptists (40 percent). See Charles Y. Glock and Rodney Stark, *Christian Beliefs and Anti-Semitism* (New York: Harper Torchbooks, 1966).

Suggested Readings

Glazer, Nathan. *American Judaism*. Chicago: University of Chicago Press, 1957.

Glock, Charles Y., and Rodney Stark. *Christian Beliefs and Anti-Semitism*. New York: Harper Torchbooks, 1966.

Goldstein, Sidney, and Calvin Goldscheuder. *Jewish Americans*. Englewood Cliffs, N.J.: Prentice-Hall, 1968.

Kramer, Judith, and Seymour Leventman. *Children of the Gilded Ghetto*. New Haven, Conn.: Yale University Press, 1961.

Schaar, Howard M. *The Course of Modern Jewish History*. New York: World, 1958.

Sherman, C. Bezalel. *The Jew Within American Society: A Study in Ethnic Individuality*. Detroit, Mich.: Wayne State University Press, 1965.

Sklare, Marshall. *America's Jews*. New York: Random House, 1971.

Wirth, Louis. *The Ghetto*. Chicago: University of Chicago Press, 1928; Phoenix Books, 1958.

ROBERT E. KENNEDY, JR.

IRISH AMERICANS*

A Successful Case of Pluralism

Is knowledge about the historical experience of European immigrants in the United States helpful in understanding contemporary American minority-group relations? Are social organizations used today by racial or linguistic minorities similar to those created by some European immigrant groups to aid their members. The immigration history of one group is particularly relevant in answering these questions—that of the Irish, especially the Irish Catholics.

In 1850 over 40 percent of all foreign-born persons in the United States had been born in Ireland (Table 1). They were the first large body of immigrants in America who were not Anglo-Saxon in culture or predominantly Protestant in religion. Because of their "non-American" ways, Irish immigrants suffered from extreme discrimination, and some of their adaptations to life in the United States, especially to life in American cities, influenced later-arriving immigrant groups for several decades.

If assimilation is the goal of a minority group, then it would seem that the Irish have succeeded. Persons of Irish birth and ancestry today

* In most instances the material presented in this paper refers to the Catholic rather than the Protestant population among the Irish in the United States. Catholics represented the majority of the Irish to immigrate in the nineteenth century and were the portion of the population most subjected to minority status.

The Reports

TABLE 1

PERCENT DISTRIBUTION BY COUNTRY OF BIRTH OF THE FOREIGN-BORN
POPULATION OF THE UNITED STATES, 1850–1920

Country of Birth	1850*	1860	1880	1900	1920
Ireland	42.8	38.9	27.8	15.6	7.5
Germany	26.0	30.8	29.4	25.8	12.1
England, Scotland, and					
Wales	16.8	14.2	13.6	11.3	8.5
Sweden, Norway, and					
Denmark	0.9	1.8	6.6	10.4	8.5
Italy	0.2	0.3	0.7	4.7	11.6
Russia, Lithuania,					
and Finland	0.1	0.1	0.5	4.7	12.2
Poland	0.0	0.2	0.7	3.7	8.2
Other	13.2	13.7	20.7	23.8	31.4
Percentage totals	100.0	100.0	100.0	100.0	100.0
Total foreign-born					
population in					
thousands	2,245	4,139	6,680	10,341	13,921

SOURCE: Nils Carpenter, *Immigrants and Their Children*, 1920 (Washington, D.C.: Government Printing Office, 1927), pp. 78–79, Table 43.
* Figures for each census year relate to countries as constituted in that year.

have assimilated into almost all aspects of American life, and many have become "Irish" in name only. But some Irish originally did not come to this country to give up their ethnic heritage; they came to create a life based on their own culture, which they felt had been denied them in their homeland. They valued the constitutional freedoms guaranteed by their adopted nation as the means for establishing separate control over their own political, educational, and religious affairs.

Many Irish immigrants in the United States also brought with them intense anti-English sentiments which, in some ways, became anti-Anglo-Saxon attitudes in this country. Far from desiring to emulate the ways of the native-born "Yank," some Irish immigrants, especially the Catholics among them, scorned elements of the then-prevailing American life style. In a nation which was overwhelmingly rural, the Irish concentrated in the larger cities. While many Protestants believed religion was a matter of individual responsibility and a personal salvation, Irish Catholics assumed the ultimate authority in spiritual matters rested not with the individual, but with a religious hierarchy. In opposition to the Jeffersonian belief in creating an informed electorate through the ideal of universal public education, Irish Catholics insisted on operating their

354

own private schools where they could educate their children as they saw fit.

Contrary to the American emphasis on monetary success as the main criterion for individual achievement, many Irish Catholic American children were brought up to value pursuits which helped others in their family or their ethnic community. In a guide to potential Irish emigrants, published in 1873, the Irish author expounded on the American virtues of hard work, moderate living, and a lifelong savings plan as the means to success, and then he defensively added:

> Be it understood that the object of the writer is not to destroy or warp any of the grand and beautiful traits of character in our race for which they are distinguished all over the world. Filial devotion, love of friends, and readiness to relieve their wants, are characteristics of our race that deserve all honor.[1]

Minority-group membership was a social reality for the Irish which often determined individual behavior. Elsewhere, for example, I have described the independent effect of minority-group status on the family size of Catholics in Northern Ireland.[2] Although several other aspects of life in Ireland have changed over the past century, the current troubles in Northern Ireland illustrate the enduring reality of Ireland's history of intergroup conflict—a history which had a direct impact on why so many Irish left Ireland for the United States. The behavior of the Irish in America is more understandable with knowledge of conditions in Ireland a century or more ago, when the forebears of most Irish Americans began arriving in this country.

Conditions in Nineteenth-Century Ireland

The hostility of many Irish immigrants to things Anglo-Saxon, their strong identity with Roman Catholicism, their rejection of rural living, and their intense concern with political power all have historical roots in their reasons for leaving Ireland. Emigration from Ireland was linked to four major topics, the first of which was the relationship between the major religious denominations.

PROTESTANTS AND ROMAN CATHOLICS

Even though the majority of the Irish population was Roman Catholic, laws once existed which discriminated against them because of their religion. The issue was one of power rather than numerical minority or majority status, with the Protestant minority being dominant. Irish Catholics lost much of their status with the passage by the English between 1695 and 1746 of what became known as the Penal Laws. As J. C. Beckett has commented: "The essential purpose of the Penal Laws . . . was not to destroy Roman Catholicism, but to make sure that its adherents were kept in a position of social, economic, and political inferiority."[3]

By the beginning of the nineteenth century the Penal Laws were gradually lifted, but social discrimination against Catholics maintained the power and privileges of Protestants over Catholics. As late as 1926 the disproportionate representation of Protestants in the better jobs was still apparent. Even though Protestants accounted for only 7 percent of the male labor force in the Republic of Ireland at that time, half of the bank officers were Protestants, as were 41 percent of the heads of commercial businesses, 40 percent of accountants, and 36 percent of lawyers.[4]

Under such circumstances a movement of Catholics from Ireland to the United States would hardly have been surprising. Given the discrimination suffered by Catholics in Ireland, however, it was difficult for them to pay their own passage across the Atlantic. This need was met in large part by the loyalty of the Irish in the United States to family and friends left behind. During the second half of the nineteenth century, Irish immigrants in the United States sent back to Ireland $260 million.[5] This money paid for at least three-quarters of all Irish emigration to the United States between 1848 and 1900, and without it Irish Catholic mass emigration to America would not have happened.[6]

LAND OWNERSHIP, EVICTION, AND FAMINE

Because of the Penal Laws, by the early nineteenth century most of the land in what is today the Republic of Ireland was owned by Protestants. They leased their land to tenant farmers who were predominantly Catholic (as was the landless laboring class). As is sometimes the case with slum landlords today, many early nineteenth-century Irish landlords tried to get as much rent from as many tenants as possible. Tenant holdings were fragmented, living standards declined, until a large segment of the rural population became dependent on a single crop for their staple food—the potato. Following a poor potato harvest, the nutritional level worsened and epidemics accompanied by starvation became increasingly common. One might ask why the Irish did not eat their other crops, or even their livestock, to avoid starvation during failures of the potato harvest? They needed to pay the rent to avoid eviction, and they had nothing to pay the rent with except their cash crops. As Irish historian George O'Brien put it:

The extraordinary spectacle of Irishmen starving by thousands in the midst of rich cornfields was thus witnessed. One case, typical of many others, is recorded of a man's dying of starvation in the house of his daughter, who had in her haggard a substantial stack of barley, which she was afraid to touch, as it was marked by the landlord for his rent.[7]

Tenants were able to resist eviction to some degree by murders, burnings, cattle mutilation, and other forms of agrarian terrorism directed against the landlord, his agents, and persons who might move into an evicted tenant's holding. Although evictions were more prevalent during famine times, contrary to what one might expect, persons officially reported as evicted made up only a small minority of all reported emigrants between 1849 and 1882.[8] The great majority of emigrants from rural Ireland did not wait for eviction before deciding to leave the country. For these individuals, the act of emigration was also a decision to give up farming as a way of life.

Between 1800 and 1879 there were eight extensive famines in Ireland, the worst one occurring between 1845 and 1848.[9] Because the 1845–1848 famine was one of the most severe in Irish history, and because at least three million persons emigrated from Ireland between 1845 and 1870 (compared with a total national population of about eight million in 1841), it is often assumed that this famine initiated mass emigration from Ireland. Actually, the famine accelerated a mass movement out of the country which was well under way by the 1820s.[10] And that mass out-migration continued for decades after adjustments to the 1845–1848 famine were over: by 1891, 39 percent of all Irish-born persons in the world were living outside of Ireland.[11]

IRISH AGRICULTURAL TECHNOLOGY

Irish Catholics may have rejected agriculture in Ireland, given the land tenure system there (as late as 1895 only 12 percent of all farmers owned their own holdings) and the destitution which periodic crop failures had brought them. But this does not explain why so few took up farming after their arrival in the United States. A major reason for their urban preferences lies in the contrast between Irish and American agricultural techniques.

Due to the fragmentation of farms which had taken place in the early nineteenth century, by 1841 four out of five Irish holdings were smaller than fifteen acres. These small farms were worked by manual methods using the spade, scythe, and wooden rake and pitchfork. The farmers did not need, and could not afford to support, a horse and the relatively expensive capital investment in horse-drawn implements.

In the United States, on the other hand, farmers were not limited by the availability of farm land. In 1862, for example, Congress passed the Homestead Act, which promised ownership of a one hundred sixty-acre tract of public land to family heads who cleared the land and lived on it for five years. Horses and horse-drawn implements were essential to exploit fully even part of such a large acreage, and by the mid-nineteenth century such horse-drawn techniques had become the dominant method of commercial agriculture in the United States.

The Irish immigrant to America during the nineteenth century may have been a farmer or a farm laborer back in Ireland, but in most cases he would have had little, if any, firsthand experience with the horse-drawn methods required to make the most of agricultural opportunities in his new nation. His lack of interest in clearing and settling previously uncultivated land on the frontier is understandable in large part on such technical grounds alone.

Many Irish immigrants also had no interest in homesteading opportunities because they were more concerned with earning a cash income as soon as possible after arrival. Often their passage across the Atlantic had been paid by a relative or friend, and some felt obligated to do the same favor for potential emigrants still in Ireland. Urban jobs, even the most menial, provided such an income, while the capital investment required to establish a homestead would have consumed any cash earnings for a period of years.

RELATIVE SOCIAL STATUS OF THE SEXES

The fourth major topic was linked to the decisions of thousands of females to emigrate: their relatively low status in Ireland. Although the situation of females had improved by the late 1950s, an Irish sociologist was still able to describe the status of teenage girls in rural Limerick in the following way:

> When a daughter reaches sixteen, if she remains on the farm, she must do a full day's work, and too often her life is one of unrelieved drudgery. . . . [Girls] are favoured neither by father nor mother and accepted only on sufferance. This is, perhaps, too strong a conclusion, and it would be better to say they are loved but not thought of any great importance.[12]

In contrast to daughters, sons in the Irish family system were given preferential treatment, second only to their father. Women and children did not eat until after the men and the older boys had had their fill, a practice which systematically made the more nutritious food and larger helpings available to the favored sex. In rural areas the division of labor also gave preference to males: Women were expected to help with the men's work, but men would be ridiculed for helping with women's work. Women were usually called out into the fields to cut turf, to plant, cultivate, and harvest potatoes, and to assist at haymaking time.[13]

Elsewhere I have argued that the dominance of Irish males over females was sufficiently extreme to result in relatively higher female mortality; several comparisons of mortality by sex, nationality, rural-urban residence, age, and cause of death all indicate that the subordinate status of Irish females did indeed increase their mortality levels from what they otherwise might have been.[14]

Because the opportunities for improving one's social status were relatively much greater for females than for males away from their families, and in urban than in rural areas, migration to urban areas appealed more strongly to Irish females than males.[15] The movement to the United States of Irish females not only made the Irish immigration stream larger than it otherwise would have been, the preference of the Irish females for cities also contributed to the urban concentrations of the Irish in their adopted country.

Nineteenth-Century Irish Immigrants

Most Irish immigrants in the United States were satisfied to remain in the eastern seaboard states throughout the second half of the nineteenth century. Almost two-thirds of all Irish-born persons in the United States in 1850 lived in just three states: New York, Pennsylvania, and Massachusetts (Table 2). Forty years later over half of the Irish-born still resided in those three states, and the relative increase in other states took place primarily among only four: New Jersey, Illinois, Connecticut, and California. The limited geographic dispersal of the Irish is understandable, given their reasons for coming to the United States. Most were rural-urban migrants not interested in settling the interior of the nation. They persisted in living in the East in spite of having been encouraged by some Irish writers of the time to take advantage of the cheap land available.

The Irish preference for urban living is understated by the state-wide figures. In 1870, for example, of all the Irish-born persons in the United States, about 16 percent were living in the New York City area alone (New York City, Brooklyn, and Jersey City, New Jersey). Besides New York, the Irish concentrated in Boston and Philadelphia in the East, Chicago in the Midwest, and San Francisco in the West (after the gold rush days). The Irish were so prevalent in these cities, in fact, that in 1870 about one in five persons living in Boston, New York City, and

The Reports

TABLE 2

GEOGRAPHIC DISPERSAL OF THE IRISH: PERCENT DISTRIBUTION
OF IRISH-BORN PERSONS BY STATE AND TERRITORY,
UNITED STATES, 1850, 1870, 1890

State	1850	1870	1890
New York	35.7	28.5	25.8
Pennsylvania	15.8	12.7	13.0
Massachusetts	12.0	11.6	13.9
Ohio	5.4	4.5	3.7
New Jersey	3.2	4.7	5.4
Illinois	2.9	6.5	6.7
Connecticut	2.8	3.8	4.2
California	0.3	2.9	3.4
Subtotals	78.1	75.2	76.1
Other states and territories	21.9	24.8	23.9
Percentage totals	100.0	100.0	100.0
Total Irish-born persons in the United States	961,719	1,855,827	1,871,509

SOURCE: United States Bureau of Statistics, *Arrivals of Alien Passengers and Immigrants in the United States from 1820 to 1892* (Washington, D.C.: Government Printing Office, 1893), pp. 90–121, Table 14.

Brooklyn actually had been born in Ireland, as had about one in six or seven persons in the populations of San Francisco, Philadelphia, and Chicago (Table 3). The sizes of the Irish ethnic communities in these cities were even larger, since the figures refer only to the Irish-born immigrants and do not include children born in the United States to Irish parents.

The importance of Irish numbers in these cities was further enhanced by the relative lack of other foreign-born groups. By the 1870s Germans were arriving in large numbers, but they dispersed themselves more widely than the Irish, many bypassing the eastern cities for the towns and farmlands of the Mississippi River valley. Almost by default, the Irish continued to compose almost two-thirds of all foreign-born persons in Boston by 1870, and about half or more of all of the immigrants living in New York City, Brooklyn, and Philadelphia (Table 3). At this time the Irish also made up the majority of foreign-born persons in several smaller cities and towns, such as Jersey City, Albany, and Providence. In such cities being a "foreigner" most often meant being Irish, and the relatively large numbers of the Irish and their children made their "non-American" ways conspicuous to the native-born Americans.

TABLE 3

URBAN CONCENTRATIONS OF THE IRISH: IRISH-BORN PERSONS AS A
PERCENTAGE OF THE FOREIGN-BORN AND THE TOTAL POPULATIONS OF
SELECTED CITIES, UNITED STATES, 1870

| City | Total City Population | Irish-Born as a Percentage of | |
		Total City Population	All Foreign-Born in City
Boston, Mass.	250,526	22.7	64.7
New York, N.Y.	942,292	21.4	48.3
Jersey City, N.J.	82,546	21.4	55.5
Albany, N.Y.	69,422	19.1	59.8
Brooklyn, N.Y.	396,099	18.7	51.1
Providence, R.I.	68,904	17.5	70.4
San Francisco, Calif.	149,473	17.3	35.1
Pittsburgh, Penna.	86,076	15.2	47.2
Philadelphia, Penna.	674,022	14.3	49.9
Chicago, Ill.	298,977	13.4	27.7

SOURCE: United States Bureau of Statistics, *Arrivals of Alien Passengers and Immigrants in the United States from 1820 to 1892* (Washington, D.C.: Government Printing Office, 1893), pp. 122–33, Table 15.

PREJUDICE, HOSTILITIES, AND DISCRIMINATION AGAINST THE IRISH

Today the Irish are not considered to be a biologically distinct race, but such was the case in nineteenth-century America. Irish persons were believed by many Americans to have certain inferior traits which were intrinsic to the "Irish race." Because this American attitude explains much of how the Irish were received, it is worth quoting at length from at least one contemporary expression of the belief. In 1852 a Massachusetts clergyman wrote a letter to a Boston newspaper urging his fellow Americans to accept the Irish because they would be useful but not competitive:

How much use are the Irish to us in America? The Native American answer is, "none at all." And the Native American policy is to keep them away. A profound mistake, I believe, for the precise reason that, in the pure blood they are so inefficient as compared with the Saxon and other Germanic races which receive them, I am willing to adopt the Native American point of view, and to speak with an *esprit du corps* [*sic*], as one of the race invaded. . . .

Now if we Americans were . . . inferior in ability . . . to the Celts, we

361

might complain. . . . But this is not true. We are here, well organized, and well trained, masters of the soil, the very race before which they [the Irish] have yielded everywhere besides. It must be, that when they come in among us, they come to lift us up. As sure as water and oil each finds its level they will find theirs. So far as they are mere hand-workers they must sustain the head-workers, or those who have any element of intellectual ability. Their inferiority as a race compels them to go to the bottom; and the consequence is that we are, all of us, the higher lifted because they are here.[16]

Some Americans were not content to let the Irish settle to the bottom on their own; they used physical coercion against the Irish and against Irish institutions. As early as the 1830s organized resistance against Irish Catholics had begun in New York and in Massachusetts, with ethnic and religious tensions often centering around the Catholic convent schools. As Hofstadter and Wallace comment: "The unfamiliar nature of convent schools in particular gave rise to all sorts of speculation about immoral behavior and to sensational rumors about secret passageways from priests' homes to nunneries, the sexual abuse of female students by confessors, and the burial of illegitimate babies in convent crypts."[17] On the night of August 11, 1834, without warning, a mob attacked the Ursuline Convent in Charlestown, Massachusetts, drove out the ten adults and sixty children, and ransacked and burned the main building and the surrounding structures. News of the incident spread quickly and reinforced many Irish in their belief of the necessity to band together in defense of themselves, their families, and their community.

Quarrels and fights between Irish Catholics and American Protestants were common beginning as early as the 1820s, and an unusually large (and lengthy) riot occurred in Philadelphia in 1844 during which both sides armed themselves with cannon. By the end of the fighting, which erupted sporadically between May and July of that year, at least fifty persons had been killed or injured, and over thirty homes and two churches had been burned down in the Irish section of the city. The riot had been sparked by Protestants incensed at a decision by the public school authorities to allow the use of the Catholic, as well as the Protestant, Bible in local schools.[18]

Paralleling open violence against the Irish was strong discrimination against their employment in any but the most menial jobs. The words, "No Irish need apply," appeared in newspaper notices beginning in the 1830s, and were only part of the problem many Irish experienced in seeking employment. There was what George Potter has called the silent conspiracy among employers not to hire Catholic Irish help: "An applicant's obvious Gaelic name or the sound of his brogue barred the door to employment, regardless of his personal qualities or qualifications, frequently on the justification that American or Protestant Irish help would not work by his side."[19]

It is an open question, however, whether more Irish were kept out of the American mainstream by discrimination, or whether more kept themselves out in their drive to establish separate religious, social, and political institutions and organizations.

IRISH AMERICAN SOCIAL INSTITUTIONS

The separatist element of the Irish immigrant population once, in 1818, went so far as to petition Congress for national aid and a piece of land on which to settle Irish charity cases at the exclusion of other groups. Congress turned down the request on the grounds that formal assignment of a national group to a particular territory could lead to similar requests by other nationalities which would fragment the nation. The noted historian of American immigration history, Marcus Hansen, remarked that "probably no decision in the history of American immigration policy possesses more profound significance, " since it established the principle that ethnic communality would have to be achieved by the voluntary action of individuals with no help from the government (Indian Americans excepted).[20]

Facing open hostility from native Americans, and prevented from establishing exclusive Irish enclaves by the action of Congress, the Irish emphasized the establishment of their own social institutions in the large American cities where most of them lived. As Oscar Handlin said of the Boston Irish:

> The flourishing growth of Irish institutions was an accurate reflection of their consciousness of group identity. . . . Unable to participate in the normal associational affairs of the community, the Irish felt obliged to erect a society within a society, to act together in their own way. In every contact therefore the group, acting apart from other sections of the community, became intensely aware of its peculiar and exclusive identity.[21]

Priority was given to establishment of the schools, churches, hospitals, and services which together, in the eyes of the Irish, constituted their Roman Catholic religious institutions. The influx of Irish immigrants after 1840 placed great strains upon the existing Catholic facilities; nevertheless, native American Catholics welcomed Irish immigrants as the means to bring about a revival of Catholicism in the United States. The Irish did not disappoint them.

The Irish enlarged or began Catholic parishes not only in the large cities, but along the transportation routes which Irish laborers helped construct into the interior. Irish immigrants and their children entered into Catholic religious vocations in such large numbers that they soon predominated in the Roman Catholic hierarchy in the United States: A study of all American Catholic bishops revealed that between 1789 and 1935, 58 percent either had been born in Ireland or had been the son of an Irish-born father.[22] Through their predominance in the American Catholic church, the Irish exercised considerable influence on American ethnic relations by playing a mediating role between the general society and the later-arriving, Catholic, foreign-born groups.[23]

Irish ethnic sentiments were especially pervasive in the controversy over Catholic parochial schools and their relation to public taxes collected for educational support. Many native Americans considered public schools the most effective instruments for Americanizing recent immigrants from Europe. The Irish, on the other hand, fresh from the experience of English-controlled schools in Ireland, insisted that only the parent had the right to decide where and how his or her children were to be educated. Compulsory public school attendance laws were denounced by Irish Catholic newspapers, which contended that education must be the work of the church and not the state. The Irish also argued that school taxes collected by the state from Catholics who operate their own schools should be returned to them. The controversy continues to this day; the net result has been that the assimilation of Catholic immigrant groups into American life was less rapid than it otherwise might have been.

While the Catholic church was open in its political opposition to public school taxes, it was often accused of using its parishioners indirectly to achieve other political ends. The connection of Irish Catholicism with organized politics has been called "Irish Catholic power," with the assumption that the Catholic hierarchy directed the behavior of Irish politicians and the votes of Irish immigrants. From this viewpoint, the separatism of the Irish was not due to their own desires, but to the actions of their religious leaders:

> The Irish peasants were likable and eager to please; they deeply desired to adjust themselves to the new culture; but their priests and bishops stood for certain separatist and non-American practices which immediately inflamed the opposition and put the whole Irish Catholic community on the defensive.[24]

This American belief was similar to the opinion once popularly held in England that the Irish "electorate was entirely under the thumb of the priesthood."[25] Actually, the historical association between the church and Irish political leaders in both countries often was one of open disagreement. Throughout the nineteenth century most Irish nationalist leaders emphasized a clear separation between church and state. The conflict of interests became most extreme in Ireland after 1916, when the Catholic hierarchy denounced the popular Sinn Fein political party and excommunicated several of its leaders.[26]

Irish political and labor leaders in the United States, as in Ireland, maintained clear limits to the authority of the church. In 1870 a popular organization dedicated to the liberation of Ireland, the Fenian Brotherhood, was condemned by the Vatican and its members threatened with excommunication. In response several Irish American newspapers urged that the Vatican's action be ignored because "the jurisdiction of the Church could not be extended properly to purely temporal questions."[27] Many priests and bishops also denounced oath-bound labor societies such as the Knights of Labor, in which the Irish were prominent, and the Molly Maguires and Hibernians, whose members often were violent participants in labor troubles. One of the first sweeping condemnations of secret societies by the church in America, in fact, was not against the anti-Catholic Masons but against "Corkonians and Connaught men" who were organizing Irish laborers on public works.

Far from being under the thumb of their priests, many Irish did not hesitate to ignore their religious leaders when they believed their secular goals were at stake. The agreement on many, perhaps most, political matters between the hierarchy and the Irish electorate sprang not from the dominance of one over the other, but rather from the fact that for decades most members of the Catholic hierarchy in the large eastern cities were Irish; they were themselves part of the Irish community and reflected the same ethnic beliefs and values as their parishioners.

IRISH POLITICAL AND LABOR ORGANIZATIONS

The Irish supported the Catholic church, through which they received spiritual and moral guidance, their children were educated, their sick and infirm were cared for, and their destitute and poverty-stricken given support and assistance. But some things the church could not provide, and the Irish were dedicated to creating organizations which would help achieve these other goals in the face of opposition from anti-Irish native Americans. They were intensely concerned with power relationships, the ability to direct their own lives and that of others:

Nothing strikes the historian of the American Irish so forcibly as their desire to wield power. As churchmen, nationalists, and politicians, they were possessed by the need to bend others to their will. Perhaps this was to be expected of a people whose homeland was subject to the world's

365

greatest empire, and whose national symbol was a weeping woman and a broken harp.[28]

To some Irish political and labor leaders, power had intrinsic rewards independent of opportunities to gain material wealth. Control over local politics was indeed the ladder scaled by many Irish immigrants and their children in their climb up out of poverty. But it should not be forgotten that for many persons in the Irish community, politics was their goal in life, and not merely the means to a better life. To these men power was built on giving and receiving loyalty, on strong organizations which could be depended on to deliver the votes, and on a pragmatism that avoided ideological extremes.

While the emotional appeals of the ardent Irish nationalist would be given deference by Irish Americans of all walks of life, even this type of idealism was shunned by the successful Irish political boss. The conflict of interests between the Irish nationalists and the Democratic Irish political bosses in the United States led to an attempt in the 1880s by Irish nationalists to win the Irish American vote over to the Republican party. But the attempt failed, as appeals to free Ireland from English rule did not carry as much weight with the Irish voter as did the patronage and political power on the local scene which was held by the Irish bosses.[29]

The Irish were successful in gaining political control in several cities not only because of their population concentrations, but also because of the experience with Anglo-Saxon political institutions, processes, and laws which they brought with them from Ireland. In Ireland they had known this form of government primarily through the Penal Laws, and the subsequent dominance of Irish affairs by either Irish Protestants or the English themselves. They had been the oppressed struggling to win political control over their own homeland. In the United States they found themselves an alienated people within the larger society, a Catholic minority in a Protestant society which shared many of the anti-Irish prejudices of the English. Given their situation, they used their knowledge of Anglo-American political structures first to gain control over local governments, and then, through the Democratic party, to influence state, regional, and eventually national politics in the United States.[30]

Through their political power, the Irish forced American politics to pay greater attention to the ethnic sensibilities of their constituents, thereby paving the way for the entry into American political life of subsequent immigrant groups. The Irish not only innovated ethnic politics in the United States, they kept control over many key political positions, especially in the Democratic party, in a way which exceeded their power on the basis of numbers alone. Their high level of political activity continued into the twentieth century,[31] and the ultimate political goal finally was won with the election of John F. Kennedy as the thirty-fifth president of the United States. Some Irish Americans consider Kennedy's election to have been the "supreme moment in the history of Irish America."[32]

Political activity provided power and some jobs; the organization of labor provided another source of power and control over potentially a larger number of jobs. The labor movement, in addition to the church and the political machine, was the third important area in which the Irish created a mediating role for themselves in American society. They were dominant in the American Federation of Labor (AFL), and produced most of the second- and third-level leadership below the AFL president, Samuel Gompers (who was of Dutch Jewish extraction).[33] The "father of Labor Day," for example, was not Gompers but an Irish American, Peter J. McGuire, a cofounder of the AFL who in 1882 proposed the idea of a national holiday to honor labor.

Until the 1930s and the drastic changes in the labor movement under Roosevelt's New Deal, successful unionization of a trade generally followed its domination by the Irish. In trades with comparatively few members but with strategic locations in industry, such as plumbing and carpentry, the Irish were able to obtain numerical dominance and bring about unionization. In other occupations with a larger number of workers, such as the teamsters and longshoremen, the Irish were able to create Irish-controlled unionization through their organizational abilities and community cohesiveness. Where the Irish were not strong, as in the steel industry and in large-scale manufacturing, no other single nationality group was able to obtain a dominant position over the workforce— the exception being the Eastern European Jews' development of strong unions in the garment industry. The heterogeneity of the workforce in other industries weakened the labor movement. The success of the Irish in unionizing the building trades, the dock workers, and the teamsters laid much of the foundation for the subsequent upsurge in the American labor movement during and after the New Deal.

TWENTIETH-CENTURY IRISH-AMERICANS

Immigrants from Ireland left an impact on American society which has persisted to this day. But what of their descendants? Did they lose their ethnic identity and gradually assimilate into the general American culture, as one might expect from the melting pot theory of American minority relations? Or is there still such a thing as a distinct, viable Irish American ethnic group in the United States?

As Moynihan has pointed out, several factors operated to bring about a decline in Irish identity in America, including the reduction in Irish immigration, the fading of Irish nationalism after the partitioning of Ireland in 1921–1922, and the relative lack of contact of the majority of American Irish with the culture of Ireland.[34] Because of the custom of patrimonial descent, individuals with family names such as O'Toole, Maguire, and Flynn are continually reminded by others of their Irish background; they are less likely to forget than those whose mother, but not father, was Irish, or those who, while of Irish descent, have surnames such as Smith, Jones, Nagle, or Costello. Being Irish in name only, however, is only a pale reflection of the intensely felt sense of Irish identity held by the immigrants themselves.

The degree of assimilation of a minority group into American society can be indicated by rates of in-marriage within the group. If most newly arrived members of an ethnic group marry native-born American persons, or immigrants from other ethnic groups, then their assimilation would be high. On the other hand, if most immigrants persist in marrying only persons born in their own country of origin, then their assimilation into the more general society would be low.

In several immigrant groups the relative lack of women born in the home country forced many foreign-born men to consider finding mates of a different national origin, including native-born American women. For this reason the in-marriage rates for male immigrants are better indicators of assimilation than those of female immigrants, who often were in short supply.

According to this measure, by 1920 the assimilation of Irish-born men in the United States was still relatively low. Although the Irish had been among the first of the large European immigrant groups, their rate of in-marriage was closer to that of more recently arrived groups. From statistics of legitimate births registered in the United States in 1920, 71 percent of the Irish-born fathers had Irish-born wives, compared with 83, 82, and 75 percent, respectively, of Italian-born, Polish-born, and Russian-born fathers whose wives had been born in their husbands' countries of origin. The figures for the earlier arrived groups of Scandinavians, British, and Germans were 48, 34, and 30 percent, respectively.[35]

Another measure of assimilation is the durability of ethnic marriage patterns among children of the foreign-born immigrants. Ireland was, and continues to be, the most extreme case of the general Western European practices of late marriage and of high proportions of persons who never marry.[36] To what degree did the American-born children of Irish immigrants continue the marriage conventions of Ireland in the United States? Compared with twelve other ethnic groups in 1950, the Irish Americans were the most persistent in continuing their late marriage and nonmarriage customs, and were quite distinct from the native white population. The proportion never married among persons aged forty-five and over, for example, was about 9 percent for both sexes in the total white population of the United States in 1950, compared with 23 percent for females, and 18 percent for males, among American-born whites of Irish parentage.[37]

In addition to marriage practices, occupational status is an important measure of the assimilation of an immigrant group and their children. While individual Irish families have been found among the very rich in America since the nineteenth century,[38] our concern here is with the Irish American ethnic group as a whole.

If an ethnic group is well assimilated into the American occupational structure, then the occupational status of its foreign-born members would be similar to that of native-born white Americans. Judging by an index of general socioeconomic status, by 1950 assimilation was high among such early immigrant groups as the English and the Germans, but remained low among the Irish foreign-born, who had essentially the same status level as immigrants from Italy and Poland.[39] Among the children of immigrants, however, the status of those of Irish descent was much improved: about the same level of status as those of English, Welsh, or Scandinavian descent, and higher than those of German, native-born American, Italian, or Polish descent.

The occupational indexes of status for Irish Americans, whether Irish-born or native-born of Irish descent, were not similar to that of the general American white population: the Irish immigrants were much lower, and their children were much higher. Upward social mobility among the second-generation Irish was higher than that of any other group, and greater than that expected by the melting pot thesis. Were Irish ethnic factors involved?

A complete answer to this question awaits future research in Irish American historical sociology. Nevertheless, at this time it seems reasonable to conclude that the important mediating role which the Irish had created for themselves in several American institutions facilitated the rise of the children of successive waves of immigrants from Ireland. Irish American dominance in American Catholic educational institutions, for example, probably encouraged Irish American students to stay in school and further their formal educations. In any case, a 1963 survey revealed that among white, Catholic, ethnic groups in the United States, the Irish had the highest proportion of high school graduates (77 percent).[40] In 1961 a young Irish American was about twice as likely to graduate from college as a typical American of any other national origin, and his choice of occupation was quite different from the average American college graduate: Irish Americans were three times more likely to be

369

lawyers than the general populations of 1961 graduates, twice as likely to be medical doctors, but only half as likely to be engineers.[41]

Judging from the persistence of marriage practices, educational accomplishments, and occupational choices, a strong sense of ethnic identity persists among many Americans of Irish descent, and influences their daily lives. They have not given up many aspects of their ethnic heritage even though they have moved up in occupational status, moved out of the central city poverty areas into the suburbs, and spread across the United States from their concentrations in a handful of large cities. While they have become middle class, many of their members remain different from their white, Anglo-Saxon, Protestant neighbors. As Andrew M. Greeley summarized the present situation of Irish Catholics in America:

> Their early arrival, their skills with the language, their political and religious power all enabled the Irish Catholics to acculturate to American society more quickly than any other group but the Jews. Indeed, they have acculturated so effectively that if there are any major differences between them and northern urban WASPs, these are rarely acknowledged explicitly on either side of the dividing line. The Irish may be "different," but neither they nor the WASPs are inclined to mention the differences very often.[42]

Conclusion

Is the history of the Irish American ethnic group a model for subsequent ethnic immigrant groups, or for racial minorities in the United States? They were considered racially inferior at one time; they suffered extreme hostility and discrimination; they gradually established their own social and religious institutions; they gained political power and forced American society to recognize ethnic concerns; they secured control over certain occupations in some cities; and their children and grandchildren were able to make substantial achievements in upward social mobility.

If the Irish are a model, then they are an example of cultural pluralism rather than complete assimilation. Irish immigrants were able to establish control over several aspects of their daily lives which was separate from the Anglo-Saxon, Protestant majority. And while many of the descendants of the Irish immigrants have virtually assimilated and acculturated into the American mainstream, others retain a sense of ethnic identity and persist in keeping distinctively different elements in their life styles.

NOTES

1. Stephen Byrne, *Irish Emigration to the United States* (1873; reprint ed., New York: Arno Press and the New York Times, 1969), p. 37.

2. Robert E. Kennedy, Jr., "Minority Group Status and Fertility: The Irish," *American Sociological Review* 38 (1973): 85–96.

3. J. C. Beckett, *The Making of Modern Ireland: 1603–1923* (London: Faber & Faber, 1966), p. 159.

4. Ireland, *Census of Population, 1926, General Report*, vol. 3, pt. 1, pp. 114–29, Table 17.

5. George O'Brien, *The Economic History of Ireland from the Union to the Famine* (London: Longmans, Green, 1921), p. 242.

6. Arnold Schrier, *Ireland and the American Emigration, 1850–1900* (Minneapolis: University of Minnesota Press, 1958), p. 111.

7. O'Brien, *Economic History*, p. 267.

8. Robert E. Kennedy, Jr., *The Irish: Emigration, Marriage, and Fertility* (Berkeley: University of California Press, 1973), pp. 30–31.

9. Cecil Woodham-Smith, *The Great Hunger* (London: Four Square Edition, 1965), pp. 32–33.

10. William Forbes Adams, *Ireland and Irish Emigration to the New World from 1815 to the Famine* (New Haven Conn.: Yale University Press, 1932), p. 111.

11. Ireland, *Censuses of Population, 1946 and 1951, General Report*, Table 21, p. 40.

12. Patrick McNabb, "Social Structure," in *The Limerick Rural Survey, 1958–1964*, ed. Rev. Jeremiah Newman (Tipperary: Muintir Na Tire Rural Publications, 1964), pp. 230–31.

13. Conrad M. Arensberg and Solon T. Kimball, *Family and Community in Ireland*, 2nd ed. (Cambridge, Mass.: Harvard University Press, 1968), pp. 33–50.

14. Kennedy, *Irish: Emigration*, pp. 51–65.

15. Ibid., pp. 66–85.

16. Edward E. Hale. *Letters on Irish Emigration* (Boston: Phillips, Sampson, 1852), pp. 53–54.

17. Richard Hofstadter and Michael Wallace, eds., *American Violence: A Documentary History* (New York: Vintage, 1971), p. 298.

18. Ibid., pp. 304–305.

19. George Potter, *To The Golden Door: The Story of the Irish in Ireland and America* (Boston: Little, Brown, 1960), pp. 168–69.

20. See Milton M. Gordon, *Assimilation in American Life: The Role of Race, Religion, and National Origins* (New York: Oxford University Press, 1964), p. 133.

21. Oscar Handlin, *Boston's Immigrants: A Study in Acculturation*, rev. ed. (New York: Atheneum, 1970), p. 176.

22. Carl Wittke, *The Irish in America* (Baton Rouge: Louisiana State University Press, 1956), pp. 88–102.

23. Gordon, *Assimilation in American Life*, pp. 216–17.

24. Paul Blanshard, *The Irish and Catholic Power: An American Interpretation* (Boston: Beacon, 1953), p. 254.

25. Brian Inglis, *The Story of Ireland*, 2nd ed. (London: Faber & Faber, 1965), p. 201.

26. Donald McCartney, "From Parnell to Pearse," in *The Course of Irish History*, ed. T. W. Moody and F. X. Martin (Cork: Mercier Press, 1967), pp. 307–12.

27. Wittke, *Irish in America*, p. 96.

28. Thomas N. Brown, *Irish-American Nationalism: 1870–1890* (Philadelphia: Lippincott, 1966), p. 133.

29. Ibid., pp. 134–51.

30. Edward M. Levine, *The Irish and Irish Politicians: A Study of Cultural and Social Alienation* (Notre Dame, Ind.: University of Notre Dame Press, 1966), pp. 6–7.

31. Andrew M. Greeley, "Political Participation Among Ethnic Groups in the

The Reports

United States: A Preliminary Reconnaissance," *American Journal of Sociology* 80 (1974): 170–204.

32. John B. Duff, *The Irish in the United States* (Belmont, Calif.: Wadsworth 1971), p. 85.

33. This discussion of the Irish in the labor movement is based primarily on William V. Shannon, *The American Irish* (New York: Macmillan, 1963), pp. 140–41.

34. Nathan Glazer and Daniel Patrick Moynihan, *Beyond the Melting Pot* (Cambridge, Mass.: MIT Press, 1963), pp. 250–51.

35. Nils Carpenter, *Immigrants and their Children, 1920* (Washington, D.C.: Government Printing Office, 1927), pp. 234–235, Tables 106, 107.

36. Kennedy, *Irish: Emigration*, pp. 139–72.

37. David M. Heer, "The Marital Status of Second-Generation Americans" *American Sociological Review* 26 (1961): 233–41.

38. Stephen Birmingham, *Real Lace: America's Irish Rich* (New York: Harper, 1973).

39. Charles B. Nam, "Nationality Groups and Social Stratification in America," *Social Forces* 37 (1959): 328–33.

40. Andrew M. Greeley, *Why Can't They Be Like Us?: America's White Ethnic Groups* (New York: Dutton, 1971), pp. 66, 67.

41. Andrew M. Greeley, "Occupational Choice Among the American Irish: A Research Note," *Erie-Ireland* 7 (1972): 4.

42. Andrew M. Greeley, *That Most Distressful Nation: The Taming of the American Irish* (Chicago: Quadrangle, 1972), p. 256.

Suggested Readings

Arensberg, Conrad, and Solon T. Kimball. *Family Community in Ireland,* 2nd ed. Cambridge, Mass.: Harvard University Press, 1968.

Glazer, Nathan, and Daniel Patrick Moynihan. *Beyond the Melting Pot.* Cambridge, Mass.: MIT Press, 1963.

Greeley, Andrew M. *Why Can't They Be Like Us?: America's White Ethnic Groups.* New York: Dutton, 1971.

———. *That Most Distressful Nation; The Taming of the American Irish.* Chicago: Quadrangle, 1972.

Handlin, Oscar. *Boston's Immigrants: A Study in Acculturation,* rev. ed. New York: Atheneum, 1970.

Kennedy, Robert E., Jr. *The Irish: Emigration, Marriage, and Fertility.* Berkeley: University of California Press, 1973.

Potter, George. *To the Golden Door: The Story of the Irish in Ireland and America.* Boston: Little, Brown, 1960.

ROSALIND J. DWORKIN

A WOMAN'S REPORT

Numbers Do Not a Majority Make

I remember, as a young girl, being told that the life of a woman was the best life possible. A woman marries and has a secure life thereafter. She does not need to compete in the cold world, but merely has to raise her children (and what woman doesn't love children?) and keep her house clean. With vacuum cleaners and washing machines, even that is easy to do. And on payday she can greet her loving husband at the door, arms outstretched and palms turned upward.

Indeed, the life of a woman, until now, was assumed by most to be pampered, indulged, and sheltered. It may seem strange to some readers now to see a report on women in this study of minority groups. A casual glance at our society would confirm the image painted to me as a youth. Isn't woman fussed over, groomed, and appreciated as though she were our most precious citizen? Men are supposed to rise in her presence, hold doors open for her, and tip their hats. This kind of deference is not usually afforded to a minority-group member. However, we are going to go beyond the casual glance and probe more deeply into the situation of women and their place in American society.

If the placement of women into minority-group status was based upon numerical disadvantage, that placement would surely be fallacious. Women comprise approximately 51 percent of our population—a slight majority. However, as we have seen previously, the criterion of numerical advantage is questionable. In the world there are many societies in which the group holding the power is not the group in the numerical majority. This was particularly in evidence in colonial Africa twenty years ago. The white ruling class was definitely a racial and cultural minority (in terms of number), but nevertheless behaved as though it were the numerical majority over the indigenous Africans. Today, even with the withdrawal of most of the colonial powers from Africa, similar circumstances can be found. In South Africa, for example, the black Africans are an oppressed people, powerless, segregated, and discriminated against by the powerful white minority. In sections of our own country we see instances in which the majority groups are oppressed. In some areas of the Southwest, where Chicanos represent the largest group of people, they are still treated as a disadvantaged minority group.

With these cases in mind, it is not difficult to reject the impossibility of minority-group status for women simply because of numbers. Rather, they reinforce the inappropriateness of a terminology (majority-minority) which denotes numerical advantage when something quite different is meant.

Were we not to use numerical superiority as a criterion for the designation of minority groups, what then ought to be used, and would it be appropriate for women? In earlier chapters it was advanced that a minority group is a group of individuals characterized by: (1) identifiability; (2) differential power; (3) differential treatment; and (4) group and/or self-awareness. If we are to accept the designation of women as a minority group, they must have each of these attributes.

In this report we shall advance the case that women are, indeed, a minority group in the process of emerging. We shall see that women fully possess the first three attributes, and that the fourth attribute (group and self-awareness) has fluctuated historically, and is now regaining salience. However, before we look at these attributes in detail, let us first consider some of the theoretical and methodological difficulties which would arise in a study of women as a minority group.

Some Problems in Conceptualizing Women as a Minority Group

THE RULE OF ENDOGAMY

Wagley and Harris[1] suggest that lines of domination-subordination may be drawn along the rules of endogamy.[2] Using the support of the Bogardus Social Distance Scale, which places marriage as the most intimate egalitarian relationship, this stance would argue that only members of groups which are seen as equal may marry. Hence, in this society,

Germans and Scandinavians intermarry with regularity because they are seen as being of approximately equal ethnic status. The rule of endogamy presents some difficulties when the minority group in question is women. Since endogamy is proscribed for women (i.e., lesbian marriages are not legal) and exogamy[3] is prescribed (marriage partners must be of opposite sexes), it could be argued that men and women must enjoy the same rank as social actors.

This argument utilizes an oversimplification of the nature of marriage and the participants in the marriage. Specifically, marriage is not the most intimate egalitarian relationship between two *individuals*. In our society, on the contrary, the traditional marriage is very male-dominated. For example, the groom promises to cherish his new wife, while the bride promises to obey. The bride traditionally surrenders her "maiden name" and acquires her husband's. Finally, they are pronounced "man and wife," she having an identity only in her relationship to him. Endless property laws, credit regulations, and divorce laws all contribute to the general picture that marriage does not represent an egalitarian relationship between man and woman.

Marriage can only be considered a bond between two equals when the unit of observation is the families so joined. When two persons marry, the bond is more than a bond between two people; it is also a bond between two families. Using the endogamy principle, the two families must be of nearly equal status. Hence marriage between man and woman can imply equal status of the families involved, while retaining a dominant-subordinant relationship between the individuals. This point is lost when we only consider the minority groups that are racially or culturally distinct. But when we admit women into the realm of minority-group status, then the implications of the marriage question on social distance scales become clearer.

Some other relationship must be found as an alternative to marriage on these scales. This relationship must be both intimate and egalitarian on the individual level, and must satisfy the scaling criteria for women as well as for racial and/or cultural minorities. Such an alternative might be club membership, confidant, best friend, or steady companion. But these are empirical questions that must be field tested before any revisions of the social distance scales can be accepted.

SIMILARITY OF SOCIAL ATTRIBUTES

The rule of endogamy causes another difficulty for researchers who are studying women. Marriage partners are usually quite similar along socioeconomic dimensions. The courting patterns are such that the marriage partner is chosen from a rather narrow pool of eligibles who are strikingly similar to oneself. The education of the married couple is usually very similar, especially at the beginning of the marriage. Although the male often continues his education (how many women earned their "PhT"—putting hubby through?), the disparity of education is usually no more than two or three years. So, too, the young couple are usually from families of similar economic background. There is some upward mobility possible through marriage, but great leaps upward are not the rule. Prince Charming usually chooses a princess to be his wife. Today, the Cinderella story remains a fairy tale.

Because of this close similarity along socioeconomic dimensions, it becomes difficult to investigate the social status of women separate from that of their spouses. Most theorists in the past have claimed that one ought not even try to separate the two. Parsons,[4] Davis,[5] and others have maintained that women do not have a status of their own, but experience one only vicariously through their spouses. Wives are considered reflections of husbands.

However, more recent research on the subject has suggested that it may be desirable and possible to separate a wife's status from that of her spouse. A study by R. Dworkin[6] has demonstrated that where this separation of statuses has been made, as in the case of income and occupational prestige, it has yielded significant results. When attempting to predict a woman's attitudes toward sex role behaviors, her own income and prestige take priority over those of her spouse under specific circumstances. For example, if one wished to predict a woman's attitudes toward sex role-related economic issues, her own income and prestige can be used to make these predictions with greater accuracy than if we used the income and prestige of her spouse. However, if one wished to predict a woman's attitudes toward sex role-related *sexual* issues, her spouse's attributes (e.g., income and prestige) can predict her attitudes better than information about her own social attributes. Unfortunately, in this study the education of the married couples was so similar that no separation could be made between the effects of the woman's schooling and those of her spouse's. While this study does illustrate the difficulty of high intercorrelations among independent variables (statisticians call this multicollinearity), especially because of the rule of endogamy, it also illustrates the importance of separating the effects of the social attributes of the spouses when possible.

INADEQUATE SCALES AND MEASURES

The neglect of women in minority-group research and in sociology as a whole has resulted in biases and omissions in scales and measures used in the discipline. We have already discussed the problems of the social distance scale when women are the subject of inquiry. There are other instances that share similar difficulties.

There is an Index of Socioeconomic Occupational Prestige[7] that was developed several years ago and is used extensively today. This index provides a relative ranking of occupations according to the prestige accorded to them. The index includes occupations from accountant to teamster and contains over two hundred twenty-five entries. However, all entries are salaried occupations in the workforce, the assumption being that only occupations in the labor force are major work activities worth sociological research, and that only these carry some measurable amount of prestige. This effectively eliminates all women who call themselves "housewives." Thus if a woman is a private household worker and is paid for her labor (i.e., she's a maid or cleaning woman), she has a prestige in the second decile. If she is unpaid for her labor (i.e., she's a housewife), she has no prestige. Researchers must then either delete her or assign her the occupational prestige of her spouse (a highly questionable procedure). In either case she has become a nonperson as far as the research is concerned.

The assumption that this type of work activity—housewife—carries no prestige evaluation or ranking is belied every time a woman says, "I'm just a housewife," or "I'm a housewife and proud of it." R. Dworkin[8] demonstrated that not only housewives, but others as well, evaluate this work activity and rank it as having a lower middle range prestige—somewhat like plumber and fireman, but lower than salesclerk, factory foreman, or student, another unpaid work activity which was also ranked.

Only by modifying scales and indexes can women be studied in a way comparable to men. Including these work activities not ordinarily considered as part of the labor force into the occupation prestige indexes has one prime advantage. Researchers are able to assess a married woman's status and keep it distinct from her spouse's status.[9] Hence we can measure mobility based upon her own achievements; we can better judge female intergenerational mobility; and we can begin to ascertain the predictive power of a housewife's own achieved status and compare it with the predictive power of her spouse's. Work of this sort has only recently begun. But we know now that is at least possible.

The Objective Status of Women: Powerlessness and Differential Treatment

It shall be my contention that women constitute a minority group because of the subjective reaction by them and to them, and because of their real, objective condition in our society. That is, we can consider women a minority group because they can be characterized as possessing the four attributes mentioned previously: identifiability, differential power, differential treatment, and group awareness.

Of the four attributes, identifiability poses the least problem. Primary and secondary sexual characteristics form a biological base for easy identification of sex. These differences have been magnified and exaggerated through fashion in clothing, hair, accessories, grooming habits, and even speech styles—all learned, extrinsic cultural traits which make possible quick gender identification whether one is listening to a voice over the telephone, approaching a figure from the rear, or viewing a figure from a great distance. One reason why the unisex fashion of the 1970s has met with such resistance from those whose preconceptions it challenges is that it reduces the accuracy and ease with which one can identify the gender of an individual before initiating interaction.

While identifiability does not pose any restriction in our designation of women as a minority group, differential power and treatment may. Therefore, to establish the existence of these attributes, we shall consider the objective position of women in the following areas: in the economy, including income and occupational distribution; in education; in the polity; and in law. These areas are most critical. One's position in the economy indicates one's possible life style and life chances, financial independence, and, in large measure, how one is viewed by others. Position within the education system is vital because of the direct linkages between education and one's economic position. A woman's position in the polity is likewise important to consider because it is through political power that groups can equalize social resources. Finally, one's legal standing pervades over all, placing limitations on (or conversely permitting) a wide range of economic, educational, and political behaviors.

OCCUPATION

It is a recurrent folk myth that women have minimal commitment to the labor force. We have all been taught to assume that a woman exchanges her graduation gown for a bridal gown. If she does choose to work after completing her education, it is surely for a brief time—time to have her "fling" before catching a husband and settling down into the "real" career of being a woman.

This myth has been far from fact since at least the 1940s. Both because of changes in the life cycle (women living longer after the youngest child reaches adulthood) and changes in the normative prohibitions and opportunities in the labor force, women have been actively participating in the world of work. Nearly one-half (43.9 percent) of all women over sixteen years of age were in the labor force in 1970.[10] Of course, the distribution by age is uneven. More than half of all women from eighteen to twenty-four and from forty-five to fifty-four are employed, with the percentage running as high as 60 percent in some age categories. Even in the peak child-rearing ages of twenty-five to thirty-four, the percentage of women in the labor force reaches nearly 48 percent.

Nor do we find confirmation of another folk myth—that women work because they are single or have no husband supporting them. True, the majority of single women (over sixteen) are in the labor force, and 40 percent of widowed, divorced, and separated women work. But nearly 42 percent of married women who have spouses present are also in the labor force. This represents a doubling since 1947, when only 20 percent of such women were employed outside the home. Nor are these all childless women, or women whose families have grown and left home, as is often assumed. Actually, nearly one-third of married women who have children under six years of age are working for a salary. These figures are presented merely to indicate that all categories of women are represented in the labor force—single, married, those with preschool children, and the previously married.

Although women are represented in great numbers in the labor force, there is still hesitance by employers to accept women as bona fide committed workers. All too many women have had similar experiences during job interviews. They are constantly asked, "Won't having a career interfere with being a mother?" and "How do you feel taking a job away from a man?"

Even though women are increasingly entering the labor force, they are not evenly distributed throughout the occupations. By far, most of the women employed (60.9 percent) are holding white-collar jobs—a far higher proportion than the percent of males (39.9 percent). Some may argue that this is evidence of favored treatment for women, since white-collar jobs are usually valued higher than blue-collar or service occupations. However, when we look into the more specific job categories we see where the inequities occur. There are very few women in managerial positions. Only 4.5 percent of employed women hold such jobs, whereas 13.1 percent of employed males hold managerial or administrative jobs. Most of the women in white-collar jobs are in clerical positions. They are the army of clerks, typists, stenographers, cashiers, and bookkeepers who are in dead-end jobs. They are the executives' secretaries and "gal fridays" who report that they often do the administrative work for their managerial bosses, but take home less pay and less pride.

And finally there are the professional occupations. These comprise the most interesting of all, because the differential treatment is more subtle and difficult to coax out of labor force statistics. There are nearly equal proportions of men and women employed in professional occupations: 13.7 percent and 14.5 percent, respectively. When we examine the distribution of men and women within the professional category, however, we once again see the results of differential treatment. Women are concentrated in the lower prestige professions: those with less pay, needing fewer qualifications, and labeled as traditionally female—nursing, teaching, and social work. Sociologists often call these the "semiprofessions." However, the United States census does not make these distinctions. Men occupy the overwhelming majority of high-status professional positions: medicine, law, dentistry, engineering, architecture, and the physical sciences.

If we focus our attention more narrowly upon a single profession, e.g., teaching, we can see still more inequities. Some 44 percent of professional women are teachers, concentrated in the preschool and elementary levels of teaching, where there is less pay, less prestige, and generally less opportunity for advancement. Men are concentrated in the high schools, which command higher salaries, more prestige, and from the ranks of which district administrators are often selected.

Thus women have been committed workers in the labor force for several years. Yet we can still observe differential treatment of working women. We have seen how women are systematically underrepresented at the higher levels of the work force.

INCOME

As one would expect, the differential treatment in the occupational structure is reflected in differential income levels. The median income for males in this country is $6,444 a year, and for females it is an amazing $2,328.[11] Some skeptics will argue that this figure represents all females, including those women who have chosen not to be in the labor force. If we were to look at the median incomes of only employed persons, the corresponding figures rise, but women still lag considerably behind men. The median income of employed males is $7,820, and of employed females it is $3,804. The wide differences in median income persist even if we exclude temporary or seasonal workers and consider only those who work the full year round. The median incomes here are $8,500 and $4,700 for men and women, respectively.

These differences remain even when we control for the effects of race. Considering males and females, blacks and whites, the census indicates that males—white and black—have higher median incomes than do females—white or black. Thus white males have a median yearly income of $6,772, followed by black males with $4,067. White females rank third with a median income of $2,374, and black females have the lowest income with the median at $2,002. The same pattern emerges with only employed persons.

As with occupations, we can learn more about discrimination in

A Woman's Report

income if we shift our vision from the gross figures to more specific occupational categories. Going back to our illustration of teaching, we see that the differentials in occupational distribution are reflected in income. At the secondary level, male median income is a full $2,000 a year greater than the female median. Even on the elementary level, where women have dominated and men have recently "broken into" the field, and thus as a group have less seniority, men lead the median income by over $500 per year.

The disparity of incomes occurs on all levels of the occupational scale. As managers, bank tellers, cooks, and janitors, wherever we have comparable data for men and women, women are distinctly paid less than men.

Part of the difference is because of variations in qualifications, seniority, and number of hours worked. Differentials due to these causes cannot be rectified until women are encouraged to improve their qualifications, gain seniority, and can work as full-time, year-round employees without such encumbrances as children and the demands of spouses.

However, not all the income differentials are reflections of these variations. Jobs that are identical, or nearly so, are often given different job titles and different salaries when they are filled by males or females. For example, you have seen waitresses and hostesses in restaurants. But have you ever seen a female maître d' hotel? I think not. And yet what is the difference (besides the pay scale) between the hostess and the maître d'? The latter makes the fancy, flaming desserts. How is it that a woman, who must make three meals a day, and must often turn out virtual banquets to please her family, when transformed into a restaurant employee cannot combine premeasured ingredients into a chafing dish and stir until warm? Of course she can. The point is that she is systematically excluded from this type of job, and this is reflected in her income.

EDUCATION

Educational achievement presents a somewhat different picture of differential treatment. Just as the academic tower is no longer only ivory in complexion, neither is it always phallic in construction. The median number of school years completed is very similar across sex, with women having a slightly higher median—12.1 years of school for women and 12.0 years for men.[12] This higher median is a reflection of the higher percentage of women than men who complete high school. A full one-third of all females have completed high school, whereas only slightly more than one-quarter of the males have. This is a function of the higher male dropout rate through past years, when males had to leave school prematurely to assume their share of the family's financial responsibilities—something the girls of a family were less frequently called upon to do.

Although women are more likely to graduate from high school, they are less likely to enter college, and once in college they are less likely to receive a degree.[13] Even fewer women go on to graduate or professional school. Only 2.2 percent of all women in the country have advanced education beyond the bachelor's degree, compared with 5.5 percent of the males.

However, these figures do not tell of the discriminatory admissions policies of many universities and the uneven distribution of scholarships and student loans. Discrimination toward women in higher education is far more subtle, including counseling women into majors which are traditionally female—education, social work, and home economics—while discouraging them from male-dominated careers in engineering, law, medicine, and the physical sciences. Subtle, too, are the other informal discriminations: difficulty in being taken seriously in group discussions and the near impossibility of being accepted as a protegée[14] by male professors. How many women students have had to force fellow students to allow them to speak in rap sessions, and then find that for all the effort the conversation continues as though they had said not a word? In some universities a woman is not even called "student." Instead she is referred to as a "coed," a term conjuring up images of frivolity, but certainly not serious scholarship. Indeed, the coed is expected to marry after graduation and if, by chance, she elects to continue her education, "everyone knows" that she isn't going for an M.A.; she is merely trying again for her Mrs.

And so, with degree in hand, the college woman steps into the world, and like her less-educated sister accepts a job in a traditionally female occupation. She may have an M.A. in English, but employers still ask if she can type.

LAW

In some measure, the discriminations against women which degrade their socioeconomic status are legal in origin. For years women have been handicapped by the "protective" labor laws. Originally designed to diminish the exploitation of women in the labor market (the assumption being that women need protection; men can take care of themselves), these laws have become a severe handicap to some working women. A mother can carry her forty-pound child, move furniture in her home, and finish her housekeeping chores late at night. But the same woman, working outside the home, legally could not carry over thirty pounds of weight, or work overtime in some states. We cannot discuss the myriad labor laws here except to say that these protective laws now work to discourage employers from hiring women, decrease the potential income of a woman laborer, and degrade women to a childlike status by assuming that they are unable, or not wise enough, to protect themselves, individually or collectively, from exploitation.

Legal standards involving rights of contract, right to credit, and property rights all assumed a childlike female incapable of making decisions or honoring financial and contractual responsibilities. Hence decisions involving any such responsibilities were placed within the prerogative of the male.

Many of the existing laws are being changed, and if the Equal Rights Amendment is passed there will be more legal changes. However, compliance with the changing law must often be forced. Women often do not know what their legal rights are, or find out only in a crisis situation, as after the death of a spouse. Even when the law is known it sometimes involves just too much effort (vis-à-vis the reward) to demand one's rights. For many it is just easier to use a spouse's credit card than to write letters, fight a computer, and sometimes even to sue in order to be granted credit in one's own name.

POLITICS

Most suffragists hailed the Nineteenth Amendment as the beginning of a revolution. The vote was the rallying point from which women would gain elective office, political appointments, and national power. However, it quickly became apparent that the right to exercise the vote was not sufficient to turn women into a voting block to be reckoned with. After passage of the Nineteenth Amendment the fervor of feminism declined and women once again returned to political powerlessness. Even today women do not constitute a serious voting block. Women tend to vote along socioeconomic lines and according to the preferences of their spouses.[15] Furthermore, women do not have the advantage of converting residential segregation into political power. Blacks in the ghettos have been able to elect black congressional figures and local political leaders because of their residential concentration into black voting districts. The sexes are not residentially segregated; each congressional district has approximately equal proportions of men and women. It is therefore harder to organize a voting block large enough to win elections without the support of male voters. The female vote, if there is one, is neutralized by the male vote.

Lacking the power of a voting block, women have been underrepresented in government on all levels. Whereas other nations of the world have been ruled by women, with India and Israel being the most recent notable illustrations, America has never had a female president and probably will not for many years to come. Citing a Gallup opinion poll,

Amundsen[16] remarks that some 67 percent of the electorate would vote for a qualified black man who was running for the party of preference, but only 54 percent would vote for a woman president. Women do not fare much better in the legislative branch of government. There have been women elected to both the House of Representatives and the Senate. The numbers have been lower than a just representation, with only sixty-five and ten women, respectively, ever elected to the houses of Congress. Most of these have initially been either stand-ins or widows of politicians.[17] Once in Congress, these women find they are excluded from both formal (high committee placements) and informal avenues of power.

Women in appointive offices have done little better. Only three women have served on the Cabinet since 1920. Similar figures tell a similar story for all levels of administrative positions in the federal government.

On the state level there have been four women who became governors. Of these the first three, Ross of Wyoming, Ferguson of Texas, and Wallace of Alabama, were stand-ins for their spouses. It wasn't until 1974 that a female, Ella Grasso, was elected on her own strengths and qualifications to be a governor of Connecticut. In that same year New York State elected a female lieutenant governor.

Women also are underrepresented on the local levels of government. No major city has had a woman mayor, although many small cities and towns have. Women are elected to serve on school boards and minor commissions, but usually not to city councils.

Even so, women are active participants in the political process. Women are often the backbone of political campaigns: they answer telephones, stuff envelopes, ring doorbells, type, and baby-sit for voters. They do everything but exercise power.

SEXISM

The system of discrimination against women is reinforced by the sexism which permeates social relationships. Beginning in childhood, females are placed routinely in the subservient position. The taunts that little boys hurl at each other are often in terms of attributing a feminine characteristic to the opponent. "You're a sissy," or "You play football like a girl" are supreme insults. The counterpart for females does not exist with the same force. For a young girl to be called a "tomboy" is at most only mildly pejorative, and is often meant as a compliment. Surely a girl who is told that she runs, climbs, fights, or plays ball like a boy is being complimented, and she accepts it as such.

These differentially insulting references are not restricted to childhood. The effect still remains in adult life. It is always an insult to attribute a feminine characteristic to a male, whereas it is usually meant as a compliment to assert that a particular woman has certain male characteristics (as long as those characteristics are not physical or sexual).

We further degrade women by the very terms used to identify them. The black man has made it clear that he is not to be called "boy." That term denies his adulthood, his adult privileges. However, we are most willing to call a woman a "girl" or "baby," thereby denying her adulthood and all the implications of adult status. Sometimes identifying names are not even in human terms. A "skirt," for example, signifies to the sexist the only important characteristic about any individual female —her sex. There are countless other examples of sexism as it occurs in our everyday life—far too many to record here. The purpose is not to itemize them all, but to sensitize the reader to some of them.

After reading reports on other minority groups, it may appear that women are objectively in a far better situation than are blacks, Chicanos, and native Americans. And this is so. Women in large numbers do hold some professional positions, and there is fuller employment among women who desire to be in the labor force.

But we must be mindful that although women live in a gilded cage, it is a cage nevertheless. Although they are treated with deference, it is the deference and consideration given one who is less able. Fathers instruct their sons, "Be good to women and take care of them, because they need a man to do things for them. So help her on with her coat." Goodness! If she can't even dress herself, what can she do?

Being placed on a pedestal is expensive. Being kept as a cute and cuddly pet costs one her sense of personhood. Independence and personal autonomy are traded in for a spouse's financial support and status. It is interesting to note that in the popular culture, even the life goals are defined differently for men than for women. A man is taught from childhood, with the lesson constantly reinforced thereafter, to seek success. He must compete in the world for his livelihood and perhaps even for his fame and glory. A woman is taught to seek fulfillment as a wife and mother. She, in essence, surrenders her opportunity to gain success, financial independence, material security—all clear and earthly things— in return for which she can seek that elusive, mystical thing called fulfillment. If she doesn't find it, the blame is placed on her. She wasn't fulfilled because she wasn't feminine enough, but never because she has been prevented from fully developing a self. The whole procedure is reminiscent of "cooling the mark out."[18] When a person has been the victim of a con game, he is calmed down by being shown that it really wasn't so bad after all, that maybe he even benefited in some way from the experience. Women are denied the opportunity to be independent, self-sufficient persons, and in return they can chase elusive fulfillment.

There is an anecdote which sums up this section rather neatly. During a lecture about sexism and the discriminations experienced by women, a male black student arose and objected, saying, "Women don't have it so bad. They can do anything their husbands let them do." He paused a moment and then, realizing what he had said, seated himself, feeling rather embarrassed.[19] Certainly this young man realized the limitations women face which are parallel to the limitations faced by those in his minority group.

Subjective Responses to Minority-Group Status

TWO FEMINIST MOVEMENTS

As we have argued throughout this book, objective discriminations and lowered life position are not sufficient for a group to be fully categorized as constituting a minority group. There must also be recognition by members of that group that they are being dealt with differentially. There must be subjective awareness of their own position and an evaluation that that position is unjust or unfair.

Women have passed through cycles of subjective awareness and then denial of their minority-group status. There are indications that women expressed concern over their status vis-à-vis men even before the American Revolution.[20] The writings of women such as Mary Warren testify to this. However, it wasn't until the abolition movement that women actively voiced their concern over the slavery issue, and then ultimately over the issue of women's rights. This led to the Seneca Falls Convention in 1848, and from there to the first great feminist movement in this country—the fight for women's suffrage. This early feminist movement was part of the general reform spirit that swept the nation. First closely aligned with the abolitionist movement, feminism later became associated with the temperance movement and social welfare causes. Degler[21] suggests that a major weakness of the feminist movement at this time was that it had no clear-cut ideology of its own. Thus women's rights became only a secondary cause for various reform groups; as such it waxed and waned with the popularity of other causes, and its gains were inconsistent and uneven.

After nearly fifty years of struggle, only four states (Wyoming, Utah, Colorado, and Idaho) had granted the vote to women. At the end of the century suffragists narrowed their goal and began to concentrate on acquisition of the vote as a precondition for other social reforms.[22] With several other states then granting the vote to women (Washington, California, Arizona, Kansas, and Oregon), attention turned to securing women's suffrage on a national level. A final drive culminated in ratification of the Nineteenth Amendment to the Constitution in 1920.

The reforms which were to follow the Nineteenth Amendment never materialized, neither for the nation generally nor for women's concerns specifically. Women, in spite of their voting potential, remained powerless and discriminated against in the labor force, in law, in politics, and in many other aspects of life.

The fire of feminism fragmented and faded, and women returned home to their traditional roles. There they remained for a generation, full practitioners of the "feminine mystique."[23] For a brief period during World War II women folded away their dish towels and picked up jackhammers, drove trucks, and built airplanes. Because of severe labor shortages, six million women[24] joined the labor force and performed in jobs hitherto unthought of for women. Attracted by good working conditions, higher pay, union representation, and a national cause, women single and married, young and middle-aged, blue collar and white, worked in the defense industries. Although this period opened unprecedented opportunities for women, there persisted a deeprooted discrimination. Women were excluded from the high-ranking occupations just as they had always been. Chafe[25] notes that women were paid according to lower pay scales than were men, and were often confined to "women's jobs." Even the presidentially appointed Women's Advisory Commission had little power to exert in behalf of women's rights in industry.

The changes produced by the war were only temporary. As the men marched home, women laid down their jackhammers and picked up the dish towel once again. The national media, which previously campaigned for women's acceptance in the labor force and overtly encouraged females to work for the cause, now reversed themselves and again espoused traditional values. Women were to stay at home, be good wives and mothers, and leave the world of work to the returning veteran. So the feminine mystique enveloped American women again, and they remained enshrouded in it until the 1960s.

In the 1960s the nation was again swept by a major reform movement: the black civil rights movement. Just as they had a century before joined the abolitionist movement, young women became active as civil rights workers. Participation in the civil rights movement had a double effect upon these young women. First, it provided them with organizational and activist experience and with strategies for activism. Second, and more crucial, while fighting for human rights and dignity for blacks, it became apparent to the young, white college women who formed the cadre of typists, envelope stuffers, and so on, that they themselves were being denied the same human rights and dignity. They became sensitized to the rejection by males within the movement. This rejection of female workers carried over to the New Left, and by the end of the 1960s small groups of women were leaving the Students for a Democratic Society (SDS) and similar New Left organizations and forming groups of their own, concerned now with women's liberation.[26] The number of these small, informal, leaderless groups expanded and formed the base of the "radical" branch[27] of the second feminist movement.

While the consciousness of the young radical woman was being raised, older women were also voicing grievances and organizing. These organizations comprise the "reform" branch of the movement and are made up of women's caucuses of professional organizations, lobbyist groups, and others which emphasize action in the legal and economic spheres.[28] The best known of these is the National Organization for Women (NOW). Formed in 1966, its membership was initially drawn from women and men in government, labor, the professions, and the communications industry.[29] It rapidly attracted the attention of the mass media, and while the small radical enclaves were just forming, NOW was receiving nationwide publicity.

Once again the issues of women's rights are in the forefront of national attention. With controversies over passage of the Equal Rights Amendment, awareness of women as a group has reached heights not experienced since the days of the suffragists. However, the membership in reform organizations remains relatively low,[30] and the numbers of radical feminists are inestimable at present.

We need now to ask, if group and/or self-awareness is an attribute of a minority group, do women share this attribute at the present time? Is this categorization as members of a minority group generally accepted among women? That is, do individuals other than spokeswomen and members of feminist organizations also view the position of women as that of a minority group? What of the huge numbers of unaffiliated?

ATTITUDES OF THE UNAFFILIATED

Research on the attitudes of women in a small midwestern city[31] can shed some illumination of this issue. Although some women view the position of females as a minority group, they had not, in 1971, reached the stage of making claims and attempting to change the situation. We can note a weak identification of women as a common group, an identification that is as yet tenuous and does not carry much commitment. Since the definition of a minority group is not a static but a dynamic phenomenon, we can best assert that, in the dimension of awareness, women as a category are in the process of *becoming* a minority group.

Attitudes of women toward feminism were assessed in two ways. First, subjects were asked questions concerned with specific points of ideology.

These points were not identified as questions about women's liberation. Ultimately these items were combined into four ideology measures: economic, sexual, personhood, and political ideology. In addition, the question was asked, "Generally, how do you feel about the women's liberation movement?" These two approaches yielded slightly different results. Women were slightly more in favor of the movement than they were against. Although 24 percent of the subjects were neutral about the movement, 49.5 percent either strongly favored it or were somewhat in favor of it; only 24.8 percent were against or somewhat against it.

As an aggregate, subjects were also slightly in favor of the economic liberation ideology. The average scores on the other measures (sexual, personhood, and political liberation ideologies) were somewhat lower, indicating attitudes slightly unfavorable toward those respective issues of feminism.

In summary, as a general phenomenon the women's liberation movement is viewed somewhat favorably, but specific issues of ideology show a range from only slightly favorable to slightly unfavorable averages.

Most women (about two-thirds of the sample of five hundred one) do perceive some discrimination against their sex, especially in the areas of employment and income. However, fewer (about one-third of the sample) have personally experienced such discrimination. Moreover, this slight agreement with the movement and the perception of discrimination have not produced committed feminists. Few (only 1 percent) were members of feminist groups. True, the opportunity to belong to such groups was extremely limited at the research site at that time. NOW had one chapter at the local university, and there appeared to be no other organizations either at the university or in the community. However, when given the opportunity to exhibit commitment of different sorts, the sample did not do so. Although the majority (53 percent) were in favor of legislation to help end discrimination against women, far fewer (only 18 percent) were in favor of activism such as marches and demonstrations. And less than 8 percent would participate personally in a demonstration for women's rights.

Thus we can hardly assert that these women define their position as a crucial problem to them, or that they perceive and are working for their own collective interests.

We could rephrase the question into a more Marxian framework by asking if women are a class. That is, do women see themselves as having commonality of goals, and problems which can only be solved through cooperation and group action rather than through competition and division?

Dahrendorf[32] has demonstrated the difficulties of defining the concept "class" and using it in an empirical fashion. In his opinion, the concept of class should be applied in only the strictest Marxist sense, and thus may not be a viable concept for postindustrial societies. Using Dahrendorf's terminology, borrowed from Ginsberg, we could say that perhaps this sample is part of a "quasi group"—an aggregate of individuals with common role interests. From this quasi group develops the interest group—the agent of group conflict which has structure, organization, and a clear membership. Within our sample we have some subjects who are members of an interest group, or who might be in the process of conversion to such a group. We have others who do not recognize group interests and commonalities and who deny the definition of women's position as a problem, either for themselves or for society.

Why is this so? In many respects small-city women resemble the peasant in Marx's "Eighteenth Brumaire."[33] They constitute a "class in itself," but have not reached the stage of a "class for itself." Like the peasants, women live in circumstances similar to each other, yet the commonality of their interests and goals is not realized. Like the peasants, women are relatively isolated from each other. They are self-sufficient within their homes, performing their tasks (producing) divorced from others doing similar work. Their social contacts with each other do not rely upon mutual interdependence for the pursuit of goals. (An occasional sharing of baby-sitting chores may be an exception among urban and suburban housewives.) Rather, interaction between women is more often an intermission—a respite from the individual pursuit of individual goals.

Although the bridge has been made for some women from "class in itself" to "class for itself"—or from quasi group to interest group—in large urban areas such as New York and Chicago, this is less the case in the smaller midwestern cities. With virtually no feminist spokeswomen on the local level, the only contact most women have had with the movement is through the mass media: television, newspapers, and magazines (especially the women's magazines such as *McCalls*, *Woman's Day*, and *Redbook*, all of which have a vested interest in the status quo). Surely the image of feminism as presented through these agencies has not been complete.

It wasn't until a year after the data in this study were collected that national feminist leaders, such as Betty Friedan and Gloria Steinem, were invited to speak at this Midwest research site. These invitations were extended by the women's association of the local university, and the audience was composed almost entirely of college students. Townswomen who had favorable attitudes toward feminism found very few supportive agencies to intensify their attitudes and deepen commitment. With activism confined to the college campus, few townswomen had the opportunity of even meeting feminists. Feminism was still seen as the club of college women and had not reached much of the noncollege community. Until it does, the definition of women as a minority group will not become generally accepted by women of all social standings.

As with any movement, the official membership of organizations does not fully represent all those sympathetic to the movement's causes and ideologies. The vast majority of women who are not members of any feminist organization nevertheless have attitudes toward the movement which range from strongly supportive to quite hostile. By eliminating those women who subscribe to a middle range of beliefs, and by looking only at the extremely supportive and extremely hostile, we can identify the social characteristics that tend to vary with agreement with feminist ideologies. Hence we can draw social portraits of the profeminist and the antifeminist.[34]

PORTRAIT OF THE PROFEMINIST

The profeminist (one who scores highly on feminist ideology) is typically a younger woman, usually under thirty, either married or single. If she is married she defines her marriage as a happy one—happier than most. She has been married for less than fifteen years, and she has no more than one child.

Although she is represented in all major religious classifications, disproportionately she either is Jewish or states she has no religion.

Superior education is the hallmark of both herself and her family. She has at least a high school diploma, and probably has gone to college. Her husband has an even higher educational attainment, with many spouses having completed college and some having been to graduate or professional schools.

Politically she is either a member of the Democratic party or an independent. She describes herself as liberal in orientation.

Occupationally the high scorer is either a student or employed in the labor force. If a student, she is probably also working. If not a student, the chances are strong that she is in a professional occupation with relatively high prestige. The employed profeminist has had an uninterrupted work pattern, beginning work during or immediately after the educative process and working still. She defines herself more in terms of her profession and/or occupation, and less in terms of being a housewife and mother. This is true even if she is not employed. The feminist housewife defines herself in terms of her occupational training, saying that she is a secretary, nurse, teacher, and so on, rather than identifying herself as a housewife.

If married, her husband has a high-prestige occupation, usually some professional position. The household income is concentrated in the middle to upper-middle income brackets.

Her parents exhibit similar characteristics. Her father is typically in a high-prestige occupation—often a profession. He has at least high school level education and probably makes well over $10,000 a year. The mother may exert a great influence upon her daughter, the profeminist. The mother is apt to have worked at some time during the daughter's period of living in her parent's home, either as a professional or a clerical worker. The mother is also well educated, having at least a high school education and often college or graduate training. Thus the mother also has the prerequisites of being a feminist.

The profeminist is alienated from traditional feminine roles and is quite concerned about her personal status. She perceives that she has been discriminated against because of her sex and supports legislation and demonstrations to further sexual equality. In this sample, however, the profeminist was not necessarily inclined to activism herself. She does know at least one member of a feminist organization, and may even belong herself. In addition, she has other friends who are in favor of the feminist movement. She perceives her husband as being favorable toward the movement as well.

PORTRAIT OF THE ANTIFEMINIST

The extremely low scorer (the antifeminist) provides a sharp contrast to the profeminist high scorer just described. She is older—at least over the college attendance years (over twenty-two). She is married or widowed. She has been married longer than her profeminist counterpart—usually over fifteen years—and she has at least two children. She defines her marriage as being about as happy as the average marriage.

She belongs to a religious denomination that is usually either Pietistic or Fundamentalist Protestant.

Her education is lower than her counterpart's. She has had some high school and probably did graduate. She may even have had some college, but left without a degree. Her spouse is better educated than she, perhaps having a college degree.

Politically she may belong to either of the two major parties, but sees herself as either "middle of the road" or somewhat conservative.

Occupationally, the antifeminist is probably a housewife. If she is employed she usually holds a clerical-type job. However, whether employed or not, she defines her chief role in life as being a wife and/or a mother. Her work pattern has been erratic. Often she worked for less than a year and then devoted her full time to marriage, children, and other activities outside the labor force. If she is working now she exhibits an early interrupted career pattern. She stopped working very early, and then returned to the labor force in her later years.

Her husband is frequently a professional, but is more likely to be in a managerial job, carrying lower prestige.

Her family of origin is more typically lower class or lower middle. Her father either owned a farm, or was in a low managerial position, or was a craftsman of some sort. Whichever was the case, his occupational prestige was lower than either her spouse's or the family of the profeminist. The family income was less than $10,000 a year when the antifeminist lived with her parents. Both parents had less education than she, having attended high school or less. The mother was most apt to be remembered as a housewife all her life. If the antifeminist recalled any occupation her mother had, it was a clerical one.

The low scorer is anomic, but not alienated from the traditional feminine role. She displays low status concern and perceives herself as status inconsistent only when she compares her status attributes with a man's. She has never personally experienced discrimination, and she does not perceive discrimination occurring to other women. She feels that demonstrations either hurt or have no effect in changing the treatment of women. She, of course, would never participate in any activist behavior on behalf of women's liberation. She does not know any members of a feminist organization. Her friends are mixed in their attitudes, but those in favor of feminism are not strongly committed to it. Her friends who are also antifeminist vocally support her. She perceives her husband as being either neutral or unfavorable toward the women's liberation movement.

Feminism and the Black Civil Rights Movement

Many metaphors could be used to approach the question of the position of women in our society. Literature on social movements, social problems, and the family all can be used to provide understandings about women. However, we maintain that women can best be studied within the framework of minority-group relations.

In particular, the extensive research on black Americans has proven useful to the study of women because of the essential similarity between the two groups. This similarity has been noted for at least a hundred years. John Stuart Mill's "The Subjection of Women"[35] points out some of these likenesses. Women are legally subordinate to men, just as a slave is subordinate to his master. Furthermore, women have no way of uniting against them, but must alleviate their personal burdens by trying to please their spouses.

Pareto[36] also pointed out, but only in passing, the similarities between women and American blacks. Gunnar Myrdal[37] suggested that

The Reports

the position of women and the position of blacks in our society are parallel (as both are with the position of children), and that the majority hold similar attitudes toward each of these groups. They are characterized by high visibility both in physical appearance and in dress, as well as calling forth behavioral expectations that are different from those of the dominant white male.

Hacker,[38] in her classic article, extended and formalized in a paradigm some of Myrdal's observations. She asserted that the two groups have many similarities other than those of high visibility. Similar also are the attributes ascribed to each of them by the majority, the accommodation techniques developed, and the discriminations to which they are subjected in the form of lower wage scales, limited job opportunities, and so on. Hacker is careful to note, however, some of the differences between the two groups, such as the social mobility possible through marriage for a woman that is not possible (generally) for a black. Hacker opens the door wider for other comparisons between the two minority groups. She casts doubt upon the composition of social distance scales which place marriage as the most intimate social relationship—an apparent truism for most minority groups, but questionable when the minority group is women, as we have already discussed.

Hacker in 1951 was one of the first sociologists to attempt to incorporate knowledge and theory from race relations into a general theoretical perspective for women. Utilizing Wirth's[39] definition of minority groups, Hacker makes the case for including women in the study of minority groups, thereby accentuating the similarities of women and other groups already under study by sociologists in the minority-group framework.

Spokeswomen for the feminist movement today have also recognized the similarities and attempted to utilize them. Gloria Steinem, for example, makes references in her speeches to these similarities and uses them to show the common interests of both the feminist movement and the civil rights movement.[40]

We must, however, be cautious, and not try to extend the similarities too far; there are differences that must also be noted. Myrdal[41] observed that while the Negro slave in the American South became a chattel and a ward, the southern woman was elevated to a cherished position as an ornament. Both were in a kind of prison, but as we have indicated, the woman's cell was padded.

Indeed, this is a meaningful difference, and not the only one. Women have not been residentially segregated in this country, while blacks have. This has meant both advantages and disadvantages. While not suffering from inferior schools (since most have become coeducational) because of de facto segregation policies, women have not been able to develop

394

clear majorities for the election of congressional representatives such as blacks have been able to do. The geographic space between women has hindered development of a "consciousness of kind" which blacks in the ghetto have developed to some extent.

There is some indication that blacks are beginning to resent the attempts of women's liberation to stress their similarities. According to LaRue,[42] there is too great a difference in degree of discrimination suffered for the similarities to be meaningful. Furthermore, she feels that feminist leaders are desirous of a parasitic relationship, benefiting from the power, legitimacy, and momentum of the civil rights movement while not contributing anything to the cause of blacks—male or female.

Whatever the subjective opinions concerning strategy, we still can make the case for similarities between the two groups while acknowledging that there are also differences, especially those of degree.

Although in different stages of development, the civil rights and feminist movements have a similar set of goals, similar ideologies, and similar organizational problems. Each movement is very diverse, having within it a proliferation of subgroups differing on specific points of ideology, but more usually differing on techniques for action and goal attainment. Both movements stress "brotherhood" or "sisterhood" of all blacks and women, respectively. They emphasize the economic, social, physical, and psychological exploitation to which they have been subjected. Each movement is attempting to reorder (to a greater or lesser degree) the social structure and social institutions in order for the members of the minority group to exercise their civil and social rights as productive members of society.

With this close similarity of the two groups, it becomes possible to apply many of the models developed for race relations to the study of women. The work of Gary Marx[43] on conventional militancy, Caplan and Paige[44] on political efficacy, and Forward and Williams[45] on blocked opportunity has all been applied to the study of women with noteworthy results.[46] Thus the study of women is enhanced by the ability to use metaphors created for a different group, but which have application to females.

Simultaneously, the inclusion of women in the study of minority groups can inform the study of minority groups. It has been a well-tested presumption that studying similar and contrasting problems in other societal settings can be of help in understanding problems in this society. Research in race relations in Brazil[47] and Barbados[48] not only adds to our knowledge of race relations in those nations, but also adds to understanding intergroup relations in our own. So, too, the study of one minority group within a particular society may add to our knowledge of not only that particular group, but other groups as well. So it is with the study of women.

For example, it has been demonstrated[49] that peers' attitudes have immense importance in predicting attitudes of a female toward feminism. Also noted was that peers exert differential influence according to: (1) the social characteristics of the peer; and (2) the marital status of the subject. When one looks at the literature in race relations, (s)he sees that there has been a long tradition—exemplified by Rose,[50] Kardiner and Ovesey,[51] and Pettigrew[52]—of stressing rejection by whites as a factor in black activism. Only more recently have researchers looked at the salience of one's own group in affecting attitudes. My own research suggests that one's own peers exert great influence, and that this is primary over some generalized majority group. Furthermore, subgroups of subjects are differentially susceptible to this peer influence. While marital status was an important differentiator for women, other minority groups would no doubt be divided along other characteristics. However, the principle is the same.

Inclusion of women in the study of minority groups will also force us to assess critically the presently used definitions, scales, and measurements, and either refine, modify, or discard them. We need to revise our emphasis on numerical advantage and racial and/or ethnic differences and endogamy, and place it on power differentials instead. Similarly, we need to revise measures such as social distance[53] to reflect the variables that are really operating, rather than spurious ones or those which appear to be salient on a commonsense level.

The inclusion of women also provides another minority-group movement which can be observed from the beginning formations through its peak and on to its possible decline. Vital also is the study of those traditional women who are rejecting the feminist movement in spite of what would appear to be benefit for all women. There may be a certain "privilege" and "freedom" in the relative subjugation of some minority statuses. The Guyanese Coloureds discussed by Gouveia[54] and the Anglo-Indians presented by Gist[55] both sided with their British overlords against the "full-blooded" native population. For this loyalty they were assured that, while they might never rise to positions of great wealth and power, they would never fall to great depths of poverty and despair. "Freedom" can be a "freedom from" the onus of certain responsibilities and consequences. In a similar vein, perhaps the fear of the Equal Rights Amendment displayed by some women is not a rejection of the gains in salary and job opportunities that might accrue from legislation, but rather fear of the loss of protection that the status of women as the "weaker sex" affords the antifeminist.

Finally, the inclusion of women also provides sociologists with one of the clearest of all minority-majority designations. In some minority groups individuals can attempt to "pass" by changing their surname, losing an accent, becoming lighter complexioned over generations, or losing some other racial characteristic. However, sex assignment is for life. Women do not have the possibility of passing. Babies are classified by sex at birth, and in this society the original classification is enforced until death (except for some rare cases). Passing is an impossibility for nearly all persons. Furthermore, one is either of the minority or of the majority: one is either male or female. There is no middle ground. While some societies have classifications for mixed racial groups such as coloured, mulatto, or mestizo, such is not the case with sex. There is no refuge of defining one's self out of a sex category; one is locked into a position with no promise of change in sex assignment. This may affect the formation of the self, attitudes toward others, and strategies for social mobility. It may also inform the study of minority groups.

The inability to pass as male is actually an advantage for the feminist movement. Even the brightest and most capable women cannot become so successful that they can be coopted by the male majority and pass, thus depriving the movement of its leadership. As women continue to enter the labor force, differences between traditional definitions of women's role and the empirical reality will become less easily rationalized. This contradiction with reality, accompanied by inability to pass and numerical advantage, will increase pressure to redefine the role of women, so that eventually we may see women converting their numerical majority base into power.

But we cannot be certain that this will happen. The liberation movement is too young and there are too many women satisfied with the protection from responsibility. To this extent there will continue to be pressures from within the minority group to accommodate to men, to acquiesce, and to nullify the effects of the movement. Compounded by the economic crisis of the present decade, the cause of women may find itself in an increasingly precarious state. "Rosie the Riveter" did accept the "feminine mystique" when job scarcity arose after World War II. It is too early to know if women have reached an irreversible stage of minority-group formation. If they have, then this stage could ultimately lead to full liberation, and numbers shall equality make.

NOTES

1. Charles Wagley and Marvin Harris, *Minorities in the New World* (New York: Columbia University Press, 1958).
2. Endogamy refers to marriage *within* one's own group. Therefore, rules of endogamy describe the pool of eligible mates.
3. Exogamy refers to marriage *outside* one's own group.
4. Talcott Parsons, "Age and Sex in the Social Structure of the United States," *American Sociological Review* 7 (1942): 604–16.

The Reports

5. Kingsley Davis, *Human Society* (New York: Macmillan, 1949).

6. Rosalind J. Dworkin, "The Female-American: Social Structure, Awareness and Ideology" (Ph.D. diss., Northwestern University, 1974).

7. Otis Dudley Duncan, 'A Socioeconomic Index for All Occupations," in Albert J. Reiss et al., *Occupations and Social Status* (New York: Free Press, 1961), 109–38.

8. Dworkin, "Female-American."

9. Of course, for those persons who do work in the labor force, occupational prestige indexes are suitable for women as well as for men.

10. Employment statistics cited in this section are taken from United States Department of Labor, *Manpower Report of the President* (Washington, D.C.: Government Printing Office, 1973).

11. Income statistics cited in this section are taken from United States Bureau of the Census, *Census of Population: 1970*, vol. 1, *Characteristics of the Population*, pt. 1, *United States Summary*—sect. 2 (Washington, D.C.: Government Printing Office, 1973).

12. Education statistics cited in this section are taken from ibid.

13. See Cynthia Fuchs Epstein, *Woman's Place* (Berkeley: University of California Press, 1971), and Janet Saltzman Chafetz, *Masculine/Feminine or Human?* (Itasca, Ill.: Peacock, 1974).

14. Cynthia F. Epstein. "Encountering the Male Establishment: Sex Status Limits on Women's Careers in the Professions," *American Journal of Sociology* 75 (1970): 965–82.

15. Chafetz, *Masculine/Feminine.*

16. Kirsten Amundsen, *The Silenced Majority: Women and American Democracy* (Englewood Cliffs, N.J.: Prentice-Hall, 1971), p. 67.

17. Ibid.

18. Erving Goffman, "On Cooling the Mark Out," *Psychiatry* 15 (1952): 451–63.

19. My thanks to Dr. Barbara Bank, of the University of Missouri, Columbia Mo., who told me this story.

20. Edith Hoshino Altbach, *Women in America* (Lexington, Mass.: D. C. Heath, 1974).

21. Carl N. Degler, "Revolution Without Ideology: The Changing Place of Women in America," *Daedalus* 93 (1964): 653–70.

22. William L. O'Neill, *The Woman Movement* (Chicago: Quadrangle, 1969).

23. Betty Friedan, *The Feminine Mystique* (New York: Norton, 1963).

24. William H. Chafe, *The American Woman* (New York: Oxford University Press, 1972).

25. Ibid.

26. Jessie Bernard, *Women and the Public Interest* (Chicago: Aldine-Atherton, 1971).

27. Jo Freeman, "The Origins of the Women's Liberation Movement," *American Journal of Sociology* 78 (1973): 792–811.

28. Ibid.

29. Ibid.

30. Ibid.

31. Dworkin, "Female-American."

32. Ralf Darhendorf, *Class and Class Conflicts in Industrial Society* (Stanford, Calif.: Stanford University Press, 1959).

33. Karl Marx, 'The Eighteenth Brumaire of Louis Bonaparte" in *Marx and Engels: Basic Writings on Politics and Philosophy*, ed. Lewis S. Feuer (Garden City, N.Y.: Doubleday, 1959), pp. 318–48.

34. Dworkin, "Female-American."

35. John Stuart Mill, "The Subjection of Women," in *Up Against the Wall, Mother . . .* , ed. Elsie Adams and Mary Louise Briscoe (New York: Glencoe Press, 1971), p. 174–88.

A Woman's Report

36. Vilfredo Pareto, *The Mind and Society* (New York: Dover, 1963).
37. Gunnar Myrdal, *An American Dilemma* (New York: Harper and Brothers, 1944).
38. Helen Mayer Hacker, "Women as a Minority Group," *Social Forces* 30 (1951): 60–69.
39. Louis Wirth, "The Problem of Minority Groups," in *The Science of Man in the World Crisis*, ed. Ralph Linton (New York: Columbia University Press, 1945), p. 347.
40. An example of this is a speech Steinem made before the Women's Association of the University of Missouri, Columbia, Missouri, in 1971.
41. Myrdal, *An American Dilemma*, p. 1073.
42. Linda J. M. LaRue, "Black Liberation and Women's Lib," *Trans-action* 8 (1970): 50–8.
43. Gary T. Marx, *Protest and Prejudice* (New York: Harper, 1967).
44. Nathan Caplan and Jeffery Paige, "A Study of Negro Rioters," *Scientific American* 219 (1968): 15–21.
45. John Forward and Jay Williams, "Internal-External Control and Black Militancy," *Journal of Social Issues* 26 (1970): 75–92.
46. Dworkin, "Female-American."
47. Roger Bastide and Pierre van den Berghe, "Norms and Interracial Behavior in São Paulo, Brazil," *American Sociological Review* 22 (1957): 689–94.
48. Raymond W. Mack, *Race, Class, and Power* (New York: American Book, 1964).
49. Dworkin, "Female-American."
50. Arnold Rose, *The Negro in America* (New York: Harper and Row, 1964).
51. Abraham Kardiner and Lionel Ovesey, *The Mark of Oppression* (New York: Norton, 1951).
52. Thomas F. Pettigrew, *A Profile of the Negro American* (Princeton, N.J.: Van Nostrand, 1964).
53. This would include scales alluded to earlier, such as the one by Emory S. Bogardus, "Measuring Social Distance," *Journal of Applied Sociology* 9 (1925): 299–308.
54. Dennis H. Gouveia, "The Coloreds of Guyana," in *The Blending Races*, ed. Noel P. Gist and Anthony Gary Dworkin (New York: Wiley, 1972), pp. 103–19.
55. Noel P. Gist, "The Anglo-Indians of India," in *Blending Races*, ed. Gist and Dworkin, pp. 39–59.

Suggested Readings

Amundsen, Kirsten. *The Silenced Majority: Women and American Democracy*. Englewood Cliffs, N.J.: Prentice-Hall, 1971.
Bernard, Jessie. *Women and the Public Interest*. Chicago: Aldine-Atherton, 1971.
Chafe, William H. *The American Woman*. New York: Oxford University Press, 1972.
Chafetz, Janet Saltzman. *Masculine/Feminine or Human?* Itasca, Ill.: Peacock, 1974.
Epstein, Cynthia Fuchs. *Woman's Place*. Berkeley: University of California Press, 1971.
Hacker, Helen Mayer. "Women as a Minority Group." *Social Forces* 30 (1951): 60–69.
Parsons, Talcott. "Age and Sex in the Social Structure of the United States." *American Sociological Review* 7 (1942): 604–16.

Name Index

401

Name Index

Name Index

Pettigrew, Thomas, 97, 396

Rivera, Julius, 165–89

Schoenfeld, Eugen, 325–51
Seale, Bobby, 161
Sherif, Muzafer, 98
Simpson, George E., 44–45
Srole, Leo, 118, 336
Stauss, Joseph, 221–53
Stonequist, Everett M., 85
Sung, Betty, 305, 306, 316

Thomas, Piri, 200, 205
Thomas, W.I., 75, 312

Tijerina, Reies, 63, 122, 183

van den Berghe, Pierre, L., 17, 64, 115, 116, 117, 118, 119, 157

Wagley, Charles, 15, 16, 17, 374–75
Warner, W., Lloyd, 118, 336
Weber, Max, 5, 35, 336
Westie, Frank, 72, 77
Wilhelm, Sidney, 47, 91, 153, 154
Wirth, Louis, 15,16, 17, 394

Yinger, J. Milton, 44–45, 79
Young, Donald, 14, 15, 17

Subject Index

405

Subject Index

Subject Index

stereotypes (*cont.*)
  defined, 73
  functions of, 73
  of Indian Americans, 227–29, 241, 242
  of Japanese Americans, 281
  majority, 83
  in paternalistic system of race relations, 116
structural pluralism, 110
Student Nonviolent Coordinating Committee (SNCC), 138–39
superordinate goals, 97
Supreme Court, U.S., 22, 38, 141, 178, 222, 235, 270, 273
tokenism, 39
tongs (Chinese organizations), 61
transmuting pot, 109

United Farm Workers, 54, 61, 90
United Jewish Appeal, 61
United Indians of All Tribes, 247–48
United Mexican American Students (UMAS), 185
Universal Negro Improvement Association (UNIA), 121
value consensus, 97
value-free science, 4, 5, 6

welfare agencies, 56–58

white supremacy, 135, 157
whites A-SP, 27, 30, 35
women, 16, 18, 27, 35, 37, 43, 373–99
  attitudes of, 388–93
  and civil rights movement, 393–95
  definition as minority, 373–77, 388, 395–97
  discrimination against, 379, 386, 387
  education of, 381–82, 391, 392
  identifiability of, 378
  income of, 380–81, 391
  and the law, 382–83
  measuring social characteristics of, 376–77
  movements of, 386–88, 397
  occupations of, 378–80, 391, 392
  in politics, 383–84, 391, 392
  similarity to spouse, 375–76
  in World War II, 387
women's suffrage, 383, 386–87
Wounded Knee, 38, 221, 250–51

Young Lords, 212

xenophobia, 72

Zionism, 122, 326, 329, 330, 332

1508-2
5-30

410